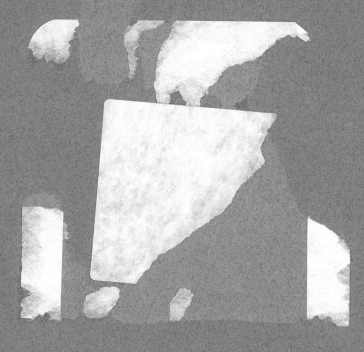

HUNGER

HUNGER

A Modern History

JAMES VERNON

THE BELKNAP PRESS OF HARVARD UNIVERSITY PRESS

Cambridge, Massachusetts, and London, England · 2007

To Mischa

Library of Congress Cataloging-in-Publication Data

Vernon, James.
  Hunger : a modern history / James Vernon.
    p.   cm.
  Includes bibliographical references and index.
  ISBN-13: 978-0-674-02678-0 (hardcover : alk. paper)
  ISBN-10: 0-674-02678-0 (hardcover : alk. paper)
   1. Poor—Great Britain—History.   2. Poor—Great Britain—Colonies—History.
3. Hunger—Great Britain—History.   4. Hunger—Great Britain—Colonies—History.
5. Food relief—Great Britain—History.   6. Great Britain—Social policy.   I. Title.
HC260.P6P47   2007
363.809171′241—dc22   2007017979

Contents

Preface

The idea for this book came to me, oddly enough, over lunch. At the Pankhurst Museum in Manchester, England, sometime in the mid-1990s, I was bemoaning to a friend the miseries of producing the infamously difficult second album, when she suggested that I make sense of the atrocious images of hunger-striking suffragettes being force-fed that hung on the walls around our table. Of course, scholars publish only a fraction of the books they imagine and discuss writing, so why did this particular conversation over lunch grow into the work you are about to read?

First, and this reason was important for someone who had started a family and begun teaching for the first time, it seemed like a relatively discrete topic, and one that my previous work on nineteenth-century English political culture had equipped me to undertake. Needless to say, it did not turn out to be the case. The further I dug, the further afield I had to venture. The hunger strike, I realized, could not be understood just in terms of a tradition of political protest in Britain. I had first to understand how hunger had acquired such a profound political charge by the early twentieth century.

The task seemed urgent for both methodological and political reasons, and the two were inseparable. I was fourteen years old in 1979, when Margaret Thatcher first became Britain's prime minister. I came of political age over the next four years, during which she articulated "Thatcherism" as a critique of the twin pillars of British social democracy—the mixed economy and the welfare state—which had defined the lives and politics of my parents' generation since the Second World War. By the time I became an undergraduate in 1984 studying politics and modern history, the miners' strike was in full swing and Thatcherism appeared to be there to stay. It was clear then that the politics of the Left was unraveling and that a good deal of intellectual work was needed to put it back together. In many ways I became a historian because as I began my doctoral work in the late 1980s, historians seemed to be at the forefront of those debates; the accounts of class formation, the forward march of the labor movement, and the rise of the welfare state about which I had been taught no longer made much sense. When I tried to imagine what a leftist politics might look like after Thatcher and tried to figure out a way past those social-historical orthodoxies, the two attempts bled into each other. Both required, I believed, a freeing of politics and history from a materialist framework that presented them as always following in the wake of socioeconomic interests forged by capitalism. Instead, embracing what we now characterize as the cultural turn, I argued that politics and history were the products of culture. The job of politics, then, was not to follow the forward march of any one class but to create constituencies of support that cut across socioeconomic interest groups, by providing them with the most credible way of understanding and experiencing the world. With the zeal of all converts, I vociferously declared that social and political historians had nothing to lose but their materialist chains. The debates were fierce, and positions became quickly and sometimes unhelpfully polarized, but intellectually it was an exciting time, when it appeared possible and necessary to rethink the nature of politics and history. So the subject of hunger and the politics associated with it was particularly attractive to me, in that it would allow me to demonstrate that even hunger, that most material of conditions, was also the work of culture—or to put it in less technical terms, that how hunger was understood shaped who actually experienced it, and how.

In the pages that follow there is no discussion of method, no rehearsal of the debates between social and cultural history. Instead of choosing a metatheoretical frame as my point of departure, I have asked two simple historical questions: How has the meaning of hunger changed over time, and what were the causes and consequences of those changes? In answering those questions, I have combined social, cultural, political, and imperial history with histories of science, technology, and other material forms, without ever trying to reconcile them in any grand framing statement. Like cultural history, social history is good at addressing certain questions, but others are better left to different traditions of scholarship. Even though I give the historical questions we ask priority over the attempt to develop or maintain methodological purity, the result is very much a product of historical practice after (and I hope beyond) the cultural turn. How else could I have explored the changing meanings of hunger? Thus, the finished work would not have been possible without the turn to cultural history; yet I could not have finished it simply as a cultural historian. *Hunger* is also a book written after the imperial turn, and although I do not agree with the now fashionable assertion that the histories of Britain and its empire were always mutually constitutive, I hope to demonstrate here that at critical moments the meanings and politics of hunger in Britain were decisively shaped in broader imperial and international contexts. Again, the questions we ask, not the territories we claim dominion over, should be our guide: sometimes they convey us to a specific parish or locality, sometimes to the region or nation, sometimes to a colony or imperial system, sometimes to an international or transnational frame.

Questions of method properly return us to questions of politics. It is my hope that tracing the changing meanings of hunger in imperial Britain will open up fresh perspectives on the rise and demise of the welfare state. My professional formation took place against the backdrop of a fundamental critique of the welfare state and a materialist social history; *Hunger* is in part my way of figuring out what is left of both of them.

*   *   *

Writing *Hunger: A Modern History* took me into many areas—chrono-
logical, geographical, historiographical—in which I was often scan-
dalously ignorant. I am bound to have made some embarrassing mis-
takes and to have neglected areas that some people consider essential,
for which I apologize in advance. Hunger, after all, is a big subject.
Many other histories—of famine relief, the Poor Law, prison and
prisoner-of-war diets, anorexia, and hunger artists—were originally
to form part of this book. I would like to thank Rebecca Jennings,
Tim Pratt, Caroline Shaw, Daniel Ussishkin, and Sarah Webster for
the wonderful research they conducted in these and other areas: my
failure to use much of it is my failure, but they should all recognize
some of the fruits of their labors.

Books, and especially books like this one, that have taken a decade
to write, mark the passage of time, the changing of the guard. I hope
that this project, begun at the University of Manchester, continues to
bear the marks of my conversations and friendships there. Thanks to
Nicky Richards for that lunch and idea at the Pankhurst Museum, to Ian
Burney, Phil Eva, Conrad Leyser, and Peter Gatrell, as well as Pat
Joyce and Chris Otter, to whose work I always seem to return for inspiration. More generally, I have tried to do justice to the wonderfully rich tradition of British social history in which I was trained at
Manchester. As I have indicated, my professional career took shape in
a critical reaction against it, yet I continue to be inspired by the big
historical questions it asked, and the sense of their political urgency.
My generation of historians, those who came of age in a world dominated by Thatcher and Reagan, need to reanimate the ambition and
passion to raise those big questions, rather than merely plug historiographical gaps.

In the end, however, this has actually ended up being a Berkeley
book. I moved here in 2000, just as I had finished the bulk of the
research, with the support of a Senior Research Fellowship from
the Economic and Social Research Council of the United Kingdom
(Award R000271073). Berkeley is in many ways the home of cultural
history, even if now many of my colleagues have long since abandoned what has become the appallingly routine work of historicizing

category crises and identity politics. I have had the good fortune to write in Berkeley's wonderfully stimulating, if exhausting, intellectual environment, where I have been blessed with colleagues and students who have asked me challenging and thoughtful questions or provided suggestive comments on various drafts or papers. All these people have made me a different and, I hope, a better historian. They can, alas, never make me as learned, curious, or intellectually generous as Tom Laqueur, whom I am immensely fortunate to have as a fellow historian of Britain and a constant catalyst to thought. My other intellectual companions must also excuse me for not providing a long list of their names, but to thank them instead as my friends, colleagues, and students in the Department of History, the Center for British Studies, and the Associate Professor Group at the Townsend Center (class of 2003), and on the editorial board of *Representations*. I must, however, thank Kenneth Carpenter by name for allowing me to interview him and for showing me, an unreconstructed humanist, around a nutritional lab.

Beyond Manchester and Berkeley, many others have also provided invaluable support. Back in Britain, David Vincent and Keith Neild were crucial in helping the project on its way, and since then I have benefited from comments and discussions with Miguel Cabrera, Ian Christopher-Fletcher, Jim Ferguson, Roy Foster, Kevin Grant, Jon Lawrence, Sonya Rose, Gareth Stedman Jones, Ann Stoler, Frank Trentmann, Judith Walkowitz, and Ina Zweiniger-Bargielowska. Unlike my first book, which no one read before it went to press, this one has profited enormously from the suggestions of people who read earlier drafts: Geoff Eley, Des Fitzgibbon, Jo Guldi, Penny Ismay, Patrick Joyce, Thomas Laqueur, Philippa Levine, Chris Otter, Caroline Shaw, Daniel Ussishkin, David Vincent, and Nicholas Hoover Wilson. Joyce Seltzer at Harvard University Press had faith in the book (and patience with its author) at the critical points, when my own faith in the project was ebbing. To have an editor who helps clarify the logic, argument, and structure of a book is a blessing indeed, for author and readers alike! Jennifer Banks and Susan Abel have ably and reassuringly shepherded the manuscript through the production process at

Harvard. Kate Barber spent the best part of her last summer at high school helping me prepare the illustrations and reclaim some order for my office, and David Anixter spent his first summer in California preparing the index. Many scholars have allowed me to read and cite their unpublished work: Laura Beers, Michael Buckley, Corrie Decker, Fiona Flett, Kevin Grant, JuNelle Harris, David Lloyd, Kaarin Michaelsen, Mark Sandberg, Daniel Ussishkin, and Don Weitzman. I have also rehearsed various arguments from this work at conferences, and I would like to thank all those who participated in those discussions. Nick Mansfield at the Labour History Museum; Phoebe Janes at the University of California, Berkeley; and Lesley Hall at the Wellcome Archive in London have all especially reminded me that no historian can operate without the support of wonderful librarians and archivists. I would also like to thank the bands—Joy Division, Echo and the Bunnymen, the Verve, and Radiohead—that have kept me going for so many years and given me hope that that difficult second album does not have to be a disappointment. In the turbulent past six years my friends and family have been a huge support. I hope that at least the three beavers—Mum, Clare, and Binni—will see a little of themselves in Chapter 7.

I began this book not long after the birth of my daughter, Mischa. I promised her then that, as her mother and brother already had books dedicated to them, this one would be for her. After that I lost both my uncle and my father in quick succession, but I also, joyfully, gained another son, Alfred, to complement the remarkable Jack. Alf is just the latest of many gifts from my wife, Ros, truly the love and inspiration of my life, who continues to teach me the art of being a human being. Words are not enough to register my thanks for all that we have, all that she has done, and all that she is. But Mischa, this one is for you. Apart from smoking, I keep my promises—so now you will never again have to ask me, innocently but mercilessly, "Haven't you finished your book yet?"

HUNGER

1

Hunger and the Making
of the Modern World

History, it appears, cannot escape hunger. In the time it takes you to read this sentence, someone will have died of it. On a daily basis twenty-four thousand people die of hunger or diseases associated with it; that is a death every 3.6 seconds. As on every other day, on September 11, 2001, when terrorists murdered 2,973 people in the United States, almost twelve times that number, an estimated 35,000, were killed by hunger around the world. Those who die of hunger are but a tiny fraction of the 820,000,000 around the globe— an eighth of the world's population—who lack adequate food and nutrition. However much we might like to think of hunger as happening elsewhere, to strangers in far-off lands ravaged by famine, it is always just around the corner. Even in the United States, the richest nation in the world, thirty-five million people are considered "food-insecure"—that is, they are not sure where their next meal is coming from. Hunger makes a visceral claim on our attention, as those who work for the myriad nongovernmental organizations (NGOs) devoted to vanquishing world hunger know all too well. It connects us in elemental ways to others, because we believe that in the modern world no one deserves to live with hunger, let alone die of it.

It was not always that way. There was a time, not so long ago, when the specter of starvation was not disturbing and the plight of the hungry commanded little attention and no sympathy. Less than two hundred years ago hunger was considered either a natural condition or an inevitable and necessary one, beyond the government of man. Then the hungry were considered not fully human; despite often being objects of Christian charity, they were figures of opprobrium and disgust, not sympathy. Their hunger, and their vulnerability to acts of nature or providence, illustrated only their lack of industry and moral fiber. Then hunger was seen as a good and necessary thing: it taught the lazy and indigent the moral discipline of labor; it taught them how to enter modernity as industrious individuals capable of competing in a market economy and providing for their families. We have come a long way since then: we no longer hold the hungry responsible for their hunger; we demonstrate our humanity by sympathizing with their suffering; we routinely lament hunger's damaging effects on the growth of the global economy; and barely a year goes by without heads of state or aging rock stars gathering to declare another war on global hunger.

This book is the history of the remarkable change in the way we have understood hunger and felt about the hungry. As an apparently unchanging biological state that has plagued human societies in all eras and on all continents, it often seems a natural and inherent part of the human condition. In this sense it has an ancient and universal history.[1] Yet hunger's perpetual presence and apparently unchanging physical characteristics belie the way in which its meaning, and our attitudes toward the hungry, change over time. The most dramatic of these changes occurred over the past two centuries—this is the modern history of hunger.

In these pages I propose to track three great transformations in the modern understanding of hunger—we might conveniently label them the divine, the moral, and the social. I focus on how, between roughly the middle of the nineteenth and the middle of the twentieth centuries, the notion of hunger as either an unfortunate if unavoidable part of God's divine plan or the necessary sign of an individual's moral failure to learn the virtue of labor was gradually displaced, if never entirely superseded, by the discovery that hunger was a collective social problem. Hunger, it was eventually recognized, was not the fault of the hungry. They were, rather, innocent victims of failing political and economic systems over which they had no control, and their hunger threatened not just themselves, but the health, wealth, and security of society as a whole. The explanation for this shift, and its effect on the ways we have tried to govern hunger, lies at the heart of this work.

The point is not to perform a now familiar cultural-historical conjuring trick that reveals as mutable some seemingly timeless and unchanging condition. The changing ways in which we have understood hunger matter because they have shaped the systems used to address it: tracing the history of one inevitably means reconsidering the history of the other. Understood in this way, the category of hunger becomes a critical locus for rethinking how forms of government and statecraft emerge and work. The three modern regimes of hunger—the divine, the moral, and the social—did not, I discovered, map neatly onto any account of the transition from the eighteenth-century ancien régime to nineteenth-century liberalism and then to social democracy in the twentieth century. The attempt to govern hunger socially, for instance, very often took remarkably liberal forms, such that forms of welfare were rarely devoid of the old impulse to discipline the hungry and hold them responsible for their own misery. We have to radically reassess how the welfare states and global institutions that emerged during the second half of the twentieth century sought to eradicate hunger, and we have to recognize just how partial and precarious their achievements were.

Imperial Britain, I argue, played a formative role in changing the meaning of hunger and the systems for redressing it in the modern era. Although the first industrializing nation had effectively rid itself of famine or large-scale subsistence crises by the late eighteenth century, hunger remained endemic within Britain, as well as throughout its expanding empire, and occupied a central place in both the English and the colonial imagination. In the late eighteenth and early nineteenth centuries Adam Smith and Thomas Malthus were the first to establish the modern political economy of hunger. While they de-

bated whether hunger was a man-made or a divinely ordained phenomenon, as well as whether the emerging market economy would
eradicate hunger or depended upon it as a spur to industry, the two
agreed that the market should be left to produce plenty or want
freely, without intervention from the state. It was also in Britain, in
the second half of the nineteenth century, that this view was first
challenged, when hunger was discovered as a humanitarian issue and
a social problem that measured the failure of the market to generate
the wealth of nations, and of the state to protect its citizens from economic downturns over which they had no control. It was in Britain
that hunger was acknowledged as an imperial and later as a global
problem requiring new forms of international redress, and there
that new political movements and forms of statecraft developed that
promised to redeem the hungry and vanquish hunger. In short, it was
in imperial Britain over the past two centuries that the story of modernity became partially organized around the conquest of hunger, or
at least its banishment to lands still awaiting "development."

As an account of the changing meanings of hunger, and modern systems for governing it, this book addresses neither why hunger still
exists on such a massive scale around the globe nor how it can be
eliminated and made history.[2] Rather than explaining the rise and fall
of hunger in the modern world, I take the nutritional history of modernity as a given. First of all, Britain's escape from famine and subsistence crises made possible a process of dynamic economic expansion that produced the first industrial nation. Second, famines of a
catastrophic nature never ceased to plague British colonies; in Britain itself, however, increased calorific intake (fueled often by cheap
foods, like sugar, siphoned from colonial possessions) and better nutrition help explain the improved standard of living and life expec-
tancy of modern Britons. All these issues are addressed in the voluminous and sophisticated literature that already deals with the history
of hunger. Instead of reexamining these processes, I focus on how
they were understood historically, and why questions about the nature of, causes for, and solution to hunger arose in the first place.

Written under the influence of various modernization theories, earlier histories of hunger were often the product of the very history I am writing, in that they reproduce the terms of debate and forms of analysis that characterized some particular stage in the changing perception of or reaction to the problem of hunger. It is no coincidence that many of them were written in the mid-twentieth century, where my historical account ends, or that they focused on Britain as the exemplar in the modern conquest of hunger.

Believing that hunger was an impediment to modernization, many scholars set out to discover how and when Europe freed itself from debilitating famines, in the hope that the European path toward modernity would offer lessons for other countries, in the still-developing world. Following a broadly Malthusian calculus, if only to refute it, they focused on how agricultural productivity improved after 1750 sufficiently to support an expanding population, in spite of bad harvests and other environmental catastrophes. Among the many accounts of this process, some focused on long-term environmental changes, some on technological developments such as new foods, forms of production, or public health measures, and still others on changing demographic patterns and household structures.[3] But all were concerned with how the escape from famine and the creation of agricultural surplus laid the foundation for the next stage of modernization, namely industrialization. No longer tied to the land, the laboring population was able to migrate to burgeoning urban and industrial centers, where, despite cyclical downturns, its standard of living gradually rose, as market competition and technological innovation drove prices down. Just as political unrest was the product of times of dearth, economic modernization led directly to the growth of social and political stability. These historians told the story of modernization, recorded earliest and most successfully in Britain, as the conquest of hunger.

This model of modernization drew upon an "optimistic" reading of Britain's precocious entry into the modern era that consciously refuted the earlier "pessimistic" account of Britain's agricultural and industrial revolutions as social catastrophes that had impoverished the

laboring classes and made hunger a perpetual part of their daily existence—one classically articulated between Friedrich Engels's *Condition of the English Working Class* (1845) and Arnold Toynbee's *Lectures
on the Industrial Revolution* (posthumously published in 1888).[4] While
the optimists dwelt on the statistical mapping of broad macropro-
cesses—the rise and fall of populations, prices and wages—the pessimists generally pointed to the human cost of social experience. As
Karl Polanyi and Edward Thompson argued during the 1950s and
1960s, the transition to a market economy displaced not only a view
of exchange relations as rooted in a network of social obligations,
but an entire class of artisans, which quickly learned that poverty
and hunger were the new disciplinary mechanism of the market.[5]
Some historians even suggested that famine, far from being a distant
memory harking back to the seventeenth century, continued to haunt
Britain's transition to an industrialized market economy.[6] Since the
1970s, a generation of historians has challenged the passion and pessimism of those earlier works, by calling on the nutritional surveys of
the late nineteenth and twentieth centuries to demonstrate that standards of living—as measured by a combination of diet, health, and income—had actually improved.[7] Although this work failed to open up
nutritional techniques to historical scrutiny, it was not simply an "optimistic" defense of economic modernization; rather, it demonstrated
the growing disparity in what the rich and the poor ate, and traced
how it was reduced, and the market once again socialized, through
the growth of the welfare state in the twentieth century.

The historically grounded social critique of classical political economy and industrialization that developed in Britain was to some extent foreshadowed by the work of nationalists in Ireland and India.
They demonstrated that the human cost also included the millions of
lives lost to colonial famines. The economic modernization of Britain, they suggested, depended on the underdevelopment of its colonial economies—a thesis later developed by many twentieth-century
critics of imperialism and liberal modernization theory.[8] The conceit
of the British, they suggested, lay in their assumption that their laws
of classical political economy were universal, that all countries had to

follow Britain's historically peculiar path to economic modernization. By the mid-twentieth century this perspective structured the late-colonial and postcolonial understanding of development as a "catch-up" economics required in those parts of the world which had suffered from the uneven nature of imperial global capitalism. Amartya Sen's seminal work on the political economy of hunger, based on his childhood memory of the famine in colonial Bengal during 1943, can be seen as part of this tradition. His insistence that famines were caused not by shortages of food, but by individuals' inability to claim "entitlements" to the available food supply, was a serious critique of the optimism that he believed characterized much postwar modernization theory. The issue, he insisted, was not one of economic growth, but of entitlement. Given his individualistic and legalistic notion of entitlements, as well as its genealogy within critiques of colonial misrule, it is not surprising that Sen has increasingly stressed the importance of political modernization and democracy as the necessary ground for the articulation of entitlements.[9]

To repeat, rather than question the actual processes and events that earlier historians have debated, I am interested in how these developments were understood culturally and politically. My sympathies are with the pessimists and their assessment of how the social experience of modernity can be sharply at odds with the optimism of macroeconomic measures, but I believe that that social experience was shaped by culture and politics. So there are two assumptions in these histories of modern hunger that I wish to question: first, that hunger was a biological condition amenable to a range of biomedical and social-scientific forms of measurement and, second, that hunger was an *effect* of broader historical forces and socioeconomic processes.

As should be already evident, I believe that hunger was never simply a condition grounded in the material reality of the human body. We have all known, however briefly and superficially, what hunger feels like. And we imagine that the horrible experience of hunger has been the same for all humans throughout time and in all places. My project is not to insist that all that is solid has melted into air, that there is no such thing as reality, that bodies are merely cultural; instead, it is to insist that hunger has a cultural history that belies its apparently consistent material form. This history matters not just because hunger hurts, but because how it has hurt has always been culturally and historically specific. We need to take seriously the very slipperiness of hunger as a category, for the modern proliferation of terms signifying its various states—ranging from starvation to malnutrition and dieting—bear witness to its changing forms and meanings. At one level, then, I am engaged in a now familiar form of cultural history, concerned with elaborating not the material causes or consequences of hunger, but its changing and historically specific meanings.[10]

Seeing hunger as a cultural category as much as a material condition (for it was always necessarily both) allows us to challenge the assumption that it is simply an illustrative consequence of other histories—namely the rise of capitalism and imperialism, or the growth of democratic systems and welfare states. Too often hunger tends to be read as the result of a preexisting set of socioeconomic interests and groups competing for entitlements in a zero-sum game, with power invariably centralized in the nation-state. In the British context, we are typically presented with an insular, national story of the making of the English working class, which a variety of political movements and parties compete to represent. These groups develop various social policies, which culminate in the advent of the welfare state and Keynesian political economy.[11] In contrast, my aim is to show how hunger generated its own history: how it became a category we moderns have used to reflect upon the world we inhabit. Through it we have transformed the ways in which we think of ourselves, our responsibilities to each other, and our relationship to the state and the market. The struggle to define and regulate hunger produced its own networks of power, its own political constituencies, its own understanding of the responsibilities of government, and its own forms of statecraft. In following the debate over the meaning of hunger and what to do about it, I have found that power resides in many unfamiliar places, seldom settling anywhere long, and that it is rarely bounded by the nation-state. It was not that hunger was an ungovern-

able problem; on the contrary, it was so amenable to a range of reforming schemes that the circuits of power multiplied around the
many locations in which the war on hunger was to be fought. Modernity may have promised that hunger would be vanquished, but its
dogged persistence produced a constant reinvention of the problem.[12]

Hunger: A Modern History, therefore, recounts how a wide array of
human actors contributed to the continual flow of new perspectives
on and solutions to the problem of hunger. In the pages that follow,
the familiar figures of political activists, economists, social scientists,
and journalists rub shoulders with nutritionists, dietary reformers,
domestic scientists, philanthropists, and the men, women, and children who hoped to be rescued from the distress of hunger. They, in
turn, found their worlds and actions shaped by material objects and
infrastructures—laboratories and manuals, ration books and menu
planners, ideal homes with efficient kitchens, and school, factory, and
civic canteens—designed to help eradicate or alleviate hunger. I follow discussions of hunger across the eclectic range of archival materials they spawned: canonical texts, political tracts, social surveys,
nutritional treatises, administrative manuals, architectural designs,
films, radio broadcasts, autobiographical testimony, songs, and cartoons. These sources help redirect our attention to areas long neglected in or omitted from the modern history of hunger: critiques of
colonial famines, the practice of hunger striking, hunger marches, accounts of childhood hunger, the spectacle of starvation as news, the
development of techniques for measuring hunger, schemes for feeding populations, and plans for increasing the efficiency of kitchens
and housewives. It is not that historians have failed to look under
these particular stones; many valuable studies have touched on these
areas, but we have yet to recognize their interdependence as part of
a broader discussion about the problem of hunger in the modern
world.

Let us now briefly return to the novelty of our modern understanding of hunger, by looking back to a time before it was imagined to be
a problem. We might start by recalling Piero Camporesi's apocalyptic

vision of a famished early modern Europe and its fevered alimentary imagination. In the centuries between the Renaissance and the Enlightenment, the continent of Europe was gripped by hunger. Processions of emaciated beggars and vagrants struggled to stay on their feet, scavenging and stealing, passing the rotting corpses of those who had stopped to rest and had not gotten up again. The survivors kept ceaselessly on the move in quest of work they were too weak to do. The perpetual pangs of hunger spawned a variety of practices—plugging the anus to keep the bowels feeling full, eating dung, drinking urine, and, of course, engaging in cannibalism—that later, in more plentiful times, came to be understood as crazed. Yet Camporesi insists that madness was attendant on hunger: illness and intoxication, often induced by putrid and rotting food, enabled people to forget the clawing pangs in their gut and the sense of impotence they caused. Even in Europe, a few centuries ago, hunger was considered an inevitable part of the human condition, for it was sent as divine retribution for man's sinful ways.[13]

Things were not so bleak in early modern England. There, hunger was less pervasive and the fatalism of the hungry was offset by their cautious patterns of reproduction, as well as by a set of paternalistic checks and charitable balances that extended well beyond the Elizabethan Poor Law.[14] By the eighteenth century these had come to inform a moral economy that legitimated food riots and a range of other plebeian "emergency routines" against hated middlemen in times of dearth.[15] We need not romanticize this moral economy to recognize the great transformation wrought by the champions of the new political economy, who believed that it was necessary to free the market from the apparently archaic obstacles of social relations and expectations. For Adam Smith, dearth and famine were human, not divine, creations, the products of markets that were everywhere in chains. Reflecting upon the recent "history of the dearths and famines which have afflicted any part of Europe," Smith argued that while the former could occasionally be the result of poor harvests or wars, the latter were only ever the consequence of "the violence of government attempting, by improper means, to remedy the inconveniences of a dearth" by compelling "dealers to sell their corn at what it supposes a reasonable price." He concluded, "The freedom of the corn trade is almost everywhere more or less restrained, and, in many countries, is confined by such absurd regulations as frequently aggravate the unavoidable misfortune of a dearth into the dreadful calamity of a famine."[16] Without such misguided interference, the market would find its natural rhythm, generate "the wealth of nations," and create a world without hunger.

In contrast, Malthus, no less a champion of the market, had a less sanguine view of its capacity to rid the world of hunger; indeed, he was not even convinced of the necessity of doing so. Malthus contended not only that the laws of nature ensured that hunger would remain a stubborn fact of modern life, but also that it was a necessary evil. Man's greater desire for sex than for food ensured that population growth would always outstrip the market's capacity to generate food. Whereas Smith had argued that famines were man-made, the consequence of undue interference in the market, Malthus saw them as natural checks on the morally weak. "Famine," he wrote, "seems to be the last, the most dreadful resource of nature. The power of population is so superior to the power in the earth to produce subsistence for man, that premature death must in some shape or other visit the human race. The vices of mankind are active and able ministers of depopulation," but should their "success be still incomplete, gigantic inevitable famine stalks in the rear, and with one mighty blow levels the population with the food of the world."[17] Regardless of his moralizing view of the hungry or his providential view of nature, both especially manifest in the later editions of his work, he consistently argued that hunger was a natural and necessary part of the world that should be left to the logic of the market, exempt from state interference.

Whereas Smith joined others in the British Enlightenment in optimistically preaching that the prospect of plenty and the desire for luxury animated labor, by the 1780s the growing ranks of the poor fueled the pessimism of those like Malthus who believed that only hunger could teach people industry: in the chilling words of Joseph Townsend, it taught "decency and civility, obedience and subjection, to the most brutish, the most obstinate, and the most perverse."[18] Consequently, Townsend and Malthus were unfaltering in their attack on the Poor Law, which, they argued, demoralized the poor and made them more, not less, dependent. In the new dispensation, hunger was to be understood in terms not of the failure to moralize the market through paternalism, charity, and the odd food riot, but of the moral character of individuals to learn the discipline of a free market. Here it drew succor from the evangelical movement that swept across Protestant England beginning in the late eighteenth century, which emphasized the sinful individual's responsibility for being poor and the necessity of atonement and salvation through hard work.[19] In the new ethic, hunger was no longer a problem deriving from the ills of political economy, but a solution to them—it had become a key disciplinary tool.

In early nineteenth-century Britain the calculated administration of poverty and hunger became critical to devising forms of statecraft to ensure that the market could operate free of the entanglements of an earlier moral economy and morality. The classic illustration of this practice was the enactment of the New Poor Law in 1834, which infamously sought to compel the poor to labor, by subjecting them to the punitive regime of the workhouse. In that degrading institution the governing principle of "less eligibility" was clearly enshrined in the insufficient diet fed to inmates, intended to supply less than "the ordinary levels of subsistence of the labouring classes."[20] The irony was that this moment of neo-Malthusian triumph (Malthus, as we have seen, was squarely against state intervention in aid of the poor) quickly turned sour; the hatred of the New Poor Law and the mobilization of opposition to it made its claim—that only hunger could remoralize the poor, by teaching them the virtue of labor—appear decidedly shaky.[21] I do not mean to suggest that in the 1840s the neo-Malthusian view of the hungry as the immoral architects of their own misery suddenly receded, for despite constant legislative revisions to the Poor Law, the inhumanities of the workhouse continued to haunt the lives of the laboring poor in Britain long after its final abolition in 1948.[22] Nonetheless, as we shall see, growing empathy for the hungry as victims caught between the dehumanizing Poor Law and a market prone to systemic failures slowly challenged its credibility, as hunger first came to be recognized as a humanitarian issue and then was discovered to be a social problem that novel forms of statecraft must redress.

Writing the modern history of hunger—how it came to be viewed and managed as a social problem—enables me to revisit what Karl Polanyi in the context of these debates described as "the discovery of society," an idea Hannah Arendt and Michel Foucault later reformulated as the history of "the social."[23] Their suggestion was that during the late eighteenth and early nineteenth centuries, the way in which the world was understood and acted upon was reimagined as a series of discrete spheres or domains—namely, economy, society, and politics—each with its own separate patterns, regularities, and norms. The critical point is that these domains were severed ontologically, so that the market was left to operate free of either social or political questions.[24] The social was the domain that addressed what contemporaries increasingly referred to as the social question: phenomena such as poverty, crime, and disease, which were seen as neither economic nor political in origin or character, but which were thought to similarly transcend the control of individuals, while shaping their lives. As the questions raised by the social were now thought to be quite separate from those of an economic or political character, they required the attention of a different type of expert, capable of developing novel investigative techniques that would shed light on and offer practical solutions to what were fast coming to be seen as a set of intractable social problems.[25] Gradually, during the mid-nineteenth century, expert investigations into these phenomena gave the social a life of its own as an entity called society: no longer just a series of unrelated questions affecting particularly problematic groups in the population, the social was viewed as a totality, a system, with its own logic (later theorized as laws), waiting to be discovered and acted upon in the name of social progress. By the late nineteenth and early twentieth centuries the individual was seen as an irreducibly social being and society was viewed as the vital connective tissue between the economy and politics. Indeed, governing the social ensured that the stability of both those domains could be maintained—a fact recognized in Britain by the creation of a system of social insurance in 1911 that subsequently formed the basis of the welfare state after the Beveridge Report of 1942.[26]

And yet during the 1980s the curious pair of Margaret Thatcher and Jean Baudrillard proclaimed the death of the social. We are now only too familiar with the neoliberal claim, most forcefully articulated by Thatcher, that there is no such thing as society—that nothing except the family should come between the individual and the market. In this case, the purpose of government is not to secure and regulate the social, but to empower individuals as consumers to take responsibility for their own education, health, and wealth, not least by opening up public services to competition and market mechanisms. Similarly, some social theorists have concluded that the social, traditionally understood in its classic modern form as systemic and territorially bounded within nation-states, no longer exists in Europe and America. Some, like Baudrillard and Bruno Latour, insist that this version of the social never did exist, that it was always an invention of modern human sciences, dependent on their framing of the class relations of industrial capitalism in the late nineteenth century.[27] Others, like Anthony Giddens and Zygmunt Bauman, suggest that the classic modern experience and understanding of the social—out of which their discipline of sociology has made a decent living—has been transformed and disaggregated into "liquid" forms of sociality by the myriad forces of globalized late capitalism and information technology.[28]

This book focuses on the largely unexamined historical gap between the formative histories of the social provided by Polanyi, Arendt, and Foucault, and the more recent theories about the death of the social.[29] The core of the book therefore focuses on the century that stretched roughly from the Great Exhibition celebration in 1851 of the bounties of empire and free trade to the Festival of Britain's more introspective vision in 1951 of a social democratically planned future; or we could see it as the period of time between the Great Hunger in Ireland and the appointment of the British nutritionist John Boyd Orr as the first director of the United Nation's Food and Agriculture Organization (FAO), charged with ending world hunger. This is an attempt to use the history of the category of hunger to rethink, from a cosmopolitan and broadly cultural historical perspective, the politics of social democracy and the welfare state in modern Britain at its current moment of crisis.

Briefly, the argument of *Hunger* is organized as follows. Chapters 2 and 3 explore the gradual unraveling of the neo-Malthusian view of hunger before the First World War as, across the British Empire, hunger first aroused humanitarian sympathy and then became an object of political protest and mobilization. Chapters 4 and 5 then examine how, from the late nineteenth century on, the emerging social and nutritional sciences made it possible to translate this new political will into actual, practical mechanisms for governing hunger socially. The forms of social welfare and intervention designed to defeat hunger that were made possible by the foregoing political and technical developments are the subject of Chapters 6 and 7. Finally, Chapter 8 reminds us of the role that people in political movements played both in democratizing these welfare regimes and in remembering the bitter experience of hunger that had made them necessary in the first place.

To some this might appear a more cumbersome way of telling the familiar story of the transition from liberal to social democracy, of how the market, once liberalized and allowed to operate freely, was reined in and brought to serve the interests of society. The difference lies in the attribution of power and agency, but also in the more critically distant view of social democracy and the welfare state that realignment affords.[30] The welfare state was never the historical monolith that nostalgic social democrats boast of or that neoliberals caricature; it was always a hybrid and precarious achievement. Acquiring the right not to be hungry rarely took predictable paths; it involved many forms of agency, within and beyond the state, that frequently cut across the nation-state, the colonial field, and transnational organizations. My hope is not only that in acknowledging this truth we will be able to understand our current tendency once again to blame the hungry for their hunger, but also that we will be better placed to consider alternative social and political formations that are not dependent upon an essentially nineteenth-century politics that was organized and conceptualized systemically. The present discontents of the hungry and the status of welfare around the globe are too crucially important for us to exempt them from historical scrutiny.

2

The Humanitarian Discovery of Hunger

These days, when we are only too familiar with the horrific spectacle of people starving to death in some distant land, it is hard to imagine a time when starvation was unnewsworthy and the hungry evoked little sympathy. As we have seen, however, in the early nineteenth century, when the theories of Malthus still held sway, hunger was thought to provide a natural basis for the moral order, in forcing the indigent to work and preventing unsustainable overpopulation. Then the hungry were objects of opprobrium, not compassion, and any attempt to alleviate their suffering was thought to make them more, not less, dependent. Not coincidentally, when the word *humanitarian* first emerged in the mid-nineteenth century, it had a pejorative connotation and implied contempt for "one who goes to excess in his humane principles."[1]

How and when did all this change? The hungry became figures of humanitarian concern only when novel forms of news reporting connected people emotionally with the suffering of the hungry and refuted the Malthusian model of causation. In this sense hunger first became news during the 1840s, but it was not until the last decades of the nineteenth century that it became firmly established as a humanitarian cause-célèbre—one that would later give rise to organizations intent on the conquest of hunger, like Save the Children and Oxfam. I am not, of course, suggesting that no humanitarian or philanthropic responses to hunger occurred earlier, but rather that they tended to be both local and personal. As others have so ably demonstrated, what was new about the modern humanitarian impulse that attached itself to various objects and causes from the late eighteenth century on was its focus on the suffering of distant strangers. The market and laws of contractual exchange established that one was both invisibly connected to strangers and accountable for the remote consequences of one's acts, while new forms of professional expertise exposed the face of human suffering and delineated its causes in ways that established the technical possibility, and thus the moral imperative, of effective ameliorative action.[2] This was the task of the new journalistic techniques and styles of reporting hunger as news that emerged in the second half of the nineteenth century. Conveying to readers the human agonies of hunger—with personal stories about helpless starving children, the anguish of a mother unable to make ends meet to feed her family, or even, later, the plight of the industrious but unemployed workingman—helped establish the moral innocence of the hungry as victims of forces beyond their control. It was the advent of reporting on hunger as news, not the birth of a new type of humanitarian person with a greater capacity for sympathy, that first began to challenge the Malthusian ethic and establish the humanity of the hungry.[3]

Hunger as News

Although the anti–Poor Law movement, by mobilizing political opposition to the New Poor Law, enabled Tory paternalists and radical workingmen to find common ground against the dismal science of political economy that had inspired the 1834 act, it was the *Times* of London that was primarily responsible for energizing a humanitarian critique calling into question the Malthusian ethic underlying it. From the outset the *Times* labeled the New Poor Law the Starvation Act, and throughout the late 1830s and 1840s articles duly highlighted—much to the chagrin of the Poor Law commissioners—the numbers and misery of those who had died of starvation after having either refused to enter the workhouse or just been released from it.[4] The reports did so by drawing on what Thomas Laqueur has described as the humanitarian narratives that emerged from coroners' inquests, detailing the life histories and the chain of events that had led particular individuals to their "death by starvation."[5] This careful individuation of suffering exposed the otherwise unimaginable horror that in Britain people had literally "died by inches": there were stories of proud but broken men thrown out of work and ashamed that they could not support their families, of women unable to feed or comfort babies crying from hunger, of children who went to the workhouse healthy but emerged skeletal figures and quickly perished. In place of any statistical accounting of the aggregate number of such deaths, a tidal wave of human stories demanded attention and sympathy. It was, the *Times* never tired of emphasizing, its duty to bring these "painful" stories to light—however "irksome" their frequency might be, or "intensely excruciating" their details—and to denounce "the system responsible for such barbarity," for of all "human afflictions and distress . . . none rends our heart, none harrows our feelings so cruelly, as . . . 'death by starvation.'"[6]

These reports challenged the Malthusian model of causation, through their insistence that those who died of starvation were not lazy, morally inadequate human beings who without hunger would never learn how to labor; they were instead innocent victims of forces and events beyond their control. Invariably, women and children were at the heart of these reports, for like Charles Dickens's Oliver Twist—whose forlorn request for more gruel remains a classic image of the inhumanity of the workhouse—they were more readily perceived as figures of sympathy and innocence than was the unemployed man.[7] Indeed, the reports in the *Times,* and its subsequent editorials, often went to great lengths not just to disarm the arguments of those "relieving officers" and boards of guardians in whose union a death by starvation had occurred, but to invert their Malthusian logic by making *them* appear morally irresponsible, incompetent, and inhumane, and stopping only marginally short of accusing them of mur-

der.[8] The negligence and brutality of Poor Law officers, and the inhumanity of their treatment of the poor, raised humanitarian fears
among those for whom workhouses had come to appear factories for
reducing fellow humans "even below the state of brutes."[9] Never was
this better illustrated than during 1845 and 1846, when the *Times*
provoked a parliamentary enquiry into the workhouse regime at
Andover, where, it was discovered, starving inmates ate putrid flesh
off bones (some reputedly human) that were supposed to be ground
for fertilizer.[10]

The *Times* was not solely responsible for rescuing the hungry from
opprobrium and pulling them into modernity as fully human beings.[11]
During the late 1840s the famine in Ireland also generated an unprecedented degree of humanitarian sympathy for those who hungered,
in large measure because of the harrowing reports of suffering published in the press. The power of these reports, many of which have
now been collected in anthologies and ably analyzed by other scholars, often lay in the use of very similar techniques for representing
the suffering of the hungry.[12] Their poignancy lay in the novelty of the
eyewitness account: travelers, philanthropists, and clergymen at the
scene who had direct experience of the suffering during the famine,
wrote up reports, often in the form of letters, for the metropolitan
press. In the case of the *Illustrated London News* these were in turn sup-
plemented by vivid images of the emaciated frames of the starving,
through which the horror of starvation was made graphically present
to readers. These reports from the front line of the famine in Ireland
were enough to prompt even some of Malthus's fiercest disciples to
reassess their unforgiving views of the hungry, as we shall see in
Chapter 3. Similarly, two decades later, in the midst of the unparalleled prosperity of "the Age of Equipoise," Lancashire's Cotton Famine produced an arguably more profound and agonized recognition
of the systemic failure of the market (for no one could say that
Lancashire's cotton industry, like Ireland, had yet to learn the discipline of the market economy or the benefits of free trade), the moral
innocence of its hungry victims and the inability of the Poor Law to
provide adequate or humane forms of relief.[13] Two sets of reports

stood out as making the human suffering of the hungry visible and generating a national, and indeed an international, humanitarian response to it: those of the *Manchester Examiner and Times* special correspondent Edwin Waugh and the letters of "a Lancashire Lad" to the *Times,* which led to the creation of the Mansion House Fund.[14] Their reports, profoundly rooted in local knowledge and expertise, were especially effective at individuating suffering by ventriloquizing the thick dialect of the hungry and despairing cotton operatives—the reporters allowed the hungry to speak directly to their readers.

By the 1880s a new generation of crusading and investigative journalists no longer required a major calamity to make hunger visible and present it as a human tragedy that required immediate action and redress.[15] Pioneered by W. T. Stead's *Pall Mall Gazette,* the "new journalism" has often been credited with transforming both the content and the form of news, not only by manufacturing "news" through shocking exposés of the social and political conditions at home and abroad, but also by presenting news in more digestible forms through human-interest stories, serialized narratives, the insertion of the journalist as a character and participant in the story, and the use of headlines, graphs, maps, indexes, and photographs. Together, these new techniques for making and reporting the news, which placed an enormous burden upon journalists as ethnographic eyewitnesses and expert investigators, were capable of elevating them to positions as special correspondents where they themselves became public figures. In the new dispensation hunger became positively newsworthy: journalists chronicling, in serial form, their descent into the abyss of the city or nation, built narrative momentum, as shocking revelation followed shocking revelation.[16] It was no longer considered "bad taste [for] people to parade their insolent starvation in the face of the rich," as one member of Parliament (M.P.) had remarked in 1887 after the infamous Bloody Sunday demonstration of the unemployed in Hyde Park.[17] Indeed, the previous year, A. S. Krausse's account of his three-week sojourn among the destitute in *Starving London,* a classic piece of new journalism that exposed a city haunted by the hunger of its poor inhabitants, was serialized in the *Globe* (the first issue of which was published on the very day of a huge meeting of the unemployed in Trafalgar Square that culminated in a riot[18]). For the next thirty years new journalists ensured that hunger remained headline news, even while the dynamics of its reporting were slowly changing. So when unemployment once again peaked only months before the hunger march was invented in 1904, the *Daily Telegraph* (whose editor J. L. Garvin had made his name as an apostle of new journalism at the *Newcastle Chronicle*) announced the organization of a relief fund for West Ham's unemployed, under the headline "The Land of Starvation" (Figure 2.1). This sensational headline and the narrative account that followed of the distress were by now hardly unusual. The report's novelty lay in its graphic use of a map which drew on the cartographic techniques that Charles Booth had pioneered in his recently completed survey of poverty in London. "The Land of Starvation" identified the "blackest depths of poverty," while acknowledging more subtle distinctions and levels of distress, ranging from the dark areas of "deepest poverty" through lighter shades for "chronic poverty" and "temporary distress."[19]

At the turn of the century, reports like these were helping transform the humanitarian discovery of the hungry into an acknowledgment that hunger had become a pressing social problem. The danger was one of scale, proximity, and reach. Although Bart Kennedy's account was the most apocalyptic in tone, its Dantean vision of hunger as a spreading cancer at the heart of the nation was typical. Shocked that hunger was so rife "in this city of incalculable wealth and riches," he warned that England (not Britain) was "a great country rotting at the very core." Hunger destroyed the vitality of Anglo-Saxon workingmen and hastened the degeneration of the imperial race, while immigrants thrived in spite of it: London's hungry children would become "fathers to the men who will be weak and unfit . . . These heirs of the mightiest empire the world has known carry with them the seeds of the destruction of that same mighty and wondrous empire." It was not just the nation's racial health and imperial preeminence that were endangered by hunger, Kennedy fumed, but social stability itself. Deluded by socialist demagogues and fueled by a hatred of the

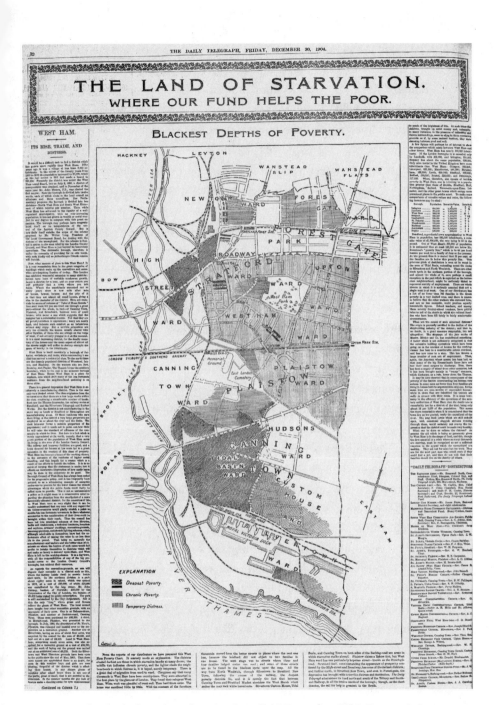

2.1. "The Land of Starvation," *Daily Telegraph*, 30 December 1904. By permission of the British Library.

"loathsome" foreign "scum" who had taken their jobs and the bread from their tables, the hungry would soon rise in bloody revolt, he warned.[20] Even though the humanitarian discoverers of hunger had dwelt on the plight of its tragic and innocent victims, it was no longer possible to imagine that the hungry were the sole victims of hunger. At the insistence of people like Kennedy, hunger instead came increasingly to be viewed as a collective social problem that promised to pull everyone into its vortex. A Salvation Army officer had presciently warned Kennedy that "the problems of the future will be social problems" and chief among them would be hunger; a few years later, on the eve of the Great War, Richard Higgs agreed, when he gave his book the title *The Heart of the Social Problem: Twelve Millions Starving; How Can They Be Fed?*[21] The appalling and undeserved human consequences of hunger, new journalists were at pains to point out, were not consequences from which their better-fed readers could any longer remain insulated. Although, as we shall see in later chapters, highly subjective techniques remained important for reporting on the human costs of hunger, the new social sciences, with their more measured and objective techniques, gradually won out in the investigation of the social costs of hunger at home.

Certainly, this crusading coverage of wars and famine, which made the new generation of journalists themselves newsworthy, increasingly drew the attention of Edwardians to the drama of starvation abroad. These men—journalists like Vaughan Nash, Henry Nevinson, and Henry Brailsford—made their reputations as "special correspondents" by championing the underdog and bringing the techniques of the new journalism to the traditional organs of the liberal press. These writers were very much part of the same liberal networks, all meeting at Toynbee Hall, enjoying the support of their patron H. W. Massingham, and writing for papers like the *Daily Chronicle,* the *Daily News,* the *Nation,* and the *Manchester Guardian.* All began their careers and made their names by writing ethnographic exposés of social conditions at home: Nash on the dockers' strike, Nevinson on the East End and South Staffordshire, Brailsford on the *Scots Pictorial.*[22] All fought the same political battles: for political and social reforms at home (most famously with Nevinson and Brailsford resigning from the *Daily News* in protest over its failure to condemn the forcible feeding of hunger-striking suffragettes) and liberal nationalist struggles abroad in the Balkans, South Africa, Russia, India, and Ireland, on which they published books chronicling their "adventures" as special correspondents. Given the previously prohibitive expenses of employing such special correspondents, these men helped form a new culture of journalism that challenged the monopoly on news from abroad by Reuters and the *Times*.[23] Indeed, the special correspondent traveling around the world filing harrowing eyewitness reports of wars, revolutions, and famines, became news in their own right, their presence itself ensuring the newsworthiness of the events they covered and a public for the recycling of their accounts in book form.

Nevinson was arguably the most energetic and productive of them all, and it is worth outlining his career, to demonstrate how the expertise of the special correspondent was forged. Having been introduced by Nash to Massingham while at Toynbee Hall, Nevinson was invited to join the staff of the *Daily Chronicle* as a war correspondent in Greece. On his return he had a brief spell as an editorial writer (with Nash) and literary editor, before being posted to Spain to cover the Spanish-American War in 1898. The following year he was posted in Ireland and France (to report on the Dreyfus Affair) and then to South Africa, where, caught in the Ladysmith Siege, he wrote harrowing reports that cemented his reputation. However, when both his friend Nash and his editor, Massingham, resigned from the *Daily Chronicle* in protest over Britain's Boer War policy, Nevinson was left isolated and, although he was sent back to Ireland and South Africa during 1901, he soon left the paper to work freelance. Work was not slow in arriving: in 1903 he was invited by the Balkan Committee to travel to Macedonia along with Henry and Jane Brailsford, who worked for the Macedonian Relief Fund; the following year *Harper's* commissioned him to undertake an "adventurous journey" that led him to investigate the slave trade in Central Africa; by 1905 he was covering the revolution in Russia for the *Daily Chronicle;* then came a brief sojourn at Massingham's *Nation,* before the *Manchester Guardian* and the *Glasgow Herald* sent him to India to cover the growing "unrest" and unfolding famine in the winter of 1907–1908; on his return he was hired by the *Daily News* to travel to Spain, to cover the Moroccan War. After his resignation from the *Daily News* in 1909, however, he struggled to obtain regular work until the outbreak of the Great War, which he covered from France on behalf of the *Manchester Guardian,* the *Daily Chronicle,* and the *Daily Telegraph.* After the war he once again took to ruffling the feathers of the establishment, by reporting on the devastating human consequences of the continued blockade on Germany after the armistice, as well as covering nationalist struggles in Ireland and speaking out frequently in criticism of British government policy there (including, as we shall see in the following chapter, the treatment of the hunger-striking MacSwiney).[24] Indeed, it is worth noting that hunger was a recurring subject for Nevinson—at Ladysmith, in Russia, in India, with hunger-striking suffragettes and Irish Nationalists, as well as in war-torn Germany—one that he frequently returned to, to illustrate the tragic human consequences of political failure.

Despite Reuters' expanding network, colonial and foreign news remained heavily dependent upon eyewitness reports—hence the power and influence of the special correspondent in the field. Eyewitness accounts had long filled the breach in the peculiarly undeveloped information system that Britain had developed in its attempt to rule the vast expanses of its empire. Nowhere had this been more apparent than during the 1857 revolt in India, when the flow of harrowing (and often wildly fantastic) eyewitness accounts from soldiers and the Anglo-Indian community to the British press often directly contradicted or exceeded those from the "official" sources.[25] The revolt proved a catalyst for the development of a rail and telegraph network in India that facilitated a more reliable flow of information. Meanwhile, knowledge of events in the rest of the empire often remained dependent upon eyewitness reports or special correspondents, as Paula Krebs has demonstrated with respect to the Boer War. Support for the war effort was galvanized by eyewitness reports from

Mafeking, South Africa, detailing the acute hunger suffered by those under siege, especially by Africans denied the meat rations afforded to Britons by Robert Baden-Powell (later founder of the Boy Scouts). Criticism of the war was, in contrast, mobilized by Emily Hobhouse's reports for the *Manchester Guardian*. She wrote of the Boer women and children held in British concentration camps, and of the starvation diets that Henry Campbell-Bannerman, the leader of the Liberal opposition, would soon famously describe as "methods of barbarism." Remarkably, government ministers sometimes depended for their grasp of events on eyewitness reports in the press: Joseph Chamberlain, the colonial secretary, in having to respond to critical questions about conditions in the concentration camps, was armed only with the very press reports that had allowed the questions to be raised in the first place.[26] Given the tenuous hold of the imperial center over an empire it was forced to govern from a distance, the power of the special correspondent in the field was considerable.

Not all reporters were blessed with the contacts of a Nevinson or a Hobhouse. Instead, many had to demonstrate the authority and reliability of the news they supplied by demonstrating at least two qualities: first-hand experience of the conditions, and compassion for the suffering. So although Krausse admitted that as "neither a missionary nor a professional philanthropist" he could lay "no claim to any special acquaintance with the subject matter" of starving London, his new-found expertise rested on the twenty-four days in which "he practically lived among the destitute poor, and every case recorded has been taken from life and actual observation."[27] This immersion in the world of the hungry, the firsthand experience of the miserable conditions in which they struggled to live, was the basis of any investigative reporter's claim to authority; for only by living alongside them and listening to their stories could an investigator truly come to understand their plight.[28] Even the seasoned reporter Nash, covering what he described as India's Great Famine of 1899–1901, claimed to have traveled so widely as to have seen "more of the superficial extent of the famine than any other person." Yet given the scale of the catastrophe, the challenge lay less in surveying "the great panorama of suffer-

ing that unrolled itself day by day" than in conveying the visceral im-
mediacy of famine: "I am writing now with the voice in my ears that I
heard this evening at the poorhouse hospital, where the sweepers
were pulling a dead child from its mother's arms."[29] In the reporting
of famine, though, none were better placed to claim they coexisted
intimately with starvation than the missionaries and relief workers
who quickly became authoritative sources of eyewitness news.[30]

Critical to the reporter's ability to immerse himself in the lives of
the hungry, to hear their stories or feel their pain, and to render both
faithfully to his public, was compassion—what Masterman described
as "sincerity."[31] A rhetoric of feeling and empathy was critical to their
claims to knowing. They had no need for a dispassionate and objective way of measuring hunger, for as men of feeling they could plainly
see pinched faces and emaciated frames. Here is Krausse's encounter
with a hungry child one cold and foggy night in Stepney:

> I was alone, and wandered many miles in search of adventures,
> which never came. Once in a street, the name of which I do not
> know, it, if written up at all, being obscured in the unlit gloom,
> I chanced upon a child, a little mite of six or seven. It was past
> ten o'clock, and this child, without either shawl or bonnet,
> stood on the narrow pavement crying bitterly . . . "What is the
> matter?" I demanded as kindly as my throat full of fog would al-
> low. "I'm so hungry" said the child. There was no false pretence
> in that avowal, no acting in the plaintive voice. Her mother
> lived "up there," pointing to a court, the entrance of which was
> half discernible in the mist, but she had gone out to try and
> pawn the last blanket, and the child was so hungry. A child's
> voice speaking like this is more terrible than all the suffering of
> mankind. Any father or mother who reads these lines will real-
> ise what it means. A little child, late at night, crying on the
> footway, in one of the most wretched districts in the East
> End—because it is so hungry. After leaving the poor girl I dis-
> covered that I had lost my way.[32]

There was no question for Krausse that the sobbing child was hungry; she had told him so, and he had recognized the sight and sound of hunger. This capacity for compassion was frequently contrasted with its conspicuous absence in others, the chief villains—those supposed to be the guardians of the poor. Kennedy was vitriolic in his account of the "hunger line" of London's soup kitchens when he described the way the Charity Organisation Society "ask[s] suffering people insolent and degrading questions . . . and does not even help them after-wards."[33] Similarly, those who filed reports from the front line of fam-ine lands bared their hearts in their copy, as they revealed their own dismay at being an eyewitnesses to unimaginable misery. Many, like Nevinson, dwelt on the anguish of being unable to help those starving to death: "When brown skeletons fling themselves flat on the ground before you, with arms outstretched beyond their heads, and faces rubbing in the dust; when they take your feet in their bones and lay their skulls upon your boots, what are you to do?"[34] Perversely, the horror of witnessing such scenes so that others might know of them presented the reporter as another object of sympathy, a different kind of victim. But then, of course, it was the very subjectivity of these re-ports that gave them their force: reliable firsthand sources demanded immediate humanitarian assistance by making readers aware of the horror and suffering.

The discovery of hunger as news quickly generated a circle of hu-manitarian virtue: the journalist proved his integrity by reporting the urgent misery of hunger and starvation; those reports elicited and created an immediate humanitarian response among readers, whose philanthropy in turn demonstrated their own virtue and redeemed the lives of the recipients.[35] Once again, Krausse's exploration of starving London for the *Globe* illustrates this dynamic well, the forg-ing of a relationship between humanitarian object and compassionate subject through the investigative report. His mission—to lead "the reader into scenes of misery such as few would believe existed in the Capital of the World" and to show them "how people, who are able and willing to work, are to-day starving for want of food"—made hunger *news* in a double sense and immediately established a bond between journalist and his intended public. Krausse took his readers with him on his self-proclaimed "mission of mercy," connecting them directly with the suffering he reported, so that before long donations flowed into the offices of the *Globe* "to feed the hungry and relieve the distressed."[36] Ambivalent about being a "messenger of relief" bearing "other people's charity," he reflected on the haphazard nature of philanthropy: how journalistic imperatives of focusing on particular cases to dramatize the human costs of hunger had meant that they alone had been singled out for his readers' charity. The remainder of his account is largely spent justifying his use of readers' donations on a soup kitchen. Krausse not only showed readers the suffering of the hungry, but he showed them that their humanitarian response had a real and immediate effect.[37]

The Changing Face of Hunger's Victims

We have seen how the techniques of new journalism helped make hunger, at home and abroad, newsworthy, but how did journalists manage to represent the hungry as deserving of, indeed entitled to, humanitarian assistance? It was of course critical that they challenge the Malthusian claim that the hungry were victims of their own moral depravity; reporters had to demonstrate that the hungry lacked food, not moral character; these were innocent victims of forces beyond their control. The first step was invariably, therefore, to expose the human costs of hunger by focusing on particular individuals and families; sometimes mentioning them by name, always by location, these descriptions of the unfortunate provided snapshots of life on the edge of starvation.[38] Near the beginning of his account, for instance, Kennedy introduces us to a family of eight, with an unemployed breadwinner. On a Saturday evening, when people with wages were returning from markets or retiring to pubs, we find this family, without bread, light, or fuel, huddled together in bed to stay warm. Typically, his sketch focuses upon the women and children of the family, who throughout the night "woke up and cried because they were hungry. The youngest child was only two weeks old. It, too, cried through hunger, because the breast of its starving mother was dry."[39] The face of hunger was invariably that of children, and only rarely of men or occasionally of mothers trying to make ends meet; it was children who could most easily be presented as unwitting and innocent victims. The sight of a starving child's body was, for Krausse, "one of the most pitiable sights in the world."[40] Innocent children starving to death in punitive famine camps or lying dead in a ditch with the jackals picking over their scanty bones became stock images in famine literature. *Cosmopolitan*'s special correspondent Julian Hawthorne, for instance, relayed to his American readers how during India's famine of 1896–1898 the occupants of a children's camp starved while the grain intended for them was stolen by their overseers. There he encountered a five-year-old whose "arms were not so large round as my thumb; its legs were scarcely larger; the pelvic bones were plainly shown; the ribs, back and front, started through the skin, like a wire cage. The eyes were fixed and unobservant; the expression of the little skull-face solemn, dreary and old. Will, impulse, and almost sensation, were destroyed in this tiny skeleton, which might have been a plump and happy baby . . . I lifted it between my thumbs and forefingers; it did not weigh more than seven or eight pounds."[41]

It was the description of starving women and children in British concentration camps provided by Emily Hobhouse that first ignited humanitarian concerns about the war in South Africa. Despite official returns revealing the escalating death rates within these camps, ministers and the "jingo" press presented the camps not as a military strategy intended, through the capture of wives and children, to force Boer men to surrender, but as a humanitarian gesture to protect those whose unmanly husbands had deserted them and left them prey to the double threat of starvation and sexually predatory natives.[42] The ineffectiveness of such claims was amply illustrated by the government's immediate appointment of the first all-woman commission, with Millicent Fawcett as its chairperson, to investigate Hobhouse's descriptions of conditions in the camps. If women and children were, as casualties of war, the principal victims of starvation, women were also thought to be the primary agents of compassion, as well as those most expert in matters of diet. It had been Hobhouse's genius to recognize that her discovery of starving women and children gained authority precisely because she was there not just as an eyewitness but as a woman. Yet not all starving women and children were equally the objects of humanitarian sympathy. Krebs reminds us of the noticeable absence of "native" African women and children in these reports and debates. The starvation of "natives," who were segregated in different camps and suffered from poorer rations, worse conditions, and greater numbers of deaths, was obscured by the spectacle of starving Boer women and children. There was no universal object of humanitarian compassion; compassion has always been contingent, a product of history and politics, time and place.

Men, then, always came last as objects of compassion. As hunger was routinely portrayed as the consequence of men's failure to support their families, men were rarely presented as victims before the Great War. On the rare occasions when men do appear, there are always extenuating circumstances to remind us that they are manly and industrious but have been reduced to objects of pity and charity through no fault of their own. Thus, Kennedy was appalled to watch unemployed dockworkers in West Ham, "with the dread, drawn-in look of hunger," at a soup kitchen, where they carefully caught every crumb and pocketed their bread and cheese to take "home to their wives and children." Here were proud men, "the backbone of our country," doing their best to support their families amid the immigrant hordes who had stolen their jobs, "wastrel aliens who are devouring the substance that belongs to our own people."[43] As a Salvation Army officer working at a soup kitchen told Kennedy: "England was being given up to the alien . . . The English working man was being starved out." In the hunger line was an old soldier who had "served his sovereign and his country," only to have "those who ruled in Westminster" decree "that England should be thrown open to the alien so that he, the Englishman, might starve . . . No, the shame lay not upon this man, but it lay upon the bold, fine, free flag of England!"[44] As we shall see in Chapters 5 and 9, it was not until after the Great War that the figure of the unemployed man moved to the center of ethnographic reports on hungry England; no longer needing a racialized other to prove their virtue as victims, at that point they became the regular human face of hunger in a way unimaginable in the 1880s. How this could happen, how the unemployed man could become a figure worthy first of humanitarian sympathy and then of social redemption, is one of the central questions of this book.

The ultimate way to humanize hunger was to photograph it. Although photography had long provided evidential force to news reports, most famously with Roger Fenton's photographic testament to William Russell's news reports for the *Times* on the Crimean War, it had always done so retrospectively.[45] According to Mike Davis, that changed in 1888, when the arrival of the "cheap, handheld Kodak Number One camera" turned every journalist, social investigator, and missionary into "a documentary photographer."[46] Nowhere was this more evident than in the missionary-produced "atrocity photos" of maimed and dismembered children in the Congo, which, displayed in the lantern lectures of the Congo Reform Association, helped generate what Kevin Grant has described as "the largest humanitarian movement in British imperial politics during the late Victorian and Edwardian eras."[47] By the 1890s, new technologies of graphic reproduction allowed photojournalism to emerge within the illustrated periodical press, and in the following decade photographs began to appear in the dailies. The *Daily Mirror* led the way in 1904, with portraits of the royal family on its front page. In the decade before the Great War photography came to be seen by ethnographically minded investigative journalists as a key mechanism for validating their exposés of otherwise seeming unimaginable social conditions at home and abroad. The camera could not lie; it appeared to provide unmediated access to its subject, to render the viewer at home as much an eyewitness as the expert ethnographer or special correspondent on the spot.[48]

It was in the colonial field, in the representation of famines in India particularly, that the force of photography was first felt. The struggle to represent the scale of Indian famines, together with the need to shock readers into humanitarian action, led first to ever more lurid accounts, and then to photographs of starving bodies and emaciated corpses.[49] Photography had long been vital to British publics' ability to picture their empire and its civilizing mission through the lantern lectures of explorers, missionaries, and teachers, but famine photography provided a radically different image of empire.[50] "Why among the pictures of famine are only those representing the dark side reproduced in England?" complained J. D. Rees, the former member of the Governor General's Council, of the photographs published by Reuters special correspondent Francis Merewether in 1898. "Why," he asked, "did we never see photographs of tens of thousands of people tolerably comfortable, and certainly not hungry, busily occupied in earning bread from the State, but only reproductions of poorhouses in which are gathered together the waifs, the strays, the halt, the lame, the blind, the aged, feeble, and infirm, the flotsam and jetsam of teeming Oriental populations?"[51] It was perhaps no coincidence that at the same time photographic publications like *The Queen's Empire,* published to celebrate Victoria's Jubilee in 1897, sought to demonstrate how in "every part of Empire we shall find some trace of the work which Britain is doing throughout the world—the work of civilizing, of governing, of protecting life and property, and of extending the benefits of trade and commerce."[52] By 1902 the Colonial Office had established its Visual Instruction Committee, to produce photographic evidence of Britain's improvement of its colonial territories that was then disseminated through lantern (slide) lectures in British schoolrooms, lecture halls, and libraries.[53] Merewether appears to have been the first to incorporate photographs into the account of his tour through India during the 1896–1898 famine. Not finding words to evoke "the awful and gruesome sights and scenes which it was his lot to witness," he published over thirty of his own photographs "taken upon the spot, to bring forcibly before the mind's eye of his readers, if any, the state and condition of the oriental races who owe their allegiance to the Queen-Empress." These images were meant to be self-explanatory, for although their placement mirrored the sequence of his journey, they generally bore little relation to the text, which rarely referred to them. The vast majority of the photos were of the usual kind taken by travelers in India—pictures of elaborate buildings, exotic bazaars, panoramic landscapes, street characters and racial types, unfamiliar customs, such as Hindu funeral pyres—but this familiar visual narrative was periodically and brutally disrupted by arresting images of starving bodies and skeletal corpses (Figure 2.2). They were intended to shock and elicit a humanitarian response; his hope was that just "one heart be touched and one purse-string loosened for the benefit of the naked and starving myriads of Hindustan."[54] Merewether had opened the floodgates to a new genre of famine photography that made a spectacle of suffering and turned the viewer into a voyeur. Not surprisingly, photography quickly became an indispensable medium for bringing the realities of famine home to a British public, and it soon focused on the suffering of starving children and the agonies of mothers unable to feed or save them (Figure 2.3). Nash wrote of "the child-like sweetness and docility" of starving Indians and how any person who had seen "half-savage parents with the death-pangs at their heart comforting their dying children . . . understands why it is that Englishmen and English-women will work for India till they drop."[55] This was, of course, a re-iteration of the imperial conceit that it was England's parental duty to civilize the childlike Indian native, but it also recalibrated the civilizing mission as one of assuming immediate humanitarian responsibility for those whose hungry cries had to be heard.

Not all famine photography was designed to provoke humanitarian reaction; it was also used to convince the humanitarian public that its donations were put to good and effective use. Four years after the famine of 1899–1900, the chairman of the *Christian Herald*'s Famine Relief Committee, Rev. J. E. Scott, published an account of the relief work he had supervised at the time. His book was full not only of "the language of eye-witnesses . . . who wrote down at the time their vivid impressions," but of many photographs "taken, as a rule, by famine relief officers and other helpers, as they went about their work among the people."[56] Dedicated to Lord Curzon and his "energetic

2.2. "India's Starving Millions," F. H. S. Merewether, *A Tour through the Famine Districts of India* (London: A. D. Innes, 1898), facing p. 185.

2.3. "Waiting for Food," Rev. J. E. Scott, *In Famine Land: Observations and Experiences in India during the Great Drought of 1899–1900* (London: Harper and Brothers, 1904), facing p. 16.

and benevolent administration," the photographs were a mise-en-scène of the famine and its relief. Unlike later photos documenting the relief operation, the early pictures of helpless, starving people and skeletal bodies lacked a specific referent; rather than record a time or place, they evoked general conditions—"Disposal of the Dead in Famine Time," "Waiting for Food," "The Horrors of Famine: Partly Eaten by Jackals While Alive"—which lent drama and a grisly authenticity to his narrative. Thus, a harrowing account of a cholera outbreak at a famine-relief camp near Godhra in May 1900 was illustrated simply by images portraying the collection and cremation of the unidentified dead (Figure 2.4).[57] Even this combination of eyewitness accounts and photographs, Scott assured his readers, failed to fully convey the "indescribable horror, an unspeakable misery," of famine, for it left out "the most pathetic, and yet most common features—the groans of the suffering, the cry of the hungry, and the pa-

2.4. Cremation of famine victims. Rev. J. E. Scott, *In Famine Land: Observations and Experiences in India during the Great Drought of 1899–1900* (London: Harper and Brothers, 1904), facing p. 106.

thetic pleading of mothers for their children."[58] And yet then came the carefully detailed photographic record of the relief in action: relief workers, famine victims being sorted on arrival at a relief center, rescued children, kitchens, "*Christian Herald* corn" ready for distribution, natives waiting to buy the grain, and finally a bishop baptizing orphans—souls as well as bodies were saved. Strikingly, Scott documented the success of this drama of humanitarian relief in a sequence of three photographs demonstrating the improving condition of orphaned children after two, three, and four months (Figure 2.5). It was, then, over a century ago that the photographic conventions that still shape our coverage of famines as news and prompt our humanitarian responses to them were first established.

Hunger has not always been news, for the hungry only became objects of humanitarian sympathy relatively recently. They first came to

2.5. Proof of the humanitarian pudding. Rev. J. E. Scott, *In Famine Land: Observations and Experiences in India during the Great Drought of 1899–1900* (London: Harper and Brothers, 1904), facing p. 162.

be viewed as victims in the middle of the nineteenth century, and by the first decade of the following century the plight of the hungry had become a principal focus of humanitarian concern, as the new journalists exposed the shocking human costs of hunger at home and abroad. Using a range of techniques—eyewitness reports, carefully individuated stories, a focus on the suffering of women and children, reportage allowing the hungry to speak for themselves, photographs of starving bodies—these journalists involved their readers emotionally and demonstrated the tragedy of those who, through no fault of their own, had to try to survive the miseries of hunger. It was only by exploding the Malthusian critique of the hungry as the architects of their own misery that journalists were able to render the hungry sympathetic figures deserving of humanitarian action. The humanitarian discovery of hunger was thus a deeply historical and highly contingent process. It reminds us that—as hunger was discovered at particular times, in specific places—the hungry were first reviled and later subject to the unpredictable ebbs and flows of moral sympathy and humanitarian attention. Yet—and this is a critical point—the humanitarian discovery of hunger helped establish the right to subsistence, or at least the belief that it was morally wrong to allow another human being to starve to death. If that new principle was unevenly applied across the British Empire, it was nonetheless distinctly cosmopolitan in conception and orientation, representing for some the culmination of a truly liberal vision of the civilizing mission of empire. As we shall see in the following chapter, it was not long before this newly conceived human right not to hunger became a reason for political mobilization. Across the British Empire a variety of political groups sought to capitalize on the defusing of the Malthusian view by extending their critique to colonial and colonizing states that had failed to protect their subjects and citizens from the ravages of hunger. It was no longer sufficient, they claimed, for hunger to be addressed solely by fickle humanitarian concern; this scourge required the attention of a properly representative government.

3

Hunger as Political Critique

As Queen Victoria opened the Great Exhibition to celebrate the prosperous modernity that free trade had delivered to Britain, census workers across the Irish Sea were discovering the horrific human cost of the Great Hunger in Ireland. It was estimated that a quarter of its eight million people had died or fled its shores.[1] For many, this enormous contrast of plenty and want within the world's first industrial nation and its closest colony, encapsulated the lessons of classical political economy taught by Smith and Malthus. While the benefits of free trade predicted by Smith were on display at the Crystal Palace, Ireland appeared to furnish Britons with a grim fulfillment of Malthus's laws of population.[2] The British conception of the Irish as a primitive and indigent peasant people had long fueled a neo-Malthusian understanding of Ireland as an overpopulated territory whose "surplus" population prevented the land reforms necessary to ensure economic growth and prosperity. Charles Trevelyan, knighted for his handling of the famine when he was an assistant secretary at the Treasury, reflected that the potato blight was "a direct stroke of an all-wise and all-merciful Providence," which had provided overpopulated Ireland with "the sharp but effectual remedy by which the cure is likely to be effected."[3] As Alan Taylor once pithily remarked, the best that can be said of officials like Trevelyan was that they "were highly

conscientious men, and their consciences never reproached them";
they acted in good faith, on the principles handed down by Smith and
Malthus, or at least the legacies afforded them following the evangelical revival and the reaction against the French Revolution.[4] The same
could be said of colonial administrators in India, who presided over
the loss of as many as fifteen million lives to famine during the last
three decades of the nineteenth century.[5] And yet by the outbreak of
the First World War this Malthusian view had been thoroughly dis-
credited. Instead, in both metropolitan and colonial settings, the effectiveness of government had come to be measured by the absence,
not the presence, of hunger and famine. This chapter is the story of
that transformation.

Clearly, as we saw in the preceding chapter, the humanitarian discovery of hunger, not least in the context of famines in Ireland and
India, was critical in first challenging the Malthusian ethic and establishing the basic inhumanity of ignoring or justifying hunger. In this
sense it was a necessary condition for the politicization of hunger: until hunger was viewed as morally wrong and inhumane, it had no
force as a basis for political critique. At the same time, the political
critique of hunger that was developed across the British Empire in
the Victorian and Edwardian period also strengthened and extended
the arguments of humanitarian critics. Their task was not simply to
neutralize the Malthusian condemnation of the hungry; it was to invert it by establishing the moral strength of those who had endured
hunger and the immorality of those who had made them do so.

In the hands of Irish and Indian nationalists, famine came to represent the inhumanity and incompetence of British rule: the British had
promised free trade, prosperity, and civilization; they had delivered
famine and pestilence. One could not condone the piles of corpses
numbering in the millions: there was no greater index of the failure
of either British colonial rule or the promise of its political economy.
Famine, the critics insisted, was not the result of the neo-Malthusian
calculus, a providential check on those who lacked the moral character to restrain their own population growth or raise themselves up by
their own industry. Rather, famine highlighted the moral strength of

those who suffered; and unnecessary colonial famines mocked the universal pretensions of classical political economy. Here the nationalist use of famine to critique colonial rule became a claim to sovereignty: they willed a new nation into existence by documenting its collective suffering.

Although no body count was made in Britain, there too those awaiting citizenship made hunger an index of political exclusion and a mark of the moral strength and fortitude of the disenfranchised. In the early years of the twentieth century, unemployed workers, many of them veterans of the recent war in South Africa, invented the hunger march to dramatize their plight. Marching to London from towns and cities from across the Midlands and industrial Northwest, they sought to demonstrate their manly strength and fitness for work, to establish that the unemployed were not unemployable but victimized by the neglect of an unrepresentative and unresponsive government. Similarly, just a few years later, in 1909, British suffragettes went on hunger strike in protest against their own exclusion from citizenship. Never before used as a vehicle of political protest in Britain or its empire, the hunger strike was a tactic designed to highlight the illegality and violence on which women's political subjection rested—a point driven home by the Liberal government's dependence upon the decidedly illiberal measure of force-feeding those on hunger strike. It was a tactic that after the First World War quickly came to form a central tactic in nationalist protest in both Ireland and India, one used similarly in both places to expose the apparent contradictions between the ostensible rule of law and the violent realities of British colonial rule. Just as the nationalist critique of colonial famines celebrated those who had the strength to endure them and the hunger march proved the moral and physical fortitude of those who could march to London, so the hunger strike demonstrated the courage of those subjugated by colonial rule. Frequently a grotesque spectacle of brinkmanship ensued: the brutal inhumanity of a state prepared to allow its subjects to die was contrasted with the willingness of the strikers to risk their own lives to further their claims to citizenship and independence.

My point is not that there was a causal connection between the critique of colonial famine, the birth of the hunger march and the practice of hunger striking; it is not that one gave way to the other, or that they depended on one another. Instead, in the specific historical moment—that stretched from the Irish famine to the era of the First World War—hunger contributed to political critique in a variety of ways. Although hunger had long been deeply carved into the lives of British subjects at home and abroad, it was its politicization at this time that gave the experience new meaning and a profound political charge. Hunger certainly hurt, but it hurt all the more when it was understood to be a result of misgovernment, rather than the unavoidable consequence of natural or providential laws. This politicization of hunger was decidedly transnational in scope: it stretched across and beyond the British Empire, yet it assumed locally specific characteristics among Irish and Indian nationalists or the unemployed workers and suffragettes of Britain. Even when they employed similar methods, such as the hunger strike, those took on different forms in each setting and drew strength from local political and cultural traditions. Yet the politics of hunger reveals more than how patterns of cultural difference inform what Ranajit Guha described as the prose of counterinsurgency.[6] Instead, hunger became the basis for political tactics and critiques that exposed the claim of the modern state to care for its subjects as founded upon an act of original violence capable of reducing them to what Agamben calls "bare life."[7]

Famine and British Misrule

In 1920s Blackburn, "Billy" Woodruff's Irish grandmother was fond of telling him that the "trouble with the English is that they can never remember what the Irish can never forget."[8] The famine, which she insisted was, to "England's shame," not a famine but a "great starvin'," was her ultimate example. It was John Mitchel, an Ulster-born Protestant, who gave Billy Woodruff's grandmother her line, by insisting in *The Last Conquest of Ireland (Perhaps)* that the famine represented an indictment of British rule and its political economy. How, he asked, could it be that "an island which is said to be an antegral [*sic*] part of the richest empire on the globe—and the most fertile portion of that empire— . . . should in five and a half years lose two and a half millions of its people (more than one-fourth) by hunger, and fever the consequence of hunger, and flight beyond the sea to escape from hunger,—while that empire . . . was all the while advancing in wealth, prosperity, and comfort, at a faster pace than ever before"?[9]

Refuting the widespread belief that the famine was an act of providence, Mitchel argued that it was manmade in England, where the potato blight was the pretext for a knowingly perpetrated genocide. Using Britain's own parliamentary reports, blue books, and census figures, he provided a litany of examples—ample harvests, exports of grain from Ireland, the profiteering use of relief supplies, the absence of British funds for relief, incompetent and murderous bureaucrats, and opportunistic Anglo-Irish landlords determined to rid themselves of unproductive tenants—that demonstrated a concerted British policy of starvation and depopulation. To blame providence or the potato blight was, he argued, to ignore that a "million and a half men, women and children were carefully, prudently, and peacefully slain by the English government. They died from hunger in the midst of abundance which their own hands had created . . . The Almighty indeed sent the potato blight, but the English created the famine."[10] No wonder, since Mitchel, that the Irish remember what the English forget.

Mitchel condemned the English for the willful inhumanity with which they adhered to the supposedly universal principles of political economy, regardless of its cost in Irish lives. At the height of the famine in 1847, he had presciently called for a specifically Irish political economy that would distinguish itself from what he described as the free-trade famine economics of the English, which ensured that if "Irishmen are hungry, it is that Englishmen may be filled."[11] His association of classical political economy with the English and famine was doubly damning; it undercut both the presumed universality of the laws of political economy and its promise to deliver the wealth of nations, at least to any nation other than England. Its advocates in the

Dublin Statistical Society (established in the same year Mitchel published his polemic) quickly denounced Mitchel's claim that political economy was identified with any one nationality.[12] Over the next two decades, however, even they began to recognize that Ireland was an "anomaly" that refused to bend to the universal laws of political economy. Seeking an explanation in the structure of Irish society for this anomaly, they became more attentive to the historical and national conditions within which markets operated.[13] Ireland, they reasoned, played by different rules than did England: in Ireland, land was inextricably tied to a broader customary moral economy that could not be reduced to market-driven conceptions of private property and the laws of contract; there the Catholic emphasis on community and family was at odds with Protestant individualism.[14] It is no accident that in the decades following the famine those intent on developing a more historically oriented political economy—one that, following List, was attentive to nationally specific paths of economic development—were Irishmen: Isaac Butt, J. E. Cairnes, Cliffe Leslie, and J. K. Ingram.[15] The famine had exposed Britain's classical political economy as a phony and irredeemably English science; it had also paved the way for a historical economics that following Arnold Toynbee would provide a searing social critique of industrialism in metropolitan Britain.[16]

Mitchel's call for an Irish political economy appears to have had less resonance than did his portrayal of a nation suffering under the yoke of unconstitutional British rule. Although such later nationalist leaders as Isaac Butt and Arthur Griffith continued to use the famine as a catastrophic example of the price Ireland had paid at the hands of Britain's classical political economy, most focused on the political causes and cultural consequences of British rule.[17] It was the economic historian George O'Brien who, turning back to the famine, powerfully reintegrated the political and the economic critiques of colonial rule. The famine, he argued, exposed the central contradiction of British rule: its insistence on treating Ireland as an indistinguishable part of Britain's free market when it came to economic policy, but as an entirely separate juridical unit when it came to the legal and political liberties afforded by the British constitution.[18] He insisted that the British imposition of free trade on Ireland as a "cure" for the famine willfully ignored the fragility of an Irish economy that had been drained of its wealth and left undeveloped since the Act of Union—and in taking this position he implicitly drew on the late nineteenth-century Indian critique of British colonial misrule.

Mitchel's portrayal of his own struggles and sacrifices, culminating with his imprisonment and deportation to a life of exile in the United States, as synonymous with those of the nation, and the people who perished during the famine, proved most enduring. Certainly, many literary and historical accounts over the next half century continually reiterated his point that the heroic suffering of Ireland during the famine had ensured its ultimate redemption; fewer, however, repeated his analysis of the Great Hunger as an unnecessary genocide.[19] Andrew Merry's description of his encounter in 1910 with Irishmen who as children had lived through the "nation's deepest misery" gives at least some of the flavor of these works: they told "of events burnt by personal suffering upon the memory . . . as if they happened yesterday . . . of difficulties too gigantic to be wholly overcome, of self-sacrifices so heroic as to be worthy of undying fame, of humanity and brotherly love reaching the highest standard, for many lives were freely laid down, and many lives, far worse than any death, were as bravely lived, for the sake of others."[20] The folk memories collected for the centenary commemoration of the famine told a less heroic tale, one that spoke to the ambivalence many felt about the national memory left in Mitchel's wake. In fact, providence, that great ally of British misrule, was routinely invoked. The famine was seen as a punishment for past misdemeanors: it struck down the extravagant, the wasteful, and the ungodly, while others were miraculously redeemed and rescued by strange events, such as the sudden and mysterious appearance of food.[21] Although some nationalists had pointed to the complicity of Catholic priests in encouraging fateful resignation to the will of providence, the Catholic Church energetically ensured that it was remembered for its humanitarian role, by transmitting countless stories of the self-sacrifices, courage, and generosity of its

priests, as well as a denunciation of evangelical Protestants for prey-
ing on the souls of the fearful and dying. The idealization of passive
suffering, of faith and martyrdom, thus made common cause with nationalist accounts of the famine.[22] A nationalist politics of hunger,
powerfully wrought by a Catholic sensibility and aesthetic, emerged
from this commemoration of the famine.[23] Later we shall see something of its power and legacy in the hunger strike of Terence Mac-
Swiney.

It was in India, however, that famine became most fully identified
with the failure of British colonial rule. After all, India, which had
long been the experimental station of British political economists and
utilitarian reformers, formed a testing ground for a range of projects like land reform that were deemed politically impossible in
Ireland.[24] It would always be in India that the promise of imperial
Britain to deliver prosperity, civility, and modernity would be most
thoroughly examined. As Malthus had taught certain East India Company officials, Charles Trevelyan among them, political economy at
Haileybury, it was hardly surprising that famines in India were officially viewed as acts of providence, checks on overpopulation of a
territory by peasants unwilling to learn the discipline of the market
economy. Providence usually took the form of "natural" phenomena
such as drought and crop failure. Recognition of this fact heightened
officials' determination to demonstrate that the colonial state could
"improve" India by mastering its natural environment, or at least temper its worst excesses, through more efficient government of its resources and people.[25] This was especially the case after the imposition
of direct rule in 1859, when the government of India accelerated the
expansion not only of major engineering projects—irrigation works,
rail networks, communication systems—but the grids of intelligibil-
ity through which the nation's resources—its territory, its people,
and the products of their labor—were understood and organized, in
texts with titles like *Moral and Material Progress Report*. As scholars now
suggest that the colonial state itself was actually forged through this
process, we should recall the centrality of famine to it.[26] Established
in the aftermath of the 1876 famine, the Famine Fund promised

investments in technical infrastructure like rail and irrigation that would improve India's rural economy and allow grain to be moved from places of plenty to places of dearth. The fund also supported the enactment of famine codes that would provide relief through public works for those unable to feed themselves but still able to work.[27] To the British way of thinking, then, colonial rule had not only rendered India less vulnerable to famine but had established a humanitarian framework for its relief when it—inevitably—struck.

This was a credo writ large in Rudyard Kipling's short story "William the Conqueror," published in 1896, on the eve of yet another famine in India. Kipling's tale describes the heroic British effort to provide relief to starving natives in famine-stricken Madras. Jimmy Hawkins, famine commissioner for the Punjab, diligently ensures that food supplies are transported by rail from his province but, alas, sends wheat and millet to rice-eating Madras. The hero of the story, Scott, an engineer in the Irrigation Department, overcomes this problem—one created not by Hawkins's oversight but by the superstitious dietary taboos of Hindus—by giving the rejected grain to goats, so that their milk can feed starving children. First published in *Ladies' Home Journal,* the story was accompanied by an illustration of Scott, as seen through the eyes of an adoring relief worker, surrounded by the plump naked children he has saved (Figure 3.1). It was a narrative that captured the myth of British colonial rule and neatly reconciled the existence of famine with the rhetoric of improvement and the forward march of the civilizing mission in India.[28]

Although after the Great Rebellion of 1857, known by some nationalists as the First War of Indian Independence, the British feared that famines would help mobilize resistance to their rule in India, that did not happen.[29] What famines did do was drive figures as diverse as Dadabhai Naoroji, William Digby, Mahadev Ranade, Romesh Dutt, and Henry Hyndman to generate powerful critiques of British colonial rule and of neo-Malthusian political economy that drew skillfully on the official reports and statistics of the colonial state's own information regime.[30] It was a strategy that forced the British not only to contest their own figures, but to rearticulate the justification for colo-

3.1. Kipling's conqueror of famine. *Ladies Home Journal,* January 1896.

nial rule according to the terms set by their nationalist critics. As the secretary of state for India, George Hamilton was forced to concede in Parliament, as another famine receded in 1901, "If it could be shown that India has retrograded in material prosperity under our rule we stand self-condemned, and we ought no longer to be trusted with the control of the country."[31]

This had been Naoroji's position for some forty years, which is why many called him, in a nod to William Gladstone, the Grand Old Man of Indian nationalism.[32] As early as 1870 he had used official statistics to show how, far from delivering prosperity and improvement, British rule had drained India of its wealth, impoverished its people, and subjected them to a series of devastating famines. There was, he argued, a good reason for which the colonial state had not included per capita income figures in its economic digests and reports: such figures would have exposed the deteriorating condition of the people. By his calculation, even in the model province of Punjab, minimum subsistence costs (thirty-four rupees) exceeded average per capita income (twenty rupees) by an alarming 80 percent. Refuting Naoroji's figures became a cottage industry among officials and apologists for the colonial state, which was eventually forced in the 1890s to include per capita income figures in the official economic records.[33] Though the colonial state had sought through the use of statistics to obscure its impoverishment of the Indian people, it could not hide the horror of famines, or escape responsibility for them. Viewing famine, like poverty, as the direct consequence of the draining away of wealth, Naoroji used it as an index of British misrule. "How strange it is," he caustically wrote, "that the British rulers do not see that . . . it is the drain of India's wealth by them that lays at their own door the dreadful results of misery, starvation, and deaths of millions . . . Why blame poor Nature when the fault lies at your own door?"[34]

In the eyes of Romesh Dutt and William Digby, the history of famines in India provided further evidence of British culpability. Whereas Dutt used the Famine Commission Reports of 1880 and 1898 to catalogue a melancholy "record of twenty-two famines within a period of 130 years of British rule in India," Digby dug deeper into colonial records, to reveal not only that the toll—twenty-six famines in the century preceding 1900—was even graver, but that the scale and frequency of famines had grown and accelerated.[35] In a classic indictment of British rule, Dutt argued that—despite forty years of direct rule in which the British had enjoyed peace, a fertile land, a loyal and industrious people, and generations of specially trained administrators—"famines have not disappeared. Within the last forty years, within the memory of the present writer, there have been ten famines in India, and at a moderate computation, the loss of lives from starvation and disease brought on by these famines may be estimated at fifteen millions within these forty years." No "other country on earth enjoying a civilized administration" would have tolerated the decimation of a "population equal to half of that of England" within a span of time so short that "men and women, still in middle age, can remember."[36] This colonial record of starvation was frequently contrasted with the era before the arrival of the British, when the people were not so pauperized as to lack the resources, material and spiri-

tual, to survive poor harvests or crop failures.[37] As the founder of
Britain's Social Democratic Federation (SDF) and great friend of Indian nationalism, Henry Hyndman, put it in his book *The Ruin of India
by British Rule,* published in 1907, a year when another deadly famine
was sweeping across India, "famines occurred in India before our conquest; but continuous famine such as now afflicts some part of India
every year was wholly unknown under Hindoo or Mohammedan
rule." It was hardly, he added, a fine testament to "the blessings of European civilisation."[38] This account of the drain on the subcontinent's
wealth and the history of colonial famines it produced would, as we
shall see in Chapter 6, resurface during the Bengal famine of 1943,
which for many represented the final nail in the coffin of British
rule.[39]

Directed against the inflated claims and violent injustices of colonial rule, the drain theory and the nationalist history of famine both
drew upon and departed from British political and economic idioms.
Although the influence of Naoroji's drain theory on economic critiques of colonial rule can not be underestimated, in its original form
it demonstrated a remarkable fidelity to traditional British constitutionalism and political economy. Three elements of the drain—the
exorbitant salaries and unproductive wealth of colonial officials; the
huge cost of maintaining a vast standing army charged with maintaining British supremacy beyond India; and the huge tax burden borne
by those denied political representation—drew directly on the arse-
nal of Britain's radical constitutionalist tradition and its critique of
"Old Corruption."[40] Moreover, Naoroji complained that Britain had
deliberately denied India the benefits of free trade, by using taxes
and tariffs to ensure an unequal exchange between India, forced to
export its raw materials cheaply, in return for expensive British
imported manufactures. If Britain only practiced the free trade it
preached, Naoroji insisted, "the result would be the re-appearance of
prosperity, accompanied by still greater prosperity for England."[41]
This was no prototheory of underdevelopment; it was a critique of
colonial rule elaborated largely within the framework of classical political economy and constitutionalist rhetoric.[42]

Not surprisingly, Naoroji's analysis had resonance in Britain, where, taken up by figures like Digby and Hyndman, it found a diverse audience that accepted British responsibility for the Madras famine in 1876.[43] Rejecting the complacent and tardy report of the Famine Commission in 1880, they proposed a reduction in taxation and military expenditure, a progressive famine fund to provide relief, and new public health programs and irrigation schemes.[44] Even Gladstone frequently evoked British misrule in India, especially the use of famine funds to wage an unjust war against Afghanistan, during the Midlothian campaign; but the hopes that his administration, as it edged toward home rule for Ireland, would advance the case for reform in India were quickly dashed. Having served as president of the newly established Indian National Congress in 1886, Naoroji, convinced that India's salvation depended on that fickle beast, the British public conscience, traveled to Britain.[45] There he worked closely with Digby, who became secretary to the British Committee of the Indian National Congress in 1889 and eventually masterminded Naoroji's election as Liberal M.P. for Finsbury Central in 1892.[46] Both Digby and Naoroji proved adept at deploying the familiar narratives and styles of the gentlemanly leader that had long dominated British reform movements, by emphasizing the sacrifices they had endured as they had labored in the wilderness to deliver the Indian nation from starvation and colonial bondage.[47] By 1899, Romesh Dutt's presidential address to the Indian National Congress further enhanced the resonance of Naoroji's drain theory among British reformers. With surely more than a nod toward Ireland, it identified crippling overassessment of land revenue and lack of investment by absentee landlords as the chief drain on Indian finances and the greatest causes of its poverty and famines. It was a case he too took to Britain, in 1900. While there he stood on many platforms with Naoroji, discussing the causes of the famine, which Dutt exhaustively demonstrated in a sweeping series of economic histories of India.[48]

Naoroji and Dutt believed, as Smith and Malthus had, that the laws of classical political economy really were universal, and that they would apply to India if the British would just stop obstructing them. The problem, they thought, was one not of political economy but of political representation; greater Indian involvement in the government of India would ensure that the drain and the obstacles it posed to the market were removed. Neither a democrat nor a critic of the free market, Naoroji, who paradoxically had once so much faith in British notions of honor, justice, and fair play, became the first to demand self-government from the Indian National Congress in 1906, just as his generation of national leaders came under pressure from those like Tilak who urged more radical analyses and militant tactics following Curzon's partition of Bengal. Although, unlike Naoroji and Dutt, Mahadev Ranade never placed famine at the center of his analysis of India's economic woes, he did develop a more critical nationalist view of the limits of classical British political economy, one that drew on the work of List.[49] In his classic 1892 lecture "Indian Political Economy" Ranade echoed Mitchel in insisting that the supposedly universal laws of classical political economy were actually nothing of the sort, but rather historically specific products of Britain's economic supremacy. Global markets were not competitive and free, but structured around Britain's comparative advantage: the supposedly natural international division of labor, in which Britain manufactured and India cultivated, was a fiction which ensured that the gospel of free trade continued to secure British domination of the global economy. In order to escape its position as a "dependent colonial economy," it was necessary to provide protection not only against the drain of wealth and materials, but *for* India's fledgling manufacturing industries, so that the economy could develop and modernize. This would entail not just a change in political representation but a new Indian vision of political economy. India would have to find its own national path to economic modernity, and Ranade hoped for an Indian political economy that was not abstracted from its social relations or from a concern for the collective welfare of society.[50] As in Ireland, it was the social that formed the basis for India's difference.

The Birth of the Hunger March

Despite the presence of figures like Dutt, Digby, and Naoroji in Britain, and despite the bridge that Hyndman provided between Indian

The Bootmakers' March on the War Office.
Scott Series Nº 618.   Walking from Raunds Nr Wellingboro to London.

3.2. The march from Raund. Gorman Collection. By permission of the People's History Museum.

nationalism and the labor movement, the politics of hunger in Britain centered on the unemployed and took the more practical form of the hunger march. Fittingly its origins lay with unemployed boot-workers. In May 1905, one hundred and fifteen of them determined to march from Raund in Leicestershire to London, to petition the War Office against undercutting the prices recommended by the National Union of Boot and Shoe Operatives and thus compelling them to work for, and live on, starvation wages (Figure 3.2).[51] A week later, inspired by their example—but against the advice of their formidable M.P., Kier Hardie, and members of the town trade council, who favored a rally at Hyde Park in support of the Unemployment Bill— four hundred of Leicester's one thousand unemployed men (including thirty from the workhouse), whose union benefit was now exhausted, followed suit.[52] The idea quickly spread. By 5 June Kier Hardie informed Prime Minister Balfour in the House of Commons that marches had now left Glasgow, Newcastle, Leeds, Liverpool, Manchester, Birmingham, and Leicester, to speed the passage of the Unemployment Bill, with the observation "It is only force which carries measures of this kind through the House."[53] In the words of Arthur Smith, secretary of Manchester's Unemployed Committee, those who were marching to London would "remain there until the Government thought it right that starving women and children should be helped."[54] In spite of these marches, and one the following January from Liverpool, it was after a march from Manchester in 1908, which never actually reached London, that the term "hunger march" was coined. "Starved off by lack of funds," the marchers reached the end of the road in Godstone, Surrey. Their charismatic leader Stewart Gray proposed to organize what he called a hunger march from London to Salisbury Plain, where he hoped to establish new farm colonies for the unemployed.[55] Then, on 14 July 1908, the *Manchester Guardian* reported that a number of the unemployed from the East End of London, "who describe themselves as 'Hunger Marchers' and state their intention of tramping under the leadership of Mr. Stewart Gray," held a meeting in Hyde Park.[56] The hunger march was born. And true to form, it had a troubled birth: the police confiscated the marchers' collection boxes.

These early hunger marches were distinguished by their militarism. As the petition carried by the Leicester marchers in 1905 informed the king: "Many of us are old soldiers . . . [and] took an active part in the late South African war . . . We are reduced to the extreme of misery and want . . . unable to fulfil one of the first duties of husbands and fathers, namely to provide food for our wives and children."[57] The injustice of Boer War veterans' returning to either no jobs or starvation wages was potent. Having risked their lives on the veldt of South Africa for the British state, they now demanded an acknowledgment of their "right to work." The committee of Liverpool's unemployed adopted that phrase as part of its name. Military discipline and organization was needed to secure this right. Leaders like the SDF agitator "General" James Gribble, who led the Raund men, and the colorful "Captain" Gibbon, who led the march from Liverpool, used their real or imagined military rank to bolster their authority.[58] Gribble's men were given a military formation, with an officer corps, an advanced cycle division, an ambulance, a band, and five companies of subaltern marchers led by "sergeants." Military discipline worked for Gribble; his men made it to London and back. It was not enough for the men that Gray marched from Manchester to London eighteen months later during the bitter winter months of January and February, although it too had a "large 'old armyman' element."[59] By the time they had left Birmingham, signs of rebellion had arisen in the ranks, including complaints about "autocratic" leaders' keeping "too tight a hold upon the purse-strings" and demanding too much of their men.[60] At Bedford fifty-eight of the seventy-four marchers accepted an offer of a free train ticket back home, while Gray assumed leadership from his hated deputy, the Independent Labour Party (ILP) activist Jack Williams, and led a "small and straggling band" to the famous private school at Eton, where he harangued its privileged pupils.

With every step they took, hunger marchers sought to refute the idea that the unemployed were morally and physically degenerate or, in a word, unemployable. Anticipating the importance of press coverage to later marches, local newspapers and the *Manchester Guardian* sent special correspondents to march with the men and provide daily reports on the privations and hardships faced and overcome: the thin and collapsing soles of the boots that gingerly navigated the frosty ridges of muddy roads, the nine-hour, thirty-mile stretches, the lack of interest or support in the towns the protesters marched through or stayed in, the empty collection boxes, the lack of food.[61] The greater the adversity, the greater the display of manly strength and moral discipline. Gray characteristically described those who followed him as "martyrs standing as beacons in oceans of blood and tears," but he then went on to "liken [himself] to a Moses seeking to free the people from bondage—not only from the extraneous Pharobe of 'organised' oppression . . . but also from the interwoven bondages of their own minds, to wit: physical and mental inertia."[62] The hunger march was thus a march as much against the forces of demoralization as against an unrepresentative government that ignored the workers' plight. Even the palpable lack of success of these early hunger marchers, their failure to meet with the authorities they petitioned, whether lowly ministers or monarchs, accentuated their heroic and manly determination. When the Leicester men reached St.

Albans, they received first a telegram from the secretary of state for home affairs, informing them that the king had refused to meet them, and then Prime Minister Balfour's declaration that "any such demonstrations of force . . . are inimical to the prospects of a bill."[63] When they reached London, the "great rally" in Hyde Park to greet them and gather support for the bill, organized by the Social Democratic Federation and the Independent Labour Party, was washed out by a thunderstorm. Yet in spite of repeated disappointments, as the men left to return to Leicester, Ramsay McDonald, the M.P. of many of the Leicester men, read a telegram from Kier Hardie describing the retreating marchers' odyssey as "heroic."[64]

The stubborn rehearsal of the constitutional process, of the right to petition for redress of grievances, and its studied refusal by those petitioned evoked a heroic tradition of constitutional protest.[65] When the secretary of state for war failed to meet the petitioning bootmakers from Raund, their leader Gribble disrupted a House of Commons debate, before being "forcibly ejected." Gray's Manchester men gamely set off, from a meeting of three thousand unemployed where they had burnt the Distress Committee in effigy, to petition the president of the Local Government Board "in favor of work being provided by the State for all willing workers."[66] As the march began to unravel, at Northampton, a desperate Gray telegraphed the queen and requested that the following postscript be appended to the king's speech: "We learn by telegraph that 75 faithful lieges [are] bearing on foot from Manchester, Birmingham and other towns a petition to us for restoration of ancient right to work . . . Some men sick, others bootless. Women and children abandoned on journey or evicted and starving along with twenty-five thousand left behind."[67] Needless to say, it did not make it into the final text of the king's speech.

When the constitutional process failed to provide work for those who had risked their lives for the nation, all that was left to attempt was an appeal for humanitarian support. When all other avenues of redress had been denied them, one of the leaders of the Leicester marchers, the Reverend Donaldson, unsuccessfully requested a meeting with the Archbishop of Canterbury.[68] Although every march had its collection boxes to support the marchers and the families they had

3.3. Storming Manchester's cathedral. Gorman Collection. By permission of the People's History Museum.

left behind, Gray made a particular point of demanding that, as the government had failed to act, the church had a duty to provide philanthropic assistance. As the congregation sang "Christians, Awake!" at Manchester Cathedral's Christmas Day service of 1907, Gray entered the pulpit with the words "I cannot understand your singing a hymn of this kind when thousands in the city are starving" and then demanded donations to establish a new farm colony for the city's unemployed.[69] Six months later, he invited church leaders and the bishop of London to lead a hunger march, and when they refused, he led forty-seven men to Canterbury to interrupt a service at the cathedral.[70] The following month, buoyed by his insistence that they should "demand food and clothes from the people who should be looking after the material and spiritual welfare of the people," fifteen hundred unemployed men marched to Manchester Cathedral and disrupted a Sunday afternoon service (Figure 3.3).[71]

The Edwardian hunger march articulated often-contradictory claims concerning the rights of veterans to jobs, the manly and moral

strength of those denied work for no fault of their own, their constitutional right to petition against a political system from which they
were excluded and which had failed to represent their interests, and
their humanitarian right to philanthropic assistance. Although there
was seemingly little cohesiveness in these marches or their claims,
that failing should not detract from the way in which they dramatized
not only the exemplary moral and manly qualities of those who hungered for lack of work, but the fecklessness of a political system that
excluded them, despite their military service to the nation, and an
economic system that had left them without work and unable to support their families. Moreover, as we shall see in Chapter 8, they had
given birth to a form of protest that would be reanimated in Britain
after the war and which was to spread to many other countries.

"Beyond Common Endurance": The Politics of the Hunger Strike

The hunger strike also had a transnational career. From tsarist Russia
the use of hunger strikes spread quickly across the British empire,
from those by suffragettes in Britain after 1909 to those by their
counterparts in Ireland in 1912, from protests against the colonial
color bar—by Gandhi in South Africa in 1913 and by Sikh migrants
to Canada in 1914—to demonstrations by conscientious objectors in
Britain and by Irish republicans in 1916, and finally to strikes by Indian nationalists after 1918.[72] Clearly, in each context the hunger
strike was adapted to a particular set of political conditions and given
an appropriate historical genealogy that heightened its purchase as a
form of protest. These differences should not obscure how suffragettes in Britain as well as Irish and Indian nationalists all used the
hunger strike to articulate a powerful critique of the illegal and violent state of their subjection by the British and the colonial state. In
doing so, they valorized hunger as an indication of moral strength,
not Malthusian weakness. They offered a contrast between their commitment to die for the cause and the immorality of a state that
claimed to have their welfare at heart yet kept them subjugated and
either force-fed them to keep them alive or simply let them perish.

The hunger strike arrived in Britain on 5 July 1909. On that day Marion Dunlop refused her prison food, in protest at the government's refusal to recognize her offense (which was writing a clause of the Bill of Rights on the walls of the Houses of Parliament) as a political, rather than a criminal, act.[73] Released after ninety-one hours on hunger strike, she was greeted by the Women's Social and Political Union (WSPU) as an exemplary figure whose protest had demonstrated her selfless commitment to the cause.[74] By the end of the month, at a meeting that had included Gandhi among the audience, Dunlop praised fourteen others who had followed her example.[75] Soon *Votes for Women* was providing weekly honor rolls for all those on hunger strike, as well as publishing accounts of their experiences.[76] These prison narratives helped establish the hunger strike as the tactic of Dunlop and the suffragettes. No reference was ever made to the masculine and Russian genealogy of the hunger strike, other than to equate the "unconstitutional" treatment of hunger strikers by the Liberal government with Russian tyranny. Instead, the suffragettes claimed that the selflessness and discipline demanded of the hunger striker made this a particularly appropriate form of protest for women. Devotion to the cause came to be measured according to a calculus of pain, suffering, and endurance: the number of times one had been force-fed, the techniques used, the level of brutality employed by prison doctors and wardresses.[77] It was a tactic that skillfully exploited the way in which the humanitarian discovery of hunger had rendered the spectacle of a starving woman morally repugnant, a reaction that the suffragettes sought to mobilize against the state which refused them the vote.

The infectious enthusiasm for the hunger strike among suffragettes soon spread to Ireland. In 1912, the British suffragette Lizzie Barker was imprisoned for throwing a hatchet at the carriage of Prime Minister Asquith in Dublin and was refused status as a political prisoner. Within two years, twenty-two Irish suffragettes had followed her by hunger striking in prison.[78] Hannah Sheehy Skeffington, one of the first to go on hunger strike, recalled that the "hunger-strike was then a new weapon—we were the first to try it out in Ireland." Consequently, she wrote, "Sinn Fein and its allies regarded [the tactic] as a womanish thing."[79] This was soon to change. During the 1920s, in the rush to assemble an exclusively male republican tradition for the hunger strike, its prior history was quickly forgotten and the hunger strikes of republican women all but ignored. Like the suffragettes, members of the Irish republican movement gendered the hunger strike in particular ways to suit their idea of who was capable of the requisite self-sacrifice and self-discipline.[80] The first male hunger strike in Ireland took place in September 1913, six months after Sheehy Skeffington's, when the socialist nationalist James Connolly refused to recognize the British government's authority to ban a meeting at which he had been arrested.[81] Republican leaders like Eamon de Valera initially expressed ambivalence toward the hunger strike; even so, between Thomas Ashe's death from being force-fed in 1917, after which forty thousand protesters flooded the streets of Dublin, and the death of Terence MacSwiney after seventy-four days on hunger strike in 1920, which "the whole world watched in anguish," an impeccably nationalist genealogy had been invented for that form of resistance.[82] It was increasingly associated not only with masculine strength and endurance but with a specifically Catholic sense of the purity and redemptive power of abstinence and sacrifice—hence the often agonized debates that surrounded discussion of whether it represented a form of suicide that violated Catholic doctrine. Subsequently, an older Irish Celtic tradition was found for the republican hunger strike, one that stretched back to the ancient custom of *Senchus Mor,* according to which a victim of debt or injustice could fast on the threshold of the house of those who had wronged him, until a settlement was reached, and its practice by Saint Patrick, the patron saint of Ireland.[83] Fortified with these "elements of the legal code of ancient Ireland, of the self-denial that is the central characteristic of Irish Catholicism, and the propensity for endurance and sacrifice that is the hallmark of militant Irish nationalism," the hunger strike was assured a significant future in the Irish republican struggle.[84]

Paradoxically, the earliest reference to the Celtic genealogy of the hunger strike I have found came not from Ireland, but from a "former resident" of British India writing in the *Manchester Guardian,* during Gandhi's fast against the proposal by the Lothian Committee to award separate electoral representation for the "untouchables" in September 1932. Claiming that it was an ascetic act through which saints brought pressure to bear upon kings and gods, and suggesting that this primitive practice had once been universal and still held sway among "simple folk everywhere and in all ages," the writer traced the provenance of hunger striking to ancient Ireland and India. Nonetheless, insisting on the Indianness of Gandhi's fast, he situated it within "the traditional mythology and philosophy of Mother India" through the custom of "sitting *dhurna,*" where, just as with *Senchus Mor,* those wronged fast until they are vindicated.[85] This account rehearsed a genealogy of the hunger strike that first appeared in the *Times* during the height of the suffragette hunger strikes in March 1913. In an article, Hutcheson Macaulay Posnett, a professor in Auckland and an early champion of comparative literature, compared the suffragettes' use of the tactic to the "barbarous and immoral" Indian practice of sitting *dhurna* that had, according to his friend, the late eminent jurist Sir Henry Maine, rightly been proscribed under the civilizing influence of the Indian Penal Code of 1860.[86] The following day George Birdwood, a retired and distinguished Indian official well acquainted with antiquarian investigations of Indian customs, disputed Posnett's account by claiming firsthand experience of the custom from his service in Bombay, where the local women had sat *dhurna* against him until he blessed them with sons.[87] Birdwood claimed that although the custom was "based on the strongest and deepest instincts of humanity" and appeared to have a universal place in mythology, it had been dying out before the much-vaunted Indian Penal Code outlawed it.[88]

It is intriguing to consider whether these discussions of *dhurna,* which themselves stretched back to the compendiums of Indian customs assembled by British administrators from the late eighteenth century, facilitated the metamorphosis of the fast into the hunger strike and its adoption as a weapon of nationalist protest in India.[89] It certainly provided an impeccably Indian genealogy for the custom. In the years following the First World War, Indian nationalists, inspired,

it seems, by events in Ireland, began a series of hunger strikes to protest the injustices of colonial rule.[90] Yet despite their frequency—and
this could well be termed the golden age of the hunger strike in
anticolonial struggles—it was Gandhi's fasts that attracted the most
attention in Britain. His emaciated frame came to embody for many
the struggle for an Indian nation, just as MacSwiney's protest came to
embody the heroic endurance of the Irish people against the inhumanity, if not necessarily the illegality, of British rule. Less than a year
after the debate in the *Times* on *dhurna,* Gandhi undertook the first of
at least fifteen significant fasts in his lifetime, all of which enacted in
different ways the trials of the Indian nation and his own claim to
moral leadership of it.[91]

Whether the fast as hunger strike was presented as a holdover
from a universal primitive practice or as the particular product of a
national history, it became effective as a weapon of political protest
only in the early twentieth century, after humanitarian considerations
had established that starving to death was unnatural, immoral, and inhumane. In that sense it is not surprising that women, one of the first
objects of humanitarian sympathy in the discovery of hunger, first
made use of the hunger strike. Like the Irish and Indian nationalists
who followed them, they sought to politically mobilize that sympathy
to highlight the illegality of the metropolitan or colonial state and expose the inhumanity and violence upon which its rule appeared to
depend. Hunger strikes invariably began as a form of constitutional
protest, an insistence that the rule of law and constitutionality had
been violated, and as a way of demonstrating that this state of exception could be maintained by only force.

In Britain the hunger strike began as a dispute over the limits and
meanings of the constitution: Dunlop was protesting against being
criminalized for rubber-stamping a clause from the Bill of Rights on
the walls of Parliament. As *Votes for Women* reminded its readers, if
"she had been a Russian defying the tyranny of the Czar and fighting
for political freedom thousands of miles away the Liberal Press of this
country would have been full of admiration for her conduct."[92] After
Dunlop, the WSPU consistently presented those on hunger strike as

champions of liberty and the English constitution, by contrast with the professedly Liberal government, whose prosecution of citizens for exercising constitutional forms of protest was equated with the tyrannical policies of tsarist Russia.

It was a task made easier first by the escalation, and then by the vacillation, in the government's response. While Dunlop had been confined to the infirmary, those who followed her were first placed in punishment cells and then force-fed. Three weeks after the home secretary, Herbert Gladstone, had authorized the use of forced-feeding in late September 1909, its first victim, Mary Leigh, gave a graphic description of being force-fed by nasal tube, an account widely disseminated in the suffragette press. As Weitzman has shown, suffragettes soon branded the government's use of forcible feeding as unconstitutional "torture," most famously in a series of gothic images that again played on the parallels with the tyrannies of the Spanish Inquisition or tsarist Russia (see, for example, Figure 3.4).[93] These images of women being held down and fed by force were used to illustrate the illiberality of a state that was dependent on violence to suppress the constitutional claims of its subjects.[94] The success of this strategy was immediately made evident by the government's successive attempts to defuse it. Less than six months after the introduction of forcible feeding, the new home secretary, Winston Churchill, effectively removed the professed cause of hunger strikes by allowing special privileges to suffragette prisoners.[95] In March 1912, however, withdrawal of these privileges by his successor at the Home Office, Reginald McKenna, prompted a fresh wave of hunger strikes, which were met with the reintroduction of forcible feeding. Faced with growing criticism of the practice, McKenna retreated once more, introducing the infamous "Cat and Mouse," or Prisoners (Temporary Discharge for Ill-Health) Act, in April 1913. Designed to replace forcible feeding, it allowed for the temporary release of hunger strikers, until they had regained their health sufficiently to resume serving their sentences. Within six months it had collapsed: those released committed new offenses and escaped rearrest.

As we shall see, the government sought to justify forcible feeding

"*Votes for Women,*" *January 28, 1910.*   *Registered at the G.P.O. as a Newspaper.*

VOTES FOR WOMEN

EDITED BY FREDERICK AND EMMELINE PETHICK LAWRENCE.

VOL. III. (New Series), No. 99.   FRIDAY, JANUARY 28, 1910.   Price 1d. Weekly. (Post Free, 1½d.)

THE GOVERNMENT'S METHODS OF BARBARISM.

FORCIBLE FEEDING IN PRISON.

In some cases, instead of nasal feeding as in the picture, the still more dangerous practice of feeding through the mouth, by a tube, down the throat, is adopted. This was done in the case of Jane Warton.

(This Cartoon is being made into a Poster, which can be obtained separately. Particulars will be found on page 274.)

CONTENTS.

THE OUTLOOK.

In view of the repeated statements which the Secretary of State has made in Parliament, he can only regard the statement that Lady Constance Lytton's release had anything to do with her rank or social position as a wilful and deliberate misrepresentation. She was released solely because she was suffering from serious heart disease, and medical treatment appropriate to her case would have involved some risk to her life.—*Mr. Herbert Gladstone to the Fabian Society, November 22, 1909.*

The extract quoted above formed part of the answer of the Home Secretary to the charge of the Fabian Society made in reference to the release of Lady Constance Lytton from Newcastle Gaol, that the reason why Lady Constance Lytton was released from prison was that forcible feeding "is an outrage too disgusting to be offered to a woman of rank." The recent imprisonment of Lady Constance Lytton in Walton Green Gaol, Liverpool, with the full accompaniment of forcible feeding and other outrages, has demonstrated incontrovertibly that it is Mr. Gladstone who has been guilty of wilful and deliberate misrepresentation.

Lady Constance Lytton's Imprisonment at Newcastle.

Lady Constance Lytton was arrested at Newcastle on October 9, 1909, for taking part in a demonstration in connection with Mr. Lloyd George's visit to the city. Her action, which involved physical violence, was a protest against the attitude of the Liberal Government to women. It was also a deliberate attempt to break down the barbarous practice of forcible feeding which was at that time being employed against a working woman—Mrs. Leigh—in Birmingham Gaol. Lady Constance Lytton, in effect, challenged Mr. Gladstone to perform the same operation on herself.

How Mr. Gladstone met the Challenge.

Mr. Gladstone behaved in the way in which bullies invariably behave. While continuing his disgraceful conduct towards working women he cringed to those in high places. He sent a specialist down to examine Lady Constance, and on the strength of an alleged serious heart disease ordered the release of Lady Constance Lytton after fifty-six hours' hunger strike. Similar treatment was meted out to Mrs. Brailsford, who, being the wife of a well-known Liberal journalist, was also a person of importance. Meanwhile, women of lower social standing were being forcibly fed in Newcastle and in other prisons of the country.

The Sequel.

Lady Constance Lytton was determined to expose the injustice involved in this "respect of persons," and she made up her mind that when a further protest was necessary she would disguise herself so that her identity was not recognised. The occasion arose on Friday, January 14. The abominable outrage inflicted on Selina Martin, a working woman, in Liverpool Gaol had stirred her to the inmost soul. She determined to make her protest against this treatment, a protest which would involve a similar ordeal for herself, and thus enable her to bring to light the foul deeds of darkness which were being perpetrated in the prison.

A Stratagem that Succeeded.

With this heroic resolve she devoted the utmost care to preparing the trap for the Home Secretary. She obtained clothes such as are worn by working girls; she as a humane act, a medical necessity forced upon it by hysterical women for whom it had a duty to care. Suffragettes consistently challenged this rationale by exposing the use of force feeding as a disciplinary device and by emphasizing the deliberate cruelty of prison wardens and medical officers. The use of handcuffs, straitjackets, and punishment cells to restrain and discipline prisoners was a frequent subject in the suffragette press. Just as visual representations invariably provided graphic images of the sadistic glee taken by brutal prison officials, so the testimonies were replete with details of their small random acts of cruelty—hair being pulled, arms and legs bruised, cheeks slapped, mouth and gums lacerated, teeth broken.[96] Some scholars have equated being force-fed with being raped: the experience of being physically overpowered and held down, of phallic tubes being forced into their mouths, noses, and throats by male doctors.[97] Certainly the vocabulary used by suffragettes to describe force feeding—an "outrage," an "assault," a "dishonour," a "degradation"— had long been used in the press to discuss sex crimes.[98] *Votes for Women* was not being salacious when it wrote movingly of "the horrible insult offered to women by this unauthorized assault upon their persons . . . of what it means to a woman to have hands laid upon her when she is offering resistance for a great principle, to be held down by force while the atrocious operation is performed upon her . . . These things can be left to the imagination of any woman."[99] When, by the summer of 1914, a number of suffragettes in Scotland's Perth prison revealed that they had been repeatedly force-fed through the rectum, nothing else could be left to the imagination. One of these, the niece of Lord Kitchener, whose pointed finger on a recruiting poster was telling people that their country needed them to volunteer for the Great War, had been subjected to "a grosser and more indecent outrage, which could have been done for no other purpose than to torture."[100] It was to prove the final, fitting climax of suffragette hunger strikes, in a horrific illustration of the illiberal violence the state exercised upon its subjects.

After the Great War Terence MacSwiney's infamous hunger strike also dramatized the difference between being a citizen of the British state and being a subject bound by its power and force. A prominent figure in the republican circles of southwest Ireland, MacSwiney became Lord Mayor of Cork and a commander of the Irish Republican Army in March 1920, following the murder of Thomas MacCurtain by the Royal Irish Constabulary. On 12 August, three days after the imposition of the Coercion Act, he was arrested, given a military trial, and sentenced to two years' imprisonment in London's Brixton Prison. Refusing to accept the legality of his trial, he began a hunger strike to "put a limit to any term of imprisonment [the government might] impose," insisting that "whatever your Government may do . . . I shall be free, alive or dead, within a month."[101] Given that since Ashe's death the British government had consistently capitulated in the face of hunger strikes, granting either political-prisoner status or release, this was not an altogether foolish gamble.[102] Yet MacSwiney raised the stakes. He demanded not political-prisoner status but recognition of the Irish Republic and the constitutional authority of its provisional government established by the Dail in January 1919. The British government, determined to maintain its authority in the wake of the Coercion Act, dug in for a show of strength, suggesting that sympathy for MacSwiney would be better directed toward the bereaved widows and children of murdered Irish policemen.[103] The stage was set for a drama that was to culminate a remarkable seventy-four days later in MacSwiney's death.

MacSwiney's hunger strike was carefully choreographed in London by his sister Mary, as well as Art O'Brien, editor of the Irish Self-Determination League's paper the *Irish Exile:* they organized vigils outside Brixton Prison, solicited support from the British labor movement and American presidential candidates, provided daily briefings for the international press, smuggled photos of the dying martyr from prison, and ensured that he was dressed in his volunteer's uniform for the guard of honor and procession through London.[104] They skillfully presented MacSwiney as a patriot battling against a cruel and inhumane colonial government by giving away his life, an inch at a time—despite the daily visits of his young, beautiful, and heart-broken wife and the prayers of their two-year-old daughter, awaiting her father's return home. Around the world, especially in Catholic countries and those touched by the Irish diaspora, this poignant drama was reported on a daily basis, often "as the most important of the news items." Demonstrations were held in support of MacSwiney in Italy, France, and the United States.[105] British critics of the government's policy of coercion in Ireland—which, like the massacre at Amritsar in 1919, appeared to confirm that colonial rule could now be sustained only by violence—were only too ready to claim that MacSwiney's treatment had "stained the name of Britain with dishonour in the eyes of the civilised world."[106]

Gandhi's fasts fit uneasily within this tradition of hunger striking to dramatize the illegality and violence of colonial rule. As I have argued elsewhere, there is no question that for him fasting was an essential component of the quest for self-rule or *swaraj,* but his vision of *swaraj* extended far beyond any legal or constitutional understanding of home rule or freedom from colonial government.[107] Rather, it evoked a freedom that could be achieved through the ethical government of the self in the pursuit of truth. Gandhi believed that India's freedom as a nation would follow when its people had reformed their souls and embraced *sarvodaya* (selfless service). Only then, from a position of moral strength, could the weapon of *satyagraha* (militant nonviolence) take effect. Without first governing the soul of the nation, home rule, in the constitutional sense, would be tantamount to accepting "English rule without Englishmen"—of rendering India "not Hindustan but Englishstan."[108] So, although Gandhi had come under the wing of Naoroji in London, and had read Dutt in tears, famine never occupied a central place in his critique of colonial rule.[109] When famines struck, as he believed they surely would, given the decimation of the moral economy of India's village communities by the British imposition of a market economy, it was the greed and extravagance of some Indians that appeared to concern him most, for these flaws were a measure of how far India had fallen morally.[110] To make India a manly nation, capable of spurning the trappings of wealth for higher communal values, would require an enormous ethical effort, a concerted obeisance to the disciplines of *swaraj* (or self-rule).

In this context, the practice of fasting became for Gandhi the supreme test of his own self-discipline and an act of penance for a sinful nation, as well as a moral challenge to British colonial rule.[111] He most clearly articulated his politics of fasting during his first notorious epic fast against the Lothian Committee's communal award of separate electoral representation for the untouchables in September 1932. Uncannily echoing the debate in the *Times* of twenty years earlier, he claimed that although fasting was "a hoary institution" in the Christian, Islamic, and Hindu traditions, it should be used responsibly and only by those like himself who had "reduced it to a science." Determined to distinguish his fast from a hunger strike—the one an act of moral force, the other a physically coercive, political act—he argued that his fasting was directed less at the government of India, whose legislation would legally entrench the stigma of untouchability, than at the Hindu community that had failed to eradicate the untouchables' position as a distinct caste. The fast was, he insisted, an act of conscience, not a political gesture: "resolved upon in the name of God, for His work, and as I believe in all humility, at His call," it was "undertaken with the purest of motives and without malice or anger against any single soul."[112] This was a position Gandhi sought to maintain even during other fasts—for instance in 1943, when his all-out fast was directed against the government of India's complete abnegation of all responsibility for the Quit India movement—when the lines dividing him from the colonial state and the grounds for protest against it were more clearly marked.[113] Given the number and regularity of his fasts, both those performed to test the limits of his own self-rule and those undertaken publicly to challenge others, they soon became synonymous with his style of leadership. They also served as a reminder of his moral claim to leadership, his particular vision of the nation, and its fight for independence from Britain.

The politics of Gandhi's fasts reminds us that if hunger strikes challenged the legitimacy of the colonial state, they did so partly by dramatizing the moral strength of people deemed unworthy of citizenship. Considerable efforts were made to portray hunger strikers as martyrs in a cause so just that it demanded the greatest sacrifice, and to contrast the purity of their motives with the cynical maneuvering of a state determined to demystify and discredit them.

After the First World War, suffragette leaders like Annie Kenney and Christabel Pankhurst ensured that those who had shown the courage and strength to sacrifice themselves on hunger strike for the cause were credited with having dealt *the* decisive blow in winning women the vote.[114] On the rare occasions when men's hunger strikes in support of the suffragettes were recalled, it was invariably to illustrate that men were incapable of the requisite spirit of selfless sacrifice and self-discipline.[115] Given that hunger artists and fasting girls had long been dismissed as hysterical frauds by an incredulous medical profession, the suffragette press had worked hard from the outset to emphasize the fidelity of those on hunger strike, how only "the rarest form of moral courage and physical self-control" allowed them to "face this martyrdom."[116] No account of a hunger strike was complete without its confession of the struggle to overcome the temptations of the flesh and the alluring plates of food left within one's cell, or the tale of the refusal to fall for the beguiling arguments and tricks of prison officials. These were presented as tests against which one's moral worth and dedication to the cause were measured. Having passed these tests, Helen Gordon, like many others, saw her jailors' use of forcible feeding, of physical force against the moral power of her protest, as a triumph: "Now they know and acknowledge that they have been beaten—they do their work—she does hers and grows morally stronger, physically weaker—their moral sense is abused, and they sicken of their job."[117] For others the hunger strike appeared to become meaningful as a test of moral character only when it culminated in forcible feeding, that "greatest trial" of their sex.[118] For Howlett the analogy of forcible feeding with rape explains the prominence suffragettes gave to resistance in their testimonies, for failure to do so would have implied complicity and moral weakness.[119] Certainly, when Mary Richardson, in the second week of one of her many hunger strikes, "felt powerless to resist" being force-fed, she was "tormented" by this "inability of mine to struggle. It seemed a moral death not to resist."[120]

The suffragette press also emphasized that women's moral strength was perceptible on a daily basis, not only on hunger strike. Drawing on the discourse of imperial motherhood, they presented women as practiced in the arts of dutiful self-sacrifice and self-denial: it was they who raised the healthy children who would become productive citizens capable of securing the future of the race, nation, and empire.[121] Although Denise Riley has suggested that this call to duty provided fresh justification for the suppression of women's political rights, many women used that language to stake a claim both to a professional career—as teachers, doctors, and inspectors—and to citizenship itself.[122] It is difficult, then, to see "a symbolic refusal of motherhood," apparent in the suffragettes' misuse of the domestic science manual *A Healthy Home—and How to Keep It* they found in their prison cells at Holloway during 1909: some, citing its prescription for fresh air, smashed their cell windows, while others inscribed poems about freedom in the pages of the manual, over its "worthy recipes."[123] Rather than reject imperial motherhood, hunger-striking suffragettes highlighted its contradictions and the impossible burdens they placed on women. *Votes for Women* frequently reported cases of infant mortality, food adulteration, the starvation wages of women engaged in small-scale, domestic production for the infamous "sweated trades," and deaths by starvation as a "terrible indictment of a social system for which men alone are responsible."[124] And several imprisoned suffragettes recorded their horror at discovering that for some of their fellow prisoners motherhood had become criminalized, that they had been incarcerated for stealing food for their children or for failing to feed them: "I only did it for my poor children!" read graffiti in Sylvia Pankhurst's Holloway cell.[125] It was not just the double standard of a state that demanded that women be imperial mothers, while denying them the proper means of doing so, or even the disciplinary nature of its forms of maternal welfare that was at issue here, but the valorization of the moral strength of those who routinely endured such impossible burdens.

Similarly, the hunger strikes of MacSwiney and his fellow Irish republicans against the illegality and violence of colonial rule were sustained by a powerful Catholic aesthetic that equated suffering and endurance with spiritual strength. There is no finer example than MacSwiney of the "sacral nationalism" that republicans consolidated after the Easter Rising. At his trial he repeated his inaugural speech as Lord Mayor of Cork, insisting that the struggle against British rule was a rivalry of endurance, not vengeance:

> It is they who can suffer most that will conquer . . . The liberty for which we today strive is a sacred thing . . . and death for it is akin to the Sacrifice of Calvary, following far off but constant to that Divine example, in every generation our best and our bravest have died . . . Because of it our struggle is holy, our battle is sanctified by their blood, and our victory is assured by their martyrdom. We, taking up the work they left incomplete, confident in God, offer in turn sacrifice from ourselves. It is not we who take innocent blood, but we offer it, sustained by the example of our immortal dead, and that Divine Example which inspires us all, for the redemption of our country.[126]

No wonder that some have suggested that MacSwiney's hunger strike was as much a religious as a political act.[127] Much was made of MacSwiney's devotion and the strength he drew from his faith; the daily visits of his chaplain Father Dominic to Brixton Prison, his taking of Daily Communion, the family's bedside reading to him of his beloved Thomas à Kempis's *Imitation of Christ*. Certainly, MacSwiney's hunger strike resonated in Catholic Ireland: masses were held, rosaries recited, vigils held outside Brixton Prison, and prayers offered across Ireland.[128] After his death, thousands flooded into the streets and cathedrals of Dublin and Cork, as well as London, where twenty thousand reportedly filed past his open casket in Southwark Cathedral and huge crowds followed the procession to Euston Station.[129] There was even a roaring trade in MacSwiney relics, such as the photo card of him "garlanded with flowers in the manner of a saint."[130] It is difficult and unnecessary here to separate religious from political practice. MacSwiney's martyrdom mobilized Catholic Ireland and appeared to make the armed republican struggle intelligible to many who had previously kept a skeptical distance. As Father Kelleher of St. John's College, Waterford, acknowledged in the *Irish Theological Times,* MacSwiney's death had not only highlighted the religiosity of the Irish people; it had "profoundly impressed the moral feelings of the entire civilised world, and won support for the Irish cause in lands where hitherto the name of Ireland had scarcely been known."[131]

The insistence on MacSwiney's faith and devotion was not entirely innocent. Ashe's death had unleashed a heated debate among Catholic theologians in Ireland on the ethics of hunger strikes, after his chaplain at Mountjoy had declared that hunger strikes were sinful, in that they amounted to willful suicide.[132] MacSwiney, who had followed this debate, believed that he had secured theological approval that his death would be deemed "sacrificial" and not "suicidal."[133] Throughout his protest it was doctrinally justified on the grounds that the "extreme injustice of British rule in Ireland" had made the hunger strike not just "exempt from moral reproach" but a heroic "act even of supernatural merit."[134] Several bishops visited him at Brixton, and there was no evidence of clerical hostility to the hunger strike in Ireland—indeed the requiem masses for him at Dublin and Cork Cathedrals attracted three archbishops and four bishops.[135]

The canonization of MacSwiney silenced those in the republican movement who believed he had shown more courage than sense, more bravery than discipline. Some clearly thought he had rendered the hunger strike obsolete as a weapon of protest—that, in republican parlance, "it had died of wounds," for now they knew "what mercy we might expect from our enemy."[136] There were even rumors that he had acted against orders by directing the hunger strike toward the impossible goal of release and recognition of the republic, rather than the achievable one of political-prisoner status. Mary MacSwiney would have none of this. After his funeral she used the memory of her martyred brother as a bulwark against not only the British but those who had forsaken his republican stand by supporting the Anglo-Irish Treaty.[137] When, in November 1922, she followed her brother's example by declaring a hunger strike to rid Ireland of the British, the Free State government was deluged with requests for her release as Cumann na mBan organized nightly vigils at the Mountjoy jail and numerous rallies. To add insult to injury, Mary's sister Anne continued what was fast becoming a family tradition, by beginning her own hunger strike outside Mountjoy after prison officials refused to allow her to visit the ailing Mary. Under a picture of Our Lady of Perpetual Succor, Anne lay behind a screen, until the government, beset by internal rifts over their policy toward Mary, relented on the twenty-fourth day of her hunger strike.[138]

It is clear, then, that suffragettes in Britain as well as Irish and Indian nationalists all deployed the hunger strike to challenge the illegality and violence of the states that kept them in subjection, yet they did so in locally very different ways, for they drew on political and cultural resources that were locally specific. This was problematic for the British and colonial states that wanted to elaborate a consistent policy regarding hunger strikes, one that would hold across the British Empire. These states were forced instead to respond to strikes in different ways, in order to dispute the various claims to high moral purpose and strength in each locale.[139] To do so, governments repeatedly used medical science to undercut mythologies woven around the miraculous powers of the hunger striker as martyr, by demystifying the physiological process of hunger striking.

This was first apparent when the introduction of forcible feeding against suffragettes was justified as a medical necessity. To begin with, the Home Office suggested that prison officials had a legal obligation to fulfill their duty of care toward subjects in their custody, or at least to prevent them from committing "the crime of suicide." In the search for precedents this legal argument quickly became wedded to a medical one: Gladstone's deputy at the Home Office, Charles

Masterman, insisted that those "contumacious and weak-minded persons" unwilling or unable to feed themselves in prisons had long been fed "artificially" by "ordinary hospital [or medical] treatment."[140] In presenting the hunger-striking suffragette as unbalanced and hysterical, the authorities presented forcible feeding as a humane, medical necessity—a justification that the prison service and its medical officers clung to in the face of criticism from professional colleagues.[141] For these important but often shadowy figures, the hunger strike provided the final demonstration of the militant suffragette's unsound mind. During Dunlop's very first hunger strike the governor of Holloway Prison wrote with indecent speed to the Home Office, suggesting that "it would not be easy to certify her as being legally insane, but I consider her to be a highly neurotic fanatic. She is probably passing through the Climacteric Period, and this is likely to aggravate her mental condition."[142] Thereafter, the neurotic and hysterical hunger striker—whose "lack of moral fibre" and "diminished will-power . . . point to the fact that she cannot be credited with a full measure of responsibility for her actions"—became a firmly established type in the reports on the condition of prisoners that besieged the Home Office over the next five years.[143] Inverting suffragette claims that the hunger strike demanded moral strength and discipline, these reports made strikers out to be gripped by hysteria that denoted moral weakness.

The suffragettes quickly responded to this medical line of defense. A week after the introduction of forcible feeding, *Votes for Women* published "Opinions of Medical Experts" on its grave dangers, citing a report in the *Lancet* from 1872 of a death caused by forcible feeding. Letters to the press from influential male medics followed, which argued that far from being an "ordinary hospital treatment," force "feeding by the methods employed [is] an act of brutality beyond common endurance," a case reiterated in a public letter to the prime minister signed by 160 medics.[144] While the Forcible Feeding (Medical Men) Protest Committee sought to keep the pressure on the home secretary, the safety and ethics of the procedure were hotly de-

bated within the leading medical journals.[145] It was in part in response
to this pressure, and the recognition of the "intolerable strain" it
placed on prison wardens and medical officers, that McKenna introduced the infamous "Cat and Mouse" Act, although in doing so he
pointedly insisted that those on hunger strike were "fanatical and hysterical women, who no more fear death in fighting what they believe
to be the cause of women than the natives of Soudan feared death
when fighting the battle of Mahdi."[146]

Just as the British government used medical science to justify the
violence of forced feeding and discredit hunger-striking suffragettes
as irrational women no better than fanatical savages, so the authorities turned to medical science to demystify the hunger strikes of its
colonial subjects MacSwiney and Gandhi. Carefully calibrated leaks
from Brixton Prison's medical officer, by suggesting that MacSwiney's
visitors had secretly supplied him with food, called into question his
apparently miraculous powers of endurance, supposedly fueled by his
faith and commitment to the republican cause.[147] The claim was
quickly rebutted by the MacSwiney camp, which asserted that it was
evidence of "a deliberate campaign of misrepresentation and false-
hood" and accused the "English press . . . [of] allowing itself to be
used as an instrument of this campaign."[148] This strategy was more
systematically evident during Gandhi's fast of 1943 in protest at the
government of India's abnegation of responsibility for the Quit India
movement, and to exert pressure on moderate Indian politicians to
take a more explicitly nationalist stance on the issue.[149] As early as
December 1940 the colonial government had been preparing how
best to respond to Gandhi's future fasts, so as to minimize their influence on both the Indian and the British publics.[150] It was first decided
to detain him in the Aga Khan's palace outside Poona (rather than in
the Yeravda jail), and a press release was prepared to document its
grandeur and comfort, as well as the extensive medical care that
would be available to the Mahatma.[151] Rather than as a life-or-death
confrontation with the colonial state, Gandhi's actions were widely
reported in Britain as the "Luxury Fast."[152] The "whole spectacle of

the *soi-disant* ascetic sitting amid palatial luxury and availing himself of all the resources of modern medical science suggests not holiness but Hollywood," opined the *Daily Telegraph*.[153]

Nutritionists were also enlisted to provide scientific explanations of how the Mahatma could guide his body safely through nutritional barriers. In India, the deeply skeptical Viceroy Linlithgow consulted doctors to satisfy himself that there was "no serious risk of his dying," and was happily reassured about the positive physiological effects of fasting by Sir Desmond Young, a provincial commissioner in the Punjab, who had experience fasting as part of a "nature cure" treatment.[154] The press in Britain followed this nutritional lead, elucidating the mechanics of Gandhi's protest in ways that eroded its semimystical aura. Thus, the *Daily Mail*'s feature on "The Nine Fasts of Mahatma Gandhi" set out to prove their unmiraculous nature, revealing how—by carefully regulating his intake of water, taking minimal exercise, and very gradually resuming a normal diet after breaking fast—Gandhi had survived eight previous fasts.[155] In the *News Chronicle* the child health expert Margaret Brady rehearsed her controversial claim that fasting was a natural and nutritionally sound treatment for pregnant women with morning sickness or ailing children.[156] Brady dispelled any mystique surrounding Gandhi's fast by suggesting that fasting for three weeks was a perfectly "normal part of some curative treatments . . . After the first day or two no great effort of self-denial or exercise of will-power is needed to continue fasting, for one has little desire for food."[157] Nutritional science had helped show Gandhi's fasts to be governed by knowable, controllable, and predictable principles and processes that required no great will-power or sacrifice.

The coup de grâce came with the revelation that Gandhi had imbibed lime juice sweetened with sugar on at least one occasion during the course of the fast. Predictably some declared this to be proof positive of the fraudulent nature of Gandhi's fast. Even the once-concerned *Daily Express* remarked that consuming a beverage with such high levels of vitamins and minerals would have marked the end of previous fasts.[158] When the end of the fast was announced three days later, Gandhi's protest had been successfully compromised by the news management of the colonial regime and a medical discourse that removed much of the wonder at the otherness of his politics of hunger. Given that Gandhi had energetically used *Young India* to contest the universal claims of British nutritionists at work in India and publicize his own dietary experiments, as we shall see in Chapter 5, the irony of this denouement was considerable. It was doubly so as famine was once again stalking India in 1943 and the nationalist critique of colonial rule was again being fashioned in part from very British resources.

Between the Irish famine and the era of the Great War the humanitarian discovery of the hunger paved the way for its mobilization as political critique. The hungry became not just objects of humanitarian sympathy, but subjects in need of political emancipation from states that failed to redress their hunger and refused to recognize them as citizens. In the second half of the nineteenth century, Irish and Indian nationalists were particularly effective in making famine the measure of their critique of British colonial rule. Nothing else exposed the hollow promises of the British Empire to deliver prosperity, civility, and modernity quite so effectively as famine: colonial rule had effectively halved Ireland's population and killed an Indian population half the size of Britain's in 1901. Having denaturalized famine, so that it could no longer be presented as a curse of nature or providence, nationalists in Ireland and India established that it was a phenomenon generated by humans: a product of a failing political economy doggedly adhered to by colonial rulers who were unwilling to concede that its supposedly universal laws were obviated by the very different social conditions of Ireland and India. In these conditions the endurance of famine and starvation by colonial subjects was represented not as a sign of moral failure to learn the discipline of the market, but as a demonstration of the remarkable fortitude that would ultimately deliver the nation from colonial bondage.

Nowhere was this inversion of natural law, with its equation of hunger with moral strength, or the brutal exposure of the violence and inhumanity of colonial rule, more apparent than in the adoption of hunger as a vehicle of political protest through the hunger march and the hunger strike. Both were tactics that appeared to defy nature and the state in equal measure. First emerging in the protests of unemployed workers and suffragettes in Edwardian Britain, these marches and strikes dramatized the illegality and violence of the state that refused the protesters citizenship and yet claimed to have their welfare at heart. As such, they were tactics well suited to the politics of Irish and Indian nationalist protest against the colonial state. Yet the politicization of hunger did not simply provide an identical and transferable critique of a state of subjection and misrule that could be leveled across the British Empire, for it assumed a different prose of counterinsurgency in every setting of its articulation, one that reflected quite distinct visions of the political nation being willed into existence. Hunger was now ready to be turned from a vehicle of political protest into a form of social government that prioritized the welfare of the hungry.

4

The Science and Calculation
of Hunger

Before 1871 it was only briefly possible, for the single year of 1839, to officially die of starvation in Britain. In that year the Registrar General's Office, established two years previously to record what was confidently expected to be the increasing health and longevity of Britons (evident from the new civil registration of births, deaths, and marriages), published its first set of results.[1] Buried away in a lengthy report was the unwelcome information that 63 of the 148,000 deaths reported that year had been caused by starvation. William Farr, the statistician and physician who had compiled the report, insisted the figure was a conservative one, given that "hunger destroys a much higher proportion than is indicated by the registers," and that "its effects . . . are generally manifested indirectly, in the production of diseases of various kinds."[2] Here were a result and an analysis that infuriated Edwin Chadwick, key architect of the New Poor Law and then its chief commissioner, who had, in an odd twist of fate, helped procure Farr his job. Farr's category of deaths by starvation challenged Chadwick's claim that the New Poor Law had made starving to death impossible in the richest and most modern nation on earth: as we saw in Chapter 2, the report provided welcome ammunition to critics of the new workhouse regime. Chadwick was quick to rebuke Farr publicly on both medical and statistical grounds. As it was notoriously difficult to single out the morbid effects of starvation, Chadwick argued, Farr's category of "deaths by starvation" was too broad; in refusing to insulate medical diagnoses of multiple causes of death from broader "social" circumstances, Farr had created a category that lacked scientific rigor and statistical precision. Not surprisingly, Chadwick prevailed; his refusal to allow deaths from starvation to be seen as a social problem ensured that by the following year it had once again become statistically impossible to die of starvation in Britain, although coroner's courts, confusingly, continued to return verdicts to that effect.

In 1871 the statistical possibility resurfaced for Londoners alone. Critics of the Poor Law unions in the metropolis, intent on exposing their inhumanity and inefficiency, as well as the growth of hunger as a social problem, demanded that the numbers of "deaths from starvation, accelerated by privation," registered by coroner's courts in each union be annually reported to Parliament. By 1908 the same logic ensured that the duty to report those results was extended to embrace all of England and Wales. Boards of guardians now had to account carefully for each death by starvation; specifically, they had to inform the Local Government Board whether the deceased had unsuccessfully applied for, or successfully received, poor relief. Accordingly, these reports delicately balanced macro forms of statistical aggregation with narrative microhistories of each individual death, provided by the coroner and the board of guardians. As Farr and Chadwick had recognized, deaths by starvation could never be merely abstract statistics; the meaning and classification of those numbers remained bound to local and personal forms of knowledge and thus remained deeply politicized. The debate Farr and Chadwick had begun over the reliability and objectivity of the reporting of deaths by starvation in the 1830s continued to rage until the final abolition of that tally in 1929.[3]

This brief history of the official record for deaths from starvation nicely captures the central theme of this chapter. As we have seen in the previous chapters, both the humanitarian discovery of hunger and its subsequent politicization—the clash between those who could find no excuse for the hungry and those who could find no excuse for hunger—relied upon at best vague and subjective definitions of hunger and how to measure it. As hunger acquired an increasingly explosive political charge in the second half of the nineteenth century, many followed Chadwick in hoping that it could be defused by the development of scientific techniques for its definition and measurement. By the late nineteenth and early twentieth centuries emergent social and nutritional sciences promised to do just that, by giving hunger a new and technical form.[4] As a consequence, it no longer had to be registered solely by the measure of human sympathy or political protest it evoked. That is to say, nutritionists developed a range of techniques that appeared to allow objective, standardized, and universal ways of defining and measuring hunger that were abstracted from the particular local, partial forms of knowledge that had rendered hunger so contentious. Social and nutritional scientists argued that with these techniques they could not only distinguish between who was really hungry and who was not, but also assess the social consequences of their hunger and, if necessary, provide practical, technical mechanisms for its redress. Support for these new forms of expert knowledge came from the Webbs, who wrote, "Our governing class . . . do not seem yet to have realized that social reconstructions require as much specialized training and sustained study as the building of bridges and railways, the interpretation of the law, or technical improvements in machinery and mechanical processes."[5]

Hunger Becomes Technical and Socially Inefficient

During the second half of the nineteenth century, nutrition, or dietetics, as it was more usually called, attracted greater attention, as researchers investigated the nexus between health, economy, and productivity.[6] Despite the persistence of other forms of dietetic expertise, the discipline taking shape in the laboratories of chemical analysts and physiologists, as well as the dietary investigations of medics, became known during the 1890s as the science of nutrition. By 1901 J. A. Hobson, Britain's leading social theorist, was predicting that this new "science of food" (the nomenclature was still in flux) would become a "tributary science" informing sociology. It would enable the social scientist to calculate principles of social efficiency by identifying standards of dietary health that would increase physical and mental productivity. Social investigators would, in turn, provide nutritionists with empirical knowledge of the dietary regimes and physical demands of different segments of the population, lending to abstract dietetic principles a specific social basis and utility.[7] Hobson's prediction was quickly realized. That same year, Seebohm Rowntree used the "new knowledge of nutrition" to measure poverty in York, by calculating how much food, and at what cost, an individual required to remain a healthy and productive member of society, and then comparing these to actual dietary practices. His work attracted widespread attention:

> In this country we know—thanks to the patience and accurate scientific investigations of Mr Rowntree and Mr Charles Booth . . . that there is about 30 per cent of our population underfed, on the verge of hunger, doubtful day by day of the sufficiency of their food. Thirty per cent! What is the population of the United Kingdom? Forty-one millions. Thirty per cent of forty-one millions comes to something like twelve millions.[8]

The abundant commentary on Rowntree's methods has remained curiously silent on the innovative nutritional calculations upon which his definition of poverty rested.[9] In his extensive discussion of the new field, Rowntree employed the at that time conventional metaphor of the human body as a motor requiring food as fuel, both to build its productive capacity (muscles, bones, and tissues) and to generate power and energy (heat and muscular strength). Drawing upon W. O. Atwater's work on the nutritional values of foods, he then outlined three different constituents of food—protein, fats, and carbohydrates—each of which served as fuel to generate a specific quantity of heat and energy known as calories.[10] Although this schema made it theoretically possible to calculate the exact quantity of fuel required for the human motor to function most effectively, there remained the practical difficulty that different bodies faced different demands as human motors, depending upon their age and sex, and the nature of the work. Focusing his attention on the productive capacity of the average male worker, Rowntree extrapolated relative "man-values" for women and children of different ages (so women's needs were calculated as 0.8 man-value, as were those of a boy aged fourteen to sixteen). Despite the more stringent standards allowed by the older work of Voit, Moleschott, and Playfair, Rowntree again followed Atwater's daily minimum standard, based on a man-value of 3,500 calories and 125 grams of protein, a requirement confirmed by D. N. Paton and J. C. Dunlop's experiments on prison diets in Scotland.[11] This conspicuous display of nutritional learning did little to obscure the difficulties of translating the abstract principles to a specific social setting. To devise the cheapest nutritionally adequate regimen, Rowntree turned to the recently revised regulations for workhouse diets, even though he acknowledged that the poor lacked the knowledge "to select a diet that is at once as nutritious and as economical" and were unlikely to embrace its vegetarian character.[12]

The next step, comparing nutritional requirements and standards to the food actually eaten by the poor, was an altogether trickier task. If nutritional science had provided a set of principles and mechanisms for calculating a minimum dietary standard, their practical utility continued to rely on less precise techniques for discovering what the poor really ate. For three weeks sampled families were required to keep detailed and exact records "regarding the quantity, character, and cost of the food consumed."[13] These journals would then be scrutinized by the case officer who was responsible for preparing detailed case notes on each family—replete with tables cataloguing weekly income, expenditures, and menus of meals served, together with a narrative description of the composition and dietary practices of the family and the condition of the home. In these case notes the weekly diet appeared as a window onto the soul of the poor: praise was heaped upon those who kept a clean, sanitary house and budgeted well enough to provide good meals, while gloomy admonishment

hung over those less adept at the arts of household management.[14]
The reports were replete with details on decor, flow of air and sunshine, size of cupboards, cooking equipment and utensils, the condition of clothes, and family eating habits. This obsessive cataloguing of
household conditions and practices dramatized the degree to which
the housewife was now seen as a key engineer of social efficiency. The
moral condescension that often permeated descriptions of individual
cases was, however, lost when these records of what the poor actually
ate, and how much it cost, were translated back into statistical tables
detailing nutritional values and position relative to the minimum
standard. And yet it was only once the stories of these families were
aggregated and presented as so many statistical columns and graphs
that it became apparent just how many people were living on less
than the minimum nutritional requirements. The tension between
two views of hunger, as a moral problem stemming from unwise
household management on the one hand and as a collective social
problem on the other, structures Rowntree's *Poverty* and plays out
across his mutually dependent modes of investigation. As we shall
see, that tension would also continue to haunt the social government
of hunger that Rowntree's social scientific techniques first made possible.

Despite the lingering moralism of Rowntree's assessment, hunger
had at last gained a scientific basis. Now that it could be defined as the
failure to reach a minimum nutritional standard, its social costs could
be precisely measured in terms of health, productivity, efficiency, and
social stability. The physiological effects on an inadequately nourished
population were plainly legible in tables showing infant mortality
rates and the number of working days lost to sickness, as well as in
reports of sickly mothers raising stunted children. An ill-fed and en-
ervated population threatened social stability and the future of the
race: "No civilisation," Rowntree warned, "can be sound or stable
which has at its base this mass of stunted human life." Having concluded that a fourth of the population was living in poverty, he believed he had identified "a social question of profound importance
await[ing] solution."[15]

Rowntree's method and conclusions were of particular interest to the Inter-Departmental Committee on Physical Deterioration, which had been set up to investigate the revelation from the director general of the Army Medical Service that during the Boer War almost two-thirds of recruits were "physically unfit for military service."[16] With no reliable anthropometric statistics to trace progressive deterioration, the committee focused on the environmental conditions, not the hereditary factors, responsible for the degeneration. Chief among these, most expert witnesses concurred, was nutrition.[17] The prioritizing of questions of food and nutrition meant that alongside the familiar professional observers of social life (journalists, teachers, health visitors, charity workers, and inspectors of factories, sanitation, and schools), appeared the new figures of social and nutritional scientists: Rowntree and Charles Booth, architect of the survey *Life and Labour in London,* both gave evidence, as did the "well-known authority on nutrition," Robert Hutchison, the author of *Food and the Principles of Dietetics.*[18] Unlike the other expert witnesses, their authority emanated, not from their proximity to or intimate familiarity with the poor, but from the comfortably objective distance from which their scientific techniques enabled them to investigate and quantify the problem of poverty and hunger dispassionately. The local case study, the statistical sample, the system of case officers trained to interview subjects, the inquiry cards on which all necessary information from each household was recorded to await aggregation into charts of statistical tables, graphs, and maps—these techniques promised objective, standardized, and thus comparable, systems of measurement over time and in different settings. Thanks largely to these experts and their methods, the committee concluded: a) that the minimum dietary requirement consisted of 3,500 calories and 125 grams of protein; b) the seriously deficient diets of many reduced their physical and mental efficiency, with grave consequences for the productivity of children at school and adults at work; c) the primary cause of this deficiency was not poverty but the ignorance of housewives who lacked knowledge of sound nutrition and efficient household management. The solution was to propose legislation that would provide the necessary "social education" for these women and school meals for children with mothers incapable of learning these lessons.[19]

The newly established authority of the social and nutritional sciences did not go unquestioned, especially by those whose expertise they had rendered marginal. C. S. Loch of the Charity Organisation Society, for example, whose work relied upon local and personal familiarity with those who sought charity, criticized Rowntree's use of "dietetics" as too abstract and "unreal, in spite of its being set down in seemingly precise statistics." Beguiled by the logic of aggregation and quantification, he argued, Rowntree had too eagerly followed Atwater's calculations of the nutritional requirements of the average man (weighing eleven stone and engaged in moderate work) and had failed to recognize the heterogeneity of the poor, who differed in age, weight, physique, and health, not to mention tastes and domestic skills. Those like the employees of the Charity Organisation Society who daily administered to the poor and knew their habits and predilections intimately were sounder and more authoritative guides than were proponents of the infant science of nutrition, which had not yet even "finally settled" how to calculate food values.[20] This reproach struck a chord with several members of the committee, who complained that nutritional textbooks had "changed every four or five years on important points."[21] It was not just that nutritionists offered competing assessments of the values of different foodstuffs, but that they appeared to be unable to agree on the qualities or function of food, let alone the quantities required to supply a minimum standard. Questioning Rowntree on these issues, the chair of the committee complained that they had heard so many "very different opinions expressed" that he had been "plunged into a morass of doubt."[22]

Other dissenting voices continued to be heard. The most compelling belonged to those like Maud Pember Reeves, who recognized the importance of nutritional science in analyzing the adequacy of diets but lamented that those who championed scientific diets and classes in household management were blind to the realities the laboring poor were facing. A poor woman, she insisted, was not inefficient or ignorant of nutritional principles; she had "but one pair of hands and but one overburdened brain . . . Give her six children, and between the bearing of them and the rearing of them she has little extra vitality left for scientific cooking, even if she could afford the necessary time and appliances." And even if she did, she would still have to contend with the well-established tastes of family members, especially the male breadwinner, who would probably "entirely refuse the scientific food." The poor assessed their diet not by its nutritional content, but by its taste.[23] As we shall see later, the insistence that food had a social and cultural meaning of its own, quite apart from its nutritional value, was to be lost for a generation, before being rediscovered by anthropologists.

The Edwardian years nevertheless marked the arrival of the social and nutritional sciences as essential to all future discussions about the measurement of hunger and its social consequences. A. L. Bowley, the professor of statistics at the London School of Economics credited with bringing sampling techniques and statistical rigor to the British social sciences, acknowledged that despite the many variables—such as the availability of food, the demands of work, types of physique, and cultural standards—"efficiency," without nutritional calculation of what constitutes a minimum diet, "is another of the words which appears to have a clear meaning, but is in reality as vague as heat or fine weather."[24] And yet on the eve of the Great War, just as nutritionists appeared to have cemented their newfound authority, the scientific and technical forms they had given to the concept of hunger began to change dramatically. The thermodynamic model that had informed Edwardian calculations of the minimum quantities of food as fuel required for the human motor was, following the discovery of vitamins and deficiency diseases, slowly challenged by a new biochemical emphasis on the quality, as opposed to the quantity, of food.

Chemical physiologists like D. N. Paton and E. P. Cathcart and their "Glasgow School," who championed the thermodynamic model, believed that as the biochemical process of metabolic combustion was unknowable, researchers should restrict themselves to observing, measuring, and calculating knowable external phenomena of food, such as fuel (carbohydrates, fats, and proteins), the energy requirements of bodies as engines operating in different environments, and their productive output.[25] Viewed in this way, nutrition was an applied science focused on discovering how much the poor needed to eat and then educating them how to eat more efficiently and healthily. By 1918, however, the discovery of deficiency diseases and vitamins led the American biochemist E. V. McCollum to declare confidently the arrival of "the newer knowledge of nutrition."[26] McCollum belonged to new generation of biochemists who, while concentrating on laboratory work, shifted attention from the quantities of food required to the qualities of particular foodstuffs and their specific physiological effects. In particular, the identification of diseases that seemed to be a consequence of specific dietary deficiencies, like beriberi and rickets, made the discovery of vitamins possible. Although Sir Frederick Gowland Hopkins and Christiaan Eijkman were awarded the Nobel Prize in 1929 for discovering vitamins, many other scientists simultaneously recognized the vital role of vitamins in promoting health. Some, following Eijkman, induced experimental beriberi and scurvy in animals; others, like Hopkins and McCollum, noted the effects of insufficient fats, proteins, and carbohydrates on the growth of rats.[27] By 1912 Casimir Funk could claim that a whole range of "deficiency diseases"—including beriberi, rickets, pellagra, and scurvy—were caused by an inadequate supply of "vitamines." Although few accepted Funk's characterization of these chemical substances as vital amines, it was increasingly clear that some mysterious "accessory food factors" were essential to health.[28] Even in Glasgow, the bastion of thermodynamic approaches, in the first Medical Research Committee funded project on nutrition, Hopkins's student Edward Mellanby determined through his experiments on puppy dogs that rickets was caused by a vitamin deficiency. We should not imagine that the thermodynamic and biochemical models were mutually exclusive or that the latter simply displaced the former. Just as biochemical research had earlier helped establish the nutritional values of foods to plug into thermodynamic calculations, so thermodynamic approaches continued to thrive long after the First World War. Nonetheless, the initial rivalry between the practitioners of the two approaches often made it impossible to find two nutritionists who agreed with each other, just at the moment when the Great War gave nutritional expertise an urgent practical relevance to the shaping of food policy.

A War of Nutrition?

The Crimean War and the Boer War had raised questions of diet and nutrition, but these were largely about the adequacy of rations to maintain the health and vitality of soldiers.[29] The First World War changed the nutritional equation by making the issue of Britain's depleted civilian food supply as urgent as that of military rations: food economy assumed an early and unprecedented prominence.[30] As early as 1905, alarmed at the decline of Britain's agricultural sector and the nation's growing dependence on imported foods, the Royal Commission on Supply of Food and Raw Materials in Time of War had concentrated on the navy's ability to keep merchant shipping lines open. Hutchison was the sole nutritionist to give evidence, and his suggestion—that food policy should be scientifically determined by calculating the nutritional requirements that would ensure the most productive soldiers and factory workers—was "totally disregarded."[31] In contrast, Germany took the lead in making nutritional science part of the armory of war. In 1914 its nutritionists were enlisted to convince the nation that, in spite of the blockade upon food supplies, Germans would not be starved into submission, for science enabled them to marshal their depleted food resources more efficiently. Their text, translated into English the following year to expose German propaganda about starving women and children, earned the praise of Augustus Waller, a professor of physiology at the University of London, for its scientific approach to the food question.[32] Later that year two colleagues at Cambridge, Hopkins (professor of biochemistry) and T. B. Wood (professor of agriculture), published a guide to civilian food economy that sought to explain its nutritional principles to skeptics who might "doubt whether the needs of the human body can be definitely expressed in pounds and ounces or other such units." Rehearsing the now familiar human motor metaphor, the guide set out in charts and tables the nutritional requirements of different groups and detailed the nutritional value of foodstuffs and their costs, with the aim of allowing readers to judge how to get most nutritional value for their money. It also, however, contained two other quite distinctive elements. First, in line with Hopkins's work on vitamins, the authors emphasized the importance of mineral salts, as well as fruit and vegetables. Second, they argued, with the help of Rowntree's survey, that because the rich ate less efficiently than the poor, it was they who would have to shoulder the burden of food economies. In doing so, they could effect a 10 percent savings in national expenditures on food, while, just as importantly, leaving cheap carbohydrate fuels like bread for those engaged in heavy manual labor.[33]

Yet official interest in the potential contribution of nutritional science to the war effort grew only slowly. It was not until March 1916 that, at the prompting of the Cabinet Committee on Food Supplies, the Royal Society established a subcommittee to flesh out Hopkins and Wood's food economy agenda.[34] The committee, which included Paton and W. H. Thompson (a professor of physiology at Dublin), along with Hopkins and Wood, was predictably sharply divided over the importance of vitamins, as well as the extent to which any wastage (generated by the process of preparing, cooking, and eating) should be incorporated into the calculation of minimum calorific requirements. W. B. Hardy, the biological secretary of the Royal Society, and the driving force behind the creation of the Physiological Sub-Committee, was compelled to remind the obstinate Paton that nutritionists would only be taken seriously as scientific experts when they had learned to speak with one voice.[35] The committee's final report achieved consensus by making three significant departures in the assessment of the state of nutritional knowledge. First, the thermodynamic emphasis on the quantities of calorific fuel required by the human motor was complemented by the somewhat grudging acknowledgment of "vitamines," which, it was agreed, "probably play an important part in maintaining the national health." Second, the relative scale of man-values was adjusted from those outlined by Atwater and used in Hopkins and Wood's *Food Economy*. Third, nutritional requirements were raised 15 percent above the immediate prewar standard of 3,400 calories, to account for the degree of wastage generated by the journey of food from the shop to the stomach. On this basis, the authors concluded that food policy should be immediately changed, given that any reduction in the food supply would "result in a decrease in the output of munitions, farm produce, and other necessary commodities." Rather than focus on food economy, policy should concentrate on "extending the bread supply" to the industrial population, which, suffering from the escalation of food prices, most depended upon it for calorific fuel; this aim, the committee argued, could be achieved by transferring the allocation of three metric tons of cereals from animal fodder to human food, a change that would also, happily, reduce the nation's dependence on imports and increase meat supplies.[36]

It was hoped that with this brokered consensus the report would establish the role of nutritional experts in the development of a scientific and efficient food policy. The outlook seemed good when, as the report was finished in December 1916, the Royal Society established a permanent and separate Food (War) Committee, with an expanded membership, to advise the Ministry of Food created by the new prime minister, Lloyd George.[37] Signs were more favorable still when Wood was appointed scientific adviser to the ministry by its new and more interventionist food controller, Lord Devonport. A nutritionist was finally established at Whitehall. But expectations were quickly dashed when in welcoming Wood the ministry's permanent secretary insisted he was at a loss to see how scientific considerations came into the food question. It was not long before Wood and the Food (War) Committee had compiled a battery of complaints: they were rarely consulted; some policies directly contradicted their advice, while others were publicly announced as having "been carefully considered by scientific people and food experts," though that was not the case.[38] By March 1917 members of the Food (War) Committee were so en-

raged at their treatment by the ministry that they considered disso-
ciating themselves from it; however, bridges were mended when
Hutchison, Paton, and Thompson were all appointed to William
Beveridge's committee planning for the introduction of compulsory
rationing. They, in turn, regularly solicited further advice from the
Food (War) Committee. Although bread rationing was introduced
against their collective scientific advice, it was based on a five-tier
sliding scale according to the physiological demands of work—a victory of sorts for the nutritionists.[39] Yet, given that in the decade before the war nutritional science had appeared poised to become an
essential tool in the art of government, nutritionists were clearly disappointed by their marginal role in determining wartime food policy.

War nonetheless provided a catalyst for nutritional research, even
if that research neatly reflected the divisions between the thermodynamic and biochemical approaches evident in the Royal Society's
Food (War) Committee. Paton's protégé at Glasgow, E. P. Cathcart,
was appointed the Ministry of Food's liaison officer with the Army
Medical Services and charged with quantifying the soldier's calorific
requirements. Cathcart was well suited to the job.[40] With the help
of a former student John Boyd Orr, he enthusiastically set about
measuring soldiers' energy requirements. Cathcart and Orr's experiments on troops in training during the last year of the war focused on
the adequacy of their diet and on how to reduce unnecessary physical
demands, thanks to more efficient marching drills and lighter packs.[41]
The Royal Society's Food (War) Committee also supported biochemical research. Plimmer, who had helped form the Biochemical Society
in 1911, was moved from his position as reader in physiological
chemistry at the University of London to analyze the nutritional
composition of common foodstuffs, so that they could be more efficiently rationed.[42] Elsewhere, the war provided other unwelcome
opportunities to investigate the relation between accessory food factors, or vitamins, and deficiency diseases. Harriette Chick and Miss
Hume at the Lister Institute helped develop food supplements (including Marmite and lime juice) whose success in treating outbreaks
of beriberi and scurvy among troops at Gallipoli and Mesopotamia in

1916 and 1917 prompted the chief physician for the hapless campaign in Mesopotamia to declare, "The great danger of Vitamin Deficiency in a ration has been demonstrated," and also, "The old idea of sufficiency of calories, or of proteins, fat and carbohydrates, is quite inadequate."[43] Chick also went to Vienna in 1919, where, amid the human wreckage caused by the continuing British blockade, she successfully treated rickets among malnourished children as a deficiency disease.[44] The same year the Lister Institute and the Medical Research Council (MRC) joined forces to appoint a committee of the leading researchers in the field to prepare the *Report on the Present State of Knowledge concerning Accessory Food Factors (Vitamines),* with Chick serving as secretary.[45]

Indeed, in 1918 the dual track of wartime nutritional research was institutionally entrenched through the Medical Research Council's creation of two separate committees on human nutrition: Cathcart chaired the Committee on Quantitative Problems in Human Nutrition, and Hopkins the Committee on Accessory Food Factors. Orr represented yet a third track. He acknowledged the superior importance of quality over quantity, but his work on animal nutrition placed greater emphasis on minerals than on vitamins. Despite the common ground, these tracks continued to shape nutritional research between the wars. This meant that every expert governmental committee was structured around the management of differences, so that competing scientific advice could be heeded or ignored at will.

Nonetheless, for advocates like Hardy at the Royal Society nutritional science came of age during the war and became an indispensable part of statecraft. It had, he insisted, revealed "the physiological basis of national efficiency, political unrest and of social security." No longer would the "imperfect nutrition of the working classes [represent] a hindrance and danger to the state," now that the technical knowledge was available to identify their minimum physiological needs and maximize their productivity as workers. The Food (War) Committee agreed, insisting that for its own health and efficiency the state should fund nutritional laboratories. In return for this investment it could expect a nutritional solution to "the labour problem in tropical and sub-tropical climates."[46] The proposal for a state-funded Human Nutrition Institute never materialized in the worsening post-war budgetary environment. Nonetheless, the development of nutritional laboratories came to characterize much of the nutritional research carried out in Britain between the wars. To an unprecedented degree the laboratory became the locus of nutritional calculation and credibility. It was hoped that in this privileged scientific space physiologists and biochemists would experiment on foods, as well as the bodies of humans and animals, in a disinterested fashion, to resolve differences and produce new universal truths of nutritional science.

Laboratory Life

Before the mid-nineteenth century, dietetic knowledge was based on codes of moral exhortation and regimens of personal experimentation that produced a cacophony of conflicting advice structured around broad and distinctly unscientific categories, such as virtue and moderation.[47] In contrast, the modern science of nutrition took to the laboratory to discover the precise thermodynamic laws governing the body and the exact chemical properties of food as fuel. There, supposedly insulated from society and its competing ideological forces, the conventions, procedures, and experimental methods of the nutritional sciences were tried, tested, and established—yet histories of nutritional science still tend to emphasize individuals and their discoveries rather than the infrastructures that made them possible. Nutritional research in laboratories had thrived after the Food Adulteration Act of 1875 had mandated the chemical analysis of foods, even though many of those laboratories remained rudimentary at best.[48] Similarly, the following year the antivivisection movement's successful campaign for the passage of the Cruelty to Animals Act (1876), which made it obligatory for those experimenting on animals to register with the Home Office, led to the immediate formation of the Physiological Society, as well as the formal recognition of laboratory space and work in medical schools and universities.[49] When a disparate group of analysts and chemists established the Biochemical Club in 1911, they followed the Physiological Society's practice of meeting in each other's laboratories, where they discussed their research, their interests, and the development of new techniques and established their professional credibility.[50] Clearly we should not view the rise of the nutritional laboratory as inevitable, for research continued to be conducted outside the laboratory, and even that which was not remained compromised by its novelty and experimental nature.[51] Even so, by the early twentieth century, the laboratory had become central to nutritionists' claim to have produced a rational science of hunger and a universal set of techniques for identifying and measuring it. By the 1920s the first nutritional laboratories built for the purpose were established with state support at the Rowett Research Institute at Aberdeen (1921) and the Dunn Nutritional Laboratory in Cambridge (1927).[52] If nutritional laboratories had become an integral part of the science of modern government, during the 1930s they also became an essential part of the food industry. Every major company boasted laboratories where the productive capacity and marketing potential of its foods were explored.[53]

As the first nutritional laboratory built for the purpose in Britain, the Rowett gives us a good sense through its design of how the field of dietary research was conceptualized and how laboratories acquired their authoritative position within that field. Built five miles outside Aberdeen, in a quiet rural setting, the Rowett was always secluded, but workers on the forty-acre experimental farm were even more sequestered on-site after the construction of a residential hall in 1930. Despite its remoteness, the Rowett was connected to the rest of the world. Seven minutes' walk from a main road, tram terminus, and train station, its workers had easy access to Aberdeen, and thus to the nation's, and indeed the world's, scientific community. Although the Rowett's reach extended across the British Empire, the world of nutritional science also came to the Rowett when in 1924, with the help of the Carnegie Corporation, it built a library.[54] Here laboratory workers were able to situate their research in relation to, and in dialogue with, experiments conducted by their colleagues in other laboratories around the world. By 1931, with the help of the Medical Research Council and the Imperial Agriculture Bureau, the Rowett began publishing *Nutrition Abstracts and Views,* to provide a global fo-

4.1. "The Rowett Institute," Rowett Institute, *First Report, 1922* (Aberdeen: Milne & Hutchison, 1922), ii.

rum for nutritional research. By the time its fifth volume appeared in 1936, it included a staggering 4,762 abstracts of papers and books in the field. Through it the Rowett provided a window onto the world of nutritional science and connected a global network of laboratories and researchers in a vibrant professional community.

The functionality of the buildings—for they were devoid of "architectural embellishments" and had "no decorative work inside"—may have made construction less expensive, but it also ensured that these edifices would be appreciated principally for the work done within them (Figure 4.1).[55] At the Rowett, Orr insisted upon the integral relation between animal and human nutrition. The experimental farm was separated from the laboratories by only thirty feet, with the workshop and metabolic rooms closest to the farm. At the center of the farm buildings were the feeding rooms where the experimental diets were prepared and weighed. The institute itself had laboratories for each branch of nutritional research on all three floors (Figure 4.2). Pride of place was given to the biochemical laboratory immediately opposite the main entrance; a larger chemical laboratory adjoined the first. The ground floor also boasted rooms for experiments

THE ROWETT INSTITUTE

Scale $\frac{1}{16}$ in. 1 ft.

Feet 10   0   10   20   30   40   50   60   70   80   90 Feet

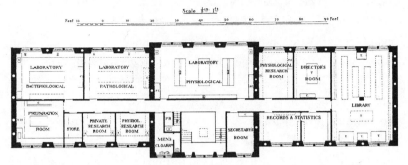

FIRST FLOOR PLAN

GROUND FLOOR PLAN

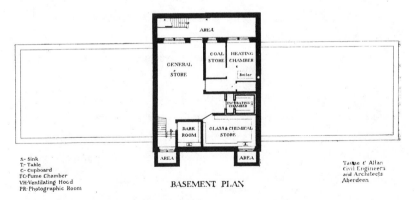

S- Sink
T- Table
C- Cupboard
FC-Fume Chamber
VH-Ventilating Hood
PR-Photographic Room

Tawse & Allan
Civil Engineers
and Architects
Aberdeen

BASEMENT PLAN

4.2. The institute's laboratories. Rowett Institute, *First Report, 1922* (Aberdeen: Milne & Hutchison, 1922), 20.

in combustion, distillation, balance, and asepsis, a bulk preparation room, the office of the experimental farm, and a large room devoted to metabolism. The basement included a darkroom and a glass and chemical store, and the first floor contained the bacteriological, pathological, and physiological laboratories, together with a room for records and statistics, a library, and the director's office. This design reflected an ideal image of the research process, with its focus on the biochemical investigations of foodstuffs and the chemical isolation and synthesis of their different elements, which led directly to the preparation of synthetic diets and the testing of their physiological effects on farm animals. Bacteriologists, physiologists, and pathologists closely scrutinized the health of the animals before the director finally authorized the production of records and the writing of papers.

Despite this coordination, each branch of investigation commanded myriad different laboratory procedures and pieces of specialized equipment. The credibility of all procedures rested on a panoply of devices, instruments, and formulas—for calculating metabolism, isolating food properties and compounds, observing cells, and measuring bodies—that enabled nutritionists on the other side of the world to run comparable experiments. Without them it was impossible to imagine either nutritionists as serious scientists or the universality of their claims. And yet since the equipment and equations never did provide entirely reliable, accurate and transferable forms of measurement and calculation, nutrition was revealed to be a historically specific science whose universality was always breaking down in the process of its constitution.[56]

Take the biochemical laboratory. It was there that pure compounds of foods were isolated through distillation or crystallization, by means of tap funnels, fractioning flasks and columns, or filter papers. Once the compounds had been purified, their chemical components—carbon, hydrogen, nitrogen, halogens, sulfur, phosphorous—were analyzed and quantified in combustion furnaces, condensers, nitrometers, or other machines or instruments, according to various methods and procedures named after their inventors (Dumas, Kjeldahl, Carius, Neumann, Meyer, or Raoult-Beckmann) and were then expressed in complex chemical formulas. The multiplication of procedures and instruments used in the quest for precision and accuracy highlighted the experimental and unsettled nature of the nascent science. Plimmer, founder of the Biochemical Society and head of the Rowett's biochemical lab, complained that even for such "a comparatively easy task" as estimating the quantity of glucose in foodstuffs, "over thirty methods have been devised by the most distinguished chemists and new ones are continually being described and advocated."[57] The discovery and analysis of vitamins led to an often bewildering proliferation in the number of procedures, pieces of equipment, and equations, as new techniques were established to measure the minuscule presence of certain vitamins in foods, the effect of preparation and cooking on those vitamins, their presence or deficiencies in animals and humans. Meanwhile, other techniques were devised to isolate vitamins, so that their chemical constituents could be analyzed and they could be reproduced synthetically. Arguably, the credibility and universality of nutritional science was restored only when the Permanent Commission on Biological Standardization at the League of Nations' Health Organization in 1931 defined an international set of four vitamin units (A, B1, C, and D) that made "the results obtained by different research workers comparable."[58]

Physiological laboratories also remained maddeningly reliant on imprecise instruments and processes. The calorific value of foodstuffs or purified compounds was measured through the use of a bomb calorimeter: a known quantity of the substance was burned in an enclosed tank of water and its heat value determined from the rise in temperature. Essentially the same technique was then applied to human or animal subjects: they were placed in a calorimetric chamber that measured the heat and carbon dioxide they produced, to determine the quantity of calorific fuel they required. Building such chambers for rats and rabbits was one thing; for humans, not to mention cows, it was quite another, especially if you wanted them to engage in vigorous physical activity. The Rowett's three metabolic rooms with calorimeters (including one for large animals) were, though costly, considered unreliable, for the subjects placed within them became anxious, and their metabolic rates increased. Indirect calorimetry was increasingly favored instead. In this technique the heat subjects generated was calculated on the basis of the quantities of oxygen they consumed and the carbon dioxide they produced. As this method required less expensive and more mobile kinds of equipment, subjects could be tested in settings more natural than a chamber and observed under conditions of acute physical strain. The Douglas bag, for instance, was a portable device worn on the back that collected carbon dioxide by means of flexible tubing connected to the subject's mouth or nose (Figure 4.3). Its valves allowed inhalation of oxygen but required a perfect seal at the mouth or nose to prevent exhaled carbon dioxide from escaping, so that it could be collected and measured and its constituents analyzed. Spirometers, allowing the simultaneous measurement of inhaled oxygen and expired carbon dioxide, were also developed. Both instruments were often used in conjunction with an ergometer (a device now sadly familiar to many of us as an exercise machine) that measured the quantities of physical exercise engaged in by the subject (Figure 4.4). However, experiments could be conducted only for short periods, for the equipment was unwieldy and uncomfortable. Given that it was impossible to measure the calorific requirements of human subjects for a full day, it was necessary to generalize from a short period of observation and assume a consistency of effort that belied the usual rhythm of a day. During work trials this was particularly problematic, because a subject was "inclined to show off, to put forward his greatest effort, instead of proceeding at his usual working rate."[59] Even universal basal metabolic rates were called into question when portable devices like the Douglas bag demonstrated that outside laboratory conditions they varied with such environmental factors as climate, clothing, and sanitary conditions.[60] New instruments and devices were constantly being invented to make up for the deficiencies of others, as the developing science struggled to establish the stable, universal, and technical definition and measurement of nutrition and hunger.[61]

Despite the proliferation of tools for nutritional measurement, they did increasingly, if haltingly, help connect the work of nutrition-

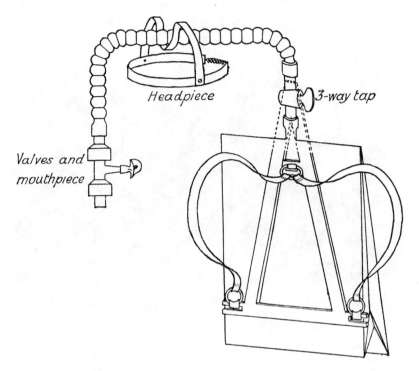

Headpiece

3-way tap

Valves and
mouthpiece

4.3. The Douglas Bag. R. H. A. Plimmer, *Practical Organic and Bio-Chemistry* (London: Longmans, Green, 1926), 511.

ists working in laboratories thousands of miles apart, through standardized systems, procedures, and units of calculation. The Cruelty to Animals Act may have helped regularize laboratory spaces and practices, but it did not prevent the principles of nutritional science from being worked out on rats, pigeons, monkeys, pigs, cows, goats, sheep, guinea pigs, and rabbits: they were fed on synthetic diets to induce deficiency diseases and then on others to cure them; the relative health and rates of growth and death of these laboratory animals were recorded on charts and in photographs; their organs were dissected and inspected, their joints x-rayed, and their blood, sweat, urine, and excrement analyzed for nutriments. They were the perfect foil for the nutritional scientist. Animals existed in virtually unlimited numbers; unlike human subjects, they could be bred as perfect specimens and maintained indefinitely in controlled conditions; they voiced no

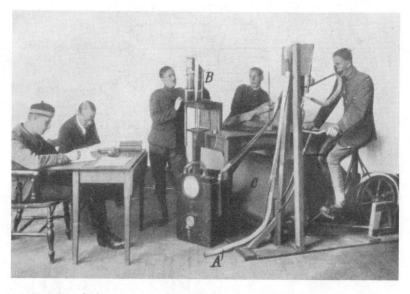

4.4. Testing with the ergometer. Sir W. G. Macpherson, W. H. Horrocks, and W. W. O. Beveridge, *Medical Services: Hygiene of the War* (London: HMSO, 1923), 2:160.

objections and had nothing to prove to investigators. Nutritional laboratories could not function without these animals. And yet the lingering question remained whether the results of experiments with laboratory animals, especially on synthetic foods, were translatable to the less controlled and more diverse human world. In this context, the eyes of nutritional scientists began to turn to the colonial laboratory as a place where they could put the universality of dietary truths to the test. The quest for a universal technical form of hunger had been forged in war and in laboratories; it was now to be extended to the empire.

The Colonial Laboratory

Nutritional science did not simply emanate from the metropolitan Britain to the colonies, where it was tropicalized.[62] As we shall see, research in the colonial laboratory was to transform British conceptions of nutrition and the science of hunger between the wars, but to talk of the colonial formation of nutritional science is to miss the complexity of a process that was inherently transnational and irreducible to the imperial relationship, however marked it was to become by it.

The Rowett Institute exemplified the transnational production of nutritional science. Founded with support from the American Carnegie Foundation as well as the British government and Scottish philanthropists, the institute and its laboratories attracted researchers from around the globe. Built to accommodate these growing ranks in 1930, Strathcona House featured stained glass windows that bore the coat of arms of every British dominion and colony. As the institute's director and a member of the Research Committee of the Empire Marketing Board (EMB), Orr traveled all over the empire, to Palestine, Kenya, Australia, and New Zealand, as well as beyond it to the United States, Belgium, Germany, and Scandinavia. Key members of his staff also joined the international circuit. Alfred Husband became head of research in Rhodesia's Department of Agriculture, and his son-in-law, David Lubbock, who had directed dietary surveys at the Rowett, went on to work at the League of Nations, and later at the United Nations when Orr became the first director general of its Food and Agriculture Organization in 1945. Rare was the nutritionist who had not worked on several continents. Like Orr, W. R. Aykroyd was a typical figure in this respect. Trained at Trinity College, Dublin, he conducted research in Canada and the Lister Institute in London before taking up an appointment at the League of Nations in 1930. In 1935, he succeeded Robert McCarrison as director of the Nutritional Laboratory at Coonor in India, a job that culminated with his membership on the Commission of Enquiry into the Bengal Famine. In 1945, at Orr's invitation, he became director of the Nutrition Division of the U.N.'s FAO, where he remained until he took a position as professor at the London School of Hygiene and Tropical Medicine in 1960. A transnational career path was not uncommon, even if other researchers rarely reached such dizzying heights.[63]

The empire proved a particularly attractive site for research. Nutritionists could learn only so much from experimenting on rats and pigs in English labs, and the empire boasted a plethora of different races with wonderfully diverse "natural" diets uncontaminated by modern commercialized foods. This heterogeneity and "primitive" purity offered a natural laboratory for discovering the key to nutritional efficiency and health. As early as 1912, D. McCay, a professor of physiology at Calcutta's Medical College, proffered a nutritional explanation for the long-acknowledged disparity in the physical stature and martial capabilities of India's different races.[64] Robert McCarrison at the Pasteur Institute in Coonor took up the agenda. Instead of focusing on the recognized manifestations of such deficiency diseases as beriberi, pellagra, scurvy, rickets, he set out to discover less visible but more widespread forms of malnutrition that lowered vitality and resistance to disease.[65] Rather than feed his rats on synthetic diets designed to manufacture specific deficiencies, he fed them on the actual diets of India's diverse regions and peoples. Reproducing India's dietary diversity in his laboratory, he compared the health and physique of its peoples with those of his rats, mapping a marked decline in their vitality as the northern diet of wheat and meat gave way to one based on rice and vegetables in the south (Figure 4.5). As cereals were replaced by rice, and animal by vegetable protein, "the manly, stalwart and resolute races of the north" gave way to "the poorly developed, toneless and supine people of the east and south." Whereas the rats fed on a Sikh diet exhibited a "remarkable freedom from disease," those fed the other diets "developed a wide variety of ailments" that while not recognized as deficiency diseases were clearly the consequence of a more general form of malnutrition.[66]

The implications of McCarrison's work were far-reaching, extending back to the shores of Albion itself. It was a decisive challenge to the Glasgow School's stance that environmental factors shaped nutritional health, for McCarrison's rats were all taken from the same stock and lived under the same controlled conditions. Rather than dismiss diseases in India as exotic peculiarities of a tropical environment, McCarrison insisted that they shared the same nutritional bases as deficiency diseases in Britain. Fed a proper diet, even the most

DIET AND PHYSIQUE OF INDIAN RACES.

Average representatives showing weight in grams of 7 groups of rats fed from the same early age on certain national diets of India. The best of these diets (Sikh) was composed of whole wheat, butter, milk, legumes, vegetables with meat occasionally. The worst (Bengalis and Madrassis) is one composed mainly of rice.

Hunza Hillman: Diet: whole cereal grains (mainly wheat), milk, vegetables and abundant fruits—apricots, etc; meat occasionally.

Tibetan Hillman: representative of dandy carriers, rickshaw-men, etc. Very hard worked. Average protein intake 175 grams daily, of which over 60% is derived from animal sources. The heat value of their diet may be as much as 6,000 calories daily (McCay).

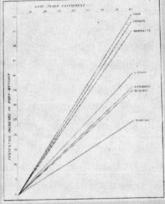

East coast cultivator: Diet: rice with dhal and vegetables and a small amount of fish, milk, and butter. Protein from 50 to 70 grams daily: calories 2,400 to 2,750 (McCay).

Percentage increase in body-weight of 7 groups of young rats, of the same initial aggregate weight fed on certain national diets of India. (vide photograph above).

Nepalese Hillman (Goorkha). Protein 120 to 130 grams, of which less than one third is derived from animal sources. Calories 3,000 to 3,200. Such people eat largely of the better class cereals—wheat, maize and good millets (McCay).

Bengali: Diet: rice, dhal, vegetables, oil with a little fish and perhaps a little milk. Protein, 50 grams daily: Calories 2,300 to 2,500 (McCay)

Mahratta

Sikh
(McCay)

Pathan

Typical of rice-eating Madrassi. Diet contains little or no animal protein. Calories low. (McCay)

4.5. In the colonial laboratory: McCarrison's rats and India's races. Sir Robert McCarrison, *Nutrition and National Health: Being the Cantor Lectures Delivered before the Royal Society of Arts 1936* (London: Faber and Faber, [1936] 1944), facing p. 18.

scrawniest, sickliest native could become a healthy racial specimen. And in a controversial conclusion unlikely to please those who maintained that Britain's colonial rule had rid India of the specter of starvation, he made the dramatic claim that although "more spectacular, endemic and epidemic diseases . . . kill their thousands yearly . . . malnutrition maims its millions."[67] Nonetheless, now that nutritionists had established the ideal diet for optimal health, responsibility also lay with the Indian people, who could redeem and modernize their lives by putting universal scientific principles before irrational local customs and "religious prejudice" in their choice of food.[68] This was a profound departure from the noted deference, even reverence, the British had often paid to Indian dietary lore and practices during the nineteenth century.[69] It also provoked Gandhi's ire. However, McCarrison's prescriptions also held good in relation to the diet of "the poorer classes in England," which compared unfavorably with that of the manly Sikhs. While the mice fed on a Sikh diet had fine, healthy physiques and "lived happily together," those fed on a "poor Britisher" diet exhibited a long list of infirmities: they were "stunted . . . badly proportioned . . . nervous and apt to bite the attendants." Moreover, they "lived unhappily together and . . . began to kill and eat the weaker ones amongst them," and they were "prone to pulmonary and gastro-intestinal disease."[70] The prognosis for the health and social stability of the British people was gloomy but not hopeless, provided that universal lessons of nutritional science could be instilled. In McCarrison's hands the science of hunger and the question of the British standard of living, what Rowntree defined as minimum human needs, had become, in part, a colonial calculation.

Indeed, during the 1920s, nutritionists played a central role in the transnational articulation of "the poor white problem." In 1927, concerned with the increasingly visible white underclass in rural America (later immortalized in the photography of Dorothea Lange for the Farm Security Administration), the Carnegie Corporation funded research on poor whites in South Africa. Five years later the report concluded that around 220,000 whites, 10 percent of the population, had been left behind by modernity. Severed "from European progress and development for many generations," they displayed characteristics—"improvidence and irresponsibility, untruthfulness and lack of a sense of duty, a feeling of inferiority and lack of self-respect, ignorance and credulity, a lack of industry and ambition, and unsettledness of mode of life"—that were assumed to indicate a tenuous hold on whiteness. Poor nutrition, though it had not caused the problem, had, by reducing the health and productivity of poor whites, removed two crucial markers of racial difference.[71] The separate report on *Health Factors in the Poor White Problem,* by W. A. Murray (who had graduated from Edinburgh with an M.B. in biochemistry before becoming senior assistant health officer in Pretoria), glumly noted that poor-white ignorance of modern nutrition resembled that of the "'raw' native." If these unfortunates could be taught that a key duty of white citizenship was sound nutritional self-government, however, all might not yet be lost.[72] Murray's report approvingly cited the work of Raphael Cilento in Australia. The director of the Institute of Tropical Medicine at Townsville, Cilento had written an influential account of the medical triumph of white settlers there, *The White Man in the Tropics,* in which he had maintained that there were no environmental limits to the health of the white race, given a decent diet and exercise regimen. Sound nutrition was the universal key to racial health and economic productivity, and its principles remained the same in the South Pacific as in Northern Europe. Cilento's influence was apparent when, in 1937, Australia's National Health and Medical Research Council was established to focus overwhelmingly on the issue of nutrition and physical fitness, practices that could ensure a healthy and productive white Australia.[73]

In some ways, then, nutritionists resembled missionaries sent from Britain, in this case to civilize colonial diets by ridding them of ignorance and superstition. The intent, however, was to save bodies, not souls—or more accurately, to improve the physical health of colonials, so that their productive capacity as workers increased. In this way nutrition made possible the discourse of colonial development. Orr was again a central figure. In 1925 he traveled to South Africa and Kenya to investigate the causes of heavy livestock losses there.

Extending his work at the Rowett on the importance of minerals to animal nutrition, Orr concluded that soil erosion and overgrazing had depleted African pastures of essential minerals. The situation called for the introduction of fertilizers to enrich the soil, and dietary supplements to restore the health of cattle. The deterioration of the land undermined its potential for "development," a growing interest of the new Cabinet Committee on Civil Research that had commissioned Orr's research in the hope it would ameliorate economic problems at home by improving the health and productivity of Kenya's native population.[74] In Kenya Orr established the integral connections between nutrition, racial health, and economic development that were to shape his vision for the FAO. There he was also struck by the rich possibilities for comparative nutritional research provided by Britain's diverse colonial subjects, after Kenya's chief medical officer, J. L. Gilks, had shown him the differences between the manly, meat-eating Masai and the enfeebled, vegetarian Kikuyu tribes.[75] Proselytizing about these possibilities on his return to London, Orr helped secure a new subcommittee of the Committee on Civil Research, devoted to nutrition, which immediately agreed to have the Colonial Office and the Medical Research Council support further research in Kenya—experimenting with fertilizers on four thousand acres of agricultural land and conducting a dietary survey of the Masai and Kikuyu.[76] In the face of Britain's worsening economic depression and the return of mass unemployment, Orr helped frame the discourse that produced the Colonial Development Act in 1929.[77]

If Orr's work made nutrition central to the discussion of colonial development, it also made Africa its primary focus throughout the 1930s: Audrey Richards's classic work on the anthropology of nutrition among the Bemba of Northern Rhodesia was published in 1932; Hailey's African Research Survey began in 1933, although the resulting report on the links between nutrition, public health, and agricultural improvement did not appear until 1938; in 1934 the International Institute of African Languages and Cultures (IIALC) at Oxford established a subcommittee on diet to facilitate a dialogue between nutritionists and anthropologists, the findings of which were first published in a special issue of its journal *Africa* in 1936.[78] The critical intersection of nutrition, public health, and agricultural development was so well established by 1936 that the Colonial Office requested reports from all its territories on the state of each. A cabinet committee, the Committee on Nutrition in the Colonial Empire (CNCE), was promptly assembled to assess these responses and frame "measures calculated to promote the discovery and application of knowledge in this field," a brief that neatly reflected the dual interest in the empire as both a nutritional research laboratory and a site for development.[79] The committee eventually delivered its report in 1939, the year after the Colonial Office, the MRC, and the IIALC had combined to conduct the most detailed nutritional survey to date in Nyasaland.[80]

The interest surrounding African nutrition and development gathered momentum from concentric local, national, and transnational networks of expertise. The ubiquitous Orr, for instance, was a member of Hailey's African Survey Committee, and the CNCE and had close ties to the IIALC Diet Committee through Gilks and Francis Kelly (both doctors had worked with him in Kenya). When Kelly returned from Kenya in 1931, he went to the Rowett and became co-director of the Imperial Agriculture Bureau and editor of *Nutritional Abstracts and Reviews,* in which capacity he helped prepare the *African Survey* for publication. Similarly, Audrey Richards and Raymond Firth, both anthropologists at the London School of Economics, not only were members of IIALC Diet Committee and the CNCE but were acknowledged for their help on the *African Survey*—hardly surprising, given that their colleague at the IIALC, E. B. Worthington, had been part of the Scientific Research Committee for the *African Survey*. Major Hans Vischer, as secretary to the Colonial Office Advisory Board on Education, and H. S. Scott, as a former director of Education in Kenya, were also both members of the CNCE who were acknowledged for their help on the *African Survey*. Despite sometimes very local and personal connections among these experts, their endeavors had considerable transnational reach. The Carnegie Corporation had funded the *African Survey,* just as it had, along with the Rockefeller Foundation, supported the work of IIALC and the Rowett. The question of the connection between nutrition, racial health, and economic development was by no means a parochially British imperial concern. Although British nutritionists took the lead in this research, it was framed by a set of questions of international interest and made possible by the transnational ambitions of American foundations and the League of Nations. Indeed, the work of a young British nutritionist, W. R. Aykroyd, at the League of Nation's Health Organization served as a catalyst for the formation of the CNCE.[81]

Building upon McCarrison and Orr's work during the 1920s, the African Survey Committee and the CNCE started from the premise that widespread malnutrition in Britain's colonies arrested their potential for economic development. These groups helped shift the discourse of colonial development away from the large-scale projects on infrastructure that had dominated the 1920s and toward investments in medical and public health schemes designed to promote the welfare of native populations, as well as to increase their health and productivity.[82] The *African Survey* was suffused with a belief in the centrality of health and education to the development of Africa's economies and to the effectiveness of its systems of government. The CNCE even went so far as to suggest that the primary cause of colonial malnutrition was not the ignorance of the natives, but an inadequate standard of living. "The problem," it concluded, "is fundamentally an economic problem. Malnutrition will never be cured until the peoples of the Colonial Empire command far greater resources than they do at present."[83] Nutritional science therefore provided one of the avenues for rethinking the political economy of empire during the 1930s and 1940s. The new ways of understanding and promoting the health and wealth of Britain's colonial subjects it provided were formally articulated in the novel coupling of terms in the title of the Colonial Development *and Welfare* Act of 1940.[84]

As a tool of colonial development, nutritional science was fundamentally transformed. In view of the sheer dietary diversity of British colonial subjects it soon became apparent that nutritional knowledge and techniques for investigating it were far from universal. Considering reports from forty-eight territories, spanning two million square miles and comprising fifty-five million people, the CNCE recognized that knowledge of their nutrition remained "necessarily imperfect and incomplete" and that even the research which had been completed had been less than consistent in the methodology and standards of measurement used.[85] Indeed, Audrey Richards argued that working in the colonial field posed particular problems that required the development of new investigative techniques. There even basic tasks were compromised: she was forced to measure the Bemba diet in the northeastern part of Rhodesia by weighing food in a suitcase "hung over the branch of a tree"; she had had no way of accounting for "snacks in the form of wild fruits . . . taken between meals"; since her time in each village was short, she had been unable to investigate the large seasonal variation in the quantity and quality of the diet; and patterns of Bemba sociability at mealtimes rendered redundant the standard technique of measuring the daily and weekly diet of a family unit.[86] The supposedly universal techniques of nutritional surveys were found wanting in the field, she concluded: "Quantitative studies of native dietaries require the development of new techniques."[87] The Nyasaland Nutrition Survey was established in 1938 to address these issues. As the first in a series of surveys on colonial nutrition to be coordinated by a new Central Nutrition Organization, the survey was established following collaborative discussions among the IIALC, the Colonial Office, and the MRC. It was specifically charged with developing a methodology and set of standards that would pull together the expertise of nutritionists, anthropologists, medics, botanists, agriculturalists, and colonial administrators and shape the work of future survey teams in the colonial laboratory. The survey soon fell apart amid personal animosities and professional rivalries, most spectacularly those between its director, the nutritionist B. S. Platt, and the anthropologist Margaret Read. Its report, which failed to develop a coherent methodology or any universal set of standards, was never published.[88]

The tension between nutrition as a biological science and nutrition as a social science lay at the heart of this debate about method. Like McCarrison and Orr, nutritionists believed that their research in the colonial laboratory, even while exposing dietary diversity, had revealed the universal requirements of the human body and the biological principles of nutritional science. It was, they insisted, diet, not culture or environment, that mattered in questions of nutritional health. The nutritional discourse of development was predicated on the belief that to modernize colonial subjects it was necessary to reform indigenous food cultures through the universal reason of nutritional science. Thus, echoing McCarrison and Orr, the CNCE complained that the "innate conservatism, prejudice, religious scruples and taboos" which characterized colonial diets were "clearly wrong and . . . a barrier to progress."[89] The new anthropology of nutrition increasingly challenged this perspective, by stressing that the locally and culturally specific social meaning of food often undercut its universal biological value. Anthropologists may have made this discovery in the colonial laboratory, but its truth, they maintained, was universal and just as apparent in Britain as in the colonies. Indeed, this was an approach that would transform British nutritional science during the 1930s and 1940s.

Audrey Richards was the critical figure here, for she was the first to question whether food choice that nutritionists dismissed as unscientific and irrational had to be eradicated from the modern diet. Rather than condemn dietary preferences as the product of primitive taboo or religious prejudice because the food was biologically inefficient, Richards explained their persistence in terms of their social function and cultural meaning. Although Richards remarked that to "venture like this on the border-line between two different sciences, biological and social, is an ungrateful task," her work was hugely influential.[90] The daughter of a senior colonial administrator in India, Richards served briefly as secretary to the Labor Department of the League of Nations Union, before conducting her doctoral work in anthropology at the London School of Economics with Bronislav Malinowski. Like Malinowski, Richards was interested in how the cultural had shaped the seemingly natural. Whereas he studied the

functions of sex in "savage" societies, she focused on the social conventions that surrounded "a biological process . . . more fundamental
than sex," namely nutrition.[91] Like Malinowski, she also suggested
that the social functions of food and sex, although more visible in
primitive cultures, were no less present in the civilizations of the
modern West.[92] Universalism, in the shape of the elaboration of the
universal laws of social anthropology, returned from the empire to
strike back at metropolitan British conceits.

Richards insisted that nutrition, as a complex social and cultural
process, should not be reduced to a technical, physiological problem.
"Man's selection of food," she argued, was determined not solely by
physiological needs, but "very largely by the habits and values which
his 'social heritage' has imposed upon him." Citing as an example
Gilks and Orr's observation that the Kikuyu in some districts did not
eat any food that was green, because they believed doing so would
impede their fleetness of foot when they were defeated by the Masai,
she suggested that the magical properties or symbolic rituals surrounding food were sometimes more important than its nutritional
value. Those who dismissed these complex social uses and cultural
meanings of food as irrational superstitions would surely fail to transform the malnourished bodies of colonial workers into those of productive and healthy modern subjects.[93]

It was a position supported by Indian Hindus angered by the way
nutritionists had dismissed their vegetarianism as the product of religious prejudice, despite its foundation upon ancient Ayurvedic principles that had long ago "actuated . . . research and investigation in
dietetics."[94] For them the challenge was not to return to those original principles, but to indigenize nutritional science and domesticate
its universal biological principles to accommodate the cultural spe-
cificities of India. Gandhi was a key figure in this debate. Turning his
own body into a nutritional laboratory, he set about his dietetic experiments with scientific rigor—ceaselessly trying not only different
diets and foodstuffs, but various modes of preparing, cooking, and
eating them, and measuring their effect on the weight and texture of
his excrement, as well as on his general health and vitality. In the

pages of *Young India* and *Harijan* he debated the success and validity of
these experiments not just with readers engaged in similar experiments (frequently chiding them for their unscientific approach and
exaggerated claims), but with nutritional scientists like McCarrison.[95]
Although Gandhi praised McCarrison's work, seeing it as a counterpart to his own dietetic experiments, he was deeply suspicious of
McCarrison's championing of milk and meat, and especially irritated
by his privileging of the Sikh diet over that of Hindus. Arguing that
the "unlimited capacity of the plant world to sustain man at his highest is a region yet unexplored by modern medical science," Gandhi al-
luded to the way in which "the fast developing researches about vitamins" could "revolutionize many of the accepted theories and beliefs
propounded by the medical science [*sic*] about food" and lend support
to his position.[96] When McCarrison, who knew a thing or two about
vitamins, countered by detailing a wealth of research on the inadequacy of vegetarian diets, Gandhi questioned its objectivity: "The tremendous vested interests that have grown around the belief in animal
food prevent the medical profession from approaching the question
with complete detachment." So compromised was nutritional science
by Western precepts that it now had to be indigenized, either by "Indian medical men whose tradition is vegetarian," or by "lay enthusi-
asts" like himself.[97] Only then, Gandhi argued, would it be possible to
understand that nutrition and dietetics were not simply a question of
physiology, but had a profound moral and spiritual basis. However
anxious Gandhi was for Indians to "free [them]selves from the tyranny of Western medicines," he knew that it was important to enter
into a dialogue with Western scientists, to appropriate and blend
their research with "Indian" knowledge. He had as little patience with
Ayurvedic physicians, who "merely repeat[ed] the printed formula" of
ancient texts instead of engaging in modern experimental research,
as with McCarrison.[98] Yet Gandhi's project to translate the claims of
Western nutritional science to India through a reinvigorated indigenous diet never managed to displace McCarrison and Aykroyd's ex-
pectation that nutritional science could help transform India into a
modern nation.

*   *   *

During the first three decades of the twentieth century our under-standing of hunger thus assumed a novel, profoundly technical, form, by contrast with previous definitions of hunger, which were highly politicized, local, and subjective. In the decades surrounding the First World War, a set of technical procedures appeared to make it possi-ble to study and measure hunger in a disinterested and scientific way. Armed with these techniques, social and nutritional scientists be-lieved they could precisely identify the amount and type of food that human bodies required in order to remain healthy, and, beyond that, to become more productive. Discussions of hunger were reduced to technical equations showing how many calories human beings re-quired and how much they would cost. Not surprisingly, nutritional science came to seem increasingly essential to modern statecraft.

Nonetheless, during the Great War, the authority and utility of nu-tritional science as a tool of statecraft was called into question, as the discovery of new vitamins and the extension of nutritional research to Britain's colonial territories cast doubt on the universality of its techniques and prescriptions. As we shall see in the next chapter, these tensions would have profound consequences for the way in which hunger was understood in Britain and around the world during the 1920s, 1930s, and 1940s. Most fundamentally, the discovery of vitamins and the gradual triumph of the biochemical view of nutri-tion allowed hunger, and eventually poverty, to be fundamentally redefined in terms of the quality of diet and health, and by reference to what became known as *mal*nutrition, rather than simply the quan-titative lack of food—that is, *under*nutrition. It is hard to overesti-mate the magnitude of this transformation or the degree to which it enabled a new social grammar for the government of hunger.

5

Hungry England and Planning for a World of Plenty

In January 1933, four years after it became officially impossible to die of starvation in Britain, two leftist newspapers, the *Daily Herald* and the *Daily Worker,* broke a story that would "explode the comfortable and superannuated belief of the tax paying classes that no one need starve in England."[1] It was in many ways an unremarkable report on the inquest of Minnie Weaving, a thirty-seven-year-old mother of seven and wife of the unemployed George Weaving. The family lived on a new housing estate in southeast London, where Minnie had tried to nourish them all on the forty-eight shillings her husband received in benefits. It was an impossible task. Although she fed her husband and children, she starved herself and eventually collapsed and died while bathing her six-month-old twins. Although the pathologist recorded pneumonia as the immediate cause of death, he noted that it would not have proved fatal had she had enough to eat; she had, he concluded, "sacrificed her life" for the sake of her children. At the inquest the coroner gave a less equivocal verdict: "I should call it starving to have to feed nine people on £2 8s a week and pay the rent."[2] In the following weeks Minnie's death became the catalyst for a debate about the condition of England and the adequacy of welfare for its hungry citizens, one that persisted throughout the 1930s and shaped social democratic planning for a world of plenty during the 1940s.

Even the usually sedate pages of the *Week-End Review* erupted into heated and prolonged debate under the headline "Hungry England"—the same title Fenner Brockway had given his exposé of the "shameful" condition of England, published the previous year.[3] Lamenting the sound and fury generated by its correspondents, the *Week-End Review* nevertheless insisted that the issues raised were "primarily technical problems." In the hands of experts capable of applying "the principle of scientific measurement" to calculate minimum human needs and their costs, the matter could be considered "outside the range of party controversy of the old-fashioned type." The paper accordingly established an "independent fact-finding" committee of inquiry, comprising "an economist [A. L. Bowley], a physiologist [V. H. Mottram], a housewife, a doctor and a social worker," to settle the debate scientifically. Far from doing so, the committee came to the conclusion that unemployment relief payments were insufficient to fund the minimum diet recommended by the Ministry of Health's new Advisory Committee on Nutrition. The findings were hugely controversial. That they also cast doubt on the credibility of the ministry's reports on the scale of malnutrition among schoolchildren—and that Mottram was a member of both committees—further inflamed matters.[4] The hungry England debate gave nutritionists unprecedented public visibility, but instead of reducing the measurement and relief of hunger to a technical matter, the debate politicized nutritional science.

Given that the political meaning of hunger could not be separated from the technical question of how to identify and measure it, the debate sharply exposed differences between nutritionists who championed newer biochemical definitions of malnutrition and those who did not. The differences led to a proliferation of technical standards that threatened to compromise the authority of dietetics, the science that claimed to have provided a universal and objective calculus of hunger. And yet the transformation of hunger into malnutrition and the emergence of social nutrition—that is, nutrition attentive to the social meanings of food and to poverty as the cause of malnutrition—made nutritional science central to the politics of the 1930s and

1940s. With a new and radically expanded definition of hunger as malnutrition, social nutritionists delineated the costs of hunger and asserted that it was preventable with a little nutritional planning. Just as nutritional science had become an indispensable force in the development of colonial societies, so it also became a vital tool of social planning in Britain that promised to deliver a society and eventually a world without hunger. The think tank Political and Economic Planning (PEP), which had emerged from the *Week-End Review*, declared, "Gradually in recent years we have ceased to regard poverty as an act of God, and come to regard it as a problem which can be analysed and treated by the same methods of science and common sense that we are trying to apply to other problems."[5]

The Rediscovery of Hungry England

The ethnographic mode of discovering hunger, with its emphasis on proximity and empathy, was revitalized between the wars in reaction against a reduction of hunger to the technical assessments espoused by the social and nutritional sciences.[6] Whereas before the war the humanitarian discovery of hunger had focused on the metropolis or foreign famine fields, during the 1930s those with a social conscience and an interest in the face of hunger went north to "old Industrial England."[7] Brockway's journey took him along the soon to be well-trodden path to Lancashire, the Black Country, Tyne and Tees, South Wales, Clydeside, and the rural Suffolk of seasonal agriculture labor. The following year Allen Hutt, covered much the same ground and discovered the "stark reality is that in 1933, for the mass of the population, Britain is a hungry Britain, badly fed, clothed and housed."[8] Orwell's *Road to Wigan Pier* came out just as social researchers who styled themselves Mass-Observers joined the now obligatory journey north to Bolton, where they hoped to document the everyday life of a "typical" northern industrial town, known first as Northtown and later as Worktown.[9] Before the Mass-Observation volunteers even encountered hunger, many were overwhelmed by the experience of the North and, like Orwell, found it a "strange country" marked by industrial "ugliness so frightful and so arresting that you are obliged, as it were, to come to terms with it."[10] Disgusted at the strange sights and smells of the North, authors frequently compared it to the colonial settings they had experienced in childhood.[11] For Tom Harrisson, cofounder of the documentary movement Mass-Observation, the Worktown project seemed an extension of his earlier work as an ornithologist in the South Pacific: "The wilds of Lancashire or the mysteries of the East End of London were as little explored as the cannibal interior of the New Hebrides or the head-hunter hinterland of Borneo."[12] Humphrey Spender, who joined Harrisson in Bolton, felt "very much a foreigner," like "somebody from another planet, intruding on another kind of life."[13]

The face of hunger changed as you went north. Alongside sacrificial mothers and innocent children was the figure of the unemployed man. Time and again it is the gaunt, hollow faces of unemployed northern men with "a constant look of strain in their expression" that the documentary movement holds up to our view.[14] At the end of his *English Journey* Priestley recalls, "Just after the Armistice, I had been sent to look after some German prisoners of war. They had a certain look, these prisoners of war, most of whom had been captured two or three years before. It was a strained greyish, faintly decomposed look. I did not expect to see that kind of face again for a long time; but I was wrong. I had seen a lot of those faces on this journey. They belonged to unemployed men."[15] No longer was the unemployed man seen as the archetypal Malthusian nightmare, the immoral and lazy architect of his family's misery. Just as the humanitarian discovery of hunger before the war had been mediated through the innocence of women and children, so these works presented the unemployed man as a victim of a market beyond his control and a political system that had failed to ensure his welfare. Of course, the Edwardian hunger marches had tried to effect the same transformation, but the documentary movement made unemployed men sympathetic figures to a much broader public.

Critical to that sympathetic response was the characterization of unemployment as a human condition, not an abstract, social-scientific

problem; here were men who bled and wept, not figures and statistics. Brockway repeatedly bemoaned the fact that statistics and "figures signify little" without some key to what they mean on a human
scale. Thus he asks his "readers who have been in the Royal Albert
Hall, London, [to] imagine it filled three times over. That would represent the workers on the Means Test in Newcastle. Imagine it filled
twelve times over. That would represent their families. It is beyond
imagination to realise the anxiety and despair and suffering they
would represent." After a long section discussing household budgets,
to demonstrate how few met Rowntree's poverty line, Brockway implored his readers to make the figures real by applying them to their
own household: "Take the last instance. A family of four existing on
14s. 6d. a week; 5s. for rent, at the lowest 1s. 6d. for coal and lighting. Allow nothing at all for clothing and household utensils and ex-
tras. That leaves 8s to provide food for two adults and two children
for a week. How can it be done without leaving actual hunger—hunger gnawing at the stomach, hunger making one dizzy and weak, hunger starving one's body and destroying one's mind?"[16] The point here
was not just to establish that hunger was a human condition which
afflicted real people but to connect his readers directly with the suffering of those people.

Other documentary accounts sought to do so by allowing the hungry to speak for themselves. As S. P. B. Mais put it in *Time to Spare*,
the book of a radio documentary about the experience of unemployment: "Few things are harder than the capacity to put yourself in the
place of someone who is suffering if you are not suffering . . . And
that is why you are about to read an account from the unemployed
themselves of what life is like when one is out of work."[17] The previous year Victor Gollancz, in his *Memoirs of the Unemployed*, had aimed
to represent "the authentic voice of the unemployed . . . the first occasion on which this voice has been heard in the long discussion of
unemployment that has dragged on for so many years."[18] In some
cases, this voice might question, like Mrs. Keen, an unemployed cotton operative from Lancashire, whether the accounts could "make
you realize what our life is like. Unless you are here, living amongst

these things, you couldn't understand—and I can't put it into words."[19] The documentary movement, however, had a touching faith in the potential of the modern technologies of radio and film to make the experience of hunger and unemployment accessible and real to audiences. As Ruby Grierson reputedly told her subjects when she was making the documentary film *Housing Problems:* "The camera's yours, the microphone is yours, now tell the bastards what it is like to live in a slum."[20]

Nonetheless, the drama of the ethnographer's encounter with hunger, so familiar to Edwardian audiences, did not disappear completely. In their determination to provide unmediated access to the experience of the unemployed, some writers believed that they could understand and convey what hunger was like only if they lived with it themselves. Although Orwell's *Road to Wigan Pier* is the iconic example, it remained routine for journalists to enter their stories as participant observers. When in 1936 a hunger march set off from Jarrow, a shipbuilding town in the Northeast devastated by unemployment, newspapers sent special correspondents to march with the men and "share their lot."[21] The dispatches reported on the conditions "we" encountered on the road, of friendships forged, and "our" determination to reach London. Ritchie Calder, in filing his last report for the *Daily Herald,* asserted, "No-one can listen to these men, as I have done, talking not of themselves but of their wives and families and of 'the man-next-door' without feeling an almost religious zeal for their cause."[22] The attempt to get underneath the skin of working-class people as a participant observer, and inside the heads of the hungry even influenced the social sciences. As early as 1933, long before the Mass-Observation movement started, Bakke stated, in his study *The Unemployed Man,* that only by sharing "their life insofar as it was possible to do so" could he discover truths not available to "cold blooded research on the basis of carefully planned questionnaires or the tabulation of recorded statistics."[23] This interest in personal experience of the psyche as affected by hunger and unemployment would help shape the nascent discipline of social psychology.[24] The documentary movement's rediscovery of hungry England in the gaunt frames of unemployed men in the North was not thus entirely at odds with the social sciences, even if it was partly animated by their reduction of hunger to technical abstractions.

Identifying Hungry England

In fact, although nutritionists had long since established the technical definition of hunger and believed that after the war their expertise would play an increasingly central role, it was not until 1931 that nutritionists were welcomed back into the fold at Whitehall, with the creation of Ministry of Health's Advisory Committee on Nutrition (ACN). Officials blamed this decade in the cold on the failure of nutritionists to agree among themselves about the existence or importance of vitamins; but as hunger and unemployment increased during the Depression, the mandarins at the Ministry of Health became convinced of the strategic value of having policies legitimated and "fortified" by "a Committee of recognized experts": this tactic would help "minimise the amount of criticism which can be directed against the Department."[25] When George Newman, the ministry's chief medical officer, eventually convened the Advisory Committee, he carefully neutralized the biochemical enthusiasm Hopkins, Mellanby, and Mottram expressed for vitamins by introducing Cathcart, Lindsay, and Greenwood's thermodynamic approach. Unsurprisingly, the committee's first memo reflected this division, setting the minimum nutritional standard at 3,000 calories and 37 grams of protein along the Cathcart and Murray scale for man-values, while grudgingly acknowledging the existence of vitamins A to D.[26]

This was the minimum standard that the *Week-End Review*'s rival committee of experts maintained could not be afforded on unemployment relief. They took issue not with the standard but rather with the presumption that it could be achieved economically. "Digestive, culinary and psychological considerations," they insisted, made that impossible: it would mean eating eight pints of porridge a day, a monotonous diet that no alimentary canal could stand.[27] Officials at the Ministry of Health were dismayed when the ACN told them that it had "no reason to dissent" from the *Week-End Review*'s report. They were in despair when the British Medical Association (BMA) established its own Committee on Nutrition, which concluded that the ACN's minimum standard should be raised to 3,400 calories and 50 grams of protein.[28] Despite Mottram's presence on this committee as well, the ACN promptly rejected the more generous BMA standard. A joint conference was hastily arranged to craft a consensus that would restore the credibility of nutritional science. A predictable tune was played: their "alleged disagreement" had been "exaggerated," their "divergences were more a matter of misunderstanding and misinterpretation than of actual fact," for there was no "fundamental disagreement on matters of scientific fact."[29] Neither the laws of nutritional science nor their method of investigation or application was disputed; rather, the two committees had had different objectives and audiences in mind. Whereas the ACN had provided average figures to guide medical officers dealing with institutional, that is school and workhouse, dietaries, the BMA's committee had focused on the minimum diet required by unemployed men and their families to maintain their health and working capacity. Any remaining difference could be accounted for by the BMA's allowance of 10 percent wastage in the nutritional value of foods, as they were purchased, prepared, cooked, and eaten by those not properly schooled in efficient household management.[30]

Instead of a resolution to the hungry England debate, in the years that followed an unprecedented politicization of nutritional knowledge took place, as the identification of malnutrition expanded the category of hunger. In 1934 both the Committee against Malnutrition and the Children's Minimum Council were established to draw attention to the scale of malnutrition and its disproportionately corrosive effect on children; in 1936 the classic texts of "the hungry thirties" were published—G. C. M. McGonigle and J. Kirby's *Poverty and Public Health,* Orr's *Food, Health and Income,* and McCarrison's *Nutrition and National Health*—all of which estimated that effectively half the population of Britain, more than twenty million people, were malnourished.[31] Political and Economic Planning, convening yet another expert committee on nutrition to review the controversy in 1936, concluded that the hungry England debate had decisively shifted the terms of discussion: "Government has ensured, with a fair degree of success, that no-one in Britain need go hungry, but hunger it is now shown is not a sufficient test, for a person getting enough bulk of food and calories to stave off hunger may still be suffering a serious deficiency of one or more protective food elements, such as vitamins, calcium or iodine."[32]

At the heart of the nutritional debate on hungry England was the question whether malnutrition was a condition, and, if it was, how it could be defined and measured. Even those who advocated an expanded definition of hunger as "malnutrition" recognized that the term had been used in a "loose and confused manner," and that this lack of precision had called into question the disinterested nature of nutritional expertise.[33] By the 1930s, as newer biochemical discoveries competed and often merged with the thermodynamic perspective, the term "malnutrition" was used variously, to describe those who suffered from a host of conditions. People who did not eat enough food, whose physique was below "normal" or locally "average" standards, or who suffered from a specific deficiency disease, as well as those whose nutritional health failed to meet the highest attainable, or "optimum," standards, might all be suffering from malnutrition. The problem of definition resolved itself into one of measurement, of how to translate the still contested laboratory knowledge about adequate diet into a technique for identifying who was malnourished—one that was transferable and could produce comparable results over time and in different countries.

These technical issues became especially politically charged after the creation of a service to provide school meals and a system of medical inspection to identify which children were deserving of them.[34] George Newman, then chief officer of health at the Board of Education, acknowledging that "no absolute standard" or "definite criteria" were in place for measuring nutritional status, nonetheless advised school medical officers to use Hutchison's clinical indicators of poor nutrition to assess "the functional efficiency and well being of the child," and then to classify his or her nutritional health as good, normal, below normal, or bad, with the latter two types being further divided into those requiring treatment and those requiring observation.[35] Critics were quick to question the reliability of Newman's standard of measurement and system of classification. The criteria for nutritional health were so broad that many other environmental factors or diseases could be seen to affect it adversely. That confusion was evident among local medical officers, who emphasized different indicators, had widely divergent ways of translating their clinical assessment into the prescribed scale, deployed their own idiosyncratic definitions of the standards, and invariably equated the "normal" with the local average. Given these problems, critics of the system never ceased to point out, it was impossible to make comparisons between localities or across time, let alone to generate reliable national figures.[36] As the medical officers despairingly pleaded for further research to identify "the clinical signs of malnutrition, for these we do not know," the BMA defended the doctors by admitting "that there exists no satisfactory and accepted routine method by which the nutritional condition or state of individuals can be assessed, and by which the findings of different observers can be compared."[37] In 1933, as these difficulties became more visible during the hungry England debate, the ACN was asked to devise a standard test for malnutrition that would help eradicate the vagaries of the existing system of measurement and classification. In the absence of a more "reliable yardstick," it continued to favor broad clinical assessments over anthropometric measurements and made only minor changes to the system of classification, which were subsequently adopted by the Board of Education.[38] It was not enough to silence the critics, including especially, but not exclusively, the increasingly forceful Committee against Malnutrition (CAM).[39] By 1940 even the Board of Education's own senior medical inspector gloomily concluded that having closely studied the last five years of returns, he had found them "so unreliable as to be valueless for any purpose . . . Clinical assessment . . . has so many intrinsic flaws that with the friction of common use it flies to pieces."[40] It was the system of classification as much as the absence of a standard of measurement that remained problematic. The Committee against Malnutrition and its allies argued that it was no longer sufficient for the ministry's category of the "normal" to be equated with the "average" or "mean" conditions of the population, for these inevitably gravitated toward the lowest common denominator of a "minimum requirement."[41] Instead, "normal" should refer to an optimal level of nutrition, to ensure that the delayed and suppressed effects of malnutrition would not later become apparent.[42] This shift from "minimum" to "optimal" standards, made possible by the discovery of malnutrition, would have dramatic consequences for how social scientists measured, and politicians governed, hunger and poverty.

The quest for a more reliable system of measuring and classifying malnutrition was not a concern unique to Britain. The League of Nations Technical Sub-Committee on Nutrition was at the forefront of attempts to provide universal standards and techniques for measuring malnutrition, just as it had been in the efforts to establish international standards for calorific requirements and the definition of vitamins, although the central role of British nutritionists in these endeavors is striking.[43] Some sense of the conflicting systems and standards already in place, which had been evident at a League of Nations conference in 1932, were later summarized by E. Burnett and Aykroyd.[44] They catalogued three basic systems of measurement—the anthropometric, the clinical, and the physiological—each with its own competing standards, techniques, and shortcomings. The complex relation between height, weight, and other bodily measurements was, for instance, expressed in no fewer than five named anthropometric "indices of nutrition," the "fallacies" of which "had been repeatedly described," even though they allowed for margins of error that ranged from 7 to 20 percent.[45] Clinical methods were no less problematic. The "Dunfermline scale," used by school medical officers in Britain before 1934, had several rivals—the Chittenden, the Pirquet, and Franzen's ACH index—each with its different systems of classification and techniques of inspection and measurement. Despite the subsequent addition of yet more anthropometric indexes of nutrition (the Bouchard, Van der Heijden, Manouvrier, Brugsch, Flesch, Pryor, McLoy, and Tuxford), another League of Nations nutritional subcommittee with a strong British flavor still found they lacked "precise or objective standards of reference." Instead, experts pinned their hopes on a new system of measurement that promised to reach beyond the limitations of the anthropometric, clinical, and physiological techniques—the vitamin-deficiency test. Designed to provide early diagnoses of malnutrition before it became clinically visible, these tests checked for deficiencies in vitamins, minerals, and proteins through a series of experiments on blood and urine samples (or, in the case of vitamin A, by a variety of competing ophthalmic tests). Although these were all "still in the experimental stage" and were limited in their application to large-scale investigations, it was hoped they would soon provide a more reliable set of standardized techniques for the identification and measurement of malnutrition.[46]

Despite these technical innovations and debates about how to identify and classify hunger as malnutrition, nutritionists remained dependent on the social sciences for measuring its hold on populations. Nutritionists could argue over the requirements for minimal or optimal standards, but dietary surveys remained essential, to ascertain whether the income of individuals or groups, or the foods they ate, met those needs. Those interested in the relation between *Food, Health and Income,* as Orr's title famously summarized it, had to combine an abstract knowledge of food values and nutritional requirements with a social investigation of what populations ate and how much money they had for purchasing food. Unfortunately, no two subjects were as shrouded in secrecy within working-class households; thus, to gain access to them, as well as accurate statistical knowledge of them, the nutritionist turned to the techniques of the social investigator.[47] Although Rowntree and Bowley had greatly improved the science of social investigation before the Great War, the collection and collation of information on the budgets and dietaries of the poor remained notoriously difficult. The process entailed a series of difficult methodological questions: how to create standardized systems of measurement that would ensure accurate results, given *both* the dependence on voluntary staff with little social-scientific training *and* the hostility, reluctance, or inability of the poor to provide detailed accounts of their weekly budgets and dietary habits.

As researchers attempted to grapple with these issues between the wars, the techniques of the dietary survey became increasingly elaborate.[48] Sampled subjects were given detailed account books in which they were expected to document all weekly income and expenditures carefully, paying especial attention to all purchases of foods—their quantities and prices. In addition, they were asked to keep a meticulous record of the household's dietary regime: who ate what, and when; how it was prepared, cooked, and eaten; what other meals or foods were eaten outside of the household (at work, at school, or at the baker's or chip shop). A set of measuring scales and jugs were provided, so that the precise quantities for each purchase, and the ingredients for every meal, could be weighed and recorded. Nothing was left to chance. The investigator (or, more accurately, his usually female assistant) would begin by weighing and recording any foods already in the house when the survey started and would end by seeing what was left. These records had to be kept for a minimum of a week, and ideally for a month, to ensure that subjects did not modify their diet, or the distribution of food within the family, to impress or flatter the investigator. It was frequently acknowledged that the longer the survey ran, the greater the burden imposed on subjects and the less the chance of securing their continuing cooperation; yet it was also hoped, as we shall see in Chapter 7, that this discipline in the art of bookkeeping and accounting would render the housewife a more efficient and scientific manager of her household resources. Armed with these records, the social investigator could calculate first the percentage of domestic income available for expenditure on food, and then, using schedules of food values and nutritional requirements, whether the money was adequate and efficiently used. No less than laboratory instruments, these inquiry cards, tables of food values, and scales of nutritional requirements were intended to enable common standards of measurement to be deployed from household to household and locality to locality. However, their utility remained frustratingly compromised by the human factor in the investigation.

Ever since the work of Booth and Rowntree, social surveys had depended on an army of research assistants to gain access to the homes of the poor and extract information from them. These assistants were very often women whose jobs as school inspectors, health visitors, and charity workers gave them a greater familiarity with the lives of the poor and a better chance of being welcomed into their homes. Although a great deal continued to rest on the personal skills, both social and observational, of the investigators, the inquiry card was designed to ensure that they left their subjective judgments behind and recorded only information that adhered to strict classifications and was capable of statistical aggregation. And yet every social survey lamented the stubborn refusal of some people to open their doors to the inquisitive gaze of their investigators. As David Vincent has so elegantly shown, privacy from prying eyes was a sacred resource for the poor: gossip and careless talk may not yet have cost lives, but they could cause a plague of inspectors to descend upon one's home and threaten an already inadequate means-tested income.[49] Even when respondents opened doors and proffered information, questions remained about its accuracy. Income was notoriously hard to compute, for it was caught up in a web of secrets between employers, men, and their wives, all fearing the financial consequences of any unintended revelation. Some investigators resorted to payments that they hoped would loosen tongues, but most researchers hoped that the charms of their research assistants or the worthiness of their investigation would do the trick. Sometimes nothing worked. Herbert Tout, son of Manchester's famous medieval historian, unusually recorded the exact proportion of families that rebutted the queries of the school attendance officers he had hired for his social survey of Bristol: it came to 7 percent of the 4,865 families approached. "There were, of course, a few cases of slammed doors," he wrote, "but nearly everywhere the investigators met with a friendly reception, and tell tales of odd cups of tea and glasses of beer offered them during the interviews. On several occasions husbands even ran after them to disclose earnings which they had not wanted to reveal in front of their wives."[50]

No less than nutritional scientists depended upon the flawed techniques of the social sciences, social scientists depended upon the flawed techniques of nutritional science. After Rowntree had established that social scientists could not measure poverty without a calculation of minimum nutritional need, their credibility rested on their ability to navigate the choppy waters of nutritional science and steer a course between its competing claims and shifting standards. Most, recognizing the absence of "unanimity among physiologists,"[51] made pragmatic choices and based their calculations on the nutritional standards laid out by the BMA, the ACN, and the League of Nations. They then translated these standards into dietaries and prices geared to local conditions, to arrive at a figure for the average cost of an adult workingman's diet—figures that varied according to the standard used, the date of compilation, and the cost of food in the chosen locality.[52] The changing standards of nutritional science posed the greatest problems for repeat studies. Rowntree's minimum standards, for instance, continually fell. In 1918 the *Human Needs of Labour* moderately revised the original standards he had set out in 1901 in *Poverty* by retaining the 3,500 calories but reducing the protein requirements from 125 grams to 115 grams, but the 1937 edition reduced calorific and protein requirements to 3,400 and 100 grams, respectively, to reflect "changes in expert opinion," not least the discovery of "protective foods." Similarly, between 1918 and 1937 his calculations in man-values for the needs of a family of three rose from 3.47 to 3.78, as the greater nutritional requirements of women and children were recognized.[53] Researchers who failed to keep up with the changes in nutritional knowledge risked having the scientific basis of their work questioned: Mottram, for instance, was scathing about Llewelyn Smith's use in *New Survey of London* of Rowntree's first set of minimum requirements and noted drily that "dietetics has undergone a marked revolution since 1901."[54]

Shared techniques of investigation enabled social and nutritional scientists to address a mutual preoccupation: whether those who failed to meet the minimum nutritional standard did so through lack of income or inefficiency. As we shall see in Chapter 7, they commonly lamented that the poor put pleasure before survival in matters of consumption. It was a criticism that infuriated those with a more immediate experience of poverty and unemployment, like Wal Hannington, who as leader of the National Unemployed Workers Movement (NUWM) organized the hunger marches of the 1920s and 1930s. Despairing about how the poor were objectified and "treated like so many test-tubes" by social and nutritional scientists, he complained that all their "talk of calories, alphabetical vitamins, proteins, carbohydrates, fats and grammes . . . sounded like a foreign language to the ordinary unemployed worker whose family was having to exist on a diet composed chiefly of potatoes, bread, margarine, tea, and condensed milk."[55] Wryly remarking that although he was not equipped to "embark upon scientific polemics with the wise men of the B.M.A. and the experts of the Ministry of Health," he did know "that the kinds of food which have been specified as the minimum requirements, are not being eaten in the homes of the workless, for the simple reason that they cannot afford to buy them."[56] Poverty, he was adamant, was the cause of hunger and malnutrition; only those ignorant of the realities of life on the breadline could suggest otherwise. Particularly "indignant at the patronising insults" of those who blamed "the ignorance of the average working-class housewife in regard to food values and in the art of cooking," he reminded those "pretentious enough to take upon themselves the right to instruct" her in the most efficient use of an inadequate income "that the working out of diets on the basis of their calorie-content and their value in vitamins is an entirely different thing from buying food which will satisfy the hunger of the family."[57]

This issue of satisfying hunger and taste, rather than nutritional requirements, became critical because it illustrated the way in which the social and nutritional sciences had ignored the social meanings and functions of food that often overlay its nutritional value. In her dietary survey of five unemployed families, Ruth Bowley, Arthur's wife, argued it was hardly surprising that the poor favored calorific meals over protein and quality, given that they had "to buy the kind of food their families will eat, and their stoves will cook."[58] Not adhering efficiently to a minimum nutritional standard, critics argued, was less a sign of ignorance or irrationality than a smart choice to satisfy hunger and the occasional taste for pleasure. In his own inimitable and patronizing way George Orwell recognized this, insisting that the unemployed "would sooner starve than live on brown bread and carrots . . . [because] when you are underfed, harassed, bored and miserable, you don't WANT to eat dull wholesome food. You want something a little bit 'tasty.'"[59] The need to satisfy entrenched tastes pointed toward the broader social and cultural meanings of food, which escaped recognition when food was reduced to its nutritional value. It was a recognition that, as we have seen, was also critical to Audrey Richard's anthropology of food, and it would be central to what came to be called social nutrition.

Social Nutrition and Planning for Plenty

Social nutritionists sought not just to ground nutritional science in social realities but to make it an effective tool of social transformation. Social nutrition had four distinctive characteristics: it embraced the expanded definition of hunger as malnutrition that shifted attention from minimal to optimal standards of nutritional health; it identified poverty, not the poor or their nutritional ignorance and dietary inefficiencies, as the primary cause of hunger; it recognized that social and cultural meanings often overlay the actual nutritional value of food; and it proposed that, armed with these insights, researchers and administrators could scientifically plan to end hunger and achieve a world of plenty. Of course, not all social nutritionists subscribed to every one of these elements, but during the 1930s and 1940s they did transform the science and government of hunger to ensure that nutritional science became vital to the task of social reconstruction during and after the Second World War.

In 1936 three texts were published whose consensus was critical to the formation of social nutrition: Orr's *Food, Health and Income,*

McGonigle and Kirby's *Poverty and Public Health,* and the League of Nations' *Interim Report of the Mixed Committee on the Problem of Nutrition.* Such was their impact that they formed the basis for Edgar Anstey's *Enough to Eat* (1936), a documentary film subtitled "The Nutrition Film," which eschewed the type of shocking images Anstey had used in his earlier *Housing Problems* in favor of a reasoned scientific tone. Its narrator, Julian Huxley, claimed that these texts had shown how science could arouse the conscience of the nation and set a new charter for improved health and nutrition. It was no wonder that they had grabbed headlines around the world. Orr had controversially claimed that 50 percent of Britain's population, 23 million people, lived on an inadequate diet and that the solution to this problem lay not in teaching the British how to eat more wisely but in ensuring that they, like those in the top income brackets, had sufficient income to eat badly and yet still reach a state of optimal nutritional health. It was poverty, both McGonigle and Kirby and the League of Nations committee agreed, that was responsible for malnutrition.[60] And poverty was, most social nutritionists agreed, the product of a dysfunctional capitalist free market. They believed that the twin problems of poverty and hunger, in Britain and all over the world, could be eradicated if the market were disciplined by scientific planning. As early as his 1934 Chadwick lecture, Orr was arguing that agricultural nutrition had made it technically possible to feed the world's entire population, and by 1939 he was claiming it could be done twenty times over.[61] With the guidance of nutritionists, "adjustments of the economic system" had to be made, however much they might "conflict with certain existing economic interests [or run] contrary to the ideals we have inherited from the past."[62] An economy based on nutritional planning would stimulate agricultural production and world trade and redistribute surpluses: it would yoke the development of economies to the welfare of populations.

There was no shortage of social nutritionists in Britain who were prepared to plan for a more plentiful future. Alongside the Committee against Malnutrition and the Children's Minimum Council, both the Fabian Society and Political and Economic Planning (PEP), which had grown out of the *Week-End Review*'s call for a national plan in 1931, established their own expert committees on nutrition. A statement by PEP nicely captured social nutritionists' zeal for planning: "To satisfy hunger where it still exists, to liquidate scarcity and to put plenty in its place . . . needs planning . . . The necessary adjustments are too large and complex, and too interdependent, to be brought about haphazardly."[63] Far from bringing politics into science, social nutritionists sought to bring science into the art of government. The complexities of modern political and economic life played out in the social domain. This was a far cry from the identification of hunger as a social problem at the turn of the century. Now that political and economic life was seen as functional only if it allowed all of society to live in plenty, government was to operate in the name of social welfare. The use of optimum, not minimum, standards of measuring nutritional health was indicative of the shift, for the optimum was to be applied to all, whereas the minimum had served to differentiate the poor and hungry as a social problem. By the late 1930s social nutritionists had thus established that poverty, not ignorance, was the chief cause of malnutrition and that only scientific planning would enable all of society to reach an optimal level of nutritional health.

A critical component of this shift was discovering why, despite the proliferation of nutritional advice and education, food habits and dietaries remained so deeply entrenched and resistant to change right across the social spectrum. William Crawford and Herbert Broadley's survey of Britons' diets, the largest ever, found in 1938 that few, regardless of income, grasped the principles, let alone the details, of nutritional science: 65 percent of those from the higher social classes and 90 percent of the lowest confessed to having no appetite for nutritional advice. Echoing Audrey Richards, Crawford and Broadley suggested that such conservatism could be explained only by taking into account the complex social and cultural meanings surrounding food. To demonstrate how "conscious and unconscious influences are at work determining the British home dietary," they took the example of a man who as a boy had so "suffered under an excess of suet puddings" that he found them repellent and banished them from his family's table as an adult.[64] Social and nutritional scientists, they argued, had been so preoccupied with identifying the bare necessities of social life that they had no way of registering, let alone reforming, seemingly irrational dietary habits. Conveniently, these authors asserted that investigating the social and psychic dimensions of food preferences made necessary a new form of expertise (their own): market research. Advertising would, in turn, persuade the consumer to adopt better nutrition. If it was anthropologists who had taught nutritionists about the complex social function of food among primitive tribes, market research and advertisers would need to take the lead in deciphering the irrational food taboos of consumers.

As America led the way, the age of mass advertising in Britain, which was pilloried by Priestley with the phrase "ad-mass" in the 1950s, was still in its infancy in the interwar years. Crawford was a central figure in promoting this new form of expertise in Britain. In 1914 he established the most successful advertising agency in Britain before the Second World War and soon assumed a leading position in various advertising organizations.[65] This prominence brought him invitations to work as a government adviser, first with the Imperial Economic Committee and then the Empire Marketing Board (where he devised the very first "Buy British" campaign in 1931), and later with the Ministry of Agriculture and Milk Marketing Board, both positions in which he would have probably encountered "Popeye" Orr.[66] A knighthood duly followed. Although Crawford's work with the EMB made him aware of "the great part food plays in the health of the people and the prosperity of the Empire," it was the recognition that a "third of our national income is devoted to the purchase of foodstuffs" that sparked his commercial interest in understanding the food market and forecasting its future trends. Crawford believed that "the advertising practitioner" having once understood the conscious and unconscious laws of the food market, would be able to direct consumers to "health-giving foods" and "assist producers and manufacturers to plan ahead and avoid wasted effort." Advertisers' "knowledge of human psychology," their capacity to "influence public opinion with the object of awakening particular desires, evoking par-

ticular actions, or establishing particular habits," would make advertising essential to raising the standard of the population's nutritional
health. The language of planning, social efficiency, racial health, and
scientific government were again in evidence, but instead of rational-
izing consumer behavior, market research sought to render it intelligible, so that manufacturers, retailers, and government agencies
could shape it.[67] The job of market researchers was not to berate the
consumer for making irrational dietary choices, but to understand
them, so that advertisers could mobilize them in support of a particular product or brand.[68]

Nonetheless, many of the investigative techniques of market research were borrowed directly from the nutritional and social sciences: the web of investigators, the inquiry cards and budget books.
In place of the amateur "statistical 'Peeping Toms'" peering "rudely
through strange windows," the research assistants of W. S. Crawford
Sales Research Services and Research Department were well-trained,
"mainly middle-aged women" who were "fully experienced in the difficult art of extracting information from the housewife" by means of
questionnaires. No fewer than 5,000 British households completed
questionnaires, a sample that dwarfed all previous dietary surveys
(Orr's survey had been based on 1,152 family budgets, culled from
eleven previous studies). The sampling was also geographically more
representative. Although Crawford and Broadley adopted the system of social classification by income as recommended by the Institute of Incorporated Practitioners in Advertising (a system, inciden-
tally, that Orr had used), they complained that it hid "the effect
of non-economic influences, such as the habits and taboos which our
social caste system imposes."[69] Accordingly, the questionnaire specifically sought information on what foods were purchased, what
meals were produced, and on the family's broader assumptions about
food. Even the system of social classification mapped out the character of each group as much by its possession of commodities as by oc-
cupation and income. Just as Richards had found that the techniques
of the dietary survey were insufficient in the colonial setting, so
Crawford and Broadley's market research predisposed them to appre-

ciate British habits and taboos. The colonial laboratory led nutritionists to redefine hunger as malnutrition, and it had generated new interest in the social meanings of food at home. As we shall shortly see,
the techniques Crawford and Broadley developed became part of the
framework of government during the Second World War. As the
Children's Nutritional Council put it, shortly before wrapping itself
up in 1946, when it claimed that the objectives it had set in 1934
were now achieved:

> Social Nutrition or Food Sociology deals . . . with the actual
> manner in which human beings, under varying conditions of
> culture and custom, choose, prepare and consume their food. It
> is concerned with the more or less fixed patterns of food habits
> and traditions, with established meal-times, with prejudices and
> taboos, with the relations between domestic and communal
> feeding, with the development of social services in the field of
> nutrition, with the regulation of all kinds of institutional feed-
> ing and with the correct methods of public instruction and en-
> lightenment about food matters. In brief, it starts with the con-
> sumer of food AS HE IS and not as we should like him to be . . .
> the student of social nutrition has to deserve the intimacy and
> confidence of those upon whom he is working. Mere curiosity
> as to "how the poor and ignorant live" should be entirely alien
> to the spirit of this emerging science.[70]

War and Reconstruction: Social Nutrition as an Applied Science

When the Ministry of Food was reconstituted at the outbreak of
the Second World War, it drew upon the expertise of the social and
nutritional sciences to an unprecedented extent, incorporating the
techniques of the dietary survey and applying the principles of social
nutrition in the effort to mold the dietary habits of the population.
Whitehall was all of a sudden awash with nutritionists, many of
whom had wasted no time in advancing the case for a scientific

food policy.[71] Although the Ministry of Health's ACN had effectively ceased to meet before the war, Hopkins, Mellanby, Cathcart, and Orr had been summoned to a meeting with Orr's old friend Walter Elliot, the minister of health, to discuss food policy in October 1939. That was the same month Jack Drummond had begun to work at the Ministry of Food as its "chief adviser on food contamination." By February 1940, a month after the introduction of rationing, Drummond had been installed as the Ministry of Food's chief scientific adviser, with a permanent staff of five. (By 1943 his staff had swollen to fourteen.) Two months later, the new prime minister, Winston Churchill, appointed Clement Attlee, his deputy and the leader of the Labour Party, as chair of the cabinet's Food Policy Committee; and a month after that, the Scientific Food Committee was established, with a familiar cast of characters that included Mellanby, Cathcart, Orr, and Platt (freshly returned from the ill-fated Nyasaland survey). Meanwhile, the Ministry of Health had continued to request advice from Mellanby and the MRC on nutritional questions; by May 1941 its chief medical officer, Wilson Jameson, had formed an influential informal committee to work with the Ministry of Food on nutritional issues. Once again this multiplication of committees inevitably sparked turf wars and generated conflicting advice that was easily ignored. Frustrated by the way in which Mellanby, Orr, and Drummond's jostling for position had kept the government from making the most of available nutritional expertise, a group of social nutritionists formed the Nutrition Society in late 1940. Within three years, the society, organized to provide practical advice on matters of nutritional policy, had grown to nearly five hundred members (much to the chagrin of Mellanby, who banned MRC-supported nutritionists from joining). It even boasted its own research bureau, designed to systematize survey work by facilitating communication between research groups and standardizing investigatory techniques.[72] The bureau, whose Advisory Committee was split into subcommittees focusing on laboratory techniques, clinical inspections, and dietary surveys, aimed to provide Drummond with coherent information to shape the government's nutritional policy.

Drummond's work at the Ministry of Food encapsulated many of the central tenets of social nutrition.[73] The nutritional needs of different segments of the population, carefully calibrated on the basis of the League of Nations calculations for optimal requirements, were used to inform the system of rationing, as well as policies on agricultural production and food imports. In addition, collaborating with the MRC's Special Diets Advisory Group, Drummond used dietary surveys to identify the nutritional requirements of particular groups—children (from infants to adolescents), expectant mothers, heavy industrial workers—and meet them through provision of vitamin foods (milk, orange juice, cod liver oil), extra rations, and expanded communal feeding (at schools, industrial canteens, and British Restaurants).[74] Drummond's senior scientific assistant, Magnus Pyke, also directed a series of surveys on the nutritional adequacy of the diets provided in industrial canteens, prisons, hospitals, and British Restaurants. The surveys were used to shape planning of meals and menus, but it was recognized that "purely nutritional considerations had to make way for national habit and tradition." Drummond's team also worked closely with the Ministry's Food Advice Division to develop menus and tastes for unfamiliar foods, thereby gently altering entrenched dietary habits, while recognizing "the psychological importance of traditional foods."[75] During the Second World War the expertise of social nutritionists and their techniques of investigation gained a central place in government planning in ways that had been unimaginable a generation earlier.

Nowhere was this change more apparent than in the work of the Wartime Food Survey. Conducted by a leading market research agency, the London Press Exchange, under the direction of Mark Abrams, its dietary surveys became so essential to the way in which the Ministry of Food formed and assessed the effectiveness of its policies that it expanded in the postwar period, first as the Family Food Survey in 1945 and then, from 1950 on, as the National Food Survey.[76] Starting in July 1940 with weekly diet logbooks collected quarterly from 1,500 urban, working-class households spread across eight localities, it steadily grew in size; continuous, more detailed records being collected from more households (peaking at 9,141 in 1943, some 31,733 people, but thereafter never falling below 5,500 households) in more locations (culminating with 89 by 1949). Despite the initial focus on the urban working class—the households of "special" dietary groups were also occasionally studied—the survey first expanded, between 1944 and 1947, to include middle-class households and eventually, in 1950, to a "complete cross-section of the population," divided into the five social-group classifications adopted by Crawford and Broadley in *The People's Food*.[77] As the largest and most ambitious dietary survey ever undertaken in Britain, it represented a remarkable technical feat. Research assistants were responsible for ensuring that families properly and accurately completed the logbook.[78] Scales were provided for weighing and measuring, so that housewives could precisely gauge and record their stocks of food. Although the quantities of foods used for specific meals, or their distribution among family members, were not recorded, the research assistant used the recorded ingredients in these meals, and the final weighing of food supplies, to double-check the accuracy of the housewives' records. Once the logbooks had been collected, information on the size and composition of the household and its consumption of particular foods at specific prices was centrally collated onto a single "transfer sheet." At this stage the agency surrendered the transfer sheet to the Ministry of Food's Statistics and Intelligence Division in Colwyn Bay, where the statistics were tabulated onto punch cards for monthly analysis by Hollerith machines, so that quantities consumed could be translated back into calculations of average nutritional intake.[79] The Wartime Food Survey incorporated a set of investigative techniques that Rowntree had first outlined half a century earlier and that social and nutritional scientists, along with market researchers, had subsequently developed between the wars. It had, as its director Mark Abrams would later claim, helped establish a central role for the empirical social sciences in the planning for and administration of the brave new world of postwar social reconstruction.[80]

Not all embraced the survey or its vision of an expertly planned government of the future. Immediately after its launch in July 1940, the survey came under fierce criticism in both the press and Parliament, although it was the minister of information, Lord Duff Cooper, and the Wartime Social Survey that took the heat, not the Ministry of Food or Abrams's London Press Exchange. It was, interestingly, Orr's friend Ritchie Calder who broke the story and led the charge against what his paper, the *Daily Herald,* dubbed Cooper's Snoopers. Others quickly followed, branding the survey an expensive and pointless exercise, whose "Nosey Parker" methods violated people's privacy and the democratic process. Duff Cooper defended the survey, arguing that it used modern scientific methods to address expert and technical questions, such as patterns of food consumption and forms of milk delivery; he had less to say in defense of its attempts to measure "morale," which had attracted the most controversy.[81] Although the controversy quickly dissipated, the following year the home intelligence operations of the Wartime Social Survey were dramatically restructured to place the emphasis on purposefully directed surveys for other ministries, rather than general opinion or morale testing.[82] If the Wartime Food Survey never attracted as much criticism as the Wartime Social Survey, a combination of the black market and working-class suspicion of researchers bearing logbooks ensured that it continued to generate hostility. Indeed, in May 1943 its survey work was actually suspended in Plymouth when the *Western Morning News* characterized its investigators as Peeping Toms snooping around the city's working-class districts.[83] The expanded survey in 1950 met with an unusually high rate of refusals to cooperate, with only 36 percent of the 6,375 households sampled returning completed logbooks.[84]

Whatever welcome the survey teams received on the doorstep, their work was critical to shaping the government's wartime publicity campaigns, or what became known as public relations. The public relations machinery of government underwent exponential growth during the war: more than four thousand staff members were employed by 1944, half of them based in the Ministry of Information.[85] Acknowledging that government surveys had been accused of "tampering secretly and illegitimately with the public mind and prying into people's personal views and habits," advocates of the system, such as PEP, argued that the two functions of public relations—surveying public opinion and seeking to mold it—were not merely consonant with the "democratic principles" but also essential to an efficient science of government.[86]

The Ministry of Food was a model for PEP's vision of the future social science of government. Its Public Relations Department, the sixth-largest in government, was in continual dialogue with its Survey Department (and through them with Abrams's Wartime Food Survey)—requesting information on general nutritional literacy, the use of specific foods, or the dietary habits of special groups—as it developed publicity campaigns and monitored their success or failure. As the deputy director of public relations at the ministry wrote to his counterpart in the Surveys Department in 1944, "most of our activities depend on knowledge of what the public, and more particularly the housewife, is doing and thinking about food problems and your surveys are one of the main reliable sources of such information available to us . . . We . . . would probably be led into wasteful expenditure were the guidance derived from them not available to us."[87] Nonetheless, as the Wartime Food Survey proved more effective at monitoring the dietary habits and deficiencies of consumers than gauging their opinions, more detailed market research was often contracted out to external agencies.[88] At the end of 1946, for instance, the advertising agency J. Walter Thompson was commissioned to investigate the reception of the ministry's publication *Food Facts,* a weekly magazine designed to inspire interest in nutrition and to elevate consumers' dietary choices. Over an eight-week period they tracked those within their sample who had remembered seeing advertisements for it, as well as those who had found the magazine helpful or had used recipes from it, and then broke down these figures by social group and geographical distribution.[89] Although the final report did not make for happy reading (in one week only 28 percent had actually seen it, a measly 8 percent had found it useful, and a paltry 4 percent had tried its recipes), the precision of the inquiry, its ability to assess the effectiveness of both specific ads and publications, was a vindication of the techniques of market research over the generalized findings of the Wartime Food Survey (by then, the National Food Survey).

As we shall see in Chapter 7, much of the work of the ministry's Public Relations Department concerned methods of arousing public interest in nutrition and encouraging citizens to improve their diets by familiarizing themselves with media on the topic or going to Food Advice Centres. A Ministry of Health survey had provided further proof that "less than half the population appear to think in terms of food values in the scientific sense." In the recognition that dietary habits were often entrenched because of the cultural associations attaching to specific foods, the campaigns sought to work with, not against, the grain of consumers' conservative dietary proclivities.[90] The aim was to nudge the citizenry toward new recipes and ingredients that took full advantage of nutritional science and "modern" cooking techniques, rather than lecture people on their ignorance and deficiencies. Now all of society, not just the poor, was the target of these interventions, which made use of advertising to cultivate consumers' desire to be nutritionally healthy, productive citizens. While citizens as consumers became responsible for securing their own nutritional health, the state was to ensure that they were able to make nutritionally informed choices in the marketplace. Regulating the extravagant and misleading nutritional claims of food ads was the Defence (Sale of Food) Regulations Order (1943), based on precise guidelines drawn up by the ministry's scientific advisers in consultation with the Medical Research Council.[91]

Most social nutritionists, however, believed that the market was not a sufficient mechanism for the reconstruction of postwar society nutritionally. Writing in the year that the Beveridge Report captured the social democratic agenda for postwar reconstruction, Orr insisted that after the war "the main function of Government will be the promotion of the welfare of the people governed, and food policy will be based not on trade interests but on the nutritional needs of the people."[92] The Wartime Food Survey had shown what nutritional planning could achieve: although the nutritional value of the *average* diet had initially fallen during the dark days of 1940–41, by 1944 it had returned to and even exceeded its prewar position—a considerable improvement for those previously most nutritionally vulnerable, the urban working class.[93] The Ministry of Food's white paper on postwar food policy hailed this triumph of planning as the key to the future. Acknowledging that poverty was the primary cause of hunger and malnutrition, it stated that the task of the emerging welfare state was to ensure that all members of society had a sufficient income to secure a healthy diet. As this was to be the responsibility of other ministries, it outlined two specific objectives for the Ministry of Food: to extend the wartime system of foods for nursing mothers and children on welfare, so that all "boys and girls of this country shall be equipped to face life in the best physical and mental condition that a full diet can secure"; and "to assist the adult citizen in choosing foods of the right nutritional value" through the regulation of advertising and food labeling, as well as "the widest measures of education and publicity." These were objectives that could neither be framed nor achieved without the techniques of the social and nutritional sciences, so it was necessary to "continue and extend . . . the dietary and nutrition surveys carried out by the Ministry of Food and Ministry of Health, and to coordinate these enquiries with related investigations sponsored by official and unofficial bodies."[94] The principles and techniques of social nutrition had come to be seen as essential to reconstructing the social fabric and health of the nation.

The Cosmopolitan Task of Social Nutrition

Social nutritionists did not see the task of social reconstruction as a uniquely British problem. Their vision was a truly cosmopolitan one that stretched from the nationalist politics of India to the wreckage of postwar Europe to the United Nations Food and Agricultural Organization.

During the 1930s nutritional science became an important means for imagining a modern and scientifically planned nationalist future for India, free of the hunger and malnutrition that had characterized

British colonial rule. If McCarrison had planted the seeds for this project by exposing the hidden scale of malnutrition in India, W. R. Aykroyd, his successor at Coonor, tended them well, Indianizing both laboratory research and personnel. When Aykroyd left Coonor in 1945 to become Orr's director of the Nutrition Division at the FAO, V. N. Patwardhan succeeded him at Coonor, an appointment that would have been inconceivable a decade earlier, when Aykroyd had assumed the position.[95] Much of the credit for this evolution also lay with the Indian Fund Association (later the Indian Council of Medical Research), whose support for nutritional research throughout the 1930s culminated in the creation of a Nutrition Advisory Committee in 1936.[96] Whoever was responsible for the flowering of Indian nutrition, it helped produce a vision of a modern and scientific Indian nation. Orr may have written the foreword to Gangulee's *Health and Nutrition in India,* but the book itself, which was dedicated to Nehru, embraced ideas of scientific planning as the only way to deliver "the rehabilitation of my country where 'for every three mouths, there are only two rice bowls.'" Simply getting rid of the British would not free India of hunger and malnutrition; a science of government was needed.[97]

Sadly, colonial rule laid the foundations for such a science of government only belatedly and insufficiently, for throughout the war the Nutrition Advisory Committee sought "to establish objectives for long-term planning by assessing the quantities of different foods required to balance the diet and indicating the changes in existing production necessary to attain this end."[98] Although the Food Department was not established until 1942 to promote the vision of a scientific food policy in India, nutritionists would soon be found in every department of public health, conducting surveys and coordinating educational measures; each province was to boast its own committee of nutritionists offering expert advice and helping to train officials, teachers, and public health workers; those suffering from deficiency diseases would be treated with vitamin supplements; vulnerable groups would be fed communally; food production would be organized around the calculation of nutritional requirements; food standards would be regulated, and new technologies used to improve food distribution.[99] The modernity of India's colonial government would be manifest in its scientific delivery of nutritional health. And yet the impetus for this new science of government came from its spectacular failure.

For many the beginning of the end of colonial rule came on 22 August 1943, when the *Statesman* in Calcutta published photographs of starving women and children on the streets of "the Empire's Second City" (Figure 5.1). Despite heavy wartime censorship by the governments of India and Bengal, news of the breaking famine had reached Britain eleven days earlier, when the *Manchester Guardian* reported that the situation was "horrible beyond description," with rotting corpses left on the streets for days. The *Statesman*'s photos made that horror real.[100] Even the official Famine Commission, of which Aykroyd was a member, commended the "valuable public service" the *Statesman* had performed in publishing "gruesome photographs of famine victims," in defiance of the Bengal Government," acquainting "the world with the horrors of the Bengal famine."[101] For many, the return of famine to India proved that the demand for national self-government was literally "a matter of life and death." Those starving and dying in Bengal, Freda Bedi wrote, should call forth more than another "cry of pain, a call to pity, a picture of another tidal wave of tears"; rather, it was henceforth essential that "every Indian see his destiny guided by patriots in a National Government of the People."[102] While the nationalist press launched relief funds and dispatched special correspondents who filed harrowing reports to generate more humanitarian contributions, the famine received remarkably little attention in Britain, where, as we shall see, attention was focused on famine in occupied Europe.[103] For nutritionists, however, the famine in Bengal provided a tragic opportunity to experiment on resuscitating starving bodies with what became known as the F-Treatment—the intravenous use of artificial or predigested proteins and minerals known as protein hydrolysates. Although only 8 percent of those who received this treatment perished (as opposed to 67 percent in the control sample), its supposedly miraculous effects were mocked in the Indian press,

5.1. Dying of starvation in the empire's second city. *Statesman,* 22 August 1943.

more concerned with a political than with a technical solution to the famine (Figure 5.2).[104] Many medics in Britain also remained unconvinced, criticizing the Famine Relief Committee's inclusion of vitamin capsules in its relief package for evoking "a fearful mental picture of ships loaded up with little capsules—when food was wanted."[105]

It was not long before the F-Treatment would be deployed in Europe, in the face of another growing humanitarian crisis. Many Britons, not just pacifists, had campaigned after 1918 against maintaining the blockade on Germany, which had caused widespread malnutrition and social unrest; and when famine spread across occupied Europe in 1940, the failure to distinguish, in the total blockade on Germany and the occupied territories, between military and civilian populations provoked alarm.[106] By May 1942 the call went out for Britain to lend assistance on humanitarian grounds to former allied nations now occupied by the Nazis. The Famine Relief Committee was formed to offer "controlled food relief" to children, nursing and expectant mothers, and invalids.[107] Parliamentary debates on the issue were held in July and November of 1943. By 1944 no fewer than 149

5.2. The "miracle" of vitamins. *Hindustan Times,* 7 November 1943.

local Famine Relief Committees had sprung up, like the one at Oxford that became known as Oxfam; 88 other interested organizations (from the Women's Institute to the Army Bureau of Current Affairs) had held meetings on the issue; 125,000 signatures had been solicited on 50 petitions; and 160,000 pamphlets and 3,000 posters had been distributed.[108]

Recruiting of the nation's leading nutritional experts—among them Orr, Drummond, Chick, and Hopkins—to the Technical Advisory Committee of the Famine Relief Committee bolstered this humanitarian mission from the outset. It helped demonstrate that the relief they advocated, "the minimum supplementary ration necessary to protect young children and nursing and expectant mothers from deficiency diseases," would not breach the blockade or hinder the war effort.[109] These experts also made it clear that occupied Europe was in a parlous state: terms such as "famine" and "starvation" were not merely rhetorical flourishes designed to grab headlines and humanitarian attention, and the Technical Advisory Committee was prepared to supply scientific proof. The Oxford nutritionist G. H. Bourne wrote his *Starvation in Europe* specifically to explain "all the technical terms used to interpret the present nutritional state of Europe to the layman." It made for grisly reading. The war had reduced some two hundred million people to dangerously deficient dietary levels across Europe. The urban working classes of Greece, Croatia, Poland, and occupied Russia were at the point of severe starvation, while the peasant diets in Serbia, Belgium, Norway, and France were seriously inadequate. Food parcels, Bourne warned, would not solve the problem: rationing would need to be maintained for some time after the war if the "pangs of hunger" in Europe were to be allayed.[110]

Nutritional science was thus critical to an internationalist vision for the reconstruction of postwar Europe. Drummond's files at the Ministry of Food were replete with reports from international conferences and humanitarian groups on the famine in Europe and the prospects for an international relief system to aid the estimated hundred million people on the brink of starvation.[111] It was not until the liberation of occupied Europe seemed possible that plans were laid for emergency feeding of its starving populations, beginning with western Holland, which was in the grip of its infamous "Hunger Winter" of 1944–45.[112] Drummond, who had been appointed to an Allied forces committee (the Supreme Headquarters Allied Expeditionary Force, or SHAEF) to advise governments on nutritional relief of the Netherlands after liberation, complained about the lack of "clear-cut advice how to resuscitate" those dying of hunger, despite the deaths of millions from starvation in "Russia, China, India and elsewhere." Nonetheless, being aware of the experiments with the F-Treatment during the Bengal famine, he encouraged the MRC to prepare units of the treatment (complete with instructions for administering them intravenously, orally, and through a nasal tube) for use by special feeding teams in western Holland.[113] He also collaborated with the Nutrition Society to generate survey teams that would accompany the liberating Allied troops, to quickly assess the nutritional status of the population and identify those most in need of the treatment.[114] Nutritionists, it now appeared, were able not only to identify the hungry and measure the degree of starvation they suffered, to bring them back from the dead.

Three weeks before teams of British nutritionists were dispatched to the Netherlands, an unexpected opportunity arose to test the efficacy of the F-Treatment when Belsen was liberated. A small team of MRC workers was immediately dispatched to the concentration camp to assess the treatment's utility and clinical success. The team's leader, Janet Vaughan, reported bad news on both fronts. It was practically impossible to administer the F-Treatment in the horrific conditions at Belsen: it could not be given intravenously, for "patients cried out at the sight of the simplest apparatus, especially as a syringe, which they knew as the prelude to death," or by nasal tube, for "patients thought it was a new form of torture," or by mouth, because the taste was so "unpleasant that most patients seemed to prefer to die rather than to go on taking" the supplements.[115] Moreover, even when it was administered, it appeared to have little beneficial effect. Recognizing that "starving people crave food and crave the familiar," Vaughan's team soon discovered that it was more effective to allow their traumatized subjects regular small doses of skimmed milk and glucose, flavored with the once-familiar tastes of coffee, tea, vanilla, or strawberry.[116] For Drummond the failure of the F-Treatment once again demonstrated "the importance and significance of the psychological consequences of food shortage." Nutritionists could not simply apply the insights of the laboratory to populations without recognizing the social meanings and associations of food.[117] When Vaughan's findings were later duplicated in the Netherlands among the inmates of an asylum at Warnsfield, the use of the F-Treatment was phased out and replaced with skimmed milk fortified with glucose and vitamin supplements. This treatment was later taken up by the United Nations Relief and Rehabilitation Administration (UNRRA) and its offshoot the United Nations International Children's Emergency Fund (UNICEF), and then codified by the Joint FAO and WHO Expert Committee on Nutrition in 1951.[118]

The role of nutritionists in postwar reconstruction was not confined to saving those dying of starvation. Indeed, expanding the work of the League of Nations' Committee on Nutrition under Orr's leadership, nutritional scientists imagined a world free of the hunger and famine that had helped generate social unrest and war in the first half of the twentieth century.[119] In wartime nutritionists had been able to use scientific techniques to increase food supplies and ensure their equitable distribution, and now it seemed that their expertise would be crucial to constructing a new world order, dedicated to securing "freedom from want of food, suitable and adequate for the health and strength of all people." This was the objective of the United Nations conference on food held at Hot Springs in May 1943 that culminated two years later in the creation of the U.N.'s Food and Agricultural Organization. When the idea of the FAO was first floated at Hot Springs, Orr was harshly critical of the proposed focus on nutritional research and education: "The hungry people of the world wanted bread, and they were to be given statistics . . . No research was needed to find out that half the people in the world lacked sufficient food for health, or that with modern engineering and agricultural science the world food supply could be easily increased to meet human needs."[120] He had once again turned to documentary film in Paul Rotha's *World of Plenty* (1943) to set out his agenda for postwar reconstruction.[121] The film was enthusiastically received at Hot Springs. The task, he argued, was to establish a world food plan that would reconfigure the world's political economy by organizing it scientifically, according to human need, not profit. Nutritionists had already done their job: they had provided scientific knowledge of the world's food needs and shown how to produce food; now politicians had to understand that "nineteenth-century economics and politics cannot carry twentieth century science."[122] There should be no retreat from the great advances made by wartime food policies in Britain and America based on nutritional planning—increased agricultural production, the management of prices, and socially equitable forms of distribution—for these techniques could now form the basis of a world food policy.[123] Orr's long campaign for a scientifically planned food policy based on human needs had extended from Britain to its empire and was now to deliver the world.

Gathering old friends and colleagues around him—including Ritchie Calder (from the *Daily Herald*), David Lubbock (his son-in-law, who had been the principal researcher behind *Food, Health and Income*), Frederic Le Gros Clark (of the Committee against Malnutrition) and W. R. Aykroyd (of the League of Nations and Coonor)—Orr laid out his plans for how nutritional science could build a "world of plenty" from the ashes of war. The postwar global shortage of food was not necessarily catastrophic, for Britain and America had both shown that even in the midst of food shortages the nutritional health of populations could be improved. With proper planning it was possible to create a new and virtuous circle of plenty—in which healthy populations produced and demanded more food—but only if the market was directed to address the nutritional needs of the entire human family.[124] This was a decisively different vision from that initially proposed for the FAO at Hot Springs, where planners hoped to shape national food policies by providing assessments of the world's food supplies and the nutritional status of different populations. (In other words, the FAO was merely to provide nation states with scientific research, in the hope that individual governments would then plan their food policies around it.) As this laissez-faire approach failed to break the hegemony of the very market that had created world hunger, Orr proposed creating a world food board that would effectively control the market, regulating the price of food commodities, buying surpluses to establish reserves or sell them to the needy, and investing in technical infrastructure and programs to develop agricultural production.[125]

After three years spent traveling the globe to rally support for this plan, without success, Orr resigned as director of the FAO in 1948, a disappointed and frustrated man. His internationalist vision was anathema in the new world order being carved out by the United States, the United Kingdom, and the Soviet Union, where the United States used its own agricultural surpluses to cultivate political and economic dependence in the recipients. Orr was furious, for instance, that the United States refused to cooperate with the United Nations over the distribution of its Marshall Plan aid. When he received the Nobel Peace Prize in 1949 for his efforts, he warned the white rulers of these countries that they faced a stark dilemma: they

5.3. Ploughing up Orr's world food plan. David Low cartoon (DL2643), *Evening Standard*, 31 October 1946. By permission of Solo Syndication and the Centre for the Study of Cartoons and Caricature, University of Kent.

could create a world in which scientific achievement and economic prowess would be measured by the war against want, or a world where those advantages were squandered in the race to cultivate spheres of influence and stockpile weapons for a war to end all wars. If the most powerful nations chose the latter route, they would be "destroyed or submerged" by the tide of misery and hunger from Asia, Africa, and Latin America. The social unrest and political turbulence it would generate could not be staved "off by the offer of technical assistance and trifling loans with political strings attached to them." Alternatively, privileged countries could "use their overwhelming industrial superiority to create a new world of plenty. In so doing they would gain a new power and prestige by assuming leadership in the march of the human family to the new age of peace and prosperity and the common brotherhood of man, which modern science has made the only alternative to the decline and fall of the Western civilization.[126] Like Orr on his path from Aberdeen to Washington, nutritional science had come a long way; it could now provide the technical basis for saving Western civilization and producing a cosmopolitan world of plenty and social stability.

Yet with Orr's world food plan in tatters, the Nutrition Division at the FAO continued the work its director, Aykroyd, had begun at the League of Nations during the early 1930s—devising standardized techniques for surveying and measuring the nutritional status and needs of the world's diverse populations.[127] Far from saving the world from hunger, nutritionists were left trying to figure out how to measure global hunger. Attention returned to development of a set of survey techniques to deliver more "accurate and comparable data." Specific challenges attached to working in "underdeveloped areas," where the unit of investigation was rarely a Western nuclear family, the persistence of barter economies made assessment of income considerably harder, seasonal variations in diet made regular "repeat" studies necessary, and investigators had to learn to rely less on record cards than on "native" intermediaries or their own observation of communities. The task was to be made simpler by the development of ever more sophisticated tables on the nutritional composition of foods. For the annual FAO assessment of the nutritive value of the world food supply, the tables were expected to harmonize competing systems for measuring carbohydrates and calories.[128] Similarly, determined efforts were made to replace the proliferating series of scales on calorific requirements that had been published during the 1930s—in which great emphasis had been given to levels of physical activity, without any means of measuring or defining that activity, and the different means of calculation and loose definitions of "minimal" or "optimal" requirements had been based on conditions in the West, thought to offer a universal "reference standard."[129] Yet the continuing attempts to deliver a universal system for measuring nutritional need were also offset by the recognition of the local and particular, social, and cultural meanings of food. Despite the apparent success of Britain and America's wartime governments in changing dietary habits and rendering them more "nutrition conscious," it was recognized that "a campaign which tries to alter existing customs abruptly often meets with an unfavourable response," such as that related by Margaret Read of her conversation with a woman in Nyasaland: "You Europeans think you have everything to teach us. You tell us we eat the wrong food, treat our babies the wrong way, give our sick people the wrong medicine. You are always telling us we are wrong. Yet, if we had always done the wrong things we should be aware of that."[130]

The journalist Malcolm Muggeridge, the angry young man of the Christian Left, pithily observed of the hungry England debate that the "under nourished soon got forgotten in the excitement of deciding what was the measure of their under-nourishment . . . [If] it had been possible to make a meal of Nutrition, many who went hungry would have been fed; but, alas, Nutrition allayed no hunger, except for self-importance and self-righteousness."[131] This seems a characteristically perceptive but ungenerous statement. Nutritional science certainly promised to technologize the study of hunger and to rid it of its local political character, by subjecting it to a series of universally applicable techniques for its identification, measurement, and management. And despite the continuing uncertainty that surrounded their accuracy, let alone their universal applicability, these techniques became essential to the understanding, discussion, and governance of hunger during the first half of the twentieth century. Within that period nutritional science went from being a novel and contested technique for the measurement of poverty in Britain to constituting a scientific basis for restructuring the global economy through the FAO. That in itself indicates that we need to take the field more seriously than Muggeridge did. The technical nutritional questions that marked the hungry England debate catalyzed both the proliferation of ethnographic studies of the suffering of the hungry and an expansive redefinition of hunger. Together these developments transformed the politics of hunger during the 1930s and 1940s, both in Britain and far beyond it.

Indeed, far from reducing hunger to a technical calculation of calories, proteins, vitamins, and man-values, nutritional science provoked a productive global debate, as nutritionists expanded the category of hunger to include not just the starving and undernourished, but the malnourished as well. The new definition of hunger as malnutrition made the quantitative calculation of a minimum nutritional standard obsolete, for only by preventively setting optimal standards was it possible truly to vanquish malnutrition. Nutritional scientists had not only broadened the definition of hunger but also raised the bar of nutritional health. If the ethnographic rediscovery of hungry England in the North had focused upon unemployed men, the technical redefinition of hunger directed attention to the particularly deleterious effects of malnutrition on children and mothers. Indeed, it made hunger into a truly global problem, not merely the preserve of particular regions or nations.

The most forceful advocates of the new definitions and standards were social nutritionists, who, set out to transform political, social, and economic life. Their discovery of malnutrition transformed the social problem of the hungry into a much larger nutritional problem for society: that is to say, hunger was no longer seen as the particular preserve of the poor, for all of society now shared the problem of maintaining and improving nutritional health. The nutritionists urged governments to plan the production and distribution of food supplies scientifically, according to nutritional need, not wealth. And nutritional scientists developed a remarkably cosmopolitan vision of the reconstruction of society, the nutritional health and welfare of populations, and the development of economies. Moreover, social nutritionists were quick to discover that foods and meals could never be reduced to solely a calculation of nutritional value. The task was to understand and adapt local food cultures to meet the universal principles of nutritional health. In the next two chapters we will see how nutritional scientists used their scientific insights to develop new forms of statecraft for the management of hunger.

6

Collective Feeding and the Welfare of Society

The history of collective feeding in Britain did not follow the logic of this book. There was no seamless progression from the humanitarian discovery of hunger to the identification of hunger as a reason for political critique and mobilization to the development of a science of hunger that calculated who should be fed what. No simple, comforting story details our emancipation of the hungry. Instead, the provision of food as a form of welfare to particular groups demonstrates how inseparable are the history of welfare and that of discipline or punishment. Michel Foucault, of course, taught us that the state first assumed the duty of welfare in disciplinary institutions like the asylum, the prison, and the workhouse, whose primary job was to punish the inhabitants. In the early nineteenth century, during the reform of these institutions, they became veritable laboratories for rather clumsy dietetic investigations into the minimum levels of nutrition needed to sustain their (preferably productive) inhabitants.[1] As we have already seen, the meager diet at the workhouse was a central instrument for enforcing its punitive principle of "less eligibility," through, as the *Times* succinctly put it in 1843, "food parcelled out in rations calculated, with the utmost nicety, to rob every meal of its quality of fully satisfying the pangs of hunger, most cautiously estimated to avoid all possible risk of the evils attendant on repletion, and less than what [England] allows to her convicted felons."[2] Initially, the Poor Law commissioners had used past practice as a basis for calculating dietaries that conformed to the principle of less eligibility, yet, beginning in the 1850s and 1860s, they increasingly drew upon the nutritional calculations of chemists and medics.[3] The punitive regimes of the workhouse and prison were specifically directed at groups considered problematic and in need of disciplinary attention and reform. However, in assuming the right to discipline them, the state also assumed an obligation for their welfare, if only to maintain them in a position of "bare life," so that punishment was still possible. In return for collective welfare and feeding, its subject populations—especially paupers and criminals—had a duty to work. It was a model that the British also exported abroad, especially in times of famine: first in Ireland with the creation of public relief during the Great Hunger, and then in India after the creation of the Famine Code in 1876.

As we shall see, collective feeding, extended to other groups and eventually to society as a whole, through community canteens and wartime rationing, was not necessarily freed in the process from its disciplinary connection. As collective feeding became common, discipline took the form less of punishment than of a new set of obligations and social responsibilities. Its champions saw the canteen as a new social form capable of producing greater health, efficiency, civility, and social solidarity.

My purpose in highlighting the disciplinary genealogy of collective feeding as a form of welfare is to complicate, not refute, accounts that present it as a form of emancipation, a direct result of the labor movement's historic struggle against hunger. Such accounts give credit to the men, or more often women, of the labor movement who campaigned for school and factory canteens, as well as for broader forms of collective feeding like the community canteen and wartime rationing. Yet agency must also be redistributed to embrace the other people—social and nutritional scientists, medics, architects, industrial designers, teachers—who not only made it technically possible for the state to assume responsibility for feeding new groups in the population but required them to do so, by showing the necessity for such intervention. The material environment of the canteen itself also helped engineer a new vision of society, even though at the same time it fell short of bringing it to fruition.

School Meals and the Factory Canteen

Clearly, collective feeding of prisoners and the poor did not stop once collective feeding for schoolchildren and workers began. The development was not sequential; the two operations were parallel, and often related. The state assumed fresh responsibility for nutrition of schoolchildren and factory workers only after experts identified the detrimental effects hunger was having on the productivity of both groups. Once again, war and the necessity to maximize the health and productive potential of populations played a critical role in ensuring the voices of these experts were heard.

With the introduction of compulsory elementary education in 1870, some of those elected to the new school boards, especially women who were first allowed to vote and hold office in this capacity, argued that as families had been deprived of their children's labor as a source of income, they had had less money to spend on food. Children were going hungry and were consequently less attentive at school. Philanthropic groups, such as the well-heeled ladies of the Manchester and Salford Ladies Health Association, the London Free Dinner Association, and the Salvation Army, first provided free school meals. Nonetheless, from its inception in 1884 the Social Democratic Federation campaigned at school board elections for universal state provision of free school meals, and during the 1890s the Independent Labour Party followed its lead. The campaign finally bore fruit twenty years after the founding of the SDF, in Bradford, where two members of the ILP, Margaret McMillan on the school board and Fred Jowett on the city council, with considerable help from the country's first school medical officer, Dr. John Kerr, successfully introduced free school meals in 1904.[4] That same year, Kerr (now chief medical officer to the London School Board) gave critical evidence to the Inter-Departmental Committee on Physical Deterioration, whose final report recommended the state provision of school meals as an effective measure for "rearing an imperial race" (or at least preventing its further physical and mental degeneration). The 1906 Education (Provision of Meals) Act, in raising property tax rates by a halfpenny, enabled (but did not compel) local authorities to supply meals for "those unable by lack of food to take advantage of the education provided them."[5] The voluntary nature of the meal service and the proviso for recovering costs from parents as well as ratepayers (both anathema to advocates of free universal provision), allowed the act to attract support across party lines. The driving forces behind it were not so much its little-known Labour sponsor W. T. Wilson as Sir John Gorst (a Conservative M.P. and an ex-minister of education) and Thomas Macnamara (a Liberal M.P. and ex-president of the National Union of Teachers).[6]

Similarly, although paternalist employers (the usual names resurfaced—Owen, Lever, Colman, Fry, Cadbury, and Rowntree) had long provided mess rooms where workers could eat their own food, it was not until the 1880s that the growing recognition of the relation between food, health, and productivity encouraged a more general interest in the feeding of workers.[7] As a well-fed workforce came to be associated with productivity, employers hired photographers to illustrate promotional brochures with shots of new canteens or mess rooms full of contented workers.[8] Mess rooms provided little opportunity for employers to improve the nutritional health, and thus productivity, of their workers, although this benefit avoided the legal complications of the 1831 Truck Act (which effectively made it illegal to count meals as a part of wages or to deduct money from wages for them without the written consent of workers). By 1914 a few employers had begun to provide canteens where food and tea were sold at cost. The imperative to increase munitions production during the Great War moved the issue of industrial canteens and worker's welfare to center stage for Lloyd George's Ministry of Munitions. It was there, in June 1915, that the Central Control Board (Liquor Traffic), reacting to concern over the lunchtime drinking habits of munitions workers and the apparent detrimental effect of alcohol consumption on productivity (as well as, in the case of women, morals), established the Canteen Committee, which assumed responsibility for the provision of canteens in government-controlled factories.

As we saw in Chapter 4, the Inter-Departmental Committee on Physical Deterioration's recommendation that the state provide school meals rested on the promise that nutritional science had finally delivered a set of techniques for identifying hungry children, and assessing the quantity and cost of food required to relieve them.[9] Accordingly, in 1907, the year after the legislation, the School Medical Service was established, under George Newman, to help identify those children in need of meals. The service was also to distinguish between those who were to have a free lunch and those who would have to meet some of the cost of meals—a distinction that helped mollify critics who charged that the act abrogated parental responsibility in favor of state maintenance of children. However, given the limited capacity the young service had to conduct inspections before the 1920s, many localities continued the old philanthropic practice of means testing, although their procedures varied enormously.[10] And by then, as we saw in Chapter 5, far from resolving the question of which children should be fed, the standards identifying and measuring hunger as malnutrition were much debated. Indeed, by the 1930s the broadened definition of malnutrition, in the hands of advocates like Le Gros Clark and the Committee against Malnutrition, had diluted the original premise that school meals were intended only for "those unable by reason of lack of food to take advantage of the education provided them." The school meal became a way of addressing the much larger question of the scale of poverty and malnutrition in "hungry England."

Moreover, without clearer standards and more consistent techniques for identifying malnutrition, the argument ran, medical inspection merely served to limit the provision of meals to a measly 2 or 3 percent of schoolchildren in haphazard and unjust ways. Only a simple means test—or provision of meals to all children—could ensure equity of treatment across localities and actively prevent malnutrition (rather than offer remedial feeding for those identified ex post facto at a medical inspection as malnourished).[11] Medical inspection, and local responsibility for defraying the cost of school meals, were abandoned in 1941, as the minister of food, Lord Woolton, ambitiously sought to expand the service to 75 percent of schoolchildren, with the bold declaration: "I want to see elementary school children as well fed as children going to Eton and Harrow."[12] By 1944 the Education Act obliged all local authorities to provide a school meals service. It retained the means test, however, to distinguish between those who were to eat for free and those who were to pay half the cost of the meal. It was not until 1968, when the means test was removed for children with three of more siblings under the age of nineteen, that Woolton's target came close to being achieved. By then just over 70 percent of schoolchildren were being fed at school, and 12 percent were eating their meals for free.[13]

The interest in and planning for the state provision of industrial canteens during the First World War involved many of the same figures and forms of expertise. George Newman chaired both the Ministry of Munitions' Canteen Committee and its Health of the Munitions Worker Committee, charged with investigating the "health and physical efficiency of workers."[14] From December on, the responsibility for implementing the committee's recommendations—chiefly to appoint women welfare supervisors and establish canteens in all controlled (and later national) factories—lay with another familiar figure, Seebohm Rowntree, who was installed as director of the ministry's new Welfare Department, a position he held until early 1917, when he was replaced by another member of the committee, Edgar Collis.[15] The committee and the department assembled an impressive array of experts. The committee appointed the well-named Dr. H. M. Vernon (a lecturer in physiology at Oxford) and Captain Greenwood (a reader in Medical Statistics at the University of London) to establish "calculating machines" and a "medico-statistical laboratory," to assess the problem of fatigue and sickness and compute the nutritional requirements for health and productivity. While Vernon concentrated on measuring optimal working hours and conditions, Greenwood addressed the discrepancy between the nutritional needs of workers and the actual content of their diet, in order to advise welfare supervisors and canteen managers on appropriate dietaries.[16] The work of Collis, Greenwood, and Vernon was heavily influenced by Rowntree's first survey of York, which they always cited. Like Rowntree, they drew upon nutritional science's conception of the worker's body as a human motor and used the Royal Society Food (War) Committee's calculations of the nutritional values of foods to stress not only the importance of carbohydrates and fats as fuel, but that of protein and "vitamines" for the proper maintenance of that motor.[17] Praising their book for emanating "the spirit of the solidarity of industrial society," Newman emphasized the social costs attributable to inadequate nutrition, for once a worker's human motor was "impaired or damaged beyond recuperation . . . his whole industrial outlook is jeapordised and he becomes by rapid stages a liability and even a charge on the State."[18] Equally critical to the efforts of the Welfare Department was Dorothea Proud's doctoral work at the London School of Economics on voluntary forms of industrial welfare, which was quickly published with a foreword by Lloyd George.

As Daniel Ussishkin has persuasively argued, these figures gave a specifically British, social-welfarist inflection to the discourse of American scientific management, one further developed after the war in the work of the Industrial Fatigue Research Board (1918) and the Industrial Welfare Society (1919).[19] By 1917 they had established no fewer than 840 canteens, feeding in excess of eight hundred thousand workers under the watchful eye of some eight hundred welfare supervisors and had secured "a marked improvement in the health, nutrition and physical condition of the workers, a reduction in fatigue and sickness, less absence and broken time, less tendency to alcoholism, and an increased efficiency and output."[20] The "industrial canteen," the *Engineer* announced triumphantly, had been "firmly established . . . as a sound business method of increasing the efficiency and productivity of the worker."[21]

Yet the brave new world of a canteen at the heart of every factory, breeding a new spirit of productivity and solidarity, quickly vanished after the armistice, when the Ministry of Munitions no longer picked up the costs; canteens were not a priority for firms dealing with the retrenchment and depression of the 1920s and 1930s. When the Second World War broke out, the work of the Ministry of Munitions' Department of Welfare during the Great War was still invoked to remind war planners of hard-learned lessons now in danger of being "forgotten or ignored," were it not for the work of the Industrial Welfare Society and the recently formed Industrial Catering Association (1937).[22] Only fifteen hundred industrial canteens had been in operation in 1939, and their advocates dearly hoped that war would again be the catalyst for their expansion (Figure 6.1). They were not disappointed. The Factory (Canteens) Order of 1940 required all firms employing more than 250 workers engaged in government or munitions work to establish canteens. By December 1943 more than ten and a half thousand were in operation, all supervised by a special Canteen Branch within the Ministry of Labour's Welfare Department. Following the extension that year of the order to all factories employing 250 workers, the number of canteens rose to almost twenty thousand by the end of the war.[23]

For all the interest in canteens as a mechanism of welfare, they were also intended to provide what the Inter-Departmental Committee on Physical Deterioration had called social education—that is, training, or one could say disciplining, in the efficiency, civility, and solidarity of society. The canteen was never simply the product of a new social ethic for governing of hunger; it actively assembled the model of the good society in whose name it acted. Champions of canteens saw them as a social laboratory, a tool of social engineering. Collis and Greenwood praised the factory canteen's "great possibilities as a social institution, where workers meet, make friends, and learn to be part of, and take part in, the life of what should be a valuable humanising influence—their industrial home," while Curtis-Bennett (citing the example of the Peckham Health Centre, of which more later) envisioned them as "centres of community activity," capable of making workers and employers "more socially-minded human beings."[24] Le Gros Clark, probably the leading figure in the canteen

6.1. "A London Underground Works Canteen in Acton, London, May 1936." By permission of Getty Images.

movement, wrote in 1948, after having helped secure a central place for the school meal program in both the British welfare state and the United Nations FAO, to insist that the school canteen should "initiate children into a social life . . . far more rich and complex than any we knew in the past." By making them "tolerant, self-reliant and easy mannered," he asserted, it had "become in every sense part of the educational system of the country."[25] By enshrining a new model of the good society, the canteen would, many hoped, help produce healthy, productive, socially adapted citizens. Yet, as we shall see, creating an appropriate moral and material environment required the attention of an ever-expanding cadre of experts bent on improving the number and quality of canteens. And yet right down to the 1950s their patchiness and poor quality seriously compromised the new vision of society they were supposed to produce.

In schools and factories it was repeatedly suggested that the school meal could train "children in habits of self-control and thoughtfulness for one another."[26] Civility was a practice that required conscientious daily practice, and school mealtimes were to provide "practical lessons in unselfishness, cleanliness and self-help," and encourage the acquisition of "gentle manners, courtesy, and respect," to foster social "harmony and happiness." If schoolchildren rarely sat down to meals at home—let alone with tablecloths, cutlery, and polite conversation—school meals would emphasize the art of civility—"washing hands and faces, singing or saying grace together, sitting at table with others and talking to them quietly, learning to handle knife and fork or spoon, and to eat in seemly fashion." Advocates hoped that these skills would then spread from the canteen to "the school, the home, even to the street" and pass "from generation to generation."[27] Teaching these forms of civility depended on suitable supervision and discipline, a regime in which pupils were expected to emulate the manners of their teachers and "monitors" or be excluded from the meal and, by extension, the social community.

In factory canteens welfare workers and canteen managers believed that the provision of a suitably civil environment made the issue of supervision moot. Dorothea Proud, for example, found "ample evidence that manners depend very largely on environment," observing the contrast between "the behaviour of girls in a well-appointed dining-room and the behaviour of the same girls in a shed. The girls who romped in the latter, who tossed food about, who threw paper on the floor, and used utensils in ways in which they were never intended, became by mere transference to a fine messroom, orderly and decorous."[28] Collis and Greenwood reported that benches, plain tables, and rough earthenware produced only "rough treatment, breakages, and bad manners," whereas "separate chairs, clean tables cloths, flowers, good cutlery and china, well chosen pictures and window curtains, nearly invariably meet with the response they deserve." In short, "give workers a canteen to be proud of," they concluded, "and the canteen will soon be proud of its workers." Considerable attention was accordingly given to questions of design and engineering: canteens should be at the heart of the work site; they should face south and overlook cultivated land; windows should be a tenth of the floor space and allow thorough ventilation; a minimum of eleven square feet of floor space was required per diner (although eight might be possible if there were more than three hundred diners). Much thought went into the design of the service counter, to ensure the speediest delivery to workers before they became unruly in line or the food went cold. It was hoped that in such environments the workers would improve themselves further by reading the contents of the reading boxes provided or listen to the occasional organized classical concert.[29] Tom Harrisson, working briefly as a welfare officer in a factory canteen during the Second World War, arranged a classical concert and marveled at the "rows of grimy men sitting rapt and motionless listening to classical and operatic music. Absolute silence and perfect order."[30]

In schools too, the material environment in which meals were served was considered critical to the aim of turning out civil and sociable citizens.[31] In part the idea was to create a sanitary and congenial space for school meals, but also to provide the physical accoutrements of civility that were often absent from the poorest homes, where food went directly from hand to mouth: tables, chairs, plates, cups, cutlery, even tablecloths and flowers.[32] It was a source of great consternation, then, that during the initial reliance on local philanthropic services, children invariably ate their meals in such inappropriate and degrading settings as church vestries, public restaurants, school playgrounds, classrooms, cloakrooms, and cellars—or worse still, on street corners or at home.[33] Even the feeding center, constructed expressly for the purpose and once heralded as a model of efficiency and civility, was soon denigrated as being too closely associated with the workhouse.[34] Increasingly, it was hoped that all schools would boast their own "bright, warm and cheerful" dinner halls or canteens, and "tables decorated with vases of flowers, [which] should seat no more than twelve, and be covered with lino or cloth. There should be chairs instead of forms . . . Tables can be laid every day with knives, forks, and spoons and tumblers of water" (Figure 6.2).[35] Yet causing this environment to materialize was a difficult,

6.2. Engineering a civil environment: full trestles and benches, Bristol, c. 1910.
Louise Stevens Bryant, *School Feeding: Its History and Practice at Home and Abroad*
(London: Lippincott, 1913).

slow, and expensive process. By 1936 only 73 out of 311 Local Education Authorities (LEAs) in England and Wales had schools with a
canteen, and they served fewer than 30,000 children in a meager 479
schools.[36] Alarmed at the patchy provision of canteens, the Board of
Education appointed the domestic scientist Edna Langley as inspector
of provision of meals arrangements in 1938. Her first report confirmed their worst fears: lack of materials and sound organization
meant that only "in a few areas can the dining service be regarded as
having definite educational value."[37]

The expansion of the school meal service during the Second World
War accelerated the development of appropriate infrastructure, as
the Board of Education, rather than local authorities, began to pick
up the cost (after 1939). By 1943 the Ministry of Works and Board of
Education had collaborated to design and produce a complete new

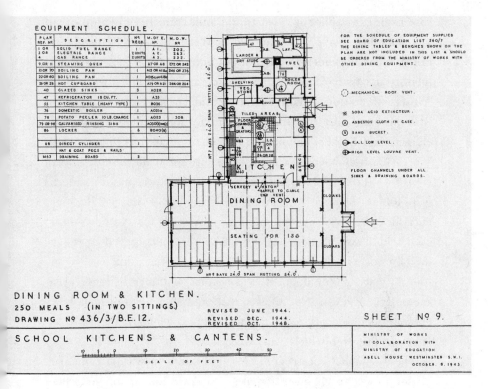

6.3. A model kitchen and canteen, 1943. By permission of the British Library, B.S.10/156.

range of canteen equipment, as well as freestanding prefabricated designs for both central kitchens and school canteens.[38] These enshrined the goals of the canteen movement: the scientific management of the kitchen area on view to the students who sat behind a cafeteria service counter, around tables of eight or ten in the well-equipped dining hall (Figure 6.3). Within six months of their launch, two to three thousand of these buildings were being produced every month, a pace that forced harassed officials at the Board of Education to find ways of expediting the planning permit process.[39] Flushed with this success, the Education Act of 1944 promised that every school would have its own dining hall, a commitment reiterated the following year in the revised school building regulations, when the new Ministry of Education began to plan a hugely ambitious building program whose cost rose from £24 million in 1947 to £55 million in 1949 to a projected £94 million in 1952. The Ministry of Works Building Research Station had initially supervised the design and construction of these new schools and their canteens, but the pace of work and the need for "closer integration of administration and [architectural] technique" were so great that the Ministry of Education formed its own Architects and Building Branch to oversee the construction program and establish detailed regulations on light, heat, and air flow in canteens.[40] In the early 1950s, when many of the newer-model canteens were found to be operating inefficiently and below capacity, the long-cherished dream of a single dining room, built for the purpose, in each school was abandoned, and LEAs were encouraged to reduce the unit costs of the building program by adopting "dual-use" dining rooms (that is, they doubled as corridors, entrance halls, or classrooms). A survey in 1956 showed that only 48 percent of schoolchildren ate school meals, a low rate partially explained by the less-than-ideal conditions in which many were served.[41]

The design and construction of school canteens was only one part of the project to engineer a civil social environment for the school meal: kitchens and dining rooms had to be equipped with appropriate hardware. Tables and chairs had to be varied and appropriate sizes, for children of different ages to be able to maintain the right posture and have enough elbow room to make appropriate use of their cutlery. And everything needed to be made from hygienic and durable materials—enamel (or later earthenware and stainless steel) plates, mugs, and cutlery, solid wooden floors, chairs, and tables (later with linoleum covers).[42] Similarly, kitchens were tiled, supplied with plentiful running water and suitable drainage, equipped with modern gas ranges, and, in accordance with the principles of scientific management, with time-saving appliances like pressure cookers, mechanical peelers, and even dishwashers.[43] Again, in 1939, alarmed at the variation in local practices, the Ministry of Works assumed responsibility for the supply of all equipment and furniture to local authorities. The ministry also produced elaborate catalogues, detailing the function, dimensions, and prices of the materials used in prefabricated kitchens and canteens.[44] Yet it was soon apparent that materials and equipment resisted orchestration into a model social environment. The much-vaunted insulated containers in which food was to be transported and served, proudly displayed at the exhibition and launch of the new kitchens in 1943, proved particularly troublesome. When full they were prone to spills and leaks (not only wasting hot food but injuring kitchen staff), and when empty the vessels suffered from condensation and rust.[45]

Buildings also creaked and groaned. Poorly insulated kitchens and canteen buildings were cold and subject to appalling condensation. The Norwich city architect repeatedly tried to solve this problem. First, he tried to insulate the buildings' ceilings, but the plaster became so wet it fell off, and cement proved only marginally more effective. He then sought to stem the flow of steam from the kitchen by placing separating doors between it and the canteen, but this only transferred the problem (and the cold) to the kitchen, where he then installed extractor fans. Eventually, when he thought to add metal covers to the sinks, conditions became "satisfactory."[46] It was hoped that such problems would become a thing of the past. In 1953, the Ministry of Education established the Advisory Sub-committee for Furniture and Equipment for School Meals to work in conjunction with the British Standards Institution Technical Committees on School Furniture and Canteen Equipment.[47] Newly designed equipment that made the most of modern materials was now to be purchased directly by LEAs (not the Ministry of Works) in the hope of bridging the divide between users, manufacturers, designers, and scientific experts. The engineering of civility required improved efforts to create an appropriate environment for the school meal, even though the endeavor was always compromised.

Since canteens were intended to produce healthy, civil, and sociable people, sanitary habits were encouraged. Lavatories and cloakrooms were provided in factory canteens, and workers were to have access to sunlight, fresh air, and good food. Workers should have an introduction to new tastes and more nutritious foods that would eventually transform their domestic dietaries as well. Ideally, for

Proud, the canteen kitchen should serve as a "domestic training school," allowing "girls" to help select menus and learn the art and science of preparing and cooking food, although she was forced to acknowledge that the "privilege is not greatly appreciated" and that the huge disjunction between facilities at work and domestic kitchens "detracts from the value of the experience gained."[48] Similarly, as social and nutritional investigators constantly bemoaned the dietary conservatism and ignorance of the poor, the school meal was seen as an opportunity to introduce children to new foods and good dietary habits, to teach them what "a dinner ought to be," so that they could adopt "wise feeding habits" and become "better fathers and mothers in consequence."[49] Commissioned to investigate how to get schoolchildren to eat their vegetables, Le Gros Clark argued that the school canteen offered an ideal forum for "training in food values" that should "go far in eradicating the settled food dislikes of most children." For instance, children could even be taught to like the dreaded swede (rutabaga), a root vegetable rich in ascorbic acid, by introducing it slowly, mashed with potatoes.[50] In Bradford it was considered "a waste of time and money" if those fed well at school returned home "to irregular, hastily prepared, unsuitable meals"; so every mother received a free book of recipes designed by the school medical officer and the superintendent of domestic subjects.[51]

The reality was, of course, considerably removed from the ideal: meals served in factories and schools were often dreadful and devoid of nutritional value. Even McNalty, Newman's successor as chief medical officer at the Board of Education, lamented the "monotony of hash, stew and soup, which in addition to being monotonous are often deficient even in calorie value, and deficient in just those elements of a well-balanced diet which a necessitous child does not get at home, such as milk, cheese, eggs, green vegetables, fruit and meat."[52] The Board of Education, although it had handed out advice on nutrition and sample menus for some time, had never done so with reference to the Advisory Committee on Nutrition; nor had school medical officers systematically inspected or approved dietaries used in schools.[53] It was not until 1941 that standards for the nutri-

tional content of school meals were finally established, and it is unlikely that much notice was taken of them until the 1944 Education
Act created the new post of school meals organizer, candidates for
which would be drawn from the new cadre of recently trained domestic scientists with knowledge of nutrition and the scientific management of kitchens. Long schedules and staffing scales were drawn
up for the veritable army of workers they were now to train in the
skills of scientific catering.[54] These new experts of the school canteen
were soon bombarded with publications offering guides to best practices in nutritional planning, sample menus, canteen management,
and kitchen organization and design, as well as advice on hygiene,
presentation, and service.[55] Nutritional expertise may have finally
been brought to bear on the preparation of school meals, but it did
not make them any more edible or attractive.

Factory canteens were not immune to these problems, either.
During the First World War, the operation of many canteens was left
to voluntary groups whose service proved distinctly unreliable. One
well-to-do volunteer complained that it was "work which would not
fit anyone else but charwomen."[56] Despite the creation of professional
welfare supervisors, the variation in standards of provision—not just
from locality to locality but from plant to plant—was huge.[57] With
their large range of duties and regions of responsibility, few supervisors could give each canteen the necessary attention. Invariably, the
daily management of canteens was left to a manager; and as everyone
recognized, the success of the operation "depend[ed] very largely
upon the individual in charge."[58] Canteen management, wrote Collis
and Greenwood, "is skilled work, and must be entrusted to an expert" capable of knowing: "(i) the value of bin cards; (ii) how to conduct portion-analysis; (iii) how to adjust the supply of *leading-lines,*
e.g. joints, and of other more paying commodities, such as tea and
puddings; (iv) the proportion of the turn-over, not exceeding 25 per
cent. spent on wages; and (v) how to adjust his selling prices so as to
obtain a gross average profit of 33 1/2 per cent on the buying prices."
Further, to be able to arrange the "menu on scientific lines" they had
to have a comprehensive and detailed knowledge of nutritional sci-

ence and food values.[59] It was a daunting task, or perhaps a hopeless one, even for lady volunteers with the best intentions.

It is not clear that the standard of meal provision improved much during the Second World War. The Industrial Welfare Society remarked on the "lack of adequate preparation and planning" that had caused many new canteens to flounder and fail. Its 1940 booklet *Canteens in Industry,* which had run to six editions by 1947, provided detailed advice on canteen planning, kitchen design, management and service, and food and diet, as well as styles and materials of flooring, furniture, and decoration. There were no surprises here: the "essential requirements are that accommodation [be] clean and bright, the food good and inexpensive, the service quick and efficient, and the atmosphere of the canteen friendly." All could be ensured with careful planning and attention to the desires of the customer.[60] That this advice was not always followed was apparent in 1943, when a new cadre of canteen inspectors was created, to ensure "improvements not only in the food but also in the storage, standard of service, methods of tea-making, and in kitchen and dining-room equipment."[61] Even this regime of inspection may have been found wanting, to judge by Lord Woolton's pointed remark six years later that industrial catering still needed to harness "the craft and skill of the cook and the knowledge of the scientist" to improve the quality of food provision.[62] Part of the problem, as with school meals, had always been attracting suitably qualified staff; before 1942 those working in canteens had been considered domestic workers with no wage controls. In 1941, the newly formed National Society of Caterers to Industry (whose members claimed to operate two thousand canteens, serving two and a half million meals a day) argued that higher professional status and better rates of pay for its staff would bring improved service. It formed a Joint Industrial Council with the Ministries of Food and Labour and, despite the quick drafting of a Catering Wages Bill, had to wait until 1945 for the Wages Board for the Catering Industry to be established.[63]

Nonetheless, factory canteens continued to be plagued by a litany of complaints: cold and unpalatable food, cramped conditions, long queues, glacial service, shortages of crockery and cutlery (which were in any case often half-washed), and no hours of opening during Sunday and night shifts.[64] The level of service at one engineering factory was so atrocious it triggered a workers' boycott:

> It was claimed that the food was cold and insufficient. Tea was very weak and one manageress had used saccharine for sweetening. The crockery was dirty, knives were rusty, while the kitchen itself and the equipment were dirty and neglected. Main complaint came from the night shift who were served on most occasions with food left over from days and heated up. Matters came to a head when bad pies were served. The stewards went with the management to the kitchen, and choosing a pie at random from a pile, cut it open, revealing the maggots who were thriving on the meal.[65]

With such stories and maggots in circulation, the appeal of canteen meals suffered! Despite the existence of 7,528 canteens serving fourteen million workers in 1942, most only served about 30 percent of those who worked in the factory, the others still preferring to go home or elsewhere to eat.[66] Everyone had a favored explanation: some claimed that the enormous expansion of the service had encouraged racketeering by small commercially run companies that were profiting from wartime conditions; others blamed the workers themselves, who were also on the make, pilfering supplies and equipment (one Midlands factory allegedly lost a third of its china in the first two months it was open).[67]

School meals were no less quick to establish, or slow to lose, their dreadful reputation (Figure 6.4). Despite some early promising signs, there is little evidence that children learned to enjoy or even tolerate nutritious foods.[68] Still, children struggled to adapt to new tastes and foods. Ernie Benson was put off brown bread for life by his free breakfasts before the Great War.[69] Even Le Gros Clark found that the hatred of green leafy vegetables was worse among older children, who had been exposed to them longer![70] The recent campaigns by ce-

6.4. Joseph Lee, "A penny more for 'is school meals and now another shilling for the tummy-ache it's given 'im . . . Coo!" (JL4200), *Evening News,* October 1949. By permission of Solo Syndication and the Centre for the Study of Cartoons and Caricature, University of Kent.

lebrity chefs—Alice Waters in the United States and Jamie Oliver in Britain—to improve the quality of school meals seem uncannily familiar. They are part of this history. It was not just the improving, nutritional foods that were unpopular. Working-class memoirs and testimonies are replete with stories of stale bread, gruel-like stews "in which floated bits of fat or grisly meat," "little bags of mystery" masquerading as sausages, lots of soggy mashed potatoes, and of course steam puddings and watery custard.[71] A recent survey tellingly titled "Why Did They Make Me Eat That?" found that 53 percent of respondents had been forced to eat school dinners they detested. Fifty-one percent claimed that their dislike of particular school foods—tapioca and cabbage were particularly reviled—continued to shape their eating habits. Unpleasant "memories of fatty roasts, spam fritters, over boiled peas and tapioca puddings (otherwise known as 'frogspawn')" abound, offset only by the cherished moments when "dinner ladies" were outwitted by the well-practiced strategies of hiding and disposing of unwanted foods between plates, in pockets, on the floor, or by trading with others.[72] Bradford's pioneers were merely the first in what became a long line of Britons involved in the campaign for school meals, who were perplexed that hungry children would often turn down the chance to eat at school, "it being no unusual thing to see a child refusing some dish with a most appetising smell to an ordinary person . . . at the same time showing it was really hungry by eating several pieces of dry bread."[73]

One key, perhaps, is that telling phrase "an ordinary person." Clearly, especially before the expansion of the service in the 1940s, those providing school meals lived at a considerable social distance from those who ate them. The meals provided, with their relentless cycle of soups, stews, or meat scraps and two overcooked vegetables, followed by a generally stodgy pudding, bore a stronger resemblance to lower-middle-class diets than to those of the laboring poor, for whom bread remained the staple of every meal and meat appeared only on weekends. The head of one of Bradford's elementary schools recalled how in 1921 a parent had told her: "Kathleen does not have dinners 'like these.' She has bread and jam and treacle. She says she will not eat any dinner today."[74] Quite apart from the alien tastes and textures of unfamiliar foods, for many, the shameful stigma of charitable soup kitchens or, worse still, the institutional reek of the workhouse lingered around school meals, much like the distinctive smell of disinfectant and boiled cabbage that they made so memorable.[75] Although families of children receiving school meals were not disqualified from voting (as those who received poor relief had been before 1918) or penalized by reductions in their relief or unemployment benefits, the medical inspection and the means test remained a hateful marker of social difference. (It remained in place until 1968.)[76] Even after the introduction of universal provision in 1944, school food continued to be experienced by many people more as a form of social punishment than as an entitlement.

The Community Restaurant: A "New Social Form"

Unlike school and factory canteens, which targeted specific groups, the community canteen or restaurant was made available to society as a whole.[77] The genesis of the idea was, again, forged by the experience of war. The labor movement's War Emergency Workers' National Committee first agitated for the creation of public kitchens or communal restaurants to provide cheap and nutritious food that would, through economies of scale, reduce the time, expense, and fuel the poor spent preparing meals.[78] That call captured the shared experience of wartime privation and—by evoking the image of these places as clean, bright, modern, and accessible to all—articulated a vision of a future peacetime democratic social contract.[79] Officials at the Ministry of Food, in vain administering campaigns for voluntary rationing and food economy, were drawn to the scheme as a way of reducing food consumption (ideally by between 10 and 25 percent) as well as improving the nutritional health and productivity of the wartime population.[80] Critical here was the influence of three women: Maud Pember Reeves, Mrs. C. S. (Dorothy) Peel, and Kate Manley. They had been hired by the ministry to form the Women's Department, which was responsible for translating the failing campaigns to economize food into practical advice to the nation's house-wives on the kitchen front. The department ended up creating and managing what became the National Kitchens Division. They brought together a range of expertise in the Edwardian social and nutritional sciences: Pember Reeves that of a social investigator and health worker among London's laboring poor; Peel that of domestic guru for the wealthier, but still not entirely comfortable, classes; and Manley that of an inspector of domestic subjects for the Board of Education.[81] They had, in the words of Peel, high hopes for the "public kitchen . . . in which food is prepared with scrupulous cleanliness, cooked with scientific knowledge, and sold at such prices as the customer can afford to pay," and were delighted when, in May 1917, the queen, with much fanfare, opened the first one on London's Westminster Bridge Road.[82] It was sufficiently successful that in February 1918 the National Kitchens Order encouraged but did not compel local authorities to adopt the scheme, by promising to cover half the start-up costs (although half of these took the form of a loan to be repaid from the projected profits of the enterprise), as well as supply standardized equipment and, of course, plenty of advice on management, dietaries, and accounting. Most important, National Kitchens were to be tailored to local purposes. They could adapt existing cooking facilities used for school meals or alter other suitable public buildings.

Appointed director of the National Kitchens Division in November 1917, F. W. ("Charles") Spencer was disappointed that so much discretion had been left to local authorities, for the success of the movement lay in their hands. An ex-alderman from Halifax, Spencer had a reputation as a student of scientific management who was allergic to waste, and he was soon lambasting local authorities, either for their failure to set up National Kitchens or for the inefficiency with which they ran them. So many reports of amateur management, dodgy cooking and, inevitably, dwindling returns flooded back to the ministry that some serious reorganization of the division was already under consideration when Spencer resigned in January 1919.[83] His successor, Kennedy Jones, a former founding editor of the *Daily Mail* who had directed the ministry's food economy campaigns beginning in 1917, inherited a mess.[84] Accounts had not been kept of all the National Kitchens operated directly by the division, leases had been taken out for buildings that were unused, and a staff of fifty-eight was quickly cut to twenty-seven, with a further fifteen positions considered unnecessary. Yet, like Spencer before him, Jones quickly discovered that despite the support of over a hundred Trades and Labour Councils, neither the Treasury nor local authorities were prepared to commit financially to the National Kitchen scheme.

The problem was simply that they were unpopular, having failed to distinguish themselves from charitable soup kitchens.[85] There were uncanny parallels: the name, the often dingy backstreet location, the voluntary assistance of lady philanthropists, and the lack of dining facilities: the kitchens merely dispensed food, so customers had to take their own receptacles and return home with food which by then was cold (Figure 6.5).[86] Their rebranding as National Restaurants made no difference to the commonly held belief that they had been "inflicted upon the poor as some kind of punishment for a crime unstated."[87] The food did not help. Even ministry officials complained that it was poorly cooked and lacking in variety and nutritional value. Although ninety-three National Kitchens had opened in 1919, Dr. Marion Phillips, who, as a member of the War Energy Workers' National Committee and the Consumer Council had been one of their most ardent supporters, concluded that women preferred to do their own cooking and found it cheaper.[88] As Peel acknowledged, the initial hope that "national kitchens would endure and become a feature of the nation's life . . . was not based on knowledge of the circumstances of the working people."[89]

Yet neither the idea of the community canteen nor enthusiasm for it dissipated. At the Pioneer Health Centre in Peckham, the cafeteria method, first developed in industrial canteens, became central to its broader project of revitalizing society.[90] The self-proclaimed "Peckham Experiment" began in 1926 when two young medics, George Scott Williamson and Innes Hope Pearse, developed a model of community health care by establishing a club. They studied the health and

6.5. National Kitchen in action. By permission of the Science and Society Picture Library.

well-being of members, as a healthy lifestyle was being actively culti-vated. Instead of treating diseases, the two pioneered preventive forms of medical care that would help develop personal vitality and a healthy society. Peckham's socially diverse population was consid-ered representative of society as a whole. Only local residents were allowed to join the center on a weekly subscription. In becoming part of the local community, the center would regenerate it, by en-couraging new forms of sociability and cooperation among families, for the family was seen as the natural unit of society. Styling them-selves as "biologists," Williamson and Pearse conceived of society as an organism: disease would render it inefficient or, worse still, cause actual disintegration. Believing that all organisms constantly evolve as they adapt to changing environments, the doctors con-tended that the health of the social body could be discerned and re-stored only by experiments in the field, not by discovery of general laws in the laboratory.[91] Consequently, Williamson and Pearse had a marked antipathy to scientific planning and insisted that their model of preventive health would be strictly voluntary, "not preached, but demonstrated."[92] There would be no directors or directives at the center; the aim was to create "auto-education in our community," where everyone took responsibility for the government of his or her own health.[93]

In 1935 the experiment moved to a center that boasted not only its own kitchen and cafeteria, but a swimming pool, a gymnasium, a theater, a game room, a lounge, a nursery, offices, laboratories, consulting rooms, and a darkroom. Designed by Owen Williams with the collaboration of Williamson, the center became famous for its modernist design (and use of concrete, steel, and glass) and as a model community health center. In fact, the two functions were inseparable: the building acted as a greenhouse for the propagation and cultivation of health. The scale of the task was enormous. Only 161 of the 1,666 members, representing some 250 families, were considered free of disease. As the rest were found to be suffering from various forms of malnutrition and deficiency diseases, questions of food and nutrition became prominent. During the 1920s the focus had been on the importance of diet in efficiently run households with healthy babies, a lesson in useful social citizenship that had attracted such vigorous support from Dorothy Peel that a room was named after her in the new center.[94] The influence of McCarrison's work on Pearse and Williamson was also increasingly evident, as the results of their research echoed his insistence on the importance of nutrition, not just to health, but to social behavior as well.[95] Indeed, food and nutrition's centrality to their experiment was apparent when in 1935 they also established an organic farm, Oakley House, twelve miles from the new center in Peckham, to produce "vital foods of high vitamin value" for its members. Modern urban life and industrial food had flattened out the formerly natural rhythms of seasonal diet and cut people off "from a natural supply of food direct from the soil."[96] On the assumption that only a "living social soil can produce food with the necessary vital qualities which can develop health in the living organism," Oakley House embraced the organic production of such key disease-resistant foods as eggs, milk, and fresh vegetables.[97]

At the new center the cafeteria became the heart of the building. On the first floor overlooking the central swimming pool area, it was designed to form the "main social feature," where members would "congregate with friends. Here all can sit and talk, read the paper over a cup of coffee or a glass of beer, and watch the dancing or other occupations of the younger folk."[98] As the focal point of the community and its forms of civility and sociability, the cafeteria encapsulated the guiding principle of the center, namely self-service as a "technique or mechanism of health" capable of "engendering responsibility . . . [and] enhancing awareness as well as increasing freedom of action."[99] There the desire for new treatments and activities would be cultivated in casual conversation among members, there new tastes and foods that were introduced could be selected willingly, instead of forced by the doctors on unwilling subjects. Since it was hoped that self-service would encourage people to emulate one another in their choice of food, no expense was spared in designing the cafeteria. The design allowed for an open plan and a self-service counter that divided kitchen from dining area, to ensure maximum mobility and visibility (Figure 6.6).[100] Without waitresses or attendants, rules or regulations, and commercially made "self-service" equipment, everything—chairs, tables, bowls, plates, utensils—"had to be designed to be handled by the members themselves." This complex and costly process proceeded by trial and error: although the original molds for an unbreakable plastic plate or saucer cost a staggering sixty pounds, they chipped repeatedly and had to be replaced eventually with a metal ones. As Pearse and Williamson recognized, "seeming trifles," such mundane details had "far-reaching significance in the type of social organization" they were hoping to develop.[101]

Although the center closed at the outbreak of the Second World War, its influence persisted. In their quest for financial support, Williamson and Pearse had energetically preached the gospel of the center all over the globe, thereby attracting the interest of the Rockefeller Foundation and Carnegie Corporation, as well as royal visits

6.6. Peckham's self-service cafeteria. By permission of Getty Images.

from Queen Mary, the Duke of Kent, and the next best thing, a visit
from Lady Baldwin, the wife of Prime Minister Stanley Baldwin.
When the center briefly reopened in 1946 with the support of the
Halley Stewart Trust, interest ran high: the doctors' book *The Peckham
Experiment* sold seventeen thousand copies, the Foreign Office commissioned Paul Rotha to make a film, *The Centre* (1947), about its
work, and the staff gave no fewer than three hundred lectures, many
on tours of the Middle East, Holland, and America. In the last fifteen
months of operation the center reportedly attracted no fewer than
twelve thousand visitors, a third of whom came from abroad.[102] In
Britain, quite apart from the influence that either its model of preventive medicine or the community center may have had on those at
the Ministries of Health and Housing at work constructing the postwar welfare state, the self-service cafeteria became the dominant

model in school canteens by 1956.[103] As we have seen, Curtis-Bennett, a historian and an advocate of the industrial canteen, looked to its example. The architect Lucy Bucknell, who had introduced Williamson's talk to the Architectural Association in 1936, also drew on it when in 1945 she collaborated with Le Gros Clark to design cafeterias that were to inaugurate the social democratic future of the community restaurant.

While Peckham closed for the duration of the war, in September 1940 the idea of the communal canteen reemerged in the form of the British Restaurant, as an emergency measure to deal with the feeding of blitzed populations.[104] In the following years the scheme was revamped and expanded, as a way of supplementing the rations of the general public, as well as targeting areas with smaller factories that lacked canteens, and schools that were unable or unwilling to provide meals. Adopting the Peckham style of self-service cafeteria was thought to be the most effective way of delivering simple but nutritious food cheaply and efficiently. As had been true of school meals and National Kitchens, local authorities were implored rather than compelled to participate. They could either take on the responsibility of provision (with repayable loans to cover capital costs) and the promise of profit; or, in a fresh departure, manage a restaurant on behalf of the ministry, which picked up all expenses and profits. Two years later, when the scheme was at its height, 2,119 British Restaurants were serving 619,000 meals a day: there were 281 in London alone.[105] In 1943, Le Gros Clark, fresh from his work for the Hertfordshire County Council on school canteens, but now director of the London Council of Social Service's Standing Committee on Communal Feeding, conducted a survey—alongside parallel investigations by the Wartime Social Survey, Mass-Observation, and the National Food Survey (as well as a nutritional survey by the Scientific Adviser's Division of the Ministry of Food)—on the popularity and social utility of the British Restaurant. He concluded, not entirely unsurprisingly: "We are here witnessing, even under the tempest of war, the emergence of a new social form," adding that a "country that has 2,000 restaurants of this nature might almost look upon them as a *social institution.*"[106]

The various other surveys agreed with Le Gros Clark that a new democratic spirit of "social cooperation" was emerging in these humble wartime restaurants.[107] Although some customers still sought to cultivate distance and privacy in their cramped conditions, others embraced what Harrisson described as the "thoroughly British and thoroughly democratic" atmosphere of "rubbing shoulders with strangers and talking to them [and] helping yourself."[108] A Mass-Observation diarist from Worcester recorded how on his first visit to a British Restaurant he had felt "in at the start of a new and wonderful experiment."[109] Le Gros Clark saw the restaurants, "democratic in price and clientele," as models of a new social community, providing "reliable and homely fare . . . selected by persons who have an eye to the dietetic interests of their customers . . . [and who] are, in most instances, so patently domesticated women preparing food for an incredibly enlarged family."[110] The "overwhelming majority" of customers wanted them to be retained after the war, and both Le Gros Clark and Tom Harrisson concurred. With new and improved premises, a more scientifically managed cafeteria service, greater variety and choice in the menu, and more dietary education, they felt, the communal restaurant possessed a bright future.

Despite such enthusiasm, this new social institution took heavily compromised forms. Forty-one of London's 281 British Restaurants were run by voluntary groups, and these Le Gros Clark studied first, considering them more representative of the standard of provision across the nation. He found a riot of improvised facilities and services, a reminder, he wrote, that "we are camping on edge of bombardment" (Figure 6.7).[111] Even though Mass-Observation's reports were unstinting in their praise for the cheap food and pleasant environment created by tables with oilcloths, vases of flowers, salt and pepper shakers, jugs of water and glasses (the London County Council's Meals Service even arranged for classical music recitals by students from the Royal Academy), Le Gros Clark's report provided a catalogue of shortcomings.[112] The buildings were adapted church halls, shops, houses, and clubs (one was even in the basement of an evacuated hospital) on predominantly residential streets. Inside, thirty were

6.7. Makeshift community restaurant in gas showroom at Bradford. By permission of Getty Images.

sufficiently bright and spacious, some even sporting fresh flowers, but at least eleven were "distinctly dull and confined," and a third of them had tables that seated eight or more, a long way from the acknowledged ideal of four. With the variety of forms of cafeteria service (only two restaurants employed waitresses), queues were always a problem, for anywhere between ten and forty people had to be served every five minutes.

Despite these difficulties, people came, ate, and left, having apparently enjoyed the experience. The forty-one restaurants served 12,350 customers daily in roughly equal proportions of men and women (not surprisingly, given the wartime demographics of the city, the men tended to be older, the women younger and unmarried). Customers were as likely to be industrial workers (28 percent) as office workers (26 percent), and a good many (14 percent) were professionals and managers or commercial shop workers. A remarkable 55 percent liked the food, and fifty-five percent found it cheap, while 33 percent praised the good service.[113] This was not entirely wishful thinking. The previous year the Wartime Social Survey had found that although only 20 percent of the population had eaten in a British Restaurant, and only 5 percent regularly, the responses were generally favorable. Mass-Observation even claimed that "if there is one thing that has impressed people about the new organizations which have sprung up in this war, it is the British Restaurant . . . there are few institutions which are more popular today."[114]

How quickly and inexplicably this initial enthusiasm evaporated! The anticipated "take-off" in numbers never materialized; between 1943 and 1947 the National Food Survey found that only 0.04 percent of the average 26.8 meals a week had been eaten in British Restaurants.[115] By 1947 only 850 British Restaurants were left, and they were withering away. In Middlesex's Yiewsley and West Drayton, the British Restaurant went from a peak of 350 meals served a day in 1943 to 100 by 1945. The inspector blamed the decline on the lack of "imagination or variation shown" in the menu, as well on as the expansion of nearby factory canteens. By October 1946 it had closed, the local council being unwilling to pick up the escalating expense for its operation.[116] Even the hopes that the restaurants running at a loss would redeem themselves by redirecting the tastes of consumers toward more nutritious food were dashed. Most managers seemed uninterested in improving the dietary habits of their customers, and nutritional surveys demonstrated that in most cases it would have been a case of the blind leading the blind.[117] Critics loved to point out that a scheme devised to provide nutritional food and modest prices delivered neither. Far from representing a triumph of democracy, the restaurants gave experts free rein in ways that were "alien to British rights and liberties": in the end, "men and women working for freedom will not be regimented into communal feeding and eating what is 'good for them' . . . No dietician will convince the man who wants a crust of bread and cheese and a pint of beer that he would be healthier and happier if he sat down in a crowded canteen and ate a 'planned' meal."[118] It was all a far cry from Peckham.

Once again, failure spurred renewed efforts to reimagine the canteen and its capacity to bring about the good society. Building on his earlier survey for the London Council of Social Services, Le Gros Clark was charged with designing the model community restaurant of the social democratic future by coordinating the expertise of managers of British Restaurants, two architects, domestic scientists and kitchen-fitting experts, as well as members of the Communal Feeding Research Group he chaired. The designs represented the accumulated wisdom derived from fifty years' experience of collective feeding. The model community restaurant would continue to serve these constituencies, but as part of the broader community: it would "maintain the productivity and efficiency" of workers in the "large mass of commercial and office labour and of labour in small industrial plants"; it would serve "the shopping housewife, the mobile or transient worker, the elderly person and the dweller of a housing estate for whom an occasional change from domestic cooking is a wholesome relaxation"; it would also provide broader social services, perhaps by feeding school children or serving as a community center. These restaurants would not merely serve the community; they would help build it, articulating the "vision of a more integrated and humanized national life." Thanks to their "atmosphere of sociability and friendly talk," they would become "the natural centre of life where community of interests can most easily be discovered and promoted" and where citizens would in turn receive a "social education" in standards of catering, cleanliness, and civility.[119]

The material design and form of the community restaurant were seen as central to the attainment of these lofty goals. Mindful of the complaints about queues, slow service, and lack of space that had plagued British Restaurants, the open-plan designs maximized not just the flow of traffic and service but the perceived space (Figure 6.8). A large entrance hall, capable of holding fifty people, ensured that lines neither stretched outside nor congested the dining area but were channeled directly toward the thirty-foot service counter,

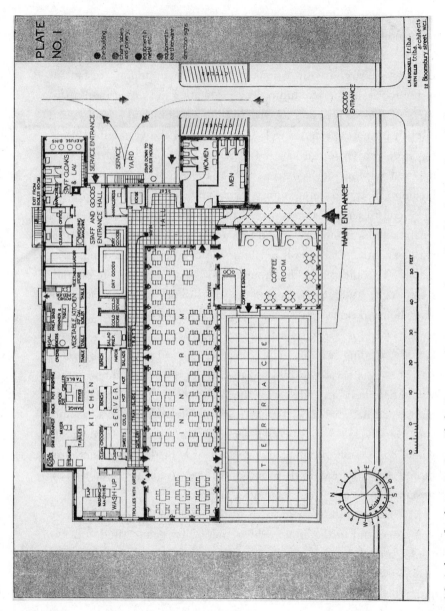

6.8. A design for dining. Le Gros Clark, *Community Restaurants in Design* (London: London Council of Social Service, 1945), 11.

where salads were to be strategically placed before hot plates and sweets. The long service counter allowed a "free" and "uninterrupted" view of the kitchen—with its own discrete spaces for storage, preparation, cooking, serving, and washing—and the "whole process of preparation." As an acknowledgment that the cafeteria system of self-service would initially be demanding for customers forced to "accustom themselves to quick decisions and estimates of total price," managers were advised to "concentrate in the early days upon the training of consumer habits," without radically disrupting the "settled habits of thought" of their customers.[120] Customers paid at the far end of the service counter, which opened onto the dining area. Tables (seating four and separated by four and a half feet) were arranged in two rows of two on either side of a central passageway. This spacing allowed diners to reach their tables with a minimum of obstruction, and trolleys to clear tables and trays quickly en route to the dishwashing area. The lavatories were located by the entrance and exit, where it was hoped they would least disrupt the flow of diners, and off the dining room were a coffee room and terrace to lend "some flavour of the 'club' atmosphere that is often appreciated by its habitues." The walls were to be painted in "bright and clear" colors that evoked "an atmosphere of gaiety and freshness," for the aim was to provide not just good food "but the pleasure of good surroundings." The hope was that by simulating the conditions in lower-class homes and encouraging friendly interaction between diners and cooking staff, a homey environment could be generated and standards of cleanliness, decorum, and civility maintained.

Clearly, the experience of war gave the impetus for these schemes of collective feeding, which particularly during the Second World War were seen as correlates to the broader system of food rationing. Rationing was the most ambitious and comprehensive form of collective feeding ever undertaken in Britain, one that demanded such unprecedented levels of state intervention in the market that it was introduced only in the very last year of the First World War, in the face of mounting unrest.[121] By contrast, the experience of food rationing during the Second World War, with its attempt to enshrine the new social democratic principles of "fair shares" for everyone and equality of sacrifice, has become part of the mythology of "the People's War," as some historians have characterized it.[122] Certainly, the Ministry of Food was assiduous in touting the success and popularity of its policy, singling out Lord Woolton and Jack Drummond as the heroic architects of wartime rationing. Woolton was the minister of food who was driven by his outrage at the way his neighbor in Liverpool had starved to death between the wars, and Drummond the scientific adviser responsible for translating the broad principle of "fair shares" into a policy of social nutritional planning.[123] If historians have subsequently qualified the ministry's rhetoric, by showing how rationing allowed profound social differences to persist, or even aggravated them—between the country and the city, men and women, the rich and the poor, adults and children—it nonetheless represented a significant new commitment to the social government of hunger.

In several respects the social logic of rationing during the Second World War replicated that of the other forms of collective feeding I have been discussing, in that it first targeted specific groups before aiming to reach the community more generally. Rationing balanced "straight" rations, in which everyone was entitled to a specified minimum quantity of food, with a points system, according to which every consumer was allowed to spend a personal allowance of "points" on additional specified foods, and a variety of "welfare" allowances and schemes that addressed the needs of particular groups, such as those engaged in heavy industrial work, nursing and pregnant mothers, and children.[124] By deploying carefully calibrated nutritional allowances, rationing combined the concern for the welfare of the general population and a continuing preoccupation with the special needs of particular groups in the interests of maintaining the health and efficiency of society as a whole. It was a level of social nutritional planning that—despite the continuing inequities generated by differing levels of access to the black market or to the yield of the sea and the countryside—ensured that the nutritional health of the population was preserved and even improved in the face of significant food shortages. Moreover, although the system of rationing elevated calculations of nutritional need and questions of welfare over wealth and access to the world of goods, it did not entirely abandon the disciplines of the market—or indeed discipline more generally. As we shall see in the next chapter, rationing as a form of welfare and collective feeding entailed its own disciplines, as the consumer was taught how to take responsibility for the nutritional health of her family by making the most of the available rations. It is the Janus-faced nature of welfare that I think explains the equivocal responses to it that are evident in the uneven acceptance or use of canteens in schools, factories, and the community, not to mention the constant complaints about the rigors of rationing, or the reluctance to claim welfare foods.[125] Thus, although Carolyn Steedman eloquently testifies about how during the late 1940s and early 1950s the "calculated, dictated fairness" of universal provision of school meals and welfare foods taught her, "in a covert way, that [she] had a right to exist, was worth something," it is never clear that it healed the silent injuries of class she first experienced when a health visitor condemned her mother for the conditions in which she was raising her children at home.[126]

7

You Are What You Eat

Educating the Citizen as Consumer

Although hunger was now largely recognized as a collective social problem, the moral critique of the hungry by no means disappeared with the rise of canteens as a form of welfare. In 1926, for example, the chief medical officer, George Newman, confidently stated, "The problem to be solved here is not the relief of poverty . . . More often it is careless mothering, ignorance of upbringing and lack of nurture than actual shortage of food which results in a malnourished child."[1] Paradoxically, the very discourse of national efficiency that had animated the attempts by social and nutritional scientists to establish hunger as a grievous social problem before the First World War also enabled rearticulation of that moral critique in more scientific and technical form. Le Gros Clark warned, even before the Second World War, "In spite of the publication in recent years of investigations in family expenditure and the relation between needs and income, many people still prefer to talk airily about 'ignorance, laziness and foolish spending' as the cause of malnutrition, rather than to take the time to do a little simple arithmetic. There is nothing occult about the economics of malnutrition."[2] Despite the growing social scientific consensus that hunger was an impediment to national efficiency, its causes remained a subject of debate in the interwar years between people who considered that the hungry were victims of their own ig-

norant and inefficient choices as consumers and people who saw
them as victims of a poverty they could not escape, given the failures
of the existing political and economic systems.

These positions (as represented by Newman on the one hand and
Le Gros Clark on the other) could be characterized as the competing
liberal and social views of the problem of hunger. The one group believed that the family and the market remained the best mechanisms
for governing hunger and that housewives had to be *made* to take responsibility for using their limited resources more efficiently; the second group thought that the state had to take responsibility for ensuring that the poor had sufficient income that they did not go hungry.
Clearly, however, these were never mutually exclusive positions. Securing the collective welfare of the hungry continued to include the
attempt to educate them as individual consumers in the principles of
nutritional health and the efficient use of resources. Very often, as we
shall see, it was the beleaguered figure of the mother and housewife
who became the target for all these endeavors and interventions. As
women were always the last to eat around the family table, they were
the first to garner responsibility for managing hunger. The history of
the social is deeply gendered.[3]

Poverty, Ignorance, and the Problem of Consumption

The social and nutritional sciences were deeply implicated when the
discourse of national efficiency reenergized a moral critique of the
hungry as the ignorant and inefficient agents of their own hunger.
Nutritionists subjected the budgets and dietaries of the laboring poor
to scientific scrutiny, singling out their inadequacies and inefficiencies
as a question of poor consumer choices as much as of poverty.
Rowntree was the first to distinguish necessary from unnecessary expenditures by identifying basic physiological needs. The degree of efficiency with which the poor made what he assumed to be rational
choices as consumers to maximize their physical efficiency largely determined whether he classified them as deserving or undeserving of
their poverty. Yet this seemingly scientific distinction between nec-

essary and unnecessary forms of consumption remained based on highly moralizing criteria. His 1901 survey of poverty in York was notoriously stringent in its translation of minimum nutritional requirements into necessary dietaries, which excluded two of the foods most treasured by the poor—beer and meat. Rowntree justified the choice on the grounds of efficiency and economy, the cost of these items not being relative to their nutritional value; but their exclusion also betrayed his Quaker sensibilities and antipathy to drink. Even though he recognized that his minimum dietary set impossible standards, given the diets and lack of nutritional knowledge customary among the poor, and although he acknowledged that those living in real poverty lacked the income to consume irrationally, he nonetheless believed that much secondary poverty was caused by "ignorant or careless housekeeping, and other improvident expenditure," not least of all on the twin evils of drink and gambling. The alleviation of poverty required "mental and moral training" as much as better wages, he felt.[4] Subsequently, when he calculated "the human needs of labour" in his eponymous publications in 1918 and 1937, he included meat and allowed expenditure on beer and tobacco (under the category of household sundries) in his definition of necessities but insisted that the poor would pay dearly for such irrational human pleasures when it came to health and fitness.[5] In using these revised standards for his second survey of York in 1942, he still insisted that although 40 percent were living below the poverty line, for 9 percent it was as a consequence of their own irrational expenditures.[6]

Rowntree was not alone in his agonized calculations of the boundaries of legitimate and rational forms of consumption. The determination of the poor to put pleasure before survival in matters of consumption became a familiar lament of social and nutritional surveys throughout the first half of the twentieth century, as they meticulously recorded "irrational" expenditures and used them as evidence of poor and ignorant housekeeping.[7] Social investigators appeared never to tire of alluding to "what can be done by a really clever housewife who takes pains to select a suitable diet," comparing her to what the Inter-Departmental Committee on Physical Deterioration dubbed the "large proportion of British housewives . . . tainted with incurable laziness and distaste for the obligations of domestic life."[8] The catalogue of incompetence was long and remained largely unchanged with regard to the poor housewife: she could not budget; her funds were routinely exhausted by Wednesday, when she was forced to make her weekly trip to the pawnshop; she preferred to buy foods in small and uneconomical quantities; she knew nothing of nutrition and invariably, preferring processed foods over fresh and traditional ones, chose the wrong kind; she had lost the art of cooking and found making meals a chore, not a pleasure—one subcontracted as often as possible to the fish and chip shop; her kitchen was devoid of proper cooking utensils, let alone suitably hygienic spaces for storage, preparation, and consumption; she, and her malnourished children with "slum stomachs," were always the last to eat, for the appetite of the breadwinning male had first to be satisfied. In short, social and nutritional scientists rarely had a good word to say about the women who ran poor households—their ignorance and inefficiency at best unnecessarily aggravated, and at worst actually caused, hunger. And it is worth emphasizing that this obsession with maternal inefficiency was shared by those who recognized the structural causes of poverty: even these experts still preached the necessity of sound household management and nutritional education for housewives.[9]

The poor much-maligned housewife was used to such criticism. Since at least the mid-nineteenth century, lady philanthropists had visited her home and offered unsolicited advice on hygiene and household management; and from the 1870s on they were joined by a proliferating number of officials and inspectors.[10] As we have seen, this veritable army of the well-to-do, familiar with the mysterious rhythms of the working-class home and experienced in gaining access to it, became key researchers for social and nutritional investigators. Yet the social and nutritional surveys of the early twentieth century presented household management less as a didactic pretext for moral exhortation than as a set of scientific procedures that required mastery. Just as the social and nutritional sciences had identified the new social responsibilities working-class housewives would need to assume to manage their household budgets more efficiently, so they provided techniques of calculation and planning for that end. In place of moral exhortation, they offered techniques for proper accounting in household budgets, rational consumption of nutritious foods, new recipes and "modern" cooking techniques, catering to the varying needs of individual family members, the scientific organization of kitchens, and generally the efficient and hygienic running of the household. Indeed, the investigations into the intricate details of working-class budgets necessarily subjected housewives to these new pedagogies. The discipline of the weekly ledgers housewives had to complete for inspection trained them in the practices of accounting and rational consumption. As we have already seen, the weekly ledgers of the inquiry card required housewives to provide increasingly detailed records of their income and expenditure: what was served at each meal, precisely how much of different ingredients and stored foods were used, how each meal was cooked, who ate them, what was left uneaten, and who ate what outside the house. Social and nutritional scientists attempted to transform housewives into subjects equipped to reflect upon and navigate the freshly quantified tasks of household management.[11]

Clearly this was not easy. During his initial survey of York, Rowntree found that only eighteen of his chosen thirty-five working-class families were capable, under careful supervision, of producing reliable records of their budgeting and food consumption.[12] Similarly, when Pember Reeves and the Fabian Women's Group studied families who were living in Lambeth on about a pound a week, the researchers found that they must first teach each woman how to keep weekly accounts.[13] After the Great War, as sample sizes of social and nutritional surveys grew larger, and techniques of measurement more sophisticated, ever-larger numbers of people were exposed to them, culminating in the Wartime Social Survey tracking of 31,733 people across 9,141 household budgets by 1943. In addition, the expansion of means-tested state benefits during the 1920s and 1930s also required that their recipients provided regular accounts of their budgets. In the words of Max Cohen, if you were unemployed, you were made to feel that you should ideally become "a calculating machine" who "would leave the Exchange devoutly determined that you would spend your money only on that small portion of extreme necessities that you could afford."[14] As social responsibility became progressively associated with rendering oneself and one's household calculable, it appears that greater numbers of people embraced, or at least reconciled themselves to, new accounting regimes. By the late 1930s Crawford and Broadley found in their survey that many of their five thousand subjects were already maintaining "housekeeping books for groceries, milk, meat, etc."[15]

In addressing household budgets, social and nutritional scientists not only created a model of and a standard for rational and efficient consumption but helped make it a new social responsibility. Housewives were expected to internalize a set of social prescriptions, which by no means simply emanated from the state, and to apply them in the marketplace and the home in ways that enhanced the family unit, rather than challenging its autonomy and independence.

Household Management and Food Economy

It is commonly held that household management came of age with Mrs. Beeton and her *Book of Household Management* in 1861, not because she was the first to address the subject, but because she codified the Victorian cult of middle-class domesticity.[16] Yet within a decade household management ceased to be seen as solely the concern of middle-class women; both renewed philanthropic interest in educating the mothers of the poor and the introduction of compulsory education put the domestic education of girls on the agenda. Domestic economy was first added to the Department of Education's Code of Regulations in 1870. Four years later grants became available to teach the subject, and by 1878 it was made compulsory for girls.[17] As cooking was deemed a vital component of domestic economy, the National Training School of Cookery was established in 1874 to produce cooking instructors who could pioneer practical instruction in elementary schools.[18] Within three years, similar cooking schools had been established in Liverpool, Leeds, Edinburgh, Glasgow, Manchester, and Leicester, and by the time the Association of Teachers of Domestic Science was formed in 1897, with its own professional journal *Housecraft,* the Board of Education accredited no fewer than twenty-seven institutions as training culinary instructors for elementary schools.[19] Cooking became increasingly prominent in elementary curricula for girls. In London, classes in cooking had been taught since 1878, but they grew rapidly after it became a grant-earning subject in 1882: by 1893 more than a hundred home economy teachers had instructed twenty-five thousand girls in ninety-nine culinary centers all over London. Similarly, although only 457 schools in all of England and Wales had begun teaching cooking in 1882, the figure had risen to 2,729 by 1897.[20] Domestic subjects, but especially cooking, began to be seen as central to education for girls, and not just because it prepared them for domestic service. According to the founder of the Liverpool School of Cookery, Fanny Calder, by cultivating "health, thrift, comfort and saving," cooking would "have a more direct effect on the welfare of the people than any other subject in the timetable of our girls' schools."[21]

The Inter-Departmental Committee on Physical Deterioration concurred. They recommended the extension of elementary classes in cooking, hygiene, and domestic economy, as well as compulsory cooking classes for girls over twelve who had left school, and called for the creation of special colleges that could produce women teachers trained in what was becoming known as the new domestic science.[22] The following year the Board of Education appointed five women, all of whom had attended the training schools, as inspectors of domestic subjects. Their first job was to conduct an inquiry into the teaching of cooking at elementary schools. Their report was published in 1907, the year George Newman, the board's new chief medical officer, was insisting on the necessity of training "girls in domestic hygiene, food values, and infant management." Its dismal findings prompted the creation of a new set of Regulations for the Training of Teachers of Domestic Subjects (1907), which emphasized the application of the scientific method to the different branches of housecraft, with particular emphasis on food values, economical cooking, and household accounting.[23] By 1914, nineteen of the board's forty-five inspectors monitored the teaching of domestic subjects to over half a million girls.[24] The launch of classes in "Home Science and Economics" at London's King's College for Women in 1908 to teach its students "the scientific facts and principles which lie at the root of the ordinary action of daily life, as well as the actual manipulation required in household and institutional management," reflected an increasingly professional ethos.[25] By 1915 the discipline was awarded institutional status as the tellingly titled Department of Household and Social Sciences. Yet despite the professionalization of domestic education and advice—also reflected in numbers of professional women incorporated into state agencies during these decades as teachers, sanitary inspectors, medical officers, health visitors, district nurses, and education inspectors—it by no means displaced the voluntary endeavor of Lady Bountifuls prepared to patronize the poor with advice on household economies.[26] The first decade of the twentieth century witnessed the emergence of new voluntary groups—including, in London alone, the Westminster Health Society (1904), St. Marylebone Health Society (1905), and St. Pancras Mothers and Infants Society (1907)—concerned with educating mothers in their new social responsibility of efficient household management.[27] In an increasingly congested field of endeavor, these volunteers took their place alongside the growing ranks of women, invariably graduates of the new culinary schools, who had been working as culinary demonstrators in the elaborate showrooms of the gas and electricity industries since the late 1880s.[28]

During the First World War both the issue of food economy and the new professional networks of culinary instructors and domestic scientists gained greater prominence in the urgent quest for economies in food consumption. Once again the war helped change the terms of discussion: food economy shifted attention away from making hungry housewives better household managers, and toward making all consumers more nutritionally efficient. The impetus for this transformation came not from the state but from the voluntary sector, in the form of the National Food Fund (NFF) and the National Food Economy League (NFEL).[29] Established at the outbreak of the war, the National Food Fund initially focused on the philanthropic provision of food for Belgian refugees and the "necessitous," but by March 1915 it had begun teaching the "principles of economy in buying, cooking, and using food," and the following October the National Food Economy League was formed as a separate but affiliated "education branch." Over the next three years, despite the "indifference if not actual hostility" of the government, the National Food and Economy League distributed 750,000 copies of its pamphlets and organized more than two thousand demonstration lectures and exhibitions at local and national fairs.[30] Meanwhile, the Board of Education, deploying the expertise of domestic subject inspectors and teachers, issued various memorandums, regulations, and pamphlets on food economy that anticipated the later food economy campaigns of the Women's Auxiliary War Savings Committee and the Board of Trade, as well as the eventual work of the Ministry of Food after its formation in December 1916.[31] The ministry's Cookery Section, responsible for the creation of National Kitchens, was also detailed to focus on the issues of food economy and nutritional education. Their growing importance was apparent from the high-profile appointment of Kennedy Jones as director general of Food Economy in March 1917, a post held from October 1917 by Arthur Yapp, the national secretary of the YMCA. When rationing was finally introduced in February 1918, the ministry's new Consumer Council continued to advise women on how to make the most of their rations. The creation of the Consumer Council was a watershed not just in the formal politics of consumption, but in the official recognition that the consumer had a vital role to play in the control of hunger.[32]

The logic of food economy for the NFF and NFEL was simple: running individual households more efficiently would reduce unnecessary waste of the nation's limited food resources. Small household economies—a little meat saved here and a little sugar there, careful husbandry of scraps to make meals, more economical forms of cooking, like stewing, that required less fuel—would amount to large and significant savings on a national level. If much of this endeavor was driven by the old but apparently timeless philanthropic tenets of thrift preached by socially elevated trustees, such as Lady Chance, the "highly qualified instructors" commissioned to lecture, demonstrate, and write on their behalf also lent it an increasingly professional air.[33] This may explain why its campaign against waste gradually shifted away from a singular focus on working-class homes, to include those of the wealthier classes.[34] Materials for working-class housewives, in recognition of the constraints on budgets and facilities, emphasized the economies that could spring from "a greater knowledge of nutritive values of food," so that "it is possible to spend 10d or 9d instead of a shilling, and yet be better fed."[35] By contrast, the "well-to-do" were chastised for "extreme incompetence" in household management, which led them to "eat more than they require." Armed with a better appreciation of the "science of food values," which the NFEL had "shorn of its difficulties and terrors and rendered perfectly easy of comprehension by even the least scientifically minded housemistress," the privileged should consume only that which was essential for "health and efficiency," and only foods that were not vital staples for the munitions-making classes.[36] The social and nutritional sciences thus not only gave sharper definitions to waste and economy, but lent the NFEL a new authority that was not dependent upon the assumed moral superiority of social position.

In hiring Pember Reeves, Peel, and Manley, the Ministry of Food also ensured that the social and nutritional sciences would play a central role in framing and conducting the food economy campaign.[37] As we saw in the previous chapter, all three were, in different ways, experts on household management as a social science, as Peel's recollections of her reading material nicely demonstrates: "Amongst the many books I studied were Mr. Beveridge's *Unemployment,* Miss Proud's *Welfare Work, The Principles of Scientific Management* by F. W. Taylor, Meredith's *Economic History of England,* Mr. Seebohm Rowntree's *Poverty,* and Booth's *Life and Labour in London, The Town and Country Labourer,* by the Hammonds, while Mr. Hutchison's *Food and Dietetics* became one of my most treasured possessions . . . I [also] made constant applications to the scientific staff of the Ministry, and especially to Sir Henry Thompson . . . for information with regard to food."[38] Nowhere do we get a clearer sense of either how the Edwardian social sciences spanned history, social investigation, scientific management, social policy, and nutritional science. Armed with this expertise, women like Pember Reeves, Peel, and Manley were instrumental in transferring issues of food economy and household management from the voluntary sector to the heart of the state in Whitehall.

Like the NFEL, as the ministry's food economy campaign drew on the social and nutritional sciences to identify targets of waste, it also concentrated its efforts on the wealthier classes.[39] Recognizing that it was "in the homes of the rich who have fuel, apparatus, and money with which to pay skilled persons to cook for them that the most glaring waste takes place," Peel organized lectures and demonstrations for "mistresses of well-to-do households" and their domestic servants, who frequently complained of their employers refusal to economize or experiment with new foods. Distancing herself from those "who preached economy to the poor, knowing nothing of their lives and the difficulties which beset them on every side," she echoed Pember Reeves's praise of the "very clever conjuring trick" by which they were able to keep "house and bring up their children on minute and fluctuating weekly incomes." When she lectured to working mothers, she invariably left feeling that she had "learned from them far more than they [had] ever learned from" her. Yet Peel also recognized that even the poor could consume more efficiently if they paid more attention to the nutritional values of food and the principles of scientific cooking.[40] It was these areas of nutritional education and culinary instruction that became the focus of her food economy work at the Ministry of Food.

The ministry's food economy campaigns were the first major intervention by the state affecting consumer choices. The scale of the campaign was impressive. As an ex–Fleet Street man, Kennedy Jones was skilled at grabbing headlines, most famously by updating George III's proclamation during the Napoleonic Wars on the reduction of bread and flour consumption and ordering it to be read at all religious services in May 1917, posted in every post office, and published in no fewer than sixteen hundred newspapers. Pledge cards and purple ribbons were distributed to those who adhered to the voluntary rationing schemes, short films were produced on the food crisis and shown at cinemas across the country, seventeen million leaflets containing nutritional advice and recipes were printed, 150 Food Economy Exhibitions were staged, and sixty demonstration shops or food bureaus were opened. Many teachers of domestic subjects toured the country distributing advice on food economy and giving cooking demonstrations.[41]

There is, however, ample evidence that consumers did not take kindly to this barrage of advice. Although some of the food economy measures met with limited success, notably the reduction in cereal consumption by 10 percent between February and June of 1917, they were not enough to prevent the introduction of compulsory rationing early in 1918. The ministry's own surveys of the effectiveness of the pledge campaign for voluntary rations in spring 1917 uncovered widespread ambivalence. Whereas 92 percent of households approached in Worthing signed the pledge, 43 percent refused in King's Lynn, and in Glasgow only two in ten families on one street in a working-class area had ever heard of voluntary rationing (and neither thought it concerned them). According to Barnett: "Those in King's Lynn who knew what the economy drive was about but refused to sign anyway gave a variety of reasons. Some thought it unnecessary to eat less, that there was plenty of food in the country. Others said they were earning good money for the first time in their lives and were going to spend it on more food, not less. Also cited was the waste of food by the army, the feeding of steak and milk to pets, the 'pampering' of German prisoners-of-war, food hoarding by the rich and delay in starting food controls by the government."[42] Many of these sentiments were echoed in letters to the press and to the ministry itself, which monitored public opinion through them.[43] Such was the hostility in Glasgow at the end of 1917 that Sir Arthur Yapp and Lord Rhondda were advised not to travel there to talk on food economy.[44]

Clearly, many resented the idea of the well-heeled and well-to-do preaching to the poor on domestic efficiency: "It is something like impertinence on the part of the people from a higher stratum of society to lecture them on food economy when perforce the most rigid economy is practised in their own families" (Figure 7.1).[45] Despite frequent use of the new cadres of professional culinary instructors, an alarming degree of tactlessness appears to have been par for the course among the ministry lecturers; even Peel recalled how at one event an audience of agricultural laborers was told by "the lady who took the chair . . . that meat was unnecessary—she advised a diet of pulses, cereals and cream!" Peel herself did not escape the opprobrium of her audiences and quickly learned "to take personal chaff with good temper" and to weather the biting wit of hecklers. In Yorkshire "a man from the back of the hall called out to my chairman, 'Sither, laad—T'Government sends the peel—happen we raather they'd send the potatoes!' While it was at a South-country town that a large man arose, and in a sleepy good-humoured voice remarked: 'But what I say is, they shouldn't send such a well-fed looking lady as you talking Food Economy!'"[46] Talks were often followed by cooking demonstrations that tried to put some practical meat on the bones of the lofty ideals and abstract theories of food economy: they were seen as the most effective way of introducing the population to new foods like tapioca, nutritionally sound recipes, and fuel-efficient cooking techniques. Peel provides some admittedly rather scant anecdotal evidence that demonstrations were more warmly received, despite the marked reluctance to accept new foods.[47] Here too, however, it appears the quality of advice was uneven at best. When the ministry's own survey revealed that in spite of having recruited thousands of domestic subject teachers from the Board of Education, many of the demonstrations taught "pre-war methods," Manley quickly recruited London County Council's culinary expert to retrain eighteen of the teachers in three weeks, before sending them out as missionaries to

7.1. W. K. Haselden cartoon (WH1318), *Daily Mirror,* 19 April 1917. By permission of Mirrorpix.com and the Centre for the Study of Cartoons and Caricature, University of Kent.

spread the gospel of scientific cooking methods among their colleagues around the country.[48]

Indeed, students of domestic science educated at the National and the various provincial training centers, as well as King's College, were in high demand during the war to fill posts as supervisors, inspectors, and managers of industrial and school canteens, National Kitchens, the Navy and Army Canteen, and the Red Cross, as well as hospitals.[49] The war had highlighted the importance of household management and the urgent need to expand the new professional corps of domestic scientists who could educate all social classes in the necessities of sound nutrition and the advantages of running an efficient kitchen. The numbers of students at King's College rose from 20 in 1914 to 104 by 1917, and the Education Act of 1918 finally placed domestic subjects and teachers—and technical, practical education more broadly—on an equal footing with their academic counterparts. By 1930, many of the training colleges in domestic subjects were formally affiliated with the Universities of London, Manchester, Liverpool, Bristol, Leeds, Durham, and Cardiff and could offer degrees, as well as diplomas, while some three thousand specialists were now teaching domestic subjects to over five hundred thousand girls in elementary schools. By the end of the decade, the Colonial Office, recognizing that the teaching of domestic science was an increasingly critical component of colonial education that would allow the linking of development and welfare, sought to increase demand for and awareness of the colonial opportunities of domestic scientists who had been professionally trained in the metropolis.[50]

Domestic Science and the Efficient Kitchen

Between the wars, domestic science, as it was now conceived, became seen as a vital mechanism for ensuring socially responsible families—that is, families whose homes were hygienic and efficient and where the women were nutritionally informed consumers who could ensure the health and productivity of their family.[51] The model family and the new materials to bring it about (the housewife could not be entirely trusted to reform herself) were on endless display, as modern, efficient kitchens and menu planners appeared in films, exhibitions, newspapers, women's magazines, and, of course, a host of domestic manuals. It was hoped that the lessons of domestic science and its new material forms would effect a silent revolution in mundane domestic practices and ensure that housewives at least knew enough about nutrition to buy and cook the right foods in the most efficient and healthy ways. Critically, social responsibility for the welfare of families was not simply ceded to the figure of the housewife; rather, it was to come about as a result of their activities as consumers in the market. If few could afford to be the model family in the ideal home with an efficient kitchen, the ceaseless modeling of domestic life encouraged all to reflect upon, and aspire to improve, their techniques of household management.

Elementary cooking classes at school and the food economy campaigns of the First World War may have introduced many women to the principles of nutrition, but it was only after the war that the vogue for domestic science allowed nutritional knowledge to be more broadly disseminated in a plethora of manuals, cookbooks, advertisements, and women's magazines and newspapers. No longer the arcane preserve of social scientists and public health workers, who continued to focus myopically on the dietary regimes of the poor, nutritional knowledge was popularized by domestic scientists determined to extend its insights socially by making all housewives aware of the importance of a balanced diet, even if they did not always understand the precise nutritional value of each foodstuff.

The two nutritionists most closely connected with domestic science programs, V. H. Mottram and R. H. A. Plimmer (with the considerable help of his wife Violet), were the most energetic popularizers of nutrition between the wars. Shortly after Mottram became professor of physiology at King's College of Household and Social Science in 1920 (where he remained until 1944), he began to publish popular nutritional manuals for housewives and domestic science teachers that drew heavily on his lectures.[52] Plimmer, who had helped found the Biochemical Society and had worked at the Rowett Institute, moved back to London in 1924 as professor of medical chemistry at St. Thomas's Medical School in London (where he too remained at the post until 1944). There he promptly began lecturing on nutrition and health for the People's League of Health, and the lectures were then published, with his wife's collaboration, in *Food,*

Health and Vitamins the following year.[53] Such was its popularity that it had gone through nine editions by 1942. Contending that "knowledge of the scientific discoveries about food is essential to the modern householder," Mottram and the Plimmers endeavored to render it intelligible to "the lay reader," to translate it into "ordinary terms for the ordinary householder."[54] Explaining the connections between diet, health, and economy lay at the heart of their project. They believed that housewives, once educated in the broad principles of nutritional science, would spend less and yet provide healthier meals for their families. In short, if every kitchen could become a nutritional laboratory and every cookbook a laboratory manual, Everywoman could be transformed into a domestic scientist.

Streams of formulas, tables, charts, and appendixes followed, designed to enable Everywoman to transform the family meal and weekly diet into a well-planned series of detailed nutritional calculations.[55] The first step was to calculate the family's total calorific requirements, the second to work out how to meet them by supplying the right proportions of fats, proteins, carbohydrates, and vitamins, and the third to translate this information into actual dietaries after referring to tables on the cost and nutritional values of specific foodstuffs. Violet Plimmer, aware of the complexity of these calculations, provided no fewer than twenty-five colored charts to illustrate how to achieve a properly balanced "square meal." The charts showed "the various constituents of a food . . . distinctively coloured like the layers of a Neapolitan ice and branded with their vitamin content . . . [so that] the nature of each foodstuff could be seen at a glance" (Figure 7.2).[56] The key, she emphasized, was not necessarily to learn the technical terms, but to be aware of the general principles, rather as one had done for the car or the wireless—principles that could then guide one in planning meals.[57] Menu planning was the crucial tool for training the housewife to become a domestic scientist; the emphasis on scheduling, structure, and routinization overlapped with the new imperative of scientific motherhood.[58] It is hard to grasp the novelty of all this nutritional calculation in our nutrition-conscious age, but just as nutritionists had given hunger a new technical form that had

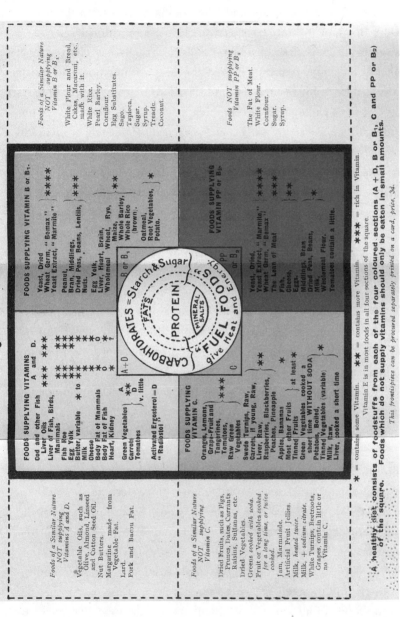

7.2. "A Square Meal," Violet G. Plimmer, *Food Values at a Glance and How to Plan a Healthy Diet* (London: Longmans, Green, 1935), frontispiece.

allowed government to address it, so they had given housewives a radically different way of thinking about feeding their families.

That it began to register and take hold is evident from the way in which food manufacturers increasingly used nutritional science to develop and sell their products. Sally Horrocks has charted how quickly the food industry enlisted the help of nutritional scientists (Mottramha d, for instance, worked for Lever Brothers before moving to King's College) to develop new production techniques for nutritionally enhanced foods that were then disseminated in technical journals such as the *Analyst, Industrial Chemist,* and *Food Manufacture.* By the late 1920s they were increasingly selling products by advertising their health-enhancing properties: Lever Brothers launched a vitamin-enriched Viking margarine in 1927, and Glaxo Sunshine Vitamin D–fortified baby milk in 1928. Colmans went a step further in 1930, when it hired nutritionists to develop an infant milk called Almata. Leaflets explaining the nutritional content of the product were distributed to nurses and health visitors, who were invited to inspect the factory laboratories and apply for free samples. The "Almata Book," which "a scientist in collaboration with a doctor and nurse" had ostensibly prepared for the public, covered a variety of topics relating to infant welfare and included the Almata Weight Chart, according to which babies' growth could be charted, and an indecent number of images of healthy babies, devoted mothers, and testimonials from delighted parents.[59] Nutritional health had become a commodity.

Much to the chagrin of nutritionists and public health workers, consumers, who had proved particularly unreceptive to nutritional instruction, appeared beguiled by the nutritional terminology of these products. Mottram and the Plimmers were vociferous critics of the commercialization of nutritional health, and George Newman at the Ministry of Health supported them. There were two chief complaints. First, as the Plimmers succinctly summarized it, the modern industrial life they called "civilisation has made it too easy to get the wrong foods of all kinds and difficult to get the foods we ought to eat." Industrially produced and processed convenience foods had displaced nature's perishable larder, in the process destroying people's

taste and generating the new "diseases of civilization" like constipa-
tion, indigestion, gastric and duodenal ulcers, gallstones, and diabe-
tes. It was these concerns that animated a new fashion of male slim-
ming. The corrupting pleasures and diseased bodies produced by the
modern food industry were compared unfavorably to the "splendid
physique and health" of the world's primitive races who still ate natural foods.[60] By the early 1930s, as George Newman was worrying that
the "indiscriminate dosing of foods with vitamins" would have disturbing and unanticipated consequences for "the balance of nutrition," the organic farming and food movement began to make significant headway, not least of all at the Peckham Health Centre.[61]
Second, in a reflection of the critique of commercial mass culture
generally, it was argued that advertisers were simultaneously manipu-
lating the gullible masses and debasing nutritional science.[62] Mottram
hoped that the domestic scientists he was teaching would train consumers to see through the spurious nutritional claims of food ads, but
he also pressed for greater regulation, so that patent foods would
have to "pass the gauntlet of expert medical opinion and not be
foisted off on a credulous public by ignorant and commercially-
minded manufacturers."[63] He had plenty of allies: PEP supported his
call for regulation to protect consumers in 1934, and it was followed
by the Committee against Malnutrition, who warned that it was fu-
tile "to carry out correct education in food values while commercial
advertising is, as at present, permitted to abuse the scientific knowledge gained."[64] Despite these complaints, there was a grudging recognition that the market had raised nutritional awareness, albeit in dis-
ingenuous and misleading ways, and that it had made consumers'
make the rational choice to consume foods that claimed to deliver
nutritional health.

As we saw in Chapter 5, William Crawford, the managing director
of Britain's leading advertising agency, advanced an altogether more
positive view of the role of advertising in promoting the nutritional
health of the population, in *The People's Food*. As advertising, he argued, was just another technique of social education, one better
suited to bringing the "abstractions of science" down to the practi-

cal level of ordinary people's everyday lives, it would form a vital "weapon which students of nutrition will undoubtedly use in striving to achieve their ideal of a healthy nation." It was a point he drove home by showing how many women—ranging from 65.9 percent of respondents in the first and wealthiest occupational group to 89.5 percent in the fifth and poorest group—remained unaffected by the proliferating dietary advice they received. Those who were interested focused on practical suggestions about recipes, dieting, and feeding children; "scientific subjects such as 'vitamins,' 'food values,' 'proper nutrition,' were seldom mentioned."[65] Few nutritionists endorsed Crawford's argument, but by the late 1930s there was a growing interest among social nutritionists in using advertising techniques for the dissemination of nutritional knowledge. Even the BMA's Committee on Nutrition had successfully made "full use of modern advertising to bring to the notice of the public" their manuals *Family Meals and Cookery* and *Doctors Cookery Book,* which had sold 127,566 and 170,654 copies, respectively.[66] This was, as we shall shortly see, to anticipate the government work of nutritionists during the Second World War, which combined sophisticated advertising campaigns on nutritional education with a framework for regulating the advertising industry's use of nutritional science.

The scientific reform of domestic life proceeded vigorously between the wars, in part because its model of the healthy and hygienic household became a commercial, as much as a civic, aspiration. At its heart lay Everywoman's dream of an efficient, labor-saving kitchen, for it was there that 60 percent of her domestic work was performed. A whole host of domestic scientists, architects, housing reformers, and commercial companies drew on theories of scientific management to design efficient kitchens that promised not only to reduce the labor of the housewife, but to improve her family's health and hygiene.[67] Not only did these kitchens make the social responsibility for producing domestic health and hygiene a commercial aspiration, but they imposed efficiency even upon those who failed to aspire, by engineering spaces that unwittingly transformed the practices of the people who worked in them.

This was evident at the *Daily Mail*'s Ideal Home Exhibition.[68] Established in 1908, the paper tried from the outset to transform household management, and its middle-class women readers whose job it was to manage domestic life, through the application of modern science and technology. The early focus on health issues of concern to women, such as health, hygiene, and child-rearing, soon merged with an interest in efficiency and saving labor. At the last exhibition before the Great War, labor-saving technologies, complete with practical lectures and demonstrations, were presented in their own section. When the Ideal Home Exhibition reopened its doors in 1920, it was with the familiar emphasis on scientific management as a way of reducing the labor it took for the housewife to provide a healthy and hygienic home. The *Daily Mail*'s publication in August 1919 of a model efficient-kitchen plan that reduced the number of steps required to make afternoon tea from 350 to 50 was followed by competitions for readers' best ideas on labor-saving devices and designs, as well as for the complete "ideal labour-saving home."[69] The winning design, built for display at the 1920 Exhibition, "contained intrinsic labour-saving design features—not just domestic appliances—to reduce both housework and maintenance. Labour-saving features were focused on the kitchen, with the various appliances being grouped to minimize work in the preparation, cooking and serving of food and in washing and house-cleaning. The heights of the cooker, table, sinks and other worktops were scientifically determined at the most suitable level for a woman of average height."[70] Given this focus on the science of domestic efficiency, it should come as no surprise that in 1919 Dorothy Peel became editor of the *Daily Mail*'s Women's Page.[71] She was the ideal candidate in the eyes of the *Mail*'s proprietor, Lord Northcliffe, not just because he engaged in antiwaste campaigns against successive governments during the early 1920s, but because she typified the women of middle England that the *Daily Mail* imagined as its readers.[72] Peel's emphasis on the new scientific ways of managing the home helped make housework a respectable activity for the salaried middle classes (coming to terms with their straitened circumstance as "the New Poor" in inflationary times, when even servants had to be let go), as well as the upwardly mobile, anxious to establish their new social credentials by running an efficient and hygienic household. This is the story of my beloved maternal grandmother, Beryl, whose copy of *Labor Saving Hints and Ideas for the Home,* published and purchased shortly after she was married in the mid-1920s, now sits on my desk.

In showcasing new designs and techniques for a scientifically managed home, the Ideal Home Exhibition associated the domestic sciences with an aspiration for modernity and a future graced by health, hygiene, and happiness. Of course, few could afford to purchase the ideal labor-saving homes on display in the *Daily Mail*'s annual exhibition, but all who went could temporarily inhabit those spaces and "fantasise that they lived the lives projected in them."[73] The catalogue for the 1924 exhibition described it as "everybody's exhibition," because in "dealing with the art of home-making, the exhibition teaches the art of living." The exhibition encouraged all to reflect on their own domestic practices, their own poorly organized kitchens and unhygienic spaces. And just to drive home the point, displays of inefficient and unhygienic "Chamber of Horrors" were often included, ranging from poorly designed utensils and appliances (1920) to a traditional Lanarkshire miner's cottage with stone floors and open range (1922) to a selection of kitchen designs from other countries (1926), showcasing an American design that was a "model of scientific arrangement," with its hygienic surfaces and labor-saving designs and devices. This heady cocktail of attractions drew ever larger numbers of visitors, growing from the 200,000 who had come to the initial exhibition of 1908 to just under half a million in 1926, 620,000 in 1937, and a peak of over a million in the postwar period.[74] The Ideal Homes Exhibition may have been the largest purveyor of model homes with efficient kitchens, but it was by no means the only one. Many others—like the Brighter Homes Exhibition or the Ideal and Happy Homes—toured the country and enabled people in even the poorest areas to envisage and momentarily inhabit the kitchen of their dreams.[75] As one historian has recently remarked, by the 1930s the planning and display of "the dream kitchen became almost a national pastime."[76]

It was one fueled by the remarkable proliferation in women's magazines between the wars as well as by competition between the gas and electric industries to provide designs and equipment for the most hygienic and labor-saving kitchen. Women's magazines went a long way toward both democratizing the ideal home, with its efficient kitchen, and popularizing scientific techniques for managing a home. *Good Housekeeping,* established in 1922, was quickly followed by a rash of similar magazines—*Women and Home* (1926), *Woman's Journal* (1927), *Women's Own* (1932), *Women's Illustrated* (1936), and *Woman* (1937)—all devoted to the new science of good housekeeping.[77] *Good Housekeeping* made labor-saving devices, modern cooking, and efficient consumption a central concern. It tested new equipment and recipes in its specially created institute on the Strand (1924) and Oxford Street Restaurant (1927), each of which boasted "a modern and properly equipped kitchen," and guided readers to the best products through the *Good Housekeeping* Seal of Approval. The practical advice on budgeting, nutrition, and meal planning that suffused its pages, often written by the staff members or graduates of King's College Department of Household and Social Science, were backed up cooking demonstrations at the institute, marketing of products like the *Good Housekeeping Diary and Account Book,* as well as competitions for labor-saving and economizing hints. The now familiar obsession with efficiency and economy encapsulated the magazine's vision of good housekeeping, from labor-saving equipment to the planning and cooking of nutritionally healthy but affordable family meals.

Although the gas industry had modeled kitchens and provided culinary demonstrations in its showrooms since the late nineteenth century, it redoubled its efforts between the wars in the face of mounting competition from electricity. Gas showrooms were redesigned to ensure that customers who came to pay their bills had to walk through a model home fully equipped with modern gas conveniences, and some companies even developed special lecture theaters, capable of seating two hundred, for their cooking demonstrations—by 1937 the Gas, Light and Coke Company had twenty-three such showrooms and had provided seventeen hundred cooking demonstrations to an estimated hundred thousand women.[78] Despite these efforts, the ideal home and kitchen were increasingly associated during the 1920s with electricity (Figure 7.3).[79] The first all-electric home was on display at the Ideal Home Exhibition in 1925, the year after Electrical Association of Women (EAW) was established to advise manufacturers on the design and use of electrical goods in the home, with the aim of providing a more efficient domestic environment.[80] Its director, Caroline Haslett, was a disciple of American apostles of the scientific management of the home Lillian Gilbreth and Christine Frederick.[81] Haslett invited Frederick to present a series of lectures to EAW in 1927, subsequently published in the EAW journal the *Electrical Age for Women,* which offered a paean to the electrical transformation of the house into an efficient space in which the housewife could work as a domestic scientist. Electrification, she argued, would elevate the kitchen to "its proper modern place as a cheerful sanitary food laboratory," where it would now be possible for the housewife "to remain neat and tidy while she does her work with step-saving and convenience."[82] The publication of her manual *The Kitchen Practical* in 1932 was followed, four years later, by the short film *Motion Study in the Home,* which showcased an electrically equipped kitchen. The film contrasted conventional preparation of a breakfast with one that followed a scientifically managed plan to maximize efficiency.[83] And to cement her reputation as the new doyenne of domestic efficiency, she took on the position of chair of the National Council of Women's newly established Council for Scientific Management in the Home in 1932. It drew upon the experience of housewives and experts of household management to set up model kitchens for the guidance of builders and consumers. As we saw in the last chapter, there was a specifically British inflection to scientific management of the home. The Council for Scientific Management in the Home, like the EAW and the Women's Gas Council, defined efficiency broadly, to include social questions of health and welfare, such as standards of nutrition, child welfare, housing, and smoke abatement.[84] It is worth recalling that during the 1930s the British Council of Gas Associations sponsored several documentary films on these issues—*Housing Problems, Enough to Eat,* and *Children at School.* The first especially had no dif-

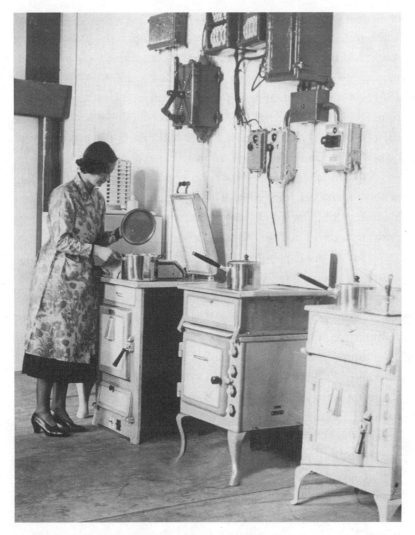

7.3. "A Demonstration Kitchen at the Electrical Women's Association, January 1939." By permission of the Science and Society Picture Library.

ficulty combining uncompromising social realism with promotion of the gas industries as a technological solution to slum housing.

Clearly, most had to be content with inhabiting their ideal kitchen in imagination, at an exhibition, or in a magazine. Few efficient kitchens materialized in actual homes, despite the tremendous expansion of Britain's public and private housing stock between the wars. By 1939 over 750,000 public council houses, 10 percent of the housing stock, had been built, and further construction that took place after the Second World War almost doubled that figure, to 17 percent by 1951. As the construction of public housing contracted in the fiscal retrenchment of the early 1920s, private developers took up the slack, building 4,000,000 new homes and raising the percentage of owner-occupiers from 10 percent in 1914 to 32 percent by 1938. An increasing number of these new homes became part of the expanding national electrical grid, which having supplied only 730,000 households in 1920, included 9,000,000 households by 1938 and was growing at a rate of 750,000 households each year.

Yet for all this expansion, the efficient kitchen made only fitful appearances in public housing. In 1918 the Ministry of Reconstruction established the Women's Housing Subcommittee, to solicit women's opinions on postwar housing design "with special reference to the convenience of the housewife": its members, inevitably, included the ubiquitous Dorothy Peel.[85] Focusing specifically upon the needs of working-class women, they concluded that a modern house required not just a bathroom and a living room (where food could be eaten, where children could play, and where adults could relax), but a room dedicated to labor-saving food preparation and economical cooking, with hot and cold running water, work spaces that were easy to clean, and a conveniently situated range. Yet the rival Tudor Walters Committee, charged with imagining plans for the homes fit for heroes that Lloyd George had promised, ignored these recommendations. It did, however, carry on an elaborate discussion of how to separate the kitchens from sculleries, and thus cooking and eating from dishwashing.[86] It was not until the 1930s that separate labor-saving kitchens began to be incorporated into public housing. Both the St. Pancras Housing Improvement Society and the London County Council implemented EAW designs in their construction of new flats. It was private developers like Wimpey, Costain, and Ideal Homestead, however, whose cheap three-bedroom semidetached houses, complete with separate bathrooms and kitchens, "dressed up with . . .

ideas from American home economics and household efficiency experts," that did the most to popularize the models of efficient kitchens on display at the Ideal Home Exhibition.[87]

By the time the 1944 Dudley Report on postwar reconstruction contemplated the design of dwellings, it was clear that women placed even greater emphasis than ever before on labor-saving design features, especially in the kitchen, for preparation of family meals.[88] An article by the architect Jane Drew, "The Kitchen of the Future," which appeared in *Women's Illustrated* in 1945, reflected the trend: "I feel that every woman agrees that household drudgery must be banished after the war and that's why I'm concentrating on kitchens."[89] Nonetheless, a PEP survey on household appliances showed that Britain lagged a long way behind the United States, with only 8.5 million gas and 1.5 million electrical cookers in operation (in other words, at least 25 percent of the population had neither), and most women still spent forty-nine hours a week on housework, even before allowance was made for shopping.[90] Not surprisingly, therefore, some women remained skeptical about efficient kitchens. One complaining to the *Builder* that the "super kitchen idea needs debunking": it owed more to science fiction than to any appreciation of the realities of domestic life.[91] The delivery of labor-saving homes, complete with efficient kitchens capable of transforming housewives into domestic scientists, was distinctly uneven. Yet the ideal was closer to realization by the 1940s, in hearts and minds if not in Formica and linoleum, than many had thought possible in 1918.

Battling on the Kitchen Front in the Second World War

During the Second World War the state, in the form of the Ministry of Food, became directly implicated in the project to make Everywoman a nutritionally informed domestic scientist and every kitchen an efficient one. It did so by drawing upon the new cadre of freshly trained domestic scientists as well as on many of the commercial techniques responsible for the popularization of domestic science between the wars. The discipline of the ration book, together with the work of the ministry's Food Advice Division, subjected consumers to new pedagogies that encouraged them to purchase and prepare foods, as well as to plan and cook meals, in the new socially responsible way—that is, efficiently and healthily. The social democratic and state-centered project of food rationing also depended, then, on educating citizens to maximize their own health and efficiency, and made those social ends an object of commercial endeavor.

The by now familiar figure of Le Gros Clark wrote a report for the Ministry of Food in 1946 praising the work of its Food Advice Division as the "first systematic effort to sustain a long-term campaign" to "instruct the public in dietetic matters."[92] Mobilizing an impressive network of nutritionists, domestic scientists, market researchers, and housewives, the Food Advice Division sought to translate nutritional science "in simple and practical terms which could be understood and applied by the average housewife," so that she could improve the nutritional health of her family through the most efficient use of available foods.[93] Despite its modest beginnings in late 1940, the division had grown considerably by the time Le Gros Clark wrote. Its headquarters boasted a staff of twenty-five dieticians and domestic scientists who, working closely with the ministry's Scientific Adviser's Division and Public Relations Department, not only operated an experimental kitchen where new foodstuffs and recipes were tested, but translated the fruits of that work into publicity materials. The media disseminating food advice, which were numerous and diverse, included bimonthly culinary calendars with topical recipes, posters, charts, and photo prints illustrating nutritional requirements and food values, books and pamphlets of recipes and basic cooking methods, periodicals aimed at domestic science teachers and others supplying food advice, short films on a variety of topics, exhibitions, lectures, and demonstrations.[94] Probably the best known of all were the regular *Kitchen Front* broadcasts on the BBC, which, appearing daily after the morning news, generated an audience of around five million listeners, "15 per cent of the available audience, and four times the audience of any other daytime talk."[95]

All these materials emphasized how greater nutritional knowledge would enable those battling on the kitchen front to reduce the waste of food, fuel, and labor, while boosting the nutritional health of their family. Key here was the discipline of menu planning. The first step was to understand the nutritional functions of what were described as the three essential food groups ("body-building," "energy," and "protective" foods), which foodstuffs belonged in each group, and each family member's differing requirements for each category. The housewife was encouraged to plan out all the meals to be provided over a week, carefully balancing the need for economy with variety, so as to satisfy the family's nutritional needs with the demand for tasty and attractive dishes. Such planning would produce a range of economies: knowing the ingredients for each meal would reduce time spent shopping; several dishes could be prepared together to save fuel and labor; food wasted in the preparation or consumption of one meal could be recycled in another (hence the popularity of soups).[96]

Drawing on its extensive use of the Wartime Social Survey and market research, the ministry recognized, in a way its food economy campaigns of the First World War had not, that, as "the average housewife does not wish to be consciously 'educated' in her craft," its publicity materials should offer "advice," not edicts.[97] Accordingly, the Food Advice Division sought to "establish direct, personal contact between the Ministry and the women of this country," tailoring its practical advice to the particular needs and circumstances of specific groups and individuals.[98] By the end of the war the Food Advice Division had assembled an extensive network for its outreach work, twenty-five regional Food Advice Organizers coordinated the tours of a further 150 qualified lecturers and demonstrators, as well as the activities of some fifty Food Advice Centres. In addition, beginning in spring 1941 local voluntary workers were recruited and briefly trained as "Food Leaders," to facilitate more direct but informal access to housewives: by June 1946 no fewer than 22,300 wore a badge to prove they were food leaders, and they could keep up to date through their own journal, *Food Leader News.*[99]

At the heart of all this endeavor were the Food Advice Centres that began opening on the main streets of larger towns from spring 1941 on: they publicized the ministry's food advice and provided a "drop-in" destination for the curious and self-improving, as well as the headquarters for regional organizers, demonstrators, and local food leaders. Radio and theater stars were hired to open the centers and attract the attention of the public, which was regaled with announcements in newspapers and cinemas, or emanating from street posters and loudspeaker vans, all promising that a short demonstration would be followed by tea and cookies.[100] Radiating advice, not instruction, the centers were designed to give no "suggestion of an Official Bureau" or "smack too much of the schoolroom," but to "look like a warm, homely kitchen; the sort of kitchen a housewife would like to drop into for help with her problems and a heart-to-heart chat." Cooking facilities were to be plain and simple (to afford no "opportunity for a poor woman to think: 'It's easy for them to cook like that with all those grand pans, but I couldn't do it'"), and nutritional advice was to "be given in simple words while explaining the cooking of homely dishes." Still, detailed and technical leaflets were also distributed. Those appointed to achieve this delicate balancing act were to possess no less than the accumulated wisdom of the social, nutritional, and domestic sciences: an "exhaustive knowledge of cookery" along with "personal experience of family cooking and the difficulties of a small, poorly equipped kitchen"; they should evince "knowledge of the technique of demonstrating," without "talking down to the women with whom they come in contact," in addition to "knowledge of the elements of dietetics," and "MOTHERLINESS: The will to serve: a keen interest in both people and food, combined with initiative and organising power."[101] Much of the burden of producing such superwomen fell on the National Training Colleges of Domestic Subjects, which were contracted to place their students as supervisors and demonstrators at Food Advice Centres, as well as to run refresher courses.[102]

It is difficult to tell how these centers actually worked in practice, or how many flocked to receive their food advice. The few detailed records we have indicate that on busy days a continual stream of up to

three hundred people dropped in to some centers, and further in-
quiries arrived by mail or telephone, whereas on other days the
stream was reduced to a trickle or even a drip, amounting to little
more than thirty enquiries.[103] Demonstrations were usually held on
one or two afternoons a week (especially on market days) and were
targeted at specific groups, like newlywed brides, young housewives
learning how to manage their households, new mothers, or even men
driven into the kitchen by their wives' wartime work. This targeting
of particular constituencies was also a feature of the demonstration
work that cultivated "contacts" with myriad groups, ranging from political clubs and religious organizations to housewives' associations
and the Women's Voluntary Service. Demonstration vans with fully
equipped kitchens were vital to this work, especially in rural areas
where alternative facilities, such as gas and electric display rooms,
school and factory canteens, or British Restaurants, were rarely available. Exhibition work was also common: booths might be rented at
local fairs and markets, as well as at larger events, such as the touring
Dig for Victory exhibition in 1944 or the *News of the World* Home
Making Exhibition and of course the *Daily Mail*'s Ideal Home Exhibition in 1947.[104] The Food Advice Centre on St. John's Road in
Battersea had just short of ninety thousand such contacts in its inaugural year, 1944, a figure that doubled the following year.

Much of this activity demonstrated the difficulties Food Advice
Centres had in reaching the majority of housewives who were not
members of a voluntary organization. The food leaders scheme was
intended to address this very problem. It represented the culmination
of the ministry's credo concerning food advice: rather than edicts
from patronizing experts or austere officials, which would be quickly
resented and soon forgotten, food advice was best spread informally:
"The average housewife is best influenced by the opinions of her
neighbours and acquaintances. The knowledge conveyed to her . . .
should have the subtle force of a change of fashion; it should pervade
her consciousness as she goes about her daily tasks."[105] As the van-
guard of food advice, food leaders had to be average members of
their community, but it was hoped that their own transformation into

badge-wearing experts, following a brief training and a subscription to *Food Leader News,* would herald a broader transformation in food habits. As "average housewives," they were expected to reach those untouched by the other work of the Food Advice Division, by inviting friends and neighbors to their own house for demonstrations or going from door to door in their localities dispensing pertinent advice and literature. In fact, fewer than half the food leaders were ever trained, and although the large majority "would be classified as housewives," most had been recruited through organizations like the Women's Voluntary Service (or WVS, which had provided the initial idea for the scheme), the Women's Institute, the National Union of Townswomen guild, and the YWCA, while the rest were professional health visitors, midwives, and domestic science teachers.[106] The food leader scheme certainly broadened the network of those dispensing food advice but it is unclear how effective it was at drawing in housewives not affiliated with a particular organization.[107]

Working closely with the ministry's Public Relations Department and the Ministry of Information, the Food Advice Division made extensive use of Mass-Observation, the Wartime Social Survey, and market research to monitor the effectiveness of its work. It did not always make for happy reading. During 1940 and 1941, for instance, Mass-Observation found that fewer than half of those they interviewed were aware of the *Kitchen Front* campaign, many of those who knew the catchphrase were unclear what it entailed, and the Kitchen Front Exhibition at Charing Cross attracted mainly middle-class men, not the working class women it was intended for.[108] Similarly, Gert and Daisy's comedic talks on food and cuisine for the *Kitchen Front* broadcast by the BBC initially went out after the six o'clock evening news, when many housewives were busy with their children—a finding that helped the Ministry of Food secure the coveted 8:15 morning slot for the broadcast.[109] Although a Home Intelligence report in 1943 indicated "considerable appreciation" for the work of the Food Advice Division, opinions varied "as to the best or most popular medium . . . On the whole, the radio and cinema seem to be liked rather better than the press; neither posters nor leaflets are thought 'to cut much ice,' and are considered by some housewives to be a waste of paper . . . except for leaflets giving food recipes or gardening hints."[110] Considerable scrutiny continued to be paid to the reception of new initiatives like the series of ads and leaflets called *Food Facts,* launched in December 1946. The British Market Research Bureau, which undertook a survey of reader responses over several months, each week interviewed a sample of between roughly a thousand and fifteen hundred housewives belonging to different social groups across the country. A depressing pattern was soon evident: fewer than 40 percent had seen the ads, fewer than 10 percent had found them helpful, and fewer than 5 percent had actually tried a suggested recipe.[111] Of course, the Food Advice Division's own network of regional food organizers and supervisors of Food Advice Centres also provided frequent, if less scientific, feedback on the success of particular campaigns and initiatives, as did the swollen mailbags of Lord Woolton and Jack Drummond.[112]

It is hard to square these gloomy assessments of the Food Advice Division's impact in transforming dietary habits and raising nutritional consciousness with the hugely positive responses to it by those like Le Gros Clark. These differences may be rooted in the contradictory results of the Ministry's own survey work. Thus, although Mass-Observation found a significant improvement in the nutritional knowledge of those attending the Kitchen Front Exhibition—with the percentage of those able to identify and distinguish between the different energy, body-building and protective food groups rising from 42.5 to 59 percent between the spring of 1940 and the autumn of 1941—little more than eighteen months later the Wartime Social Survey study of two thousand consumers concluded that "large numbers of people have no scientific knowledge of dietetic food values."[113] Nonetheless, by 1946 the Midlands regional food organizer was asserting that it "has to a very large extent become part of the national habit to think of food in terms of its value; its place in the national interest can be assessed by the fact that the cartoonists and joke writers have found it essential to include this interest in food among their jokes."[114] Certainly, many of the letters and telegrams sent to Jack

Drummond showed an impressive grasp of nutritional science.[115] Similarly, reminiscences of wartime childhoods are rarely complete without some mention by the authors of their mothers' struggles on the kitchen or food front, experiments with new foodstuffs and recipes, or attendance at various culinary demonstrations.[116]

Just as the objective of the Food Advice Division was to translate the principles of nutritional science into practical dietary advice by promoting the concept of meal planning, so the discipline of the ration book itself imposed certain rules and obligations on the housewife that forced her to plan her weekly shopping for supplies, if not necessarily her family's meals. Some forty-four million ration books were issued in September 1939 to cover every member of the population, but the harassed housewife was left to coordinate the different allowances for adults, infants, and children, to procure food to meet those allowances through the different mechanisms of "straight" rationing and "points" rationing, and to secure unrationed foods on a first-come, first-served basis (Figure 7.4).[117] We know little about how housewives adapted to these new disciplines but, despite the existence of a thriving black market, which we should be careful not to romanticize as simply a sign of resistance, it appears that for the most part they did so remarkably well. Or at least they coped, resigned to the idea that their struggles were a necessary part of the war effort.[118] The long lines and inadequate supplies, not the necessity of planning budgets and dietaries, were the most frequent causes for complaints, although the waiting in lines highlighted the hollowness of claims that the planning was labor-saving.[119] It was the demands of standing in lines—as well as its unfairness—that formed the initial focus for the animosity of predominantly middle-class women's organizations—the Mothers League and the British Housewives League. With the extension of peacetime rationing in 1946, however, and especially the rationing of bread, they redirected their critique toward a more general attack on food controls and the overbearing and un-English intrusion of the state into domestic life.[120] Given that the scientific management of the home had come to be equated with the efficiency of the middle-class housewife, the hostility toward state control and the

7.4. The harassed housewife calculating rations. *News Chronicle,* 1940. By permission of Solo Syndication.

continuation of austerity measures, not hostility to food advice and meal planning, were the factors that drove some local branches of the British Housewives League to protest outside Food Advice Centres.

However weary some women had grown of the discipline of the ration book, they were to enjoy no respite in the postwar years from the injunction to plan meals. New manuals and guides were produced by the Ministry of Food and the Association of Teachers of Domestic Subjects for the instruction of canteen managers, schoolchildren, and housewives charged with ensuring the nutritional health of postwar society. Written by Magnus Pyke (of the ministry's Scientific Adviser's Division) and Le Gros Clark, the publications demonstrated not only the centrality of nutritional expertise to the science of meal planning but the continued determination to find ways of making its complexities accessible through practical demonstrations, tables, charts, and quizzes.[121] Indeed, meal planning was increasingly a sign of how women's contribution to the kitchen front had helped elevate what the *Coventry Evening Telegraph* described as "the new domestic science as against the old 'housework'" and its task in the project of social reconstruction.[122] By the late 1940s cooking for the family had become integrally associated with meal planning and efficient management in the kitchen: "The principle of to-day's Family Cooking is based on a well-organised kitchen, forecast shopping, planned menus and, of course, adequate knowledge of food values and general diet in relation to individual family requirements."[123]

In 1947, Helene Reynard, who had been warden of King's College of Household and Social Science for the past two decades, took stock of the public career of domestic science in Britain and its place in the project of postwar social reconstruction. "It is obvious," she wrote, "that the health, comfort, and to a great extent the happiness, of the entire population depend on the success with which housewives perform their functions of home-makers and housekeepers." The organizing principles of domestic science—economy, efficient organization, and sound nutrition—had ensured not only that a "well-planned . . . clean and well-ordered" home and an "adequate, nourishing, varied and attractive diet" were now within the reach of every family, but that they were now also widely applied in the social work of public institutions. The extension of communal catering in schools, factories, hospitals, and prisons, the expansion of domestic science curricula in schools and training colleges, and the commercial marketing of efficient kitchens and nutritional health had created a plethora of well-remunerated new posts for the trained domestic scientist. To meet this need, the 1944 Education Act ensured that domestic science was taught to all girls in primary school, and that the majority of secondary schools would now include it as a component of the School Certificate Exam. No fewer than fifteen training colleges offered three-year diplomas, with tuition fees covered by government grants from 1946 on, and the Universities of Bristol and London offered undergraduate and postgraduate degree courses.[124]

Some citizens, of course, rejected the idea that the health, happiness, and prosperity of all depended upon the housewife's ability to master the techniques of domestic science. These critics found the disciplines of rationing and meal planning profoundly un-English, a violation of the very liberties that the war was being fought to defend. Devon's delightful wartime tirade against the ministry on behalf of all those "who enjoy their food and dislike being told officially what, when and where they shall eat" pointedly promised "no attempt to re-educate taste or re-align habit in eating" and certainly no "formulas or charts with 'planned' diets which most people have tried without great enthusiasm." Devon made jokes at the expense of Glossop's luckless medical officer of health, whose infamous "super diet" included the "Glossop Health Sandwich," made of wholemeal bread, an ounce of cheese, meat, or dried yeast mixed with half an ounce of vitaminized margarine, mustard, and cress (or tomato or raw carrot): "It would be stupid to suggest that an expert in vitamins and correct diet does not know what is really good for you . . . [but] if the Glossop menu is an 'elixir' of life, I am not sure that I want to prolong my life indefinitely." Concluding that the experts were really "cranks," the author of *Let's Eat!* warned that if they got their way, traditional and much-loved, tasty foods like fish and chips and the roast beef of old England would be lost forever.[125] He would not have mourned the steady flow of closures of Food Advice Centres that followed their transfer to local authorities' control in 1949, or the dissolution of the Food Advice Division in 1952 or the abolition of the Ministry of Food in 1954 after the final cessation of food rationing.

Although the critics of rationing and food advice presented themselves as engaged in a David-and-Goliath struggle, championing the market-driven consumer against the colossus of state controls, the Ministry of Food and its "cranks" had actually ceded much control over diet to the citizen-consumers. The ministry's unparalleled use of market research and advertising encouraged citizens to consume in more rational and self-improving ways. The ads did so not least of all by making nutritional health seem desirable: they promised women beauty, youthful zest, and happy children, and men strength and vitality. As the commercial marketing of foods had attracted a great deal of criticism from nutritional experts for willfully misleading consumers, the Ministry of Food was adamant that its food advice was scientifically accurate and that its scientific advisers would help regulate food advertising. Although the 1938 Food and Drugs Act had pro-

vided a regulatory framework to control the composition and labeling of foods, its powers had been suspended on the outbreak of the
war, thereby leaving the way open for commercial manufacturers to
make exaggerated claims about the nutritional properties and benefits of their products, often by appropriating the government's own
jingles and slogans.[126] It was not just that many labels were outdated
and depended upon unjustifiable claims, or that they used such vague
and misleading descriptions as "tonic," "nourishing," and "natural," but
that they often implied "that a food has a dietetic or nutritional value
when in fact the value is insignificant."[127] Determined to help "the
housewife in making an intelligent choice from the foods available,"
the ministry issued the Defence (Sale of Food) Regulations Order in
1943, which for the first time set particular standards that labels and
advertisements had to meet. Precise nutritional quantities had to be
specified, not just for the product as a whole, but for each individual serving, and a code of practice with precise guidelines was
drawn up by the ministry's scientific advisers in consultation with the
Medical Research Council.[128] Henceforth, consumers were advised
how to procure their nutritional health through the market and
were protected from anyone trying to exploit their hard-won nutritional knowledge. This marked a significant shift. Ensuring nutritional health was no longer simply about instructing citizens how to
be rational consumers. Instead, individuals were encouraged to govern their own nutritional health by purchasing the appropriate foods.
If scientific experts defined nutritional health, advertisements represented the benefits accruing to anyone who had achieved it, and manufacturers developed ever more nutrition-conscious products and labels. The role of government and of formal politics more broadly
became one of facilitating informed consumer choice and ensuring
that all the necessary information and the proper regulatory framework were available to support the responsible consumer. This occurred during the emergence of a social democratic state, and that
confluence that might lead us to reassess the contention that the failure of social democratic politics in Britain, marked by the two pro-
tracted periods of Conservative government in 1951 and 1979, lay in

the failure to engage with the commercial desires of its citizens, especially women.[129] We have to recognize that the welfare state's concentration on the subject of consumption elevated the political status of the housewife, albeit as a servant of her family. The shift was evident in the proliferation of such organizations such as Women's Institutes, Townswomen's Guilds, the Women's Voluntary Service, and the British Housewives League—dedicated to the mobilization of housewives as key actors in the new society.

8

Remembering Hunger
The Script of British Social Democracy

On 24 November 1947 the formidable Bessie Braddock, Liverpool's first female M.P. and a veteran of its unemployment struggles between the wars, rose in the House of Commons to join the debate on the second reading of the National Assistance Bill. It was an iconic moment. The bill marked the end of the reviled Poor Law, and labor movement activists had fought long and hard to see that day. The minister, Aneurin ("Nye") Bevan, whose political career had been fashioned in the fight to substitute welfare and security for the fear generated by poverty and unemployment, professed himself honored to sponsor a bill he described as the copingstone of the new welfare state. He reminded the House of the horrors of the workhouse and its association of poverty with sin and criminality.[1] But it was Braddock, once described by Sylvia Pankhurst as the finest platform orator in the country, who bore most eloquent testimony to the painful memories that had helped forge the bill.

> Let us remember the queues outside the Poor Law relief offices, the destitute people, badly clothed, badly shod, lining up with their prams—many of the men lining up with their kit-bags which they had carried during the 1914–1918 war—for the week's rations of black treacle and bread. Bread was then issued

once a week—and we know what bread is, even in the best of times, when it has been kept for a week. These are the things we are repealing . . . These things remain with us. We remember them . . .

I have looked forward to the time when the Poor Law would be abolished ever since 1906, when I had my very first recollections of people starving. I was taken, at the age of seven, into the central area of Liverpool where the women of the Socialist movement, even then, were looking after people who were in poverty. They used to make soup every day and take it down to the central area of the city in a van and distribute it, and a piece of bread, to those who were hungry and waiting for it at a cost of a farthing a bowl. I have always remembered since then the terrible tragedy and horror on the faces of those in the queue when the soup was finished and there was no more to be sold. . .

I am glad that I have lived to see this day and to have had a share in the agitation—because agitation it had to be until this Government came into power . . . I hope that the working class movement will be able now to forget the horrors of the past in the joy of realising that we are living in a country that is going to produce for the benefit of the citizens as a whole.[2]

As Braddock demonstrated, the battle against hunger and poverty was central to the labor movement in Britain, and the memory of their shameful indignities would play an important role in legitimating the achievement of social democracy. Recalling past struggles, suffering, and sacrifices had long endowed the labor movement with a sense of destiny, but following the Labour Party's electoral victory in 1945 a series of histories were produced to reassure people that "Labour would continue on its forward march because it knew well the lessons of the hard road already travelled."[3] Hunger became a familiar landmark on this road to renewal, and its defeat, especially the passing of the decade that became known as the hungry thirties, became a critical part of the story of British social democracy in the decades following 1945. No less than the narratives of the labor movement, victory over hunger permeated the autobiographies and testimony of Britons who came to measure their affluence by their distance from it. As Geoff Eley has written of postwar British film, the poverty of the thirties became "a sign for the difference and desirability of the present . . . The imagery of dismal hardship, mass unemployment, and hunger marches defined an unacceptable past that could not be repeated, a misery that required collective action and responsibility."[4] This chapter is less concerned with the advent of social democracy as a political settlement than with how memories of hunger generated and sustained a story of social democracy in the postwar years that validated its achievements. Clearly, however, as Braddock recognized, the two were intertwined and, I will argue, all the more so because in the immediate postwar decades the welfare state in its infancy remained in a precarious state.

Let us return to the hunger marches that later came to epitomize the social democratic memory of the thirties, even though these were protests by unemployed workers who were at best marginal to the institutions of the labor movement. As we saw in Chapter 3, the hunger march had been invented to demonstrate that the unemployed were victims of a failing economy and governmental neglect, but after the Armistice the National Unemployed Workers Movement embraced this form of protest to demand either jobs or adequate welfare—"work or full maintenance."[5] Despite its predominantly communist leadership, the NUWM dwelt less on elaborating an economic critique of unemployment as the inevitable product of capitalism than on contesting the often punitive welfare regimes that surrounded the unemployed and demanding their right to full maintenance on welfare. The NUWM's hunger marches were rarely successful in extracting concessions from government, the standard by which most historians have judged them. The more remarkable achievement of the marches was to invert the logic of welfare by claiming it as part of the commons, a social right, rather than as a form of discipline aimed at recalcitrant social groups. The NUWM transformed the politics of welfare between the wars and, in doing so, created the conditions for the emergence of the Beveridge Report in 1942. That report, with its call for a universal system of social insurance and welfare, in turn laid the foundation for the postwar social democratic welfare state.

Paradoxically, because the NUWM was long ignored and reviled by the labor movement, hunger marching only became respectable in 1936, when Ellen Wilkinson, Labour M.P. for Jarrow, famously led a march to London to protest at the scale of unemployment in the town. Whereas the hunger marches of the NUWM had been represented as revolutionary threats to the rule of law and the British constitution, the march from Jarrow was widely seen as a valid protest against unemployment because it was deliberately styled as a crusade (not a hunger march) that expressed the interests of a locality (not a class) with cross-party support from the town council. And yet, Wilkinson's debt to the NUWM was clear from the opening sentences of her book about the march, *The Town That Was Murdered,* when she insisted that the "poverty of the poor is not an accident, a temporary difficulty, a personal fault. It is the permanent state in which the vast majority of the citizens of any capitalist country have to live. That is the basic fact of the class struggle [underlying] . . . the modern labour movement."[6] Despite Wilkinson's talk of class struggle and the failures of capitalism, the Jarrow crusade generated more publicity than all the preceding hunger marches put together. It has been subsequently almost sentimentally evoked by historians to capture the zeitgeist of the "hungry thirties."[7] The relocation of the hunger march and the once detestable figure of the unemployed man from the margins to the sympathetic center of British political culture during the 1930s portended a remarkable transformation—it meant that the hunger march, and indeed the defeat of hunger more generally, would occupy a central place in the story of British social democracy.

Only Cowards Starve in Silence

The NUWM made the hunger march *the* form of protest by the unemployed between the wars. Alongside the national hunger marches

it organized in 1922, 1929, 1930, 1932, 1934, and 1936 were others
animated by specific local or regional conditions and grievances.[8] In
November 1927 miners from South Wales, with Bevan's support,
marched to London to protest the growing numbers of unemployed
in their ranks. The following autumn they were on the road again,
this time to the Trade Union Congress in Swansea, while their counterparts in Scotland marched to Edinburgh to highlight the inequities
of poor relief and unemployment benefits. The summer of 1933 was
marked by a spate of local and regional marches, generally concerning the amount of relief administered by the new county Public Assistance Committees (in Scotland to Edinburgh, in Lancashire to Preston, in Nottinghamshire and Derbyshire to Derby, in Yorkshire to
Wakefield, and in South Wales to Bridgend).[9] Labor historians deserve much credit for rescuing these marches from their previous neglect, as well as for emphasizing how their adaptability as a form
of protest enabled the NUWM to target particular elements of or
changes to the administration of relief.[10] Whereas the organization on
its first march in 1922 had demanded work or full maintenance at a
nationally uniform rate of thirty-six shillings, its second march in
1929 took aim at the detested "not genuinely seeking work" clause of
the Unemployed Insurance Act of 1927, and in 1932 the march was
directed against the infamous means test introduced the previous October.

It is impossible to doubt the punitive nature of much of the relief
for the unemployed between the wars. The aim of punishing people
who were out of work ran counter to their own insistence on welfare
as a right. Although social insurance, introduced in 1911 and extended in 1920 to cover eleven million workers, established the right
of the insured to unemployment benefits, the limited amount and duration of those benefits (initially fifteen shillings a week for fifteen
weeks) forced even insured workers to apply for the "extended"
benefits introduced in 1921 (which lengthened the duration of relief
to a maximum of forty-seven weeks and included meager allowances
for dependent women and children). Because extended benefits were
funded from the public purse, not from contributory social insur-

ance, they transformed benefits claimants into applicants for relief or "assistance." Welfare officials, instructed to make it a deterrent, means-tested eligibility for this assistance: far from disappearing, the Poor Law's infamous principle of less eligibility was expanded. On the sliding scale of relief, unemployment benefits always paid less than a living wage, and poor relief or unemployment assistance always paid less than benefits. Even after eligibility was restricted through imposition of the "not genuinely seeking work" clause in 1927 and of the household means test in 1932, the amount and duration of relief were further abridged by a 10 percent reduction in benefit rates in 1931 (though they were restored to the full amount in 1934) and by the replacement of extended benefits with "transitional" benefits lasting just twenty-six weeks. No wonder that, as the London Kino Group's silent and haunting documentary film *Bread* (1934) made apparent, the unemployed continued to experience their "relief" as a form of punishment. It was not just the inadequacy of relief (even in real terms, as prices fell), but the bewildering proliferation of regulations and procedures (between 1920 and 1934 twenty-one pieces of legislation affecting unemployment insurance were enacted), as well as the demeaning treatment of applicants, who had to prove they were genuinely seeking work or have their household income means-tested. Burnett aptly summarizes the situation: "Unemployment relief beyond the insured period was discretionary, not a right; in effect it involved a test of 'character' of the claimant, who became a supplicant forced to accept the conditions laid down."[11] The short-lived replacement of local boards of guardians with Public Assistance Committees in 1929 was intended to prevent Labour-controlled boards, like the board of guardians at Poplar in London, from establishing a more generous regime toward the unemployed. The Public Assistance Committees (PACs) continued to be constituted locally and thus failed to impose the desired centralized, nationally uniform scale of relief. A national scale finally came about in 1934, in the heat of the hungry England debate, when the new Unemployment Assistance Board tried to establish one based on scientific definitions of the minimum.[12] The uproar was so great, however, in areas whose PACs had more generous scales, especially over use of the hated means test to assess the aggregate minimum household income, that the new national scale was not enforced until 1937, and the more locally generous allowances were grandfathered in.

The NUWM sought to establish the right of the unemployed to welfare by insisting, like their Edwardian predecessors, that this was no way to treat veterans. Military service was an early and critical component in activists' articulation of the right to either work or welfare. As in continental Europe, in Britain unemployed veterans mobilized politically after 1918, and the NUWM had its origins in their discontent.[13] In the early 1920s, Wal Hannington, the leader of the NUWM, liked to refer to it as a "great army of ragged, half-starved, unarmed men," and those who joined the struggle had to swear an oath of allegiance to "the great army of unemployed."[14] Seventy-five percent of the participants from Manchester on the first hunger march in 1922 were reputed to be ex-servicemen. At the rally in Trafalgar Square at the culmination of the march, speaker after speaker—like Jack Riley, the leader of the contingent from Kent—returned to the injustice done to men who had returned from the Great War only to find that their jobs had vanished: "They asked us in 1914 to go to war, and I was one of the damned mugs that went. They said we were going to fight for liberty. What liberty did we fight for? The only liberty we fought for was the liberty to starve."[15] Even though on later marches the proportion of veterans inevitably fell, they continued to occupy an iconic place in the movement, not just because the sense of betrayal remained potent, but because those who had done their duty believed they had earned the right to work or full maintenance (Figure 8.1). As we shall see, it was no accident that two-thirds of those *selected* for the Jarrow march were veterans of the Boer War or the Great War.

Not surprisingly, militarism remained a central component of the NUWM's hunger marches. District councils engendered local contingents for the march, which coordinated preparations for others marching through their locality. Contingents were divided into companies of twenty, each with its own leader, who represented them on

FROM THE VALLEYS

8.1. The face of the hungry veteran. *The Socialist,*
November 1936, British Library of Political and
Economic Science, London School of Economics,
B1/5/58.

the Contingent Control Council, which met each evening to review
the health of marchers, review plans for the next day, and take any
necessary disciplinary action against marchers who had violated the
rules. Contingents marched in crisp "army style," with ten minutes'
rest each hour, and always advanced in unison on their arrival at the

appointed destination, where they were met by a reception committee. Each contingent boasted its own quartermaster, in charge of securing the requisite equipment for his men (boots, overcoat, blanket, knife, fork, spoon, spare shirt and underwear, razor, soap, and pint cup), coordinating the work of a designated cobbler, the field kitchen (staffed by cooks and cleaning assistants and equipped with portable boilers and supplies transported by truck), an ambulance section dispensing first aid, and a fatigue squad to clean up halls where the men slept.

These meticulous military preparations were designed to maintain the morale and discipline of the marchers, critical if the marches were to affirm the manly and moral strength of the unemployed. Every step was intended to challenge the insinuation, propagated in much of the press, that the unemployed were physically and morally dissolute, that they were the lazy, apathetic, and irredeemable.[16] Leaders and supporters always stressed the strength and discipline of the marchers. No account was complete without its paean to their suffering, and their determination to continue in spite of it, bloodied but unbowed: in worn boots and rain-soaked clothes that froze solid onto the men's frames, the marchers persevered for thirty miles or so through deep snow, blistered feet numb with pain. These appalling conditions were portrayed as tests of the men's strength and resolve (Figure 8.2).[17] Their commitment gave the lie to the charge that men without work were apathetic: "We refuse to starve in silence" and "Only cowards starve in silence" were popular sentiments on the marchers' banners. "Years of poverty have undermined their strength but not their morale," Nye Bevan wrote of the 1936 march: "These are not mendicants come to beg alms from the so-called prosperous South, but dignified, disciplined bands of representative men, the workers' own plenipotentiaries extraordinary."[18] The marches demonstrated that the unemployed would no longer cower in shame and plead for charity; they could march with pride and discipline to demand at least decent and humane forms of relief, if not always work or full maintenance. Challenging the stigma of pauperism so long associated with the provision of relief, with its often petty and degrad-

8.2. Bloody but unbowed—Lancashire hunger marchers, 1932. By permission of the Science and Society Picture Library.

ing discipline, was one of the NUWM's most important achievements.[19] The NUWM was equally energetic in pursuing the politics of welfare between marches. It sought to make sense of the bewildering series of changes and the labyrinthine regulations that surrounded welfare assistance for the unemployed, and at local tribunals it represented more than two thousand people faced with a reduction in benefits.[20]

Given the military and macho culture of these early hunger marches, it was not surprising that women were conspicuously absent from them. After all, these marches championed the right of unemployed men to maintain their status as family breadwinners by obtaining work or relief, even though the issue of welfare provision and the maintenance of families was very much women's territory. When Mary Docherty asked Hannington whether she could join the

NUWM's second national hunger march in 1929, he bluntly replied, "No, nae women were allowed."[21] Yet later that year the NUWM created a women's department under the direction of Maud Brown, and she secured women's limited participation in the third national Hunger March.[22] What really brought women into the fold was the hated effects of the means test on family life, and the disqualification of 179,888 married women from unemployment relief under the Anomalies Act of June 1931.[23] In 1932, some fifty women, ranging in age from sixteen to sixty-three, marched from Burnley to London and into the mythology of the movement. Brown appears to have been successful at forcing the NUWM to recognize that a particular politics of welfare surrounded women, and especially wives of unemployed men. She was able to secure the leaders' support, beginning in the mid-1930s, for higher benefits for pregnant and nursing mothers.[24] Yet deep down the hunger march remained an inveterately masculine phenomenon. Women were not even allowed on the Jarrow march. Ellen Wilkinson, who was to attract much attention as the only woman on the march, believed they would "add complications," for it was "not going to be a luxury cruise. It will be hard work and every man we take must be fit."[25] Women's involvement undercut the image of the hunger march as a display of the strength and dignity of unemployed men struggling to support their families and protect them from the punitive welfare regimes of the "baby-starving government." The right to welfare they articulated was based on the assumption that the needs of the unemployed man always came first.

Unlike their Edwardian predecessors, hunger marchers between the wars were citizens. For the NUWM the hunger march was a sign of democratic failure and was made necessary by Parliament's inability to represent the interests of the unemployed or address the problem of unemployment. The vote, long promised as the salvation of the disenfranchised, the tool by which workers would ensure that government served their interest, had turned out to be effectively worthless. This did not mean that voters eschewed a political solution. Indeed, they emphasized not only the constitutionality of their protest, but their determination to work through constitutional channels. Since 1922 the NUWM had used the traditional persuasion of moral force: marchers, carrying a petition of demands, collected signatures in support of them on the way to London. At the culmination of each march came a request that a deputation be allowed to meet with the prime minister or members of the cabinet, or from 1930 on, to present a petition to the House of Commons. These requests were always refused on the grounds that a) there were already constitutional channels for the unemployed to air their grievances through their M.P.'s; b) the NUWM was itself unrepresentative, because its leaders were the stooges of Moscow (a point underlined by the failure of the labor movement to give its blessing to the marches before 1934); and c) deputations and appearances before the House of Commons could not help redress their problems. As prime minister during the 1934 hunger march, Ramsay MacDonald took a rather different position from the one he had taken in 1905, when he had supported the hunger march of his constituents from Leicester; he insisted, "[It] is merely trifling with the distress that unemployment is causing right now, to induce people to come marching to London, implying that they can force the Prime Minister, the Cabinet, and the House of Commons to see them."[26] These refusals worked to substantiate the NUWM's claim that the unemployed might now be citizens but remained effectively disenfranchised and unrepresented by the Parliament they had helped elect.

MacDonald's complaint that the NUWM was exploiting and exasperating the suffering of the unemployed became a familiar refrain, one lent additional force by the portrayal of the NUWM leaders as communists taking orders directly from Moscow.[27] Only communists, it was implied, would exploit the unemployed for their own political purposes and impose unnecessary suffering upon already vulnerable people. Indeed, such was the hostility of the national press to the NUWM until 1934 that its hunger marches went largely unreported in the papers (unless they recorded the numbers of men who had abandoned the march), with the exception of the *Daily Herald* and the *Daily Worker*, until the marchers reached London.[28] There is even evidence that in 1932 and 1934 the Metropolitan Police appealed to the

newsreel companies not to cover the marches and used the BBC to
advise people to stay away from their rallies in London.[29] Representing the NUWM as a communist organization helped justify the
close surveillance and increasingly repressive policing of their activities.[30] Quite apart from the frequent arrest and imprisonment of its
leaders (Hannington served five sentences in ten years),[31] violent
clashes occurred in Manchester and Glasgow during October 1931,
in Castleford (where an NUWM member was killed following a police baton charge at a demonstration against the means test), as well
as in Birkenhead and Belfast (where two were shot dead and fifteen
wounded by gunshot) in the late summer and autumn of 1932. Paradoxically, although these police actions prompted the creation of the
National Council for Civil Liberties, which argued that constitutional
meetings were being illegally and violently disrupted by the state,
they also helped cement the image of the NUWM as a communist-
inspired, violent "mob," little better than Moseley's fascists.[32] In response, the NUWM shifted responsibility back to the government, by
claiming that it was the government that had caused the unemployment and then failed to address the misery of unemployed. Worse
still, the government had deliberately adopted punitive policies toward hunger marchers—in particular the insistence that boards of
guardians offer marchers only the meager "casual diet" (two slices of
bread and margarine and a cup of tea or cocoa at breakfast and sup-
per), and the denial of relief under the "not genuinely seeking work"
or the parish residency clause for poor relief. Probably the greatest
tactical victory for the NUWM came in 1934. The introduction of
the scientifically calibrated universal scale for assistance, which reduced the income of half of its recipients, sparked such protest that it
was partially abandoned.

The critique of the punitive nature of welfare had greater force
thanks to the NUWM's insistence that unemployment was a national
class experience: at any moment a member of the working class
could be reduced to misery by the inhumanity of those dispensing relief. While successive governments sought to provincialize the problem of unemployment and its relief, as specific to certain industries,

groups of workers, or regions (or what came to be designated in 1934 as "distressed areas"), the NUWM used the hunger march to demonstrate the national extent and scale of unemployment.[33] Each march enacted the coming together of the unemployed nation, as local contingents swelled the ranks and the different tributaries (which flowed not just from the industrial heartlands but from Norwich, Hereford, Plymouth, Southampton, Brighton, and Canterbury) all converged on London (Figure 8.3). Geography mattered, but it was the human scale of the tragedy of unemployment that mattered most. "The trickle of these little streams from all parts of the country," declared the leader of the men from South Wales on the first national hunger march in 1922, "will awaken the public to the fact that we are not a newspaper paragraph, or a recorded statistic, but men who wear boots and clothes, who eat, drink, sleep, love and laugh and cry like themselves."[34]

It was not until 1934 that the tide of public opinion began to turn, no doubt aided by the revelations of the privations of unemployment during the previous year's hungry England debate. The 1934 march attracted substantially more attention and favorable comment, even in unlikely quarters, like the *Economist* and the *Times*.[35] It has been suggested that the arrival of the 1934 march in Cambridge radicalized students, by providing some with their first view of the poverty and unemployment of the northern working class.[36] The novelty of these encounters of two social worlds, the old two nations, North and South, hunger and privilege, is palpable, and it worked both ways. Invited to dine in Cambridge colleges during the 1936 hunger march, the men from Durham and Newcastle tasted "the first real salmon and the first real chicken any of us have ever eaten in our lives."[37] Barbara Cartland recalled the mutual shock apparent when the NUWM staged a protest in the Savoy's Grill Room in 1937: "The poor things were in rags; they looked tired and exhausted. They didn't make a sound; they just gazed around in disbelief, overwhelmed by the fountain, the opulence, the atmosphere. The people having tea just sat there, still, looking upper-class; nothing was said. There was an uncanny silence."[38] The classic image of this encounter

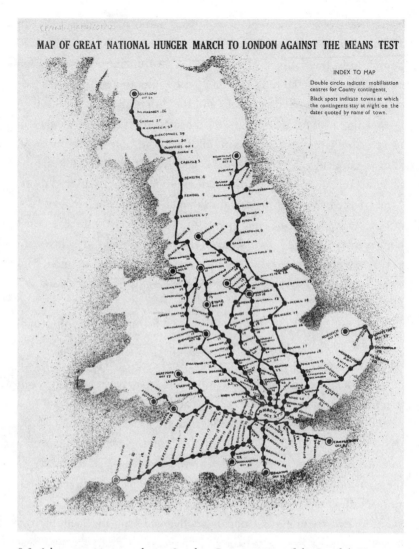

8.3. A hungry nation marches to London. By permission of the People's History Museum.

between two nations and two classes is Thomas Dugdale's painting *The Arrival of the Jarrow Marchers in London*, in which one views their rally in Picadilly from the perspective of a high-society lady watching from her window in the Ritz (Figure 8.4). Her curious but nonchalant gaze downward upon the undifferentiated mass of marchers as-

8.4. *The Arrival of the Jarrow Marchers in London,* oil painting by P. C. Dugdale. By permission of the trustees of the Geffrye Museum.

sembled below, and the lack of interest shown by her male companion, is neatly inverted back upon the decadence of this opulent couple.

Within the space of a few years the politics of hunger marching had shifted from demonizing the NUWM marchers as a dangerous rabble led by communists to denigrating the cruel indifference of London's high society toward the honest men from Jarrow. Indeed, the march from Jarrow was to receive the sort of favorable reception that Hannington and the NUWM could have only dreamed of.[39] Certainly, by consulting with Hannington, Wilkinson learned much about how to disarm the critics who argued that hunger marches were unconstitutional and that they exploited the suffering of the un-employed. Only five hundred of twelve hundred applicants were se-lected to respond to questions "concerning their domestic affairs, their army service and their health" and then submitted to inspection by the borough's medical officer. Of those, only two hundred were eventually selected for the march, 62 percent of whom were veter-ans.[40] Those selected had to agree to comply with the rules of the march, to follow instructions, and to remain "sober at all times and also not to take part in any collection without the approval of the marshall."[41] In return, they were well cared for by an impressive sup-port staff of cooks, a barber, two medical students from the Inter-Hospital Socialist Society, mechanics, and truck drivers. Trucks car-ried the cooking equipment and the men's kit bags, and all the men had been supplied with boots, socks, and spare soles, as well as a wa-terproof groundsheet that doubled as a cape in wet weather. Com-panies eager to publicize their brands donated food, cigarettes, and medicine. Early reports were so effusive about the health of the men and the beneficial effects of the regimen of regular meals, fresh air, and exercise that some worried they had created the wrong impres-sion of conditions back in Jarrow. Wilkinson, however, insisted that healthy, well-fed marchers gave the lie to those who had branded them "ill-clad and under-fed" at her own Labour Party conference, not to mention cabinet ministers who, Wilkinson complained, "weep 'crocodile tears' about the hardships of the march when the men are being fed as they have never been fed since they last worked."[42]

Whereas the NUWM's marches had always been tainted by the smear of communist exploitation of the unemployed, Wilkinson was determined to ensure that the march from Jarrow was seen as repre-sentative of the whole town, not a specific party or class. The town council's all-party March committee made much of its nonpartisan nature.[43] In adherence to this gospel of neutrality, the very term "hun-ger march" was studiously avoided, so as to distinguish it from the politics of the NUWM march that had set off from Glasgow on the same day.[44] Instead, the Jarrow march was described in religious terms, as a "crusade" to publicize the plight of the town and present its petition to Parliament; the marchers, blessed in a joint service of the town's Anglican and Catholic churches, were frequently referred to as pilgrims or "Jarusaders."[45] It was not a distinction entertained by the government, which issued a statement lumping both marches together as unnecessary and unconstitutional:

> In the opinion of the Government such marches can do no good to the causes for which they are represented to be undertaken. They are liable to cause unnecessary hardship to those taking part in them and are undesirable . . . In this country, governed by a Parliamentary system where every adult has a vote and every area has its representative in the House of Commons to put forward grievances and suggest remedies, processions to London cannot claim to have any constitutional influence on policy.[46]

There followed an avalanche of complaints from people who would ordinarily have defended the government position. The bishop of Sheffield declared the march a "very English and constitutional thing," while the chairman of the Leeds Conservative Party described it as a "constitutional and orderly appeal," sentiments echoed by Major E. G. Whitaker, Sheffield's Conservative agent, who thought it "a good thing . . . whether my head office likes it or not."[47] Even the *Spectator* and the *Times* defended the right to march and petition Parliament as "an ancient, a valuable, a well-recognised right," commending the Jarrow crusade (but pointedly not the NUWM march) for having "enlisted a large amount of public sympathy."[48] As Wilkinson asked, "With the blessing of the bishop, priests and clergy, subscriptions from business men, the paternal interest of the Rotary Club and the unanimous support of the Town Council, could anything have been more constitutional?"[49] The marchers had, she claimed, "exhausted every kind of parliamentary pressure," and their petition now "bore the hopes of the women and children whom the marchers had left behind."[50]

This emphasis on the constitutional, classless, and nonpartisan nature of the march secured it unprecedented coverage in the national press. Several local papers sent reporters on the march to lend their reports a more ethnographic flavor, a trend later mimicked by the national press. Consequently, reports increasingly tended to focus on the human drama of the march and its principal characters—Paddy the mascot dog, the mouth organ band, "smiler" John Hanrey, Boer War veteran George Smith—in ways that generated interest, sympathy, and news momentum. At the center of all the coverage was the diminutive figure of Wilkinson, or, as she was more often referred to, "wee Ellen," "our Ellen," or "brave Ellen." Alongside Councillor Riley in his bowler hat, the image of Wilkinson, the only woman allowed on the march, a slight figure among burly men, gamely leading them forward, walking stick in hand, became emblematic (Figure 8.5). The press speculated how long she would last on the march, and she was repeatedly interviewed, not about the politics of unemployment but about her height, her love of sports, her choice of footwear, her blisters, and her exhaustion.[51] By the time brave Ellen and her fellow Jarusaders reached the outskirts of London, they were "preceded by a battery of cameras, escorted by a posse of police, pursued by a crowd of spectators."[52] Hannington and the NUWM's hunger marches never received such attention.

Despite the studied refusal to employ the term, the Jarrow crusade was a hunger march. Its purpose was to provide what Wilkinson described as a "picture of a walking distressed area" and to show, in the words of the bowler-hatted Riley, "the kind of men who are unemployed in Jarrow," who if given the chance were obviously "all fit and capable of doing a day's work."[53] The very elements that were supposed to distinguish the Jarrow march from other hunger marches—its nonpartisan focus on a town, not a class, that had been "murdered"; its plea for work, as opposed to a protest against inadequate and punitive forms of relief—enabled it to capture the public imagination in ways that finally legitimated the hunger march as a

8.5. "Wee Ellen" and the men on the Jarrow crusade. By permission of Getty Images.

form of peaceful, constitutional protest. Jarrow quickly came to represent the acceptable, even sentimentalized, face of the determined hunger marcher, bravely battling against the indignity and injustice of unemployment. It cast such a long shadow over the NUWM marches that Barbara Cartland remembered the NUWM's protest at the Savoy in 1937 as the work of the men from Jarrow.[54] Even though it was the NUWM that had made the hunger march an effective weapon for claiming welfare as a right, it was the Jarrow march that came to exemplify the battle against unemployment and hunger during the thirties and the achievements of social democracy after the Second World War.

That achievement, we must remember, was a precarious one, and not simply because the Labour Party's election victory in 1945 did not represent a landslide, as we have recently learned, despite the size of its parliamentary majority.[55] The foundational text of the welfare state, the Beveridge Report of 1942, may have outlined a universal system of social insurance and welfare, but the five giant evils from which William Beveridge wished to protect the population—Want, Squalor, Ignorance, Idleness, and Disease—were described in a censorious series of euphemisms that would not have been out of place a century earlier and failed to exonerate their victims of responsibility for their plight. Of course, advocates of the system of welfare that Beveridge imagined did indeed quickly translate its purpose in more positive terms, as the defeat of poverty and the promotion of housing, education, work, and health. Yet Beveridge's foundational text remained caught between the conception of welfare as a necessary social right and the conception of welfare as a form of disciplinary care: the former protecting the innocent from systemic failures beyond their control, the latter disciplining those who had failed to protect themselves from these misfortunes. In many ways it was absolutely "the last and most glorious flowering of late Victorian philanthropy."[56] In the decades following the creation of the welfare state, then, it seemed necessary to legitimate it by remembering the hungry thirties and narrating the story of social democracy as the defeat of hunger.

History, Memory, and the Hungry Thirties

Hunger and poverty have always been with us, but they are discovered and remembered at particular historical moments.[57]

> The title of a work written by Mr. Fisher Unwin in 1904 has fastened on the decade that saw the railway boom and the repeal of the Corn Laws the stigma of "the hungry forties," and only the other day a magazine called *Womanfare* referred to the decade before the recent one as "the hungry thirties." A legend is growing up that the years 1930–39 were marked throughout by misery. In the next generation "the hungry thirties" may be common form.[58]

As T. S. Ashton reminded us, it was only in the first decade of the twentieth century that free trade campaigners came up with the idea of the preceding century's "hungry forties" in the battle against the protectionism that was part of Chamberlain's tariff reform campaign in the run up to the 1906 election.[59] Determined that no one would "ever again vote to bring that curse back upon us," the publisher T. Fisher Unwin, son-in-law of that great apostle of free trade Richard Cobden, collected testimony from those who could remember the story he wanted to tell of the miseries of life before the repeal of the Corn Laws in 1846. In 1904 he published a selection of these "interviews" under the title *The Hungry Forties: Life Under the Bread Tax. Descriptive Letters and Other Testimonies from Contemporary Witnesses.* His wife, Jane Cobden Unwin, the daughter of the great Cobden himself, wrote an introduction contrasting the widespread experience of hunger before repeal with the half century of plenty that followed.[60] This story, endlessly reiterated at political meetings, where veterans of the "hungry forties" would be displayed or engaged as speakers, imprinted the term upon the political unconscious, and historians and novelists have ever since uncritically reproduced the phrase as a contemporary description of the 1840s.[61] Like Ashton, I suggest that the idea of the "hungry thirties" was similarly invented and quickly naturalized in the decades following the Second World War.

After that war, when social democracy across Europe appeared to carry all before it, Ashton cooperated in Friedrich Hayek's attempt to prevent left-leaning intellectuals from giving economic liberalism and capitalism a bad name. A Manchester School liberal, and thus an optimistic-minded economic historian, he derided those who had sustained Arnold Toynbee's pessimistic assessment that standards of living had deteriorated with the advance of industrialization in Britain.[62] As the "standard of living controversy" raged among historians during the postwar years, Ashton realized that those who talked of the hungry thirties did so to celebrate the achievements of social democracy and the welfare state. Although accounts of the decade produced immediately at its close did not make use of term, they did characterize

Auden's "low dishonest decade" as marked by persistent unemployment and the rise of fascism, symptoms marking the failure of both
the market and politics.[63] This sentiment gathered momentum in the
early years of the war, when leftist intellectuals like J. B. Priestley,
George Orwell, and Humphrey Jennings valorized "the people," urging them to fight not just against fascism but for a social democratic
future in which there would be no return to the grinding poverty,
hunger, and unemployment of the 1930s.[64] When, in February 1943,
the Labour M.P. James Griffith made a motion urging Churchill's
wartime government to adopt Beveridge's proposals, he reminded
the House of Commons, "Our people have memories of what happened at the end of the last war, memories of the period of depression, memories of the unemployment, frustration, poverty and distress."[65] The phrase "Never Again" became the rallying cry for the
construction of the postwar welfare state by Clement Attlee's Labour
government of 1945–1951, and Griffith became the minister responsible for introducing Beveridge's universal system of social insurance
through the National Insurance Act of 1946.[66]

As the speech by Braddock quoted earlier illustrates, throughout
Attlee's administration, when its achievements were attenuated by
continuing austerity measures, the Labour Party assiduously cultivated memories of the thirties as those "unhappy years" of poverty
and unemployment for which the Conservatives were responsible.
Thus Bevan, on the eve of the inauguration of the National Health
Service, his greatest achievement, reminded his audience in one of his
most famous and controversial speeches:

> In my early life I had to live on the earnings of an elder sister
> and was told to emigrate. That is why no amount of cajolery
> and no attempt at ethical or social seduction can eradicate from
> my heart a deep burning hatred for the Tory Party that inflicted
> those bitter experiences. So far as I am concerned they are
> lower than vermin. They condemned millions of first-class peo-
> ple to semi-starvation. Now the Tories are pouring out money
> in propaganda of all sorts and are hoping by this organised sus-

tained mass suggestion to eradicate from our minds all memory
of what we went through. But, I warn you young men and
women, do not listen to what they are saying now. Do not listen
to the seductions of Lord Woolton. He is a very good salesman.
If you are selling shoddy stuff you have to be a good salesman.
But I warn you they have not changed, or if they have they are
slightly worse than they were.[67]

In more sober and measured tones, the Labour Party manifestos for
the 1950 and 1951 elections warned that those dark days "must never
come again."[68] Their 1951 manifesto invited voters to "contrast Britain in the inter-war years with Britain to-day," adding, "Then we had
mass unemployment; mass fear; mass misery. Now we have full employment. Then millions suffered from insecurity and want. Now we
have social security for every man, woman and child."[69] During the
1950 election, images of the once reviled hunger marchers adorned
Labour posters, and youthful voters were told, "Ask Your Dad," so
that he would tell them "about his 'bitter memories' of the thirties."[70]
Evoking the hunger of the thirties became politically less effective, as
the Conservatives embraced the reaction against the "queues, controls and rationing" of the postwar austerity measures and delivered a
new era of consumption and affluence that brought them three successive election victories.[71] By 1956 the *Sunday Express* was even con-
fident enough to publish a picture of a thirties hunger march with the
caption "Could this happen again?" because they knew their readers
would answer in the negative.[72] Yet as revisionist voices on the Left
earnestly debated whether Labour's defeats were the consequence of
a sociological sea change in which newly affluent workers were turning away from the politics of class to embrace consumption, the thirties were again evoked as a moment when hunger and deprivation
had provided a clear script for class struggle and solidarity.[73]

It is in this context that we must consider the steady stream of
working-class autobiographies, testimony, and reminiscences, mainly
from childhood, about the experience of poverty and hunger before
the Second World War that were published in the decades that fol-

lowed it. Members of the working class, in whose name the state now claimed to govern, were increasingly encouraged to speak for themselves, to narrate the story of their salvation under social democracy from the hunger of the thirties.[74] Describing this process as statesponsored autobiography, Carolyn Steedman has traced its institutional origins to the classroom, where creative writing was taught during the 1950s as a form of "ethical self-cultivation" in which children came to understand themselves by narrating their experiences and sharing them with others.[75]

It was not just in the classroom that the working class was being told to speak. The 1950s were marked by the proliferation of attempts to document and represent the realities of lower-middle- and working-class life, for example, the rash of familiar "kitchen sink dramas" of "angry young men" eager to escape their parents' suffocating experience of class.[76] Most influential, however, was Richard Hoggart's lament for the working class of his interwar childhood, after its desecration by American mass culture, and his account of his education as a way out of it. *The Uses of Literacy* (1958) became a seminal text for a New Left perplexed by the reformation of class in the face of rising affluence, consumer capitalism, and the expanding influence of mass media.[77] Much was made of the emergence of an authentic working-class voice and its alleged debt to that pillar of postwar social democracy, the 1944 Education Act.[78] Given that the act still condemned most at the age of eleven to preparation in secondary schools for a life of manual labor, the extension of adult education through institutions like the Workers Education Association (WEA) perhaps did more to facilitate working-class self-expression.[79] In the WEA the central figures of the New Left—Richard Hoggart, Raymond Williams, and Edward Thompson—first made their living, recovering working-class history and culture from "the enormous condescension of posterity" and handing it back to their students within a script of redemption.[80] Higher education expanded following the Robbins Report of 1963—student numbers doubled by 1970, with the provision of universal grants and the development of a number of more democratic campuses. The expansion extended the reach of the narrative of class redemption and provided a natural, if still "up-rooted and anxious," home for many self-styled organic intellectuals, like Hoggart.[81]

Beginning in the late 1960s, a host of cultural organizations and strategies materialized that were designed to reclaim working-class experience and empower workers to speak for themselves. As Steed-man has demonstrated, the diverse set of practices that surrounded adult education, community publishing and theater, documentary filmmaking, the folk movement, oral history, and of course women's groups, "operated on the assumption that the subaltern could speak, that through the articulation in spoken or written words, the dispossessed could come to an understanding of their own story. That story—that life—could by various means be returned to the people who had struggled to tell or to write it, and be used as a basis for political action."[82] Many of these practices were closely related, as Steedman's own account of her working-class childhood in 1950s Britain illustrates.[83] She was the recipient of an education under the 1944 Education Act (and also, thanks to Ellen Wilkinson, free milk and dinners at school), an undergraduate in the late 1960s at the new Sussex University, where she studied social history in the Thompsonian mode, and a feminist member of the History Work-shop collective—a forum "in which socialist intellectuals might not only integrate with, but also grow out of the culture and politics of working people themselves."[84] It is worth remarking on the whiteness of the subjects of this experiment. The attempt to recuperate and give voice to the English working-class experience of hunger cannot be divorced from the fall of the empire and the slow transformation of working-class communities into more colorful, multiracial neigh-borhoods. Nostalgia for a world of class solidarity that was lost disguised the active exclusion of people who could not share the Englishness of the remembered past and the script of class redemp-tion it afforded.[85]

As Chris Waters has noted, "hundreds of working class autobio-graphical reminiscences were collected, edited, printed, and dissemi-nated by community publishers in Britain during the 1970s and

1980s."[86] Many of these, like Alice Foley's *A Bolton Childhood*, flowed directly from the tributaries I have mapped.[87] Ernie Benson's recollections of his childhood in Leeds between the wars, aptly titled *To Struggle Is to Live*, published by a Newcastle community publisher in 1979, begins with profuse thanks to his WEA mentors and the Federation of Workers, Writers and Community Publishers.[88] When, the following year, Benson published the second volume, *Starve or Rebel*, Jack Lindsay, the frighteningly prolific Marxist author and WEA stalwart, could still complain, "We have few sustained records by working class men or women of their lives, their struggles, their awakening consciousness of their social position." Benson, a trade unionist, communist, and NUWM member, was in Lindsay's eyes "the real thing," an authentic voice of "the hardships, conflicts, struggles, through which they [the working class] have lived."[89] Similarly, Kathleen Dayus, whose autobiography of a childhood in the Birmingham slums between the wars, was described as speaking "with an authentic working-class voice." Local archivists and social historians went in search of that authenticity when they began collecting oral testimony during the 1970s.[90]

So how was the authentic experience of hunger and poverty before the coming of the welfare state remembered? Christopher Waters has shown that, unlike tales of self-improvement that marked Victorian working-class autobiographies, those produced in the second half of the twentieth century dwell nostalgically on worlds now lost.[91] It is certainly striking how most of them focus only on childhood or early adulthood, invariably ending with the Second World War, rather than proceeding to the authorial present. They progress by accumulating anecdotes, rather than by establishing narrative momentum over time. Although nostalgia is often a central aspect of autobiography, reminiscences, and testimony, it was hard to be nostalgic about hunger: as the miner Jimmy Jones recalled, "When you reminisce, . . . ah . . . I do this myself, mind, you reminisce about the better things in life more than the bad things."[92] Memories of hunger were heavily freighted and difficult to recall. An anonymous citizen of Bolton, born into a family of seven in 1903, knew hunger all too well. Her father, a bleacher, was frequently off work through sickness, and he died young. Married life was not much better, for her husband was unemployed for most of the "grim, very grim" 1930s: "They say they were the good old days, but they weren't."[93] For Mary Burnett, the eldest of ten children and thus charged with helping her mother put food on the table, those were just "terrible" times.[94] In Oldham between the wars children "were so damn hungry that they couldn't get up and run about": the plague of hunger and unemployment were always there "just there waiting to touch you."[95] It could not have gotten much worse for a NUWM activist who, born in 1901, lost his father in the First World War and shortly afterward his mother and eldest sibling. Four children were left to battle for survival:

> We are living longer now, through better times, people are a lot taller, there's a lot of difference in everybody, there isn't as much sickness as there were then, people have had a better life, they've been able to keep themselves fitter. Then, everybody we used to . . . was less than they are now, five, six, seven, eight, ten inches less than they are now, and scraggy, all of them, all little . . . Everybody was more or less thin because there were malnutrition . . . Things was very, very bad . . . Children died young because they didn't get the food. There were a family called Worthington, and she lost about four children through, errr, mainly malnutrition. The government wouldn't accept that, but that's what it was, definitely . . . There were a lot of kids bow-legged and deformed, and more than you ever see now. There was a lot of poverty all the way around, and it was terrible. We don't want to go back to those days.[96]

These memories of the hunger of the thirties were not merely recorded from the relative safety and prosperity of the postwar years; they were continually compared with them. In Carolyn Steedman's postwar childhood, hunger and poverty "hovered as a belief. It existed in stories of the thirties, in a family history" that enabled her mother to remind her, "Not being hungry and having a warm bed to lie in at night, I had a good childhood, was better than other people; was a *lucky* little girl."[97] The hungry thirties came to signify the deprivation that staked out subsequent prosperity, the hunger once known, now past.[98]

Yet "never again" does not fully capture the sentiment of these memories of hunger. There was often a tension between the remembrance of happy childhoods and the misery of the conditions in which those childhoods were lived. Having spent much of her autobiography describing a childhood of considerable hardship in the East End before the Great War, Grace Foakes reflected: "To many it may seem that we lived a miserable existence, but I do assure you that this was not always the case. I never worried then over the conditions as I saw them. I, along with the rest of the children, was carefree, happy, noisy, cheeky and cheerful."[99] She suggested that many compensations were to be found in the tight bonds of community, which grew still closer when poverty and hunger descended. The lament for the lost ties of mutuality and community that pervades much of the genre serves as a critique of a more prosperous present, where each looks after his own. Even though Mary Dagnah recalled how children at her school collected their "cup of Bovril and a thick wedge of dry bread cup" before returning home to empty plates and bare cupboards, she added, "As I remember, they all seemed quite happy and there was the attitude of 'what you've never had, you never miss' . . . Everyone helped each other; there was a good deal of sharing, doors were never locked and no-one tried to keep up with the Joneses."[100]

Remembering hunger often produced this dichotomy between celebration of the subsequent material gains that had rendered dearth a childhood memory and mourning for the cultural values lost in the process. Those who had hungered as children appreciated the newfound affluence of postwar Britain. Arthur Barton's memories of his hungry childhood in the Jarrow of the thirties shaped his experience as an affluent adult after the war. "I find that . . . I take a peculiar pleasure in unpacking the groceries and filling up the larder, that wasted food makes me angry, that my pleasure in Christmas plenty is tempered with the memory of my mother giving me, as so many did,

her food on the pretext that she had already eaten."[101] A common
refrain, other than that food had tasted better when it had been
scarce, was those who had never gone without now took abundance
for granted.[102] William Woodruff, pillorying contemporary dietaries,
captures this spirit well when describing the "hunger mentality" that
gripped his Blackburn childhood between the wars. When there was
a little more money in the house, he remembered,

> We gorged . . . Nobody was accused of gluttony. Few bothered
> about their waistlines, not even my sisters. We didn't shy away
> from fatty meat. If we did, father quickly ate it . . . All meals
> with us were favourite meals. There was an earthy naturalness
> about our eating. There was a vigour about it: "'unger's t' best
> sauce." We champed and chewed with relish. The smacking of
> lips, belching and sucking of fingers were all ignored, so was
> slurping hot tea out of a saucer. To eat and drink one's fill was
> to be blessed.[103]

The natural reactions the hungry had to food stands in contrast to the
artifice of worry about waistlines and manners; the plentiful present
can be appreciated only through the lens of hunger past. Relish for a
rare family feast, or brief period of plenty, returns again and again in
these accounts.

In keeping with the social democratic framework in which working-class self-expression was encouraged in the postwar period, hunger was always remembered in social terms. Remarkably, autobiographical accounts contain little discussion of what it felt like to live
with constant hunger or to inhabit a hungry body. For these we must
turn to the autobiographies of hunger strikers, where the heightened
sense of smell and taste, the weakness and exhaustion, the coldness
and fever, the violent headaches and dizziness, the depression and
sense of desolation, are described at length.[104] The exception is the
early, stylized account by Max Cohen (with a nod to Knut Hamsun)
of his struggle against unemployment and hunger, where a delirious
anxiety and obsession with food, from which neither walking nor

reading could distract him, gave way to "an emptiness of the brain
and of the spirit" and an "intolerable weakness and fatigue."[105] Testimonials about hunger were concerned less with the self and the sense
of interiority than with the social community in which hunger was
endured.[106] There is an amazing symmetry to the details in these texts
about how hunger was managed across the institutions that dominated working-class life in the first half of the twentieth century: the
family, the street, the corner shop, the market, the fish and chip shop
or pie shop, the pawnshop, the church, the school, the Poor Law
Guardians. Against this social backdrop of the everyday rhythms of
family life in small communities the experience of hunger was nar-
rated. As Hoggart knew well, it was the local, the concrete, and the
personal that made sense of working-class life, not the "mass of abstractions" they were told out to give their lives meaning.[107]

Several autobiographies feature stray relatives, family friends, or
acquaintances who preach the gospel of socialism and promise the
day when no one will hunger, but they are usually marginal figures or
local "characters."[108] An exception is Ifan Edwards's account of his
struggle to survive poverty between the wars, which culminates in a
tale of conversion and redemption: he swapped the *Daily Mail* for
Marx. "Hunger and wretchedness are excellent tutors," he wrote;
"they make the basic wrongness of things stand out clear and hard;
they drive the brain to think in a different, unaccustomed, and harsh
manner; they quicken the perception of sham and humbug and cant
and irrelevancy; they take the scales from the eyes and the rust from
the reasoning faculty, and the false gods are abashed in their presence."[109] Similarly, the labor movement changed Ernie Benson's understanding of a life of hunger. His aptly titled autobiography, *Starve
or Rebel,* recounts how, through the Communist Party and NUWM,
he absorbed the narrative of class struggle that gave meaning to his
experience of hunger. But generally politics are remarkably absent
from postwar autobiographies. When it did register, it was an object
of suspicion and ambivalence. Max Cohen was so "electrified" by the
great torrent of a hunger march flooding through the streets of London in 1932 that he joined it: "The tramp of thousands of feet seemed

to make the very road-way tremble and vibrate. The roar of shouted slogans crashed against the walls of the office buildings and thundered against the sky . . . We dispersed with optimism, sure of victory."[110] This was no epiphany for Cohen but a temporary moment of hope amid the otherwise hopeless toil of the unemployed. William Woodruff watched the men from Blackburn set off on this march—a "pilgrimage of grace," his communist mentor called it (fittingly, as some had fasted for a day so they could take Communion before they departed). They returned a month later, thinner and, another friend remarked, looking "licked": "For all the notice that was taken of 'em, they might as well have stayed home and marched round the park."[111]

The heroes of postwar autobiographies were not hunger marchers or leaders of the labor movement, but ordinary men and women who struggled daily to feed their hungry children. Rather than rehearse abstract debates about the causes of hunger and who was responsible for it, these texts dwell on the far-from-simple business of surviving it. Of course, tales of endurance and survival reflected the writer's gender: women tended to detail the struggle of everyday domestic life—of shopping, cooking, pawning, making do, and mending; men focused on the quest for or experience of work, only mentioning food when it is absent, or when descriptions of eating can be rendered heroically.[112] For men and women alike, the script of hunger was a dramatization of small heroic acts remembered: a child's crafty theft of a longed-for tasty morsel, the fooling of an inspector or philanthropist, or, above all, the sacrifices and ingenuity with which mothers made ends meet, in spite of their invariably hopeless, drunken, and violent husbands.[113] The story of *Angela's Ashes* has been told many times before.

Just as mothers stood on the front line of the struggle to put food on the table, they appear at the heart of most autobiographical accounts of hungry childhoods. In these texts, as in life, there is simply no escaping the heroism of mothers. Hoggart's elegy to his mother, and his characterization of the composite working-class mother, "devoted to the family and beyond proud self-regard," is particularly striking, even though he warns against rendering these women as heroic figures.[114] Those who followed were less careful, painting a seemingly idealized picture of their mothers' superhuman efforts in keeping the family show on the road. Characteristically, the adored mother takes on even more heroic and saintlike qualities because she either has to raise the children on her own or raise them while battling against at best a distant and detached husband or at worst a violent and alcoholic one.[115] So often in these accounts the father is the villain of the piece: it is he who is seen to have failed to bring home the bacon (and not always as a consequence of forces beyond his control); it is the father who eats first and best, while his hungry children look on;[116] it is he who is too proud to apply for relief.[117] Mothers, in contrast, always worked their fingers to the bone. It was they who made up for the family's inadequate income by any means possible. It was they who ingeniously made it last the week through the weekly set of "calculations" with the pawnshop and local shopkeepers, not to mention displayed a talent for preparing cheap but filling food. Even when mothers are portrayed less lovingly, their children always show a devoted respect for them, a recognition that the burden of the family's survival fell on them.[118] Both Nancy Sharman's and Pat O'Mara's mothers were frequently hospitalized when that burden became too overwhelming; others lived with persistent complaints for which the doctor was never called. Even when Grace Foakes's mother was finally certified as having tuberculosis and given a fortnight's supply of cod-liver oil and malt, "she very seldom took it and it was kept instead for us children."[119] This sacrificial maternal economy was most evident at the table, where mothers are always remembered as eating last, if at all. Jean Rennie's mother "kept us clean and tidy and well-fed . . . We didn't starve, although I can remember my mother saying often that she wasn't hungry. Mothers do say that."[120]

Next to the heroic labors and sacrifices of mothers, the ingenuity of hungry children is perhaps the most frequent theme. Petty theft was a common survival strategy, though it assumed a variety of forms and had different motives and outcomes.[121] Thefts ranged from stealing apples from orchards on a visit to the country to hit and runs at local shops; from well-orchestrated and repeated larceny to the spontaneous but later guilt-ridden snatch; and parental reactions to pilfering ranged from a warm welcome for the booty to a savage scolding when the spoils were discovered. Thieving was portrayed as not merely beyond reproach, but necessary. One example must suffice. Kathleen Dayus, with her brother and sister, had arrived late at school, where they missed her free breakfast. On their way home from school, fueled only by the bread and drippings they had had the night before and "very, very, very hungry," they gazed longingly at the "pig's pudding, hot meat pies, hocks, tripe and cake of every sort" on display in a shop window. With "saliva dripping down our chins," complaining that such food should not be "on show when [they were] so hungry," they decided to act: two of them looked out, while one of them stole a roll of pig's pudding and some meat pies. "I don't think I ever tasted anything like that meat pie. It was delicious."[122] If hunger gave children permission to write their own laws for survival, it also created opportunities for small acts of generosity between families, friends, and siblings. These small gestures of kindness, often among people for whom hunger was never far from the door, were invariably remembered as involving an element of sacrifice that marked a sense of solidarity and community that was subsequently lost.[123]

This solidarity stood in marked contrast to the cruelty and inhumanity of those who sat in judgment on these families and determined the level of welfare relief they could receive. Noticeably in the autobiographies, men who had to face the indignities doled out by officials at the Labour Exchange, the Public Assistance Committee, and the Courts of Referees never had a good word to say about them. "Their main concern," recalled Joe Loftus, "was to cut you down and pay out as little as possible, not even your entitlement, to keep you at arm's length by humiliation, by assuming you guilty of willful idleness before you even opened your mouth."[124] Such accounts are not abundant; indeed, the shameful indignities are part of the silent injuries of class that men, even though they felt emasculated in the process, had to endure for their families' sake—indignities that their families began to understand only when relief or means-test officers turned up at the door asking awkward questions and eyeing treasured heirlooms that could be sold. It was this rich seam of resentment and bitterness that the NUWM mined in demanding the right to welfare. Yet while these postwar autobiographies and testimonials mobilized the evidence of experience to evoke the hunger of the thirties, they did not necessarily legitimate the script of social democracy. Although they emphasized the material achievements of the postwar welfare state, a sense of the cultural loss incurred from the waning of the old community solidarity often offset them.

Nonetheless, the vast majority of these childhood recollections of the hungry thirties were produced after historians, following Ashton's lead, had attacked with determination what C. L. Mowat described as the "myth, sedulously propagated later, of the 'hungry thirties.'"[125] The experience of hunger had been central to Britain's liberal-left industrial, labor, and social historians steeped in Toynbee's pessimistic account of the industrial revolution. The nomenclature and focus may have changed, but the sentiment had not. As we saw in Chapter 1, ever since Toynbee, for historians engaged in the controversy over standard of living the battleground had been the eighteenth and nineteenth centuries. This point had been decisively confirmed in the debates of the 1950s and 1960s between the pessimistically inclined Anglo-Marxists like Edward Thompson and those, like Ashton, whom he characterized as optimistic and econometric-minded friends of capitalism.[126] As the idea of the hungry thirties became more established, however, that battleground moved to the social history of the interwar years, and particularly to the experience of plenty or want of the thirties. With remarkable speed, a revised and more optimistic account of the decade had achieved historiographical orthodoxy by the 1970s: the experience of unemployment and hunger was confined to localized pockets of deprivation; want was offset by plenty, as rising standards of living were reflected in improved nutrition and falling infant mortality rates; the decline of old staple industries was offset by the rise of new industries; the plight of working-class men was counterbalanced by the advances among women, who produced and consumed the goods of the new industries.[127]

It was no coincidence that the hungry thirties were demytholo-
gized at the very moment when the cracks in the postwar social democratic settlement had begun to show. During the 1970s, politicians
and intellectuals of the New Right gathering around Enoch Powell,
Keith Joseph, and Margaret Thatcher increasingly valorized the thirties as the last decade before a mixed economy, the welfare state, and
the retreat from empire had created a culture of dependency that
rendered self-reliance redundant for individuals and nationalized industries alike. While Norman Tebbit was minister of employment
in Mrs. Thatcher's first administration, the unemployment figures
reached levels similar to those of the thirties. In 1981 Tebbit made a
remark that became infamous, to the effect that when his father had
then been out of work, he had gotten on his bike and looked for
work; he had not demanded the right to welfare and become dependent upon the nanny state. In response, historians of the Left, determined that the "present phase of serious unemployment should not
be clouded by a false perspective with respect to its most immediate ancestor and obvious analogue," insisted that revisionist accounts
of the thirties depended uncritically on the claims of government
sources.[128] Historians were paying renewed attention to the politics of
unemployment during the 1930s and to the history of hunger marching. Stephen Constantine concluded his study the year before Tebbit's
speech by emphasizing, "[For] many people the memory of those
years remains close and bitter, and they resent the return to a high
rate of unemployment."[129] When the specter of Thatcherism had
finally apparently vanished, with the electoral victory of Blair's New
Labour Party in 1997 (a victory that briefly drew parallels with Labour's victory of 1945), historians again sought to retrieve memories
of the hungry thirties.[130] Remembering that harrowing decade still
remains central to the program of British social democracy.

Conclusion

As I was writing this book, friends and colleagues often asked me why I chose to end it in the 1940s, at the very time when all over the world hunger had become the primary concern and persistent problem of welfare states, colonial and postcolonial states preoccupied with development, and a host of transnational humanitarian organizations. The answer is implicit in the question itself; after the 1940s Britain's role in shaping the history of hunger became increasingly marginal. This is not to say that the British influence ceased to be important, or to subscribe to tired laments about the decline of Britain.[1] Of course, the achievements and failures of the British welfare state in its battle against hunger were not fully apparent until the 1960s. In that decade, social scientists rediscovered the persistent features of poverty, in part by redefining it in terms of relative deprivation rather than by Rowntree's absolute measure of a poverty line for minimum nutritional standards.[2] Similarly, despite the rapid pace of decolonization in the decades following the Second World War, Britain's policies of colonial development had ensured that former colonies remained closely tied to its economy even after independence. Similarly, British-based nongovernmental organizations neatly repackaged the old imperial conceits of the civilizing mission, by leading the now global war against hunger.[3] Thus, there was no magical moment after the 1940s when hunger vanished from Britain and its empire, or when Britons stopped thinking about the conquest of world hunger. In the wake of the Second World War, particularly with the failure of Orr's vision of the FAO, Britain lost its central place in the modern cultural history of hunger. This change, as we saw in Chapter 1, took place at the very moment when Britain's model of modernization was held to be exemplary.

It has been my contention that, far from being a timeless and un-changing condition, hunger, along with the meaning that people gave to it and therefore the systems used to govern it, underwent a series of dramatic transformations between the late eighteenth and the mid-twentieth centuries. Broadly speaking, although the classical political economy of Smith and Malthus had established hunger as an avoid-able, man-made phenomenon, rather than the curse of nature or providence, their view of hunger removed responsibility for its con-trol from the state. Their claim being that the market must be free to generate either plenty or want, neo-Malthusians soon came to blame the continuing presence of the famine on the laziness and moral weakness of the hungry. Thereafter, I have shown, hunger was one of the core dilemmas of British liberalism that helped determine where the boundaries would be drawn between the market and the state, the subject and the citizen, the individual and the collective, the nation and the empire.

These dilemmas deepened when the humanitarian discovery of hunger during the second half of the nineteenth century challenged the neo-Malthusian dismissal of the hungry as the authors of their own misery—a discovery that enabled hunger to become grounds for political critique and mobilization. In the wake of the New Poor Law and the Irish famine, journalists and social innovators developed new techniques to represent the innocent suffering of the hungry. By giv-ing it a human face, they ensured that hunger, both at home and abroad, became a focus of humanitarian concern before the Great War. Colonial nationalists in Ireland and India, together with suffra-gettes and unemployed protesters in Britain, mobilized this new-found sympathy for the hungry by turning hunger into a symbol of the failure of British liberalism and Britain's colonial states. Yet hunger remained a vague object for human sympathy or political outrage until, at the turn of the twentieth century, social investigators enlisted the new science of nutrition to offer a precise definition and measure the extent and social costs of hunger. A complex amalgam of human endeavor with scientific techniques and apparatuses—the statistical sample, the calorimeter, and the inquiry card in the hands of the trained researcher or interviewer—enabled social and nutritional scientists to establish that hunger was a pressing social problem and that, to counteract it, new forms of social welfare would be required. Social concerns had initially prompted punitive governmental intervention to reform the hungry. Humanitarians, political activists, and social and nutritional scientists subsequently fostered a more democratic social view of hunger, as the responsibility of society as a whole.

A final ironic twist to the story brings us almost full circle, to face our current predicament with the welfare state. The forms of welfare devised in response to the reinvention of hunger as a social problem were often adapted from the disciplinary methods of institutions like the workhouse, predicated on lessons in social efficiency and responsibility. During the first half of the twentieth century, the labor movement, especially unemployed workers, who were the most exposed to hunger, laid claimed to a less punitive view of welfare as a right, in ways that anticipated the creation of the welfare state after the Second World War.

When nutritionists redefined hunger as malnutrition after the First World War, it was no longer perceived as the problem of the poor alone but was instead reconceptualized as a nutritional challenge for all. From this perspective, the effort to curb hunger, no longer restricted to welfare, was ceded back to individual consumers, responsible for promoting their own nutritional health. If one takes into account the twisted logic of its formation, the welfare state was thus a precarious achievement that required a good deal of shoring up through reminders of how it had rescued its citizens from the misery and hardship of the hungry thirties that had preceded it. Until very recently, allusions to the hunger of the 1930s were almost as common a feature of social democratic Britain as parents' admonitions to their children to eat up their food or it would be sent to those starving in Africa.

This history of the changing ways in which hunger was understood and governed in modern imperial Britain makes it possible to reconsider the politics of social democracy and the welfare state in a number of ways.

First, following Foucault, I have highlighted the disciplinary roots of welfare regimes, which grew out of efforts at collective feeding first undertaken at such institutions as prisons and workhouses. The hunger strike was in part a rejection of the state's claim to care for those it sought to punish. Rather than present discipline and welfare as naturally opposed to each other, or indeed as developing sequentially, I have tried to show that they were mutually dependent on and constitutive of each other. Of course, as Foucault showed us, discipline and welfare were used to equip laboring subjects for life in the market economy. We might extend this thesis further, to recognize the importance of market mechanisms for the forms of welfare I have traced, specifically the discipline to make socially responsible choices—whether at the self-service canteen or in planning, purchasing, and preparing family dietaries. In emphasizing the hybrid forms of welfare, I have endeavored to demonstrate that liberalism and social democracy did not depend on historically separate forms of statecraft—any more, presumably, than our current neoliberalism does—but that each reworked and recombined elements of the other.

Second, the state was by no means always at the center of the various forms of welfare designed to secure the nutritional health and efficiency of society. Time and again we have seen how humanitarians, philanthropic groups, private employers, and local political parties mobilized a diverse set of experts from the social and nutritional sciences. Some of the tools at their disposition reached into the home: women's magazines, domestic science manuals, and menu planners,

as well as exhibitions of ideal homes and efficient kitchens. Govern-
mentalization of states of welfare, emphasizing standards of socially
responsible conduct, restructured everyday life around the family and
the figure of the housewife. Yet even when certain types of welfare—
like the collective feeding of workers and schoolchildren—began to
be sponsored by the state, they often remained dependent upon local
initiative and voluntary endeavor. Rather than simply a novel social
dispensation for the relief of hunger, collective feeding generated notions of solidarity and civility, of the good society in whose name it
operated. Figures like Orr and Le Gros Clark considered themselves
activists for defeating hunger on the technopolitical front. They, like
the many other technicians of social life who delivered meals to communities, in some ways produced a model of the social that did not
merely prefigure the postwar British welfare state but actively helped
create it.

Third, agency did not rest solely with technical experts like Orr
and Le Gros Clark. It also extended to material objects, from the inquiry cards of social investigators to the laboratories of nutritional
scientists to canteens to nutritional menu planners. The material production of the good society relied on means that were often partial,
uneven, or compromised, for conditions varied enormously from locality to locality. It is worth emphasizing how these materials had a
different historical rhythm: forms of expertise come and go, but the
material environments they help construct endure far longer. Perhaps
the unevenness and the disciplinary antecedents of welfare help explain the continuing ambivalence many felt toward distribution of relief. Social theorists may talk of the death of the social, yet we still inhabit its increasingly shabby infrastructure.

Fourth, it will be apparent that my account represents a significant
challenge to the powerful and enduring narrative of the labor movement's heroic struggle to achieve social democracy. Although it will
hardly mollify my critics, I want to emphasize that if I have paid less
attention to the contributions of those in political movements, it is
not from any desire to downplay them. The social may not have been
the product of political mobilization, but it did quickly become the

object of it. The initial orientation of radical and labor politics may have been backward, out of a wish to restore the lost rights of the commons, but from the late nineteenth century on, the Left began to look forward, and to transform the often punitive practices of welfare into social rights. It is fitting that my modern history of hunger ends by showing how effective was the claim to the welfare of life as the bare minimum of what makes us human and social.

Fifth and finally, from the outset it was clear that a history of hunger would require me to open up the relation between the provision of welfare in Britain and its broader colonial and transnational dimensions. In the colonial laboratories of South Asia and Africa British nutritionists discovered the deficiency diseases that redefined hunger as malnutrition at home. Many of these scientists subsequently were at the forefront of the war against hunger in Britain and played leading roles in international nutritional programs and transnational organizations like the Carnegie Corporation, the League of Nations, and the United Nations, as well as in the framing of the Britain's Colonial Development and Welfare Acts of the 1940s. The literature on colonial development and European welfare has treated them as discrete topics, yet historically their objectives were never separate. They were not merely historically contingent: they actively shaped and enabled each other. Contrary to what current apologists for liberal empire maintain, late British colonialism took distinctly welfarist forms. Yet its achievements were so partial that after independence the task was to make good on the colonial state's unfulfilled promise of welfare and development.

In this modern history of hunger, then, I have taken the opportunity to revisit what in the British context historians have long called the crisis of liberalism and the advent of social democracy and welfare state. I have endeavored to show that although hunger helped produce the crisis of liberalism, in both its domestic and imperial forms, it led not to the collapse of liberalism but to a reconfiguration in which liberal and social democratic forms of governing hunger coalesced. The result was a state that claimed the welfare of society, at home and abroad, as its primary objective. It is a history that appears to offer some hope politically. For too long we have accepted the self-legitimating claims of both social democrats and neoliberals that the welfare state was a totalizing, monolithic structure, when in fact it was never entirely either statist in form or welfarist in orientation. If we cannot historically separate forms of welfare from discipline or the market on the one hand, or the state from other forms of rule on the other, we can no longer ask simply whether we are for or against welfare, for or against the state. Instead, we might be able to imagine a new form of politics, whether local, national or global, that eschews systemic analysis for strategic interventions to ensure the democratic nature and the welfare of society.

Notes

Index

Notes

1. Hunger and the Making of the Modern World

1. See T. K. Rabb and R. I. Rotberg (eds.), *Hunger and History: The Impact of Changing Food Production and Consumption Patterns on Society* (Cambridge: Cambridge University Press, 1985); L. F. Newman (ed.), *Hunger in History: Food Shortage, Poverty and Deprivation* (Oxford: Blackwell, 1990); Sharman Apt Russell, *Hunger: An Unnatural History* (New York, Basic, 2005).

2. I write in the aftermath of the Make Poverty History campaign. See also Jeffrey Sachs, *The End of Poverty: Economic Possibilities of Our Time* (New York: Penguin, 2005).

3. On long-term environmental changes, see Emmanuel Le Roy Ladurie, *The*

Peasants of Languedoc (Urbana: University of Illinois Press, [1966] 1974); *Times of Feast, Times of Famine: A History of Climate since the Year 1000* (New York: Doubleday, [1967] 1971).

4. Thomas McKeown, *The Modern Rise of Population* (New York: Academic, 1976); Peter Laslett, *The World We Have Lost* (New York: Charles Scribner's Sons, [1965] 1984); E. A. Wrigley and R. S. Schofield, *The Population History of England, 1541–1871* (Oxford: Blackwell, 1981). The foundations for this "optimistic" reading of industrialization were laid by J. H. Clapham, *Economic History of Modern Britain,* 3 vols. (Cambridge: Cambridge University Press, 1926–1938), but it was consolidated after the war by T. S. Ashton, *The Industrial Revolution* (London: Oxford University Press, 1948); F. A. Hayek, *Capitalism and the Historians* (Chicago: University of Chicago Press, 1954); W. W. Rostow, *Stages of Economic Growth: A Non-Communist Manifesto* (Cambridge: Cambridge University Press, 1960); and R. M. Hartwell, *Industrial Revolution and Economic Growth* (London: Methuen, 1971). On hunger as a determinant of political mobilization and protest, see Max Beloff, *Public Order and Popular Disturbances, 1660–1714* (London: Oxford University Press, 1938); W. W. Rostow, *British Economy in the Nineteenth Century* (Oxford: Clarendon, 1948). On the genealogy of this critique, see D. C. Coleman, *Myth, History and the Industrial Revolution* (London: Hambledon, 1992), 1–43; Philip Connell, *Romanticism, Economics and the Question of "Culture"* (Oxford: Oxford University Press, 2001); Stedman Jones, *An End to Poverty? A Historical Debate* (London: Profile, 2004), chaps. 5 and 6.

5. Karl Polanyi, *The Great Transformation: The Political and Economic Origins of Our Time* (Boston: Beacon, [1957] 2001); E. P. Thompson, *The Making of the English Working Class* (London: Gollancz, 1963).

6. Although their studies were notably confined to preindustrial contexts of the Scottish highlands and the wartime conditions of the 1790s, see Roger Wells, *Wretched Faces: Famine in Wartime England, 1793–1801* (Gloucester: Sutton, 1988); and T. M. Devine, *The Great Highland Famine: Hunger, Emigration and the Scottish Highlands in the Nineteenth Century* (Edinburgh: Donald, 1988).

7. John Burnett, *Plenty and Want: A Social History of Diet in England from 1815 to the Present Day* (London: Nelson, 1966); D. Oddy and D. Miller (eds.), *The Making of the Modern British Diet* (London: Croom Helm 1976); Oddy and Miller (eds.), *Diet and Health in Modern Britain* (London: Croom Helm, 1985); Jay Winter, "Unemployment, Nutrition and Infant Mortality in Britain, 1920–1950," in Winter (ed.), *The Working Class in Modern British History* (Cambridge: Cambridge University Press, 1983); Charles Webster, "Hungry or Healthy Thirties?" *History Workshop Journal* 13 (1982), 110–129; R. Floud, K. Wachter, and A. Gregory, *Height, Health and History: Nutritional Status in the United Kingdom, 1750–1980* (Cambridge: Cambridge

University Press, 1990); Roger W. Fogel, *The Escape from Hunger and Premature Death, 1700–2100* (Cambridge: Cambridge University Press, 2004).

8. Mike Davis, *Late Victorian Holocausts: El Niño Famines and the Making of the Third World* (London: Verso, 2002); Manu Goswami, *The Production of India: From Colonial Economy to National Space* (Chicago: Chicago University Press, 2004), chap. 7.

9. Amartya Sen, *Poverty and Famines: An Essay on Entitlement and Deprivation* (Oxford: Clarendon, 1981); Sen, *Development as Freedom* (New York: Knopf, 1999). For a sustained critique of Sen's work, see Michael Watts, "Hour of Darkness: Vulnerability, Security and Globalization," *Geographica Helvetica* 57, no. 1 (2002): 5–18.

10. I draw here on a rich vein of interdisciplinary scholarship, much of it inspired by feminist histories of the body. Nancy Scheper-Hughes, *Death without Weeping: The Violence of Everyday Life in Brazil* (Berkeley: University of California Press, 1992); Susan Bordo, *Unbearable Weight: Feminism, Western Culture and the Body* (Berkeley: University of California Press, 1993); Maud Ellmann, *The Hunger Artists: Starving, Writing and Imprisonment* (Cambridge, Mass.: Harvard University Press, 1993); Joseph Alter, *Gandhi's Body: Sex, Diet, and the Politics of Nationalism* (Philadelphia: University of Pennsylvania Press, 2000).

11. For examples, see Keith Laybourn, *The Evolution of British Social Policy and the Welfare State, 1800–1993* (Keele, U.K.: Keele University Press, 1993). For more nuanced histories of Britain's mixed economy of welfare, see Pat Thane, *Foundations of the Welfare State* (London: Longman, 1996); Derek Fraser, *The Evolution of the British Welfare State: A History of Social Policy since the Industrial Revolution* (Houndmills, U.K.: Macmillan, 2003); Bernard Harris, *Origins of the British Welfare State: Society, State and Social Welfare in England and Wales, 1800–1945* (Houndmills, U.K.: Macmillan, 2004).

12. An insight gleaned from Arturo Escobar's *Encountering Development: The Making and Unmaking of the Third World* (Princeton, N.J.: Princeton University Press, 1995), chap. 4.

13. Piero Camporesi, *Bread of Dreams: Food and Fantasy in Early Modern Europe* (Chicago: Chicago University Press, 1989); Camporesi, *The Land of Hunger* (Cambridge: Polity, 1996).

14. Peter Laslett, "Did the Peasants Really Starve? Famine and Pestilence in Pre-Industrial Society," in *The World We Have Lost*, 113–134; John Walter, "The Social Economy of Dearth in Early Modern England" in J. Walter and R. Schofield (eds.), *Famine, Disease, and the Social Order in Early Modern Society* (Cambridge: Cambridge University Press, 1989).

15. E. P. Thompson, "The Moral Economy of the English Crowd in the Eighteenth Century," and "The Moral Economy Revisited," in *Customs in Common* (New York: New Press, 1991), 260–261. See also A. Randall and A. Charlesworth (eds.),

Moral Economy and Popular Protest: Crowds, Conflict and Authority (New York: St. Martin's, 2000).

16. Adam Smith, *An Inquiry into the Nature and Cause of the Wealth of Nations* (London: Methuen, [1776] 1904), bk. 4, chap. 5: 46, 78, http://www.econlib.org/LIBRARY/Smith/smWN15.html.

17. Rev. Thomas Malthus, *An Essay on the Principle of Population* (London: J. Johnson, 1798), chap. 7, http://socserv2.socsci.mcmaster.ca/~econ/ugcm/3ll3/malthus/popu.txt.

18. Joseph Townsend, *A Dissertation on the Poor Laws* (Berkeley: University of California Press, [1786] 1971), 27. "In general," Townsend wrote, "It is only hunger which can spur and goad them [the poor] on to labour . . . It is not only a peaceable, silent, unremitted pressure, but, as the most natural motive to industry and labour, it calls forth the most powerful exertions" (23–24). On the economic thought of the British Enlightenment, see Roy Porter, *The Creation of the Modern World: The Untold Story of the British Enlightenment* (New York: Norton, 2000); Joyce Appleby, *Economic Thought and Ideology in Seventeenth-Century England* (Princeton, N.J.: Princeton University Press, 1978).

19. Gertrude Himmelfarb, *The Idea of Poverty: England in the Early Industrial Age* (London: Faber and Faber, 1984); Boyd Hilton, *The Age of Atonement: The Influence of Evangelicalism on Social and Economic Thought, 1795–1865* (Oxford: Clarendon, 1988); Mitchell Dean, *The Constitution of Poverty: Toward a Genealogy of Liberal Governance* (London: Routledge, 1991).

20. Poor Law Commissioners, *Second Annual Report of the Poor Law Commissioners for England and Wales* (London: W. Clowes, 1836), 63.

21. The still-classic account is Nicholas Edsall, *The Anti–Poor Law Movement* (Manchester: Manchester University Press, 1971).

22. On the long history of the poor laws, see Lynn Lees Hollen, *The Solidarities of Strangers: The English Poor Laws and the People, 1700–1948* (Cambridge: Cambridge University Press, 1998); David Englander, *Poverty and Poor Law Reform in Britain: From Chadwick to Booth, 1834–1914* (London: Longman, 1998).

23. Polanyi, *The Great Transformation;* Hannah Arendt, *On Revolution* (London: Faber and Faber, 1963); Michel Foucault, "On Governmentality," *Ideology and Consciousness* 6 (Autumn 1979): 5–22. For a useful comparison, see Claire Edwards, "Cutting Off the King's Head: The 'Social' in Hannah Arendt and Michel Foucault," *Studies in Social and Political Thought* 1, no. 1 (June 1999): 3–20.

24. Agamben reformulates and dehistoricizes this process by arguing that from Aristotle onward, the structuring dialectic of citizenship was the relation between the granting of democratic liberties by the sovereign and the reinscription of disciplinary, biopolitical power over the body of the citizen. Giorgio Agamben, *Homo*

Sacer: Sovereign Power and Bare Life (Stanford, Calif.: Stanford University Press, 1998).

25. Mary Poovey, *Making a Social Body: British Cultural Formation* (Chicago: Chicago University Press, 1995).

26. It is a history suggestively if schematically sketched in Nikolas Rose, *Powers of Freedom: Reframing Political Thought* (Cambridge: Polity, 1999).

27. Jean Baudrillard, *In the Shadow of the Silent Majorities* (Cambridge, Mass.: MIT Press, 1983); Bruno Latour, *We Have Never Been Modern* (Cambridge, Mass.: Harvard University Press, 1993).

28. Anthony Giddens, *Modernity and Self-Identity: Self and Society in the Late Modern Age* (Cambridge: Polity, 1991); Zygmunt Bauman, *Liquid Modernities* (Cambridge: Polity, 2000). For useful discussions of these developments in social theory, see Patrick Joyce (ed.), *The Social in Question: New Bearings in History and the Social Sciences* (London: Routledge, 2002); Nicholas Gane (ed.), *The Future of Social Theory* (New York: Continuum, 2004).

29. For similar attempts in other European contexts, see Jacques Donzelot, *The Policing of Families* (New York: Pantheon, 1979); Paul Rabinow, *French Modern: Norms and Forms of the Social Environment* (Cambridge, Mass.: MIT Press, 1989); George Steinmetz, *Regulating the Social: The Welfare State and Local Politics in Imperial Germany* (Princeton, N.J.: Princeton University Press, 1993); David G. Horn, *Social Bodies: Science, Reproduction, and Italian Modernity* (Princeton, N.J.: Princeton University Press, 1994).

30. Here I draw on and extend the work of feminist scholars: Gisela Bock and Pat Thane (eds.), *Maternity and Gender Policies: Women and the Rise of the European Welfare States, 1880–1950* (London: Routledge, 1991); Susan Pedersen, *Family, Dependence and the Origins of the Welfare State: Britain and France, 1914–1945* (Cambridge: Cambridge University Press, 1993); and Gail Lewis, *"Race," Gender, Social Welfare: Encounters in a Post-Colonial Society* (Cambridge: Polity, 2000).

2. The Humanitarian Discovery of Hunger

1. *Oxford English Dictionary* (Oxford: Oxford University Press, 1989 2nd ed.), http://www.oed.com/; Raymond Williams, *Keywords: A Vocabulary of Culture and Society*, rev. ed. (New York: Oxford University Press, 1983), 150–151.

2. Thomas L. Haskell, "Capitalism and the Origins of the Humanitarian Sensibility," in Thomas Bender (ed.), *The Anti-Slavery Debate: Capitalism and Abolitionism as a Problem in Historical Interpretation* (Berkeley: University of California Press, 1992), 105–160; Thomas Laqueur, "Bodies, Details and the Humanitarian Narra-

tive," in Lynn Hunt (ed.), *The New Cultural History* (Berkeley: University of California Press, 1989), 176–204.

3. For two recent and challenging reflections on this theme, see Luc Boltanski, *Distant Suffering: Morality, Media and Politics* (New York: Cambridge University Press, 1999); Jenny Edkins, *Whose Hunger? Concepts of Famine, Practices of Aid* (Minneapolis: University of Minnesota Press, 2000).

4. Between 1837 and 1849 the *Times* reported fifty-eight such cases and published fourteen leading articles on the subject, even though, as we shall see in Chapter 4, the Poor Law commissioner and key architect of the act, Edwin Chadwick, ensured that the Registrar General's annual returns of births and deaths did not include the category of death by starvation.

5. Thomas Laqueur, "Bodies, Details and the Humanitarian Narrative," in Lynn Hunt (ed.), *The New Cultural History* (Berkeley: University of California Press, 1989), 176–204.

6. *Times,* 23 December 1846, 4; and 22 January 1844, 4; John Lhotsky, *On Cases of Death by Starvation and Extreme Distress among the Humbler Classes Considered as One of the Main Symptoms of the Present Disorganization of Society* (London: John Ollivier, 1844), 1–2; emphasis in the original. Lhotsky's text reproduced many of the *Times* reports of these individual deaths. *Times,* 20 November 1846, 4.

7. Charles Dickens's *Oliver Twist* was first published in 1837. *Times,* 19 November 1842, 4.

8. *Times,* 27 November 1846, 4; 29 December 1846, 4; and 4 January 1847, 4. "This is a most cruel addition to the catalogue of barbarous murders (for they are nothing less) which the New Poor Law has been the means of perpetrating." *Times,* 22 June 1842, 7.

9. Lhotsky, *On Cases of Death by Starvation,* 2.

10. Ian Anstruther, *The Scandal of Andover Workhouse* (London: Bles, 1973); Parliamentary Papers (1846), vol. 663–1, *Report of the Select Committee on Andover Union.*

11. The radical and Chartist press also highlighted, using many of the same techniques of representation, the inhumanity and barbarity of a system that produced these deaths from starvation. My claim is that the *Times* gave rise to a new and quite different humanitarian critique and humanitarian public.

12. Melissa Fegan, *Literature and the Irish Famine 1845–1919* (Oxford: Clarendon 2002), chap. 3; Margaret Kelleher, *The Feminization of Famine: Expressions of the Inexpressible?* (Durham, N.C.: Duke University Press, 1997), chap. 1; John Killen (ed.), *The Famine Decade: Contemporary Accounts, 1841–1851* (Belfast: Blackstaff, 1995); Steve Taylor, "Views of the Famine," at http://vassun.vassar.edu/~sttaylor/FAMINE/.

13. The classic account is W. O. Henderson, *The Lancashire Cotton Famine*

1861–1865 (New York: Augustus Kelley, [1934] 1969). W. L. Burn, *The Age of Equipoise: A Study of the Mid-Victorian Generation* (London: Allen and Unwin, 1964).

14. Many of these are extracted at length in John Watts, *The Facts of the Cotton Famine* (London: Simpkin and Marshall, 1866).

15. On the "New Journalism," see Jo Baylen, "The Press and Public Opinion: W. T. Stead and the 'New Journalism'" *Journalism Studies Review* 4 (July 1979); Joel Weiner, *Papers for the Millions: The New Journalism in Britain, 1850s–1914* (New York: Greenwood, 1988); Judith Walkowitz, *City of Dreadful Delight: Narratives of Sexual Danger in Late Victorian London* (Chicago: Chicago University Press, 1992), chap. 3; Laurel Brake, *Subjugated Knowledges: Journalism, Gender and Literature in the Nineteenth Century* (New York: New York University Press, 1994), chap. 5; Mark Hampton, *Visions of the Press in Britain, 1850–1950* (Urbana: University of Illinois Press, 2004).

16. In what follows I draw particularly from A. S. Krausse, *Starving London: The Story of a Three Weeks' Sojourn among the Destitute* (London: Remington, 1886) first serialized in the *London Globe;* Robert Sherard, *The White Slaves of England: Being True Pictures of Certain Social Conditions in the Kingdom of England in the Year 1897* (London: James Bowden, 1898), originally serialized in *Pearson's Magazine;* C. F. G. Masterman, *The Condition of England* (London: Methuen, [1909] 1960), much of which had been published by the *Nation,* the periodical he had founded in 1907 with a campaigning "new Liberal" brief.

17. Quoted in Walkowitz, *City of Dreadful Delight,* 29.

18. Afterward several leaders of the Social Democratic Federation were arrested and tried for conspiracy, but acquitted, and Joseph Chamberlain, as president of the Local Government Board, relaxed the conditions for the granting of outdoor relief in London. See Jose Harris, *Unemployment and Politics: A Study in English Social Policy, 1886–1914* (Oxford: Oxford University Press, 1972), 55–56.

19. *Daily Telegraph,* 30 December 1904, 12. Charles Booth, *Life and Labour of the People in London* (London: Macmillan, 1892–1897); the maps are now available online at http://booth.lse.ac.uk/.

20. Bart Kennedy, *The Hunger Line* (London: Werner Laurie, 1908), 117, 33–44, 59, 38. See also Krausse, *Starving London,* 34; Sherard, *White Slaves of England,* 114; Arnold White, *Efficiency and Empire* (Brighton: Harvester, [1901] 1973), 100; William Booth, *In Darkest England, and the Way Out* (London: Salvation Army, 1890), 18.

21. Richard Higgs, *The Heart of the Social Problem: Twelve Millions Starving; How Can They Be Fed?* (London: Stead's, 1913); Kennedy, *The Hunger Line,* 41. See also Rev. William Sirr, *Workless and Starving: Brief Considerations upon the Burning Questions of the Day* (Plaistow, U.K.: Church Press, 1906).

22. H. Llewelyn Smith and Vaughan Nash, *The Story of the Dockers' Strike* (London: Garland, [1889] 1984); H. W. Nevinson, *Neighbours of Ours* (Bristol: J. W.

Arrowsmith, 1895); *In the Valley of Trophet* (London: Dent, 1896). Angela John's *War, Journalism and the Shaping of the Twentieth Century: The Life and Times of Henry W. Nevinson* (London: Tauris, 2006) appeared too late to be consulted here.

23. For a discussion of the different roles of the "foreign" and the "special" correspondent, see Lucy Brown, *Victorian News and Newspapers* (Oxford: Oxford University Press, 1985), chap. 10. On Reuters, see Michael Palmer, "The British Press and International News, 1851–1899," in G. Boyce, J. Curran, and P. Wingate (eds.), *Newspaper History from the Seventeenth Century to the Present Day* (London: Constable, 1978), 205–219; and Donald Read, *The Power of News: The History of Reuters* (Oxford: Oxford University Press, 1999).

24. H. W. Nevinson, *Scenes in the 30 Days War between Greece and Turkey, 1897* (London: Dent, 1898); Nevinson, *Ladysmith: The Diary of a Siege* (London: Methuen, 1900); Nevinson, *A Modern Slavery: Narrative of a Journey in West Central Africa (Angola) and the Portuguese Islands of San Thome and Principe during 1904–5 to Investigate Slavery and the Slave Trade* (London: Harper and Brothers, 1906); Nevinson, *The Dawn in Russia, or Scenes in the Russian Revolution* (London: Harper and Brothers, 1906); Nevinson, *The New Spirit in India* (London: Harper and Brothers, 1908). The armistice was another subject on which Nevinson echoed Brailsford. See Henry Brailsford, *Across the Blockade* (London: Allen and Unwin, 1919); and Brailsford, *After the Peace* (London: Leonard Parsons, 1920). For Nevinson's own glamorized version of his life, see Nevinson, *Changes and Chances* (London: Nisbet, 1923); Nevinson, *More Changes, More Chances* (London: Nisbet, 1925); and Nevinson, *Last Changes, Last Chances* (London: Nisbet, 1928).

25. C. A. Bayly, *Empire and Information: Intelligence Gathering and Social Communication in India, 1780–1870* (Cambridge: Cambridge University Press, 1999); Tim Pratt, "Ernest Jones' Mutiny: The People's Paper, English Popular Politics and the Indian Rebellion 1857–58," in Chandrika Kaul (ed.), *Media and the British Empire* (Basingstoke, Eng.: Palgrave, 2006), 88–103; Ernest Jones, "English Popular Politics and India, 1857–1858" (M.A thesis, Manchester, 1999).

26. Paula Krebs, *Gender, Race, and the Writing of Empire: Public Discourse and the Boer War* (New York: Cambridge University Press, 1999), 38–39.

27. Krause, *Starving London,* iii.

28. Sherard's *White Slaves of England* entailed two months research within six manufacturing centers across the North and Midlands. Note how both tried to make their subjects "speak for themselves" by quoting directly from reported conversations. Krause, *Starving London,* i, iii.

29. Vaughan Nash, *The Great Famine and Its Causes* (London: Longmans, Green, 1900), v, 85–86. See also the harrowing reports of the *Englishman's* correspondent, quoted in William Hare, *Famine in India: Its Causes and Effects* (London: King & Son, 1901), v.

30. See Rev. J. E. Scott, *In Famine Land: Observations and Experiences in India during the Great Drought of 1899–1900* (London: Harper and Brothers, 1904), x–xi. On the wider role of missionaries in bringing news of the empire back home to Britain, see Susan Thorne, *Congregational Missions and the Making of an Imperial Culture in Nineteenth-Century England* (Stanford, Calif.: Stanford University Press, 1999); Kevin Grant, "Christian Critics of Empire: Missionaries, Lantern Lectures and the Congo Reform Campaigns in Britain," *Journal of Imperial and Commonwealth History* 29 (2001): 27–58.

31. Masterman, *The Condition of England*, 1.

32. Krausse, *Starving London*, 50–51.

33. Kennedy, *The Hunger Line*, 61–63. "Be in want yourself," he warned his readers, "and apply to them, and all that you will get will be insult and a detective skill in the way of prying into your private affairs." See also Krausse, *Starving London*, 19–20.

34. Nevinson, *More Changes, More Chances*, 251.

35. Nash was explicit in regularly imploring his readers to dig deep into their pockets and resist what we now know as "compassion fatigue." See, for instance, his plea for Indian famine relief in May 1900, when humanitarian generosity had been overtaken by patriotism and events in South Africa; the Mansion House Famine Relief Fund raised just 7 percent of a parallel Lord Mayor's War Fund. Nash, *The Great Famine and Its Causes*, 186–187; Mike Davis, *Late Victorian Holocausts: El Niño Famines and the Making of the Third World* (London: Verso, 2002), 164.

36. Krausse, *Starving London*, 142, 46. Such was Krausse's identification with his readers that, he said, it "caused me in all my explorations to imagine their presence" (76); accordingly, he continually slipped from "I" to "we" in his reports.

37. Krausse's initial strategy was to publish the names and addresses of the families on whose plight he had reported, so that readers could visit them and validate his account with their own eyes. He abandoned this method when the families found themselves deluged by philanthropic donations. Ibid., 45–46, 75. For a stinging critique of the haphazard nature of newspaper relief funds, see Sirr, *Workless and Starving*, 13.

38. Statistics and maps, though effective in demonstrating the scale of the problem, tended to dehumanize hunger and suggest that it happened not to individuals but to territories or abstract populations. On the inadequacy of statistics in representing human catastrophe of famine, see Nevinson, *New Spirit of India*, 144; and F. H. S. Merewether, *A Tour through the Famine Districts of India* (London: A. D. Innes, 1898), vii.

39. Kennedy, *The Hunger Line*, 4.

40. Krausse, *Starving London*, 70–71.

41. Quoted in Davis, *Late Victorian Holocausts*, 157.

42. Krebs, *Gender, Race, and the Writing of Empire*, 62.

43. Kennedy, *The Hunger Line*, 110, 112, 27–29. For a less racialized defense of the unemployed man, see Sirr, *Workless and Starving*, 5.

44. Kennedy, *The Hunger Line*, 38, 20–21.

45. Jennifer Green-Lewis, *Framing the Victorians: Photography and the Culture of Realism* (Ithaca, N.Y.: Cornell University Press, 1996).

46. Davis, *Late Victorian Holocausts*, 147–148.

47. Grant, "Christian Critics of Empire," 28.

48. Judith Walkowitz, "The Indian Woman, the Flower Girl, and the Jew: Photojournalism in Edwardian London," *Victorian Studies* 42, no. 1 (1998–99): 3–46; Seth Koven, "Dr Barnado's 'Artistic Fictions': Photography, Sexuality and the Ragged Child in Victorian London," *Radical History Review* 69 (Fall 1997): 6–45; John Taylor, *A Dream of England: Landscape, Photography and the Tourist's Imagination* (Manchester: Manchester University Press, 1994); John Tagg, *The Burden of Representation: Essays on Photographies and Histories* (Amherst: University of Massachusetts Press, 1988).

49. Famine photography is a surprising absence in the literature. See Clark Worswick and Ainslee Embree, *The Last Empire: Photography in British India, 1855–1911* (New York: Aperture, 1976); and Judith Mara Gutman, *Through Indian Eyes* (New York: Oxford University Press, 1982); *Shifting Focus: Photography in India, 1850–1900* (London: British Library, 1995).

50. James Ryan, *Picturing Empire: Photography and the Visualization of the British Empire* (Chicago: University of Chicago Press, 1997), 184.

51. J. D. Rees, *Famine Facts and Fallacies* (London: Harrison and Sons, 1901), 10.

52. H. O. Arnold-Foster (ed.), *The Queen's Empire: A Pictorial and Descriptive Record* (London, 1897), x, cited in Ryan, *Picturing Empire*, 184.

53. Sir John Halford Mackinder, *India: Eight Lectures* (London: George Philip & Son, 1910).

54. Merewether, *A Tour through the Famine Districts*, viii.

55. Nash, *The Great Famine and Its Causes*, 85.

56. Scott, *In Famine Land*, x–xi.

57. "The smell of burning bodies kept me awake a greater part of last night, and even as I write, one of my workers calls out that a man is dying under the hedge of the compound . . . Whichever way we turn we discover these ghastly corpses, twisted and bloated, in almost every position which agony can produce. Cart-load after cart-load arrives at the poor-house . . . During the last few days a thousand bodies have been picked up." Ibid., 36.

58. Ibid., 196. Although famine photos allowed the reader to inhabit a position

as eyewitness momentarily, the way they were framed within a broader narrative reaffirmed the expertise of the narrator.

3. Hunger as Political Critique

1. Jeffrey Auerbach, *The Great Exhibition: A Nation on Display* (New Haven, Conn.: Yale University Press, 1999). On the debate surrounding the demographics of the Irish famine, see Cormac O'Grada, *Black '47 and Beyond: The Great Irish Famine in History, Economy, and Memory* (Princeton, N.J.: Princeton University Press, 1999). Precise figures may be less important than the role that famine played in the Irish nationalist imaginary; indeed, when deaths are measured in millions, precision seems an overrated virtue.

2. In fact, Malthus's position on Ireland was considerably more complex. See Thomas Malthus, "Newenham and Others on the State of Ireland," *Edinburgh Review* 24 (July 1808), illuminatingly discussed in David Lloyd, "The Political Economy of the Potato," in *Ireland's Orifice* (forthcoming).

3. Sir Charles Trevelyan, "The Irish Crisis," *Edinburgh Review* (January 1848): 320. Trevelyan had made his name reforming India's trade duties, education, and civil service. For a different revisionist account, see Robin Haines, *Charles Trevelyan and the Great Irish Famine* (Dublin: Four Courts, 2004).

4. A. J. P. Taylor, "Genocide," in *From Napoleon to the Second International: Essays on Nineteenth-Century England* (London: Hamilton, 1993), 153. See Gareth Stedman Jones, *An End to Poverty? A Historical Debate* (London: Profile, 2004); and Boyd Hilton, *The Age of Atonement: The Influence of Evangelicalism on Social and Economic Thought, 1795–1865* (Oxford: Oxford University Press, 1988).

5. Mike Davis, *Late Victorian Holocausts: El Niño Famines and the Making of the Third World* (New York: Verso, 2001).

6. Ranajit Guha, "The Prose of Counter-Insurgency," *Subaltern Studies,* vol. 2 (New Delhi: Oxford University Press, 1983).

7. Giorgio Agamben, *Homo Sacer: Sovereign Power and Bare Life* (Stanford, Calif.: Stanford University Press, 1998).

8. William Woodruff, *The Road to Nab End: An Extraordinary Northern Childhood* (London: Abacus, 2003), 236. This was an adage that encapsulated the differing responses to the sesquicentennial commemoration of the famine on either side of the Irish Sea. It was big business in Ireland, where a welter of new museums, television and radio shows, books, and Web sites were produced, but it hardly registered in Britain, except among those who stridently insisted there should be no formal retroactive apology by the British government. Roy Foster, *Irish Story: Telling Tales and Making It Up in Ireland* (New York: Allen Lane, 2001).

9. John Mitchel, *The Last Conquest of Ireland (Perhaps)* (Glasgow: Cameron, Ferguson, n.d.), 8. Published in 1860, the book drew heavily on his earlier work in *United Irishmen,* as well as other nationalist analyses during the famine itself, but nonetheless assumed an iconic status that helped it shape memories of the famine. Graham Davis, "Making History: John Mitchel and the Great Famine," in P. Hyland and N. Sammels (eds.), *Irish Writing: Exile and Subversion* (New York: St. Martin's, 1991); James Donnelly, "The Construction of the Memory of the Famine in Ireland and the Irish Diaspora, 1850–1900," *Eire-Ireland* 31, nos. 1–2 (1996): 26–61.

10. Mitchel, *The Last Conquest of Ireland (Perhaps),* 219.

11. John Mitchel (ed.), *Irish Political Economy* (Dublin: Irish Confederation, 1847), iv. See also Isaac Butt, *A Voice for Ireland: The Famine in the Land* (Dublin: James McGlashan, 1847). I draw heavily here on Thomas A. Boylan and Timothy P. Foley, *Political Economy and Colonial Ireland: The Propagation and Ideological Function of Economic Discourse in the Nineteenth Century* (London: Routledge, 1992), esp. chap. 6. For a broader analysis of how literary critiques of the famine produced an emphasis on the national particularities of Ireland and its economy, see Gordon Bigelow, *Fiction, Famine, and the Rise of Economics in Victorian Britain and Ireland* (Cambridge: Cambridge University Press, 2003), chap. 4.

12. See the work of one of its founders, the professor of political economy at Queen's College Belfast, William Hancock, *Three Lectures on the Question: Should the Principles of Political Economy Be Disregarded at the Present Crisis?* (Dublin: Hodges and Smith, 1847).

13. Boylan and Foley, *Political Economy and Colonial Ireland,* 135–137. R. D. Collinson Black, *Economic Thought and the Irish Question, 1817–1870* (Cambridge: Cambridge University Press, 1960). By 1855 the Dublin Statistical Society had become the Statistical and Social Inquiry Society of Ireland, the first organization dedicated to social science in the British Empire. There is no reference to it in Lawrence Goldman, *Science, Reform, and Politics in Victorian Britain: The Social Science Association 1857–1886* (Cambridge: Cambridge University Press, 2002).

14. This historicist reading was encapsulated in the multivolume work *The Ancient Laws and Institutes of Ireland: "The Brehon Law"* (Dublin: A. Thom, 1865–1901), the first two volumes of which were edited and introduced by William Hancock. There are obvious parallels with Henry Maine's work on India—see his *Ancient Law: Its Connection with the Early History of Society and Its Relation to Modern Ideas* (London: John Murray, 1861)—a connection explored by Clive Dewey, "The Rehabilitation of the Peasant Proprietor in Nineteenth-Century Economic Thought," *History of Political Economy* 6, no. 1 (1974): 17–47. See also S. B. Cook, *Imperial Affinities: Nineteenth Century Analogies and Exchanges between India and Ireland* (New Delhi: Sage, 1993), chap. 3.

15. On List and the national economists' critique of classical political econ-

omy, see Roman Szporluk, *Communism and Nationalism: Karl Marx versus Friedrich List* (Oxford: Oxford University Press, 1988); Bernard Semmel, *The Rise of Free Trade Imperialism: Classical Political Economy, the Empire of Free Trade and Imperialism, 1750–1850* (Cambridge: Cambridge University Press, 1970), chap. 8; and G. M. Koot, "T. E. Cliffe Leslie: Irish Social Reform and the Origins of the English Historical School of Economics," *History of Political Economy* 7, no. 3 (1975): 312–336.

16. Arnold Toynbee, *Lectures on the Industrial Revolution of the Eighteenth Century in England* (London: Longmans, Green [1884] 1894); Alon Kadish, *The Oxford Economists in the Late Nineteenth Century* (Oxford: Clarendon, 1982).

17. For the way in which this privileging of the political and the cultural has been reproduced by historians of Irish nationalism, see Stephen Howe, *Ireland and Empire: Colonial Legacies in Irish History and Culture* (Oxford: Oxford University Press, 2002), 61–62.

18. George O'Brien, *The Economic History of Ireland from the Union to the Famine* (London: Longmans, 1921), 585.

19. Chris Morash, *Writing the Irish Famine* (Oxford: Clarendon, 1995); Melissa Fegan, *Literature and the Irish Famine, 1845–1919* (Oxford: Clarendon, 2002).

20. Andrew Merry, *The Hunger: Being Realities of the Famine Years in Ireland, 1845 to 1848* (London: Andrew Melrose, 1910), 2–3.

21. Roger J. McHugh, "The Famine in Irish Oral Tradition," in R. D. Edwards and T. D. Williams (eds.), *The Great Famine: Studies in Irish History, 1845–52* (New York: New York University Press 1957); Cathal Poirteir, "Folk Memory and the Famine," in Poirteir (ed.), *The Great Irish Famine* (Dublin: Dufour, 1995): 219–231.

22. Louis J. Walsh, *The Next Time: The Story of 'Forty-Eight* (Dublin: Gill and Son, 1919). On the Catholicized nationalist ethic of sacrifice and martyrdom, see the Kevin Toolis, *Rebel Hearts: Journeys within the IRA's Soul* (London: Picador, 1995), 339.

23. The forgetting of the famine in Protestant Ulster is part of the story yet to be told. Between 1841 and 1851 Ulster's population fell by a recorded 374,493. Howe, *Ireland and Empire,* 39. On the historiography of famine and its tortuous politics and silences, see Patrick O'Farrell, "Whose Reality? The Irish Famine in History and Literature," *Irish Historical Studies* 20 (1982): 1–13; Niall O'Ciossain, "Was There 'Silence' about the Famine?" *Irish Studies Review* 13 (1995–96): 7–10.

24. Eric Stokes, *The English Utilitarians and India* (Oxford: Clarendon, 1959).

25. Bipan Chandra, *The Rise and Growth of Economic Nationalism in India 1880–1905* (New Delhi: People's, 1966), chap. 1; S. Ambirajan, *Classical Political Economy and British Policy in India* (New York: Cambridge University Press, 1978), chap. 3; Davis, *Late Victorian Holocausts,* chaps. 1 and 5.

26. Gyan Prakash, *Another Reason: Science and the Imagination of Modern India* (Princeton, N.J.: Princeton University Press, 1999); Nicholas Dirks, *Colonialism*

and the Making of Modern India (Princeton, N.J.: Princeton University Press, 2001); Manu Goswami, *Producing India: From Colonial Economy to National Space* (Chicago: University of Chicago Press, 2004). For the less well-developed Irish parallel, see Patrick Carroll-Burke, "Science, Power, Bodies: The Mobilization of Nature as State Formation," *Journal of Historical Sociology* 9, no. 2 (1996): 139–167; "Material Designs: Engineering Cultures and Engineering States—Ireland, 1650–1900," *Theory and Society* 31 (2002): 75–114. See also James C. Scott, *Seeing Like a State: How Certain Schemes to Improve the Human Condition Have Failed* (New Haven, Conn.: Yale University Press, 1999).

27. In a voluminous literature, see especially Hari Shanker Srivastava, *The History of Indian Famines and the Development of Indian Famine Policy, 1858–1918* (Agra: Sri Ram Mehra, 1968); Navtej Singh, *Starvation and Colonialism: A Study of Famines in the Nineteenth Century British Punjab, 1858–1901* (Delhi: National Book Organisation, 1996); and N. Neelakanteswara Rao, *Famines and Relief Administration: A Case Study of Coastal Andhra, 1858–1901* (New Delhi: Radha, 1997).

28. See Robert Wallace, *Lecture on Famine in India* (Edinburgh: Oliver and Boyd, 1900); J. D. Rees, *Famine Facts and Fallacies* (London: Harrison and Sons, 1901); *Report of the Indian Famine Commission, 1901,* Parliamentary Papers (London: His Majesty's Stationery Office [HMSO], 1901); and A. Loveday, *The History and Economics of Indian Famines* (London: G. Bell and Sons, 1914).

29. John McLane, *Indian Nationalism and the Early Congress* (Princeton, N.J.: Princeton University Press, 1977).

30. The classic account is Chandra's *Rise and Growth of Economic Nationalism.* Several of these figures had direct personal experience of famine. It would be worthwhile to study the formative effect of famine on India's political class. For some examples, see Meera Kosambi (ed.), *Pandita Ramabai through Her Own Words: Selected Works* (New York: Oxford University Press, 2000), 247–260; Panchanan Saha, *Shapurji Saklatvala: A Short Biography* (Delhi: People's, 1970). My thanks go to Praachi Deshpande and Manu Goswami for these citations.

31. Quoted in Chandra, *Rise and Growth of Economic Nationalism,* 27.

32. Rustom Mansani, *Dadabhai Naoroji: The Grand Old Man of India* (London: Allen and Unwin, 1939); Munni Rawal, *Dadabhai Naoroji: A Prophet of Indian Nationalism, 1855–1900* (New Delhi: Anmol, 1989).

33. Goswami, *Producing India,* 225–231. A similar debate surrounded the statistical recording of deaths by starvation. As famine-relief schemes increased during the 1880s, so too did the determination of colonial officials to prove their worth by avoiding the recording of famine mortalities as death by starvation.

34. Dadabhai Naoroji, *Poverty and Un-British Rule in India* (Delhi: Government of India, [1901] 1969), 212, 126. On Naoroji's drain theory, see Birendranath

Ganguli, *Dadabhai Naoroji and the Drain Theory* (New York: Asia Publishing House, 1965); Chandra, *Rise and Growth of Economic Nationalism.*

35. Romesh C. Dutt, *Famines and Land Assessments in India* (London: Paul, Trench and Tubner, 1900), 1; William Digby, *"Prosperous"British India: Revelation from Official Records* (London: Fisher Unwin, 1901), 17.

36. Dutt, *Famines and Land Assessments in India,* 16; Dutt, *The Economic History of India,* vol. 1, *Under Early British Rule* (Delhi, [1901] 1960), xxiii.

37. See, for example, Naoroji, *Poverty and Un-British Rule in India,* 628.

38. H. M. Hyndman, *The Ruin of India by British Rule* (London: Twentieth Century, 1907), 13.

39. On the "drain," see Amy Moore, *Hunger and Deadlock in India* (London: Socialist Commentary, 1943); K. Santhanam, *The Cry of Distress: A First-Hand Description and an Objective Study of the Indian Famine of 1943* (New Delhi: Hindustan Times, 1944); Freda Bedi, *Bengal Lamenting* (Lahore: Lion, 1944); K. C. Ghosh, *Famines in Bengal, 1770–1943* (Calcutta: India Associated, 1944). Digby's dedication in *"Prosperous"British India* was reproduced in Santosh Kumar Chaterjee, *The Starving Millions* (Calcutta: Asoka Library, 1944), iii, as well as in Vicky's *Nine Drawings by Vicky* (London: Modern Literature, 1944), 12.

40. On British constitutionalism, see James Vernon (ed.), *Rereading the Constitution: New Narratives in the Political History of England's Long Nineteenth Century* (Cambridge: Cambridge University Press, 1996); James Epstein, "Constitutionalist Idiom," in *Radical Expression: Political Language, Ritual and Symbol in England, 1790–1850* (New York: Oxford University Press, 1994). Nicholas Dirks has recently suggested that the origins of the nationalist critique of the drain lay in Edmund Burke's attack on the corruption of East India Company officials like Warren Hastings. Nicholas B. Dirks, *The Scandal of Empire: India and the Creation of Imperial Britain* (Cambridge, Mass.: Harvard University Press, 2006), chap. 4.

41. Naoroji, *Poverty and Un-British Rule in India,* 630–631.

42. As such, it was designed to appeal to the Manchester School free traders for whom empire was both economically and morally wrong. Donald Winch, *Classical Political Economy and Colonies* (Cambridge, Mass.: Harvard University Press, 1965); Semmel, *The Rise of Free Trade Imperialism;* John Cunningham Wood, *British Economists and the Empire* (London: Croom Helm, 1983).

43. William Digby, *The Famine Campaign in Southern India, 1876–1878* (London: Longmans, Green, 1878); H. J. Hyndman, *The Indian Famine and the Crisis in India* (London, 1877).

44. Mary Cumpston, "Some Early Indian Nationalists and Their Allies in the British Parliament, 1851–1906," *English Historical Review* 76 (1961): 279–297. Davis, *Late Victorian Holocausts,* 54–59.

45. A position that Digby shared. See his *"Prosperous"British India,* 136–137.

46. Naoroji was defeated in his first election as Liberal candidate in Holborn in 1886, when Lord Salisbury infamously declared: "I doubt if we have yet got to that point of view where a British constituency would elect a black man." Mansani, *Dadabhai Naoroji,* 263–266; Antoinette Burton, "Tongues Untied: Lord Salisbury's 'Black Man' and the Boundaries of Imperial Democracy," *Comparative Studies in Society and History* 43, no. 2 (2000): 632–659. On the networks of Indian nationalists and their supporters in London, see Jonathan Schneer, *London 1900: The Imperial Metropolis* (New Haven, Conn.: Yale University Press, 1999), chap. 8.

47. On Digby, see his *"Prosperous"British India,* 18; and Naoroji, *Poverty and Un-British Rule in India,* 624. On the varied tropes of gentlemanly leadership in Victorian Britain, see John Belchem and James Epstein, "The Nineteenth-Century Gentleman Leader Revisited," *Social History* 22 (1997): 173–192.

48. Dutt, *Famines and Land Assessments in India;* Dutt, *The Economic History of India,* 2 vols. (New Delhi: Ministry of Information, [1902] 1970); J. N. Gupta, *Life and Work of Romesh Chundra Dutt* (London: Dent, 1911).

49. Goswami, *Producing India,* chap. 7.

50. Ranade, "Indian Political Economy," in Chandra (ed.), *Ranade's Economic Writings,* 336–338; Chandra, *The Rise and Growth of Economic Nationalism in India,* chap. 14.

51. Remarkably, the only accounts we have of these early hunger marches are John Gorman, *To Build Jerusalem: A Photographic Remembrance of British Working Class Life, 1875–1950* (London: Scorpion, 1980) and Jess Jenkin's recent and excellent *Leicester's Unemployed March to London, 1905,* occasional papers no. 2 (Leicester: Friends of the Record Office for Leicestershire, 2005).

52. *Manchester Guardian,* 15 May 1905, 8; and 17 May 1905, 4.

53. Ibid., 9 June 1905, 7.

54. Ibid., 22 May 1905, 4; and 5 June 1905, 8.

55. Ibid., 6 July 1908, 6. On farm colonies for the unemployed, see Gareth Stedman Jones, *Outcast London: A Study in the Relations between Classes in Victorian Society* (Oxford: Clarendon, 1971).

56. *Manchester Guardian,* 14 July 1908, 14.

57. Gorman, *To Build Jerusalem,* 75.

58. Captain Gibbon, also formerly Professor Valdo of Sanger's Circus, led a march of ten delegates from Liverpool's Right to Work Committee in protest against the Unemployed Workmen's Act. Gibbon gave circus escapology performances to raise money along the way. One hundred and fifty marchers arrived in London but were met with stony silence by London's trade and labor organizations. *Manchester Guardian,* 18 January 1906, 14; 29 January 1906, 11; and 9 February 1906, 8.

59. Ibid., 22 January 1908, 4; 23 January 1908, 3; 24 January 1908, 7; 25 January, 1908, 10; 27 January 1908, 7; 28 January 1908, 14; 30 January 1908, 10; and 1 February 1908, 10.

60. *Manchester Guardian,* 30 January 1908, 10. "They had to march thirty-two miles the previous day on a piece of dry bread and were without money to buy tobacco or writing paper." Ibid., 29 January 1909, 5.

61. See, for example, ibid., 24 January 1908, 7.

62. "The Chat Moss Colony," *Manchester City News,* 2 August 1907.

63. *Manchester Guardian,* 19 May 1905, 8.

64. Gorman, *To Build Jerusalem,* 77.

65. James Vernon, *Politics and the People: A Study in English Political Culture, 1815–1867* (Cambridge: Cambridge University Press, 1993), chap. 8.

66. *Manchester Guardian,* 20 January 1908, 12; "Unemployed March to London," *Manchester City News,* 25 January 1908.

67. *Manchester Guardian,* 30 January 1908, 10.

68. Ibid., 13 June 1905, 10. On Labour churches, see Mark Bevir, "The Labour Church Movement, 1891–1902," *Journal of British Studies* 38 (1999): 217–245.

69. *Manchester Guardian,* 26 December 1907, 7; and 28 December 1907, 6. Six months earlier he had been sacked as manager of the experimental Chat Moss Farm Colony by Manchester's Distress Committee.

70. Ibid., 6 July 1908, 6.

71. Gorman, *To Build Jerusalem,* 81.

72. On the hunger strike as a transnational phenomenon, see Kevin Grant, "Hunger Strikes and Fasts in Britain and the Empire, c. 1909–1935," in D. Ghosh and D. Kennedy (eds.), *Decentering Empire: Imperial Structures and Globalization in the Era of Globalization* (Delhi: Longman Orient, 2006). Similar territory is covered less convincingly in Sharman Apt Russell, *Hunger: An Unnatural History* (New York: Basic, 2005).

73. For the most influential accounts, see Lisa Tickner, *The Spectacle of Women: Imagery of the Suffrage Campaign, 1907–1914* (London: Chatto and Windus, 1987); Maud Ellmann, *The Hunger Artists: Starving, Writing, and Imprisonment* (Cambridge, Mass.: Harvard University Press, 1993); Caroline Howlett, "Writing on the Body? Representation and Resistance in British Suffragette Accounts of Forcible Feeding," *Genders* 23 (1996): 3–41; and Barbara Green, *Spectacular Confessions: Autobiography, Performative Activism, and the Sites of Suffrage, 1905–1938* (New York: St. Martin's, 1997). I have also benefited from the doctoral work of Don Weitzman at Berkeley and JuNelle Harris at Harvard.

74. See, for examples, *Votes for Women,* 16 July 1909, 933; 23 July 1909, 981; and 30 July 1909, 1014.

75. Grant, "Hunger Strikes and Fasts in Britain and the Empire, c. 1909–1935."

76. For characteristic accounts, see *Votes for Women,* 20 October 1909, 67; or 3 December 1909, 154.

77. On the calculus of pain, the tabulation of days without food or water, the number or weeks of forced feedings, the charting of lost weight, see Green, *Spectacular Confessions,* 96–97. Olive Wharry held the longest hunger strike, of thirty-one days, without being force fed; see Sylvia Pankhurst, *The Suffragette Movement: An Intimate Account of Persons and Ideals* (London: Virago, [1931] 1977), 441.

78. George Sweeney, "Irish Hunger-Strikes and the Cult of Self-Sacrifice," *Journal of Contemporary History* 28 (1993): 424; Rosemary Cullen Owen, *Smashing Times: A History of the Irish Women's Suffrage Movement, 1883–1922* (Dublin: Attic, 1984), 63; D. Norman, *Terrible Beauty: A Life of Constance Markievicz* (London: Hodder and Stoughton, 1987); James S. J. Healy, "Suffragette Hunger Strikes, 1909–1914," *Horizons* 16 (Summer 1982): 65–76.

79. Quotations from Owen, *Smashing Times,* 63; and Ellmann, *The Hunger Artists,* 12.

80. A point well made in "Suffraging in the Streets," in Don Weitzman, *The Politics of Suffrage: A Comparison of the Chartist and Women's Suffrage Movements in Britain* (Berkeley: University of California, forthcoming). See also Sandra Stanley Holton, "Manliness and Militancy: The Protest of Male Suffragists and the Gendering of 'Suffragette' Identity," in Angela V. John and Constance Eustance (eds.), *The Men's Share? Masculinities, Male Support and Women's Suffrage in Britain, 1890–1920* (London: Routledge, 1997); Charlotte Fallon, "Civil War Hunger-Strikes: Men and Women," *Eire-Ireland* 22, no. 3 (1987): 75–91; Fallon, *Soul of Fire: A Biography of Mary MacSwiney* (Cork: Mercier, 1986).

81. Sweeney, "Irish Hunger-Strikes and the Cult of Self-Sacrifice," 424.

82. The phrase is George Dangerfield's, from *The Damnable Question: One Hundred and Twenty Years of Anglo-Irish Conflict* (Boston: Little, Brown, 1976), 343. See Sweeney, "Irish Hunger-Strikes and the Cult of Self-Sacrifice," 426; Charles Townshend, *Political Violence in Ireland: Government and Resistance since 1848* (Oxford: Clarendon, 1983), 314–317; Daniel Corkery, "Terence MacSwiney: Lord Mayor of Cork," *Studies* 9 (1920): 512–520; Moirin Chavasse, *Terence MacSwiney* (London: Burns and Oates, 1961); Francis J. Costello, *Enduring the Most: The Life and Death of Terence MacSwiney* (Dingle, U.K.: Brandon, 1995). A mass hunger strike began in Cork on the day of MacSwiney's arrest, and several strikers outlasted him, but they were commanded to stop by Arthur Griffith. Chavasse, *Terence MacSwiney,* 171; Charles Townshend, *The British Campaign in Ireland, 1919–1921* (Oxford: Oxford University Press, 1975), 122.

83. David Beresford, *Ten Dead Men: The Story of the 1981 Irish Hunger Strike*

(London: Grafton, 1987), 14–15; Padraig O'Malley, *Biting at the Grave: The Irish Hunger Strikes and the Politics of Despair* (Belfast: Blackstaff, 1990), 26; Ellmann, *The Hunger Artists,* 12–13.

84. O'Malley, *Biting at the Grave,* 25. Later republican hunger strikers, like Bobby Sands in 1981, had a profound sense of the historic nature of their struggle. See O'Malley, *Biting at the Grave,* 50, 57; Tom Collins, *The Irish Hunger Strike* (Dublin: White Island, 1986), 119; Allen Feldman, *Formations of Violence: The Narrative of the Body and Political Terror in Northern Ireland* (Chicago: University of Chicago Press, 1991), 215–219.

85. *Manchester Guardian,* 14 September 1932, 12.

86. By hunger striking, the suffragettes had shown themselves to be no better than "barbourous Indians" [*sic*]; *Times,* 11 March 1913, 14. Posnett trained as a barrister in Ireland before becoming a professor of classics and English literature at University College, Auckland.

87. On Birdwood's distinguished career as a medic, botanist, curator, journalist, and administrator, see http://64.1911encyclopedia.org/B/BI/BIRD-WOOD_SIR_GEORGE.htm

88. *Times,* 12 March 1913, 12.

89. For examples of antiquarian discussions of *dhurna,* see J. A. Dubois Abbé, *Hindu Manners, Customs and Ceremonies,* 3rd ed. (Oxford: Clarendon, 1906). Not all highlighted the links between *dhurna* and its Western counterparts, but Yule and Burnell's *Hobson-Jobson,* a famous glossary of Anglo-Indian words and phrases, provided copious information on the history of any Indian customs it listed, including illustrative examples from a variety of experts. See A. C. Burnell and H. Yule, *Hobson-Jobson: A Glossary of Anglo-Indian Words and Phrases,* W. Crooke, ed. (Delhi: Munshiram Manoharlal, [1886] 1968); *dhurna* entry, 315–316.

90. Grant, "Hunger Strikes and Fasts in Britain and the Empire, c. 1909–1935."

91. David Arnold, *Gandhi* (Harrow: Longman, 2001), 181–182; Joseph S. Alter, *Gandhi's Body: Sex, Diet and the Politics of Nationhood* (Philadelphia: University of Pennsylvania Press, 2000), 28.

92. *Votes for Women,* 16 July 1909, 933. The clause read: "It is the right of the subject to petition the King, and all commitments and prosecutions for such petitioning are illegal."

93. Weitzman, "'Suffraging in the Streets.'" In the House of Commons, Philip Snowden suggested to the home secretary that he "should make an application to Spain or Russia in order to adopt the most brutal and up-to-date methods of barbarism"—an allusion to Campbell-Bannerman's critique of British tactics during the Boer War. *Hansard* 11 (27 September 1909): 926.

94. A critique that echoed the campaigns against the Contagious Diseases Acts

and compulsory vaccination, see Judith Walkowitz, *Prostitution and Victorian Society: Women, Class and the State* (Cambridge: Cambridge University Press, 1980); Philippa Levine, *Prostitution, Race and Politics: Policing Venereal Disease in the British Empire* (London: Routledge, 2003); Nadja Durbach, *Bodily Matters: The Anti-Vaccination Movement in England, 1853–1907* (Durham, N.C.: Duke University Press, 2004).

95. Rule 243a allowed suffragettes the privileges of political prisoners, without affording them political prisoner status. It did not apply to male suffrage-rights protesters, who continued their hunger strike.

96. Constance Lytton and Jane Warton, *Prisons and Prisoners: Some Personal Experiences* (London: Heinemann, 1914), 269–270; Helen Gordon, "The Prisoner: An Experience of Forcible Feeding" [1911] in Marie Mulvey Roberts and Tamae Mizuta (eds.), *Perspectives on the History of British Feminism. The Militants: Suffragette Activism* (London: Routledge, 1994), ix–x, 49.

97. Tickner, *The Spectacle of Women,* 107; Ellmann, *The Hunger Artists,* 33.

98. Harry Cocks, *Nameless Offences: Homosexual Desire in the Nineteenth Century* (London: Tauris, 2003), chap. 3.

99. *Votes for Women,* 17 October 1913, 34.

100. Ibid., 7 August 1914. Pankhurst, *The Suffragette Movement,* 580. On her release, the victim, Fanny Parker, was discovered to have swelling and rawness in the genital region. See June Purvis, "The Prison Experiences of Suffragettes in Edwardian Britain," *Women's History Review* 4, no. 1 (1995): 123.

101. Arrested on four charges, he was found guilty of possessing seditious documents and an RIC cipher. Chavasse, *Terence MacSwiney,* 143–146, 151.

102. Most recently in mid-April, when those interned on hunger strike in Mountjoy and Wormwood Scrubs were released in the midst of a general strike on their behalf, despite the insistence two days earlier by both Bonar Law and the Attorney General for Ireland that the strikers would not be released under any circumstances. See *Hansard* 127 (1920): 1559–1570, 1643–1646, 1810–1821; *Cork Examiner,* 15 April 1920, 5.

103. Various compromise positions were explored in both Dublin and London, not least by King George V. D. G. Boyce, *Englishmen and Irish Troubles: British Public Opinion and the Making of Irish Policy, 1918–1922* (London: Jonathan Cape, 1972), 89. *Manchester Guardian,* 27 August 1920, 3.

104. Costello, *Enduring the Most,* 160–161, 184–187; Fallon, *Soul of Fire,* 46–55.

105. Quoted from the *Daily News* in Chavasse, *Terence MacSwiney,* 159.

106. Quoted in Costello, *Enduring the Most,* 174. The Peace with Ireland Committee was formed on the day of MacSwiney's death; its members included George Bernard Shaw and Henry Nevinson, who covered MacSwiney's hunger strike, along with Henry Brailsford, for the *Daily Herald.* See Henry W. Nevinson, *Last Changes, Last Chances* (London: Nisbet, 1928), 175–177. On violence and the not-so-strange

death of liberal vision of empire in postwar Britain, see Jon Lawrence, "Forging a Peaceable Kingdom: War, Violence, and Fear of Brutalization in Post–First World War Britain," *Journal of Modern History* 75, no. 3 (2003): 557–589.

107. Tim Pratt and James Vernon, "'Appeal from This Fiery Bed . . .': The Colonial Politics of Gandhi's Fasts and Their Metropolitan Reception in Britain," *Journal of British Studies* 44, no. 1 (2005): 92–114. As in that article, the focus here is on Gandhi's fasts in 1932 and 1943, for these were, remarkably, the only ones widely reported in Britain.

108. Mohandas K. Gandhi, *Indian Home Rule* (Madras: Ganesh, 1922), 25; originally published as *Hind Swaraj, or Indian Home Rule* (Natal, 1910).

109. Mohandas K. Gandhi, foreword to Mansani, *Dadabhai Naoroji,* 7; Gandhi, *Indian Home Rule,* 12–14, 105.

110. Drawing upon metropolitan critics of political economy and industrialism like Maine and Ruskin, Gandhi looked beyond the 'dark age' of British 'civilization' with its competitive materialism and lust for wealth and technology that had beguiled so many Indians. Gandhi, *Indian Home Rule,* chap. 7, "Why Was India Lost?" See Alter, *Gandhi's Body,* 23; Santhanam, *The Cry of Distress,* 6–7.

111. Mohandas K. Gandhi, *The Story of My Experiments with Truth* (Ahmedabad: Navajivan, 1929), 157; Gandhi, *The Collected Works of Mahatma Gandhi,* vol. 24 (Ahmedabad: Navjivan Prakashan, [1924] 1994), 95–99.

112. Pyarelal, *The Epic Fast* (Ahmedabad: Mohanli Maganlal Bhatt, 1932), 101, 113, 117.

113. On Gandhi's motivations, see Francis G. Hutchins, *Spontaneous Revolution: The Quit India Movement* (Delhi: Manohar Book Service, 1977), 311–318.

114. Annie Kenney, *Memoirs of a Militant* (London: Routledge, [1924] 1994), 145; Sylvia Pankhurst, *Unshackled: The Story of How We Won the Vote* (London: Routledge, [1959] 1994), 142–143.

115. See Weitzman, "Suffraging in the Streets"; and Holton, "Manliness and Militancy."

116. For a comparison of Dunlop to the hunger artist Saaci, see *Votes for Women,* 16 July 1909, 950. On fasting girls, see W. Vandereycken and R. Van Deth, *From Fasting Saints to Anorexic Girls: The History of Self-Starvation* (New York: New York University Press, 1994). The quotations on forcible feeding are from in Henry Brailsford, "Letter to a Liberal Member of Parliament," in Roberts and Mizuta, *Perspectives on the History of British Feminism,* 2–3, 4.

117. Gordon, "The Prisoner," 46, 58–59, 19–20.

118. Ellmann, *The Hunger Artists,* 35; Mary Jean Corbett, *Representing Femininity: Middle-Class Subjectivity in Victorian and Edwardian Women's Autobiographies* (Oxford: Oxford University Press 1992), 165.

119. Howlett, "Writing on the Body?"

120. Mary R. Richardson, *Laugh a Defiance* (London: Weidenfeld and Nicolson, 1953), 171; Sylvia Pankhurst, *My Own Story* (London: Evelyn Nash, 1914), 334.

121. There is a vast literature on the subject, but the classic statement is Anna Davin's "Imperialism and Motherhood" reproduced in F. Cooper and A. Stoler (eds.), *Tensions of Empire: Colonial Cultures in a Bourgeois World* (Berkeley: University of California Press, 1997), 87–151.

122. Denise Riley, *"Am I That Name?" Feminism and the Category of "Woman" in History* (Basingstoke, U.K.: Macmillan, 1988), chap. 4.

123. Jane Marcus (ed.), *Suffrage and the Pankhursts* (London: Routledge, 1987), 1–2. Francis Vacher, who wrote *A Healthy Home,* was a medical officer and health and food adulteration inspector in Cheshire. On suffragette responses to it, see JuNelle Harris, "'The Women's Way': Gender and Political Protest in Suffragette Hunger Strikes, 1909–1914," paper presented at the Northeast Conference on British Studies, Concordia University, Montreal, Canada, 27–28 October 2000, 11; Weitzman, "Suffraging in the Streets."

124. See, for example, *Votes for Women,* 17 January 1913, 235.

125. Pankhurst, *The Suffragette Movement,* 441. For a discussion of the position of crimes of maternity in suffragette prison narratives, see Weitzman, "Suffraging in the Streets," 21–23.

126. Quoted in Chavasse, *Terence MacSwiney,* 132–133.

127. Patrick O'Farrell, *Ireland's English Question: Anglo-Irish Relations, 1534–1970* (London: Batsford, 1971), 290.

128. Chavasse, *Terence MacSwiney,* 165–167; Costello, *Enduring the Most,* 173. For reports of a demonstration of ten thousand outside Brixton Prison and its violent disruption by police, see *Daily Mirror,* 26 August 1920, 3; *Daily Herald,* 26 August 1920, 1. See also *Daily Herald,* 27 August 1920, 1. Events recalled by Billy Woodruff's grandmother are described in Woodruff, *The Road to Nab End,* 237.

129. *Daily Herald,* 29 October, 1920, 1. On the "unprecedented" scenes in Dublin and Cork, see *Cork Examiner,* 1 November 1920, 1, 5.

130. O'Farrell, *Ireland's English Question,* 291.

131. Quoted in Chavasse, *Terence MacSwiney,* 156.

132. Canon John Waters was also professor of theology at Clonliffe College. For the debate in the *Irish Ecclesiastical Record* between August 1918 and May 1919, see Sweeney, "Irish Hunger-Strikes and the Cult of Self-Sacrifice," 426–427; Chavasse, *Terence MacSwiney,* 153–157. Thereafter, the British government was quick to portray republican hunger strikers as violators of the Catholic faith. *Daily Herald,* 26 August 1920, 1.

133. Costello, *Enduring the Most,* 189.

134. P. J. Gannon, "The Ethical Aspect of the Hunger Strike," *Studies* 9 (1920): 448; A Catholic Priest, *The Ethics of Hunger Striking* (London: Sands, 1920), 9.

135. He was also buried in Cork Cathedral's republican plot, honors not bestowed on hunger strikers since Ashe. The Irish church shifted position after the creation of the Irish Free State; see Sweeney, "Irish Hunger-Strikes and the Cult of Self-Sacrifice," 428–431.

136. Ernie O'Malley, *The Singing Flame* (Dublin: Anvil, 1978), 250; Costello, *Enduring the Most,* 152–153.

137. Although she immediately toured the United States with MacSwiney's wife, Muriel, Mary MacSwiney quickly established herself as the exclusive guardian of his legacy, even abducting Terence's child from Muriel, who had forsaken republican politics for communism and Ireland for continental Europe and had refused to bring her daughter up as a Catholic. Angela Clifford, *Muriel MacSwiney: Letters to Angela Clifford* (Belfast: Athol, 1996). My thanks go to Roy Foster for this appalling footnote to the story.

138. On Anne's hunger strike, see *Cork Examiner,* 27 November 1920, 5. On the government's wavering position and opposition to it, see Fallon, "Civil War Hunger-Strikes," 77–80.

139. On the attempts to elaborate a policy on hunger strikes across Britain and its empire, see Grant, "Hunger Strikes and Fasts in Britain and the Empire, c. 1909–1935."

140. *Hansard* 11 (27 September 1909): 925–926; (28 September 1909), 1094; and (6 October 1909), 2000–2001.

141. On the important role of medical women in this debate, see Kaarin Michaelsen, "'Like Hell with the Lid Off': British Medical Women and the Politics of Forcible Feeding, 1909–1914," paper presented at the Pacific Coast Conference on British Studies, Stanford University, Stanford, California, 6–8 April 2001.

142. See his reports of 6 and 8 July 1909, in NA, HO 144/1038/180965.

143. These words referred to Phyllis North (aka Olive Wharry), on 8 July 1914. She was described on 19 June as "a highly hysterical individual," and on 1 July as "obstinate and hysterical." See NA, HO 144/1205/221873.

144. *Votes for Women,* 1 October 1909, 2; Pankhurst, *The Suffragette Movement,* 318. On the direct targeting of individual prison medics, see *Votes for Women,* 12 November 1909, 106.

145. A. Savill, C. Mansell-Moullin, and Sir V. Horsley, "Preliminary Report on the Forcible Feeding of Suffragette Prisoners," *British Medical Journal,* 31 August 1912, 505. Forcible Feeding (Medical Men) Protest Committee, Petition to Home Sec., 7 July 1914. NA, HO 45/10726/254037. Horsley and Mansell-Moullin were the leading figures behind both the initial 1909 memorial and the formation of the Forcible Feeding (Medical Men) Protest Committee. Mansell-Moullin's wife, Caroline, was a member of the WSPU and served time in prison. Michaelsen has

counted fifty-six articles on the subject in the *British Medical Journal* between October 1909 and November 1913, "nearly double the number published on any other subject." This is less surprising than it might at first seem, given that in 1908, 538 of the 553 women on the Medical Register had signed a petition in support of woman's suffrage. Michaelsen, "'Like Hell with the Lid Off.'"

146. It was the chairman of the Prison Commission, Sir Evelyn Ruggles-Brise, who wrote of the "intolerable strain" on the prison services. NA, PCOM 7/355 to Home Office, 7 January 1913, NA. McKenna's words are taken from Pankhurst, *The Suffragette Movement,* 568.

147. Costello, *Enduring the Most,* 195–196. See also the similar arguments over the alleged forced feeding of MacSwiney, *Hansard* 133, 19 and 21 October 1920, 769–771, 1051–1053.

148. Costello, *Enduring the Most,* 198. On the day of MacSwiney's death the government released a letter intended to incriminate him in the production of hand grenades the previous May.

149. See Hutchins, *Spontaneous Revolution,* 311–318.

150. R. Tottenham, Circular Note from Additional Secretary, Home Department, Government of India, to Provincial Governors, 18 January 1941. OIOC, R/ 3/1/290.

151. R. Tottenham, Memorandum from Additional Secretary, Home Department, Government of India, to J. M. Sladen, Secretary to the Government of Bombay, Home Department, 6 December 1940, OIOC, R/3/1/290; "Very Secret" letter from R. Tottenham, Additional Secretary, Home Department, Government of India, to J. M. Sladen, Secretary to the Government of Bombay, Home Department, 16 December 1940, ibid.

152. *Daily Mail,* 4 March 1943, 2.

153. *Daily Telegraph,* 4 March 1943, 4.

154. John Christie, *Morning Drum* (London: British Association for Cemeteries in South Asia, 1983), 87. Recollections of Bill Cowley, Punjab, India Civil Service, District Officers Collection, OIOC Mss Eur f180/66 (entitled "Peacocks Calling"), 116.

155. *Daily Mail,* 13 February 1943, 2.

156. Claims elaborated the following year in her books: Margaret Brady, *Having a Baby Easily* (London: Health for All, 1944) and *Health for All: Ration Time Recipe Book* (London: Health for All, 1948). On the popularity of fasting cures, see Bernard MacFadden, *Fasting for Health: A Complete Guide on How, When and Why to Use the Fasting Cure* (New York: MacFadden, 1925); Rev. Walter Wynn, *Fasting, Exercise, Food and Health for Everybody* (London, 1928); Alfred Layton, *Fasting for Perfect Health* (London: Lutterworth, 1928). Diet culture for men spread in the 1920s; see Ina Zweiniger-Bargielowska, "'The Culture of the Abdomen': Obesity and Re-

ducing in Britain, c. 1900–1939," *Journal of British Studies* 44, no. 2 (April 2005): 239–273.

157. *News Chronicle*, 15 February 1943, 2.

158. *Daily Express*, 1 March 1943, 1.

4. The Science and Calculation of Hunger

1. Unlike the decennial census, these data enabled the calculation of laws of mortality and mobility. John Eyler, *Victorian Social Medicine: The Ideas and Methods of William Farr* (Baltimore, Md.: Johns Hopkins University Press, 1979); Lawrence Goldman, "Statistics and the Science of Society in Early Victorian Britain: An Intellectual Context for the General Register Office," *Social History of Medicine* 4, no. 3 (1991): 415–434.

2. Farr's position was supported by Richard B. Howard, *An Inquiry into the Morbid Effects of Deficiency of Food: Chiefly with Reference to Their Occurrence amongst the Destitute Poor* (London: Simpkin, Marshall, 1839). On the Chadwick-Farr debate, see D. V. Glass, *Numbering the People: The Eighteenth Century Population Controversy and the Development of Census and Vital Statistics in Britain* (Farnborough, U.K.: Saxon, 1973), 146–167; Christopher Hamlin, "Could You Starve to Death in England in 1839? The Chadwick-Farr Controversy and the Loss of the 'Social' in Public Health," *American Journal of Public Health* 85, no. 6 (1995): 856–866.

3. "Starvation Tables Memo to Mr. Rucker (Home Office) from Registrar General," 7 September 1929, p. 5, NA, RG26/13; Mary Poovey, "Figures of Arithmetic, Figures of Speech: The Discourse of Statistics in the 1830s," *Critical Inquiry* 19 (Winter 1993): 256–276; Theodore Porter, *Trust in Numbers: The Pursuit of Objectivity in Science and Public Life* (Princeton, N.J.: Princeton University Press, 1995); Ian Burney, *Bodies of Evidence: Medicine and the Politics of the English Inquest, 1830–1926* (Baltimore, Md.: Johns Hopkins University Press, 2000), 64–65.

4. On the "technologization" of hunger, see Jenny Edkins, *Whose Hunger? Concepts of Famine, Practices of Aid* (Minneapolis: University of Minnesota Press, 2000).

5. Sidney and Beatrice Webb, quoted in G. R. Searle, *The Quest for National Efficiency: A Study in British Politics and Political Thought, 1899–1914* (Oxford: Blackwell, 1971), 85.

6. The now classic account is Anson Rabinbach's *The Human Motor: Energy, Fatigue and the Origins of Modernity* (Berkeley: University of California Press, 1990). See also Jane O'Hara-May, "Measuring Man's Needs," *Journal of the History of Biology* 4, no. 2 (1971): 249–273; Harmke Kamminga and Andrew Cunningham (eds.), *The Science and Culture of Nutrition, 1840–1940* (Amsterdam: Rodopi, 1995).

7. J. A. Hobson, *The Social Problem: Life and Work* (London: Nisbet, 1901), 265, 267, 266.

8. Speech by the future Liberal prime minister Campbell-Bannerman at Perth in 1903, quoted in A. F. Wells, *The Local Social Survey in Great Britain* (London: Allen and Unwin, 1935), 70–71.

9. See Raymond Kent, *A History of British Empirical Sociology* (Aldershot: Gower, 1981); Martin Bulmer (ed.), *Essays on the History of British Sociological Research* (Cambridge: Cambridge University Press, 1985); E. P. Hennock, "The Measurement of Poverty: From the Metropolis to the Nation, 1880–1920," *Economic History Review* 40, no. 2 (1987): 208–227; and M. Bulmer, K. Bales, K. Kish Sklar (eds.), *The Social Survey in Historical Perspective, 1880–1940* (Cambridge: Cambridge University Press, 1995); David Englander and Rosemary O'Day (eds.), *Retrieved Riches: Social Investigation in Britain, 1840–1914* (Aldershot: Scholar, 1995).

10. As director of the Department of Agriculture's Experimental Station in Connecticut, Atwater, who oversaw the publication of some fifty-eight studies on human nutrition between 1895 and 1907, was the driving force in nutritional research at the time. Kenneth Carpenter, "The 1993 W. O. Atwater Centennial Memorial Lecture: The Life and Times of W. O. Atwater (1844–1907)," *Journal of Nutrition,* 124 (1994): 1707–1714; Dietrich Milles, "Working Capacity and Calorie Consumption: The History of Rational Physical Economy," in Kamminga and Cunningham, *Science and Culture of Nutrition,* 75–96.

11. B. Seebohm Rowntree, *Poverty: A Study of Town Life* (London: Macmillan, 1901), 97–98.

12. See Rowntree's lengthy discussion on the relative values of meat and vegetarian diets, ibid., 240–243.

13. Ibid., ix.

14. For a characteristic example, see Budget No. 9, detailing the life of a family of three—a father aged twenty-seven, a mother aged twenty-two, and their ten-month-old baby—surviving on eighteen shillings a week when the head of household, a laborer, had work. Ibid., 277.

15. Ibid., 304. These sentiments are echoed, less carefully and scientifically, in Arnold White *Efficiency and Empire* (Brighton: Harvester, [1901] 1973), 105; and Richard Higgs, *The Heart of the Social Problem: Twelve Millions Starving: How Can They Be Fed?* (London: Stead's, 1913).

16. *Report of the Inter-Departmental Committee on Physical Deterioration,* vol. 1, *Report and Appendix* (London: HMSO, 1904), v.

17. "A striking consensus of opinion was elicited as to the effects of improper or insufficient food in determining physique, and this factor was acknowledged by every witness to be prominent among the causes to which degenerative tendencies might be assigned, though in one or two case its relative importance was thought liable to exaggeration." Ibid., 39.

18. The work of other nutritionists, Paton and Dunlop at Glasgow, as well as

that of Atwater, was also mentioned. See the evidence of Drs. Chalmers, Macken-zie, Niven, and Eicholtz, as well as Rowntree and Loch, in *Minutes of Evidence Taken before the Inter-Departmental Committee on Physical Deterioration,* vol. 2. Robert Hutchison, *Food and the Principles of Dietetics* (London: Edward Arnold, 1900), was the standard work in Britain. First published in 1900, it was reprinted three times in 1901, and again in 1902 and 1904. The second edition of 1905 was reprinted in 1906, 1909, and 1910; the third edition of 1911 was reprinted in 1913 and 1914; the fourth edition of 1916 was reprinted in 1918 and 1919. It went through three further editions, in the last of which V. H. Mottram rewrote the earlier chapters. Robert Hutchison and V. H. Mottram, *Food and the Principles of Dietetics* (London: Edward Arnold, 1933).

19. *Report of the Inter-Departmental Committee on Physical Deterioration,* 41.

20. Ibid., 111.

21. *Minutes of Evidence,* 2:259, 260.

22. Ibid., 202.

23. Maud Pember Reeves, *Round about a Pound a Week* (London: Virago, [1913] 1979), 174, 131. For a less compelling critique, see Arthur Shadwell, *Industrial Efficiency: A Comparative Study of Industrial Life in England, Germany and America,* vol. 2 (London: Longmans, Green, 1906), 229.

24. A. L. Bowley, *The Nature and Purpose of the Measurement of Social Phenomena* (London: King & Son, 1915), 167, 171. See also the influential A. L. Bowley and A. R. Burnett-Hurst, *Livelihood and Poverty: A Study in the Economic Conditions of Working-Class Households in Northampton, Warrington, Stanley and Reading* (London: Bell and Sons, 1915).

25. David Smith, "Nutrition in Britain in the Twentieth Century" (Ph.D. diss., University of Edinburgh, 1986). On the Glasgow School, see D. Smith and M. Nicholson, "The 'Glasgow School' of Paton, Findlay and Cathcart: Conservative Thought in Chemical Physiology, Nutrition and Public Health," *Social Studies of Science* 19 (1989): 195–238.

26. E. V. McCollum, *The Newer Knowledge of Nutrition: The Use of Food for the Preservation of Vitality and Health* (New York: Macmillan, 1918).

27. For useful histories of the discovery of vitamins, see Leslie Harris, "The Discovery of Vitamins," in J. Needham (ed.), *The Chemistry of Life: Eight Lectures on the History of Biochemistry* (Cambridge: Cambridge University Press, 1970), 156–170; and Kenneth Carpenter, *Beriberi, White Rice, and Vitamin B: A Disease, a Cause, and a Cure* (Berkeley: University of California Press, 2000).

28. C. Funk, "The Etiology of Deficiency Diseases," *Journal of State Medicine* 20 (1912): 341–368; Funk, *The Vitamines,* trans. H. E. Dubin (Baltimore, Md.: Williams and Wilkins, 1922); F. G. Hopkins, "Feeding Experiments Illustrating the Importance of Accessory Food Factors in Normal Dietaries," *Journal of Physiology* 44

(1912): 425–460. For an account of the debate over nomenclature, see J. C. Drummond, "The Nomenclature of the So-Called Accessory Food Factors (Vitamins)," *Biochemical Journal* 14 (1920), 660.

29. Alan R. Skelley, *The Victorian Army at Home: The Recruitment and Terms and Conditions of the British Regular, 1859–1899* (London: Croom Helm, 1977), 63–68.

30. I draw here on the unpublished doctoral work of Michael Buckley at University of California, Berkeley, on food economy campaigns during the First World War.

31. One member of the commission needed to have the word *calorie* explained. L. Margaret Barnett, *British Food Policy during the First World War* (London: Allen and Unwin, 1985), 8.

32. Paul Eltzbacher (ed.), *Germany's Food: Can It Last? The German Case as Presented by German Experts,* trans. S. Russell Wells (London: University of London Press, 1915), xiii. On the politics of the blockade and for a parallel account of the politics of food in wartime Germany, see, respectively, Paul C. Vincent, *The Politics of Hunger* (Athens: Ohio University Press, 1985); Belinda J. Davis, *Home Fires Burning: Food, Politics, and Everyday Life in World War I Berlin* (Chapel Hill: University of North Carolina Press, 2000).

33. T. B. Wood and F. G. Hopkins, *Food Economy in War Time* (Cambridge: Cambridge University Press, [1915] 1917), 4, 35, v–vi.

34. It was a subcommittee of the Committee on Physiology, itself a belated addition in June 1915 to the Royal Society's war committees on physics, chemistry, engineering and "war trades," established twelve months earlier.

35. Cited in David F. Smith, "Nutrition Science and the Two World Wars," in David F. Smith (ed.), *Nutrition in Britain: Science, Scientists and Politics in the Twentieth Century* (Routledge: London, 1997), 146.

36. "Report of the Physiology (War) Committee of the Royal Society on the Food Supply of the United Kingdom," Cd. 8421 (1916), later published by T. B. Wood as *The National Food Supply in Peace and War* (Cambridge: Cambridge University Press, 1917), 2, 12, 13, 14–15.

37. The fullest account of this committee is Mikulas Teich, "Science and Food during the Great War: Britain and Germany," in Kamminga and Cunningham, *Science and Culture of Nutrition,* 213–234.

38. Quoted in Smith, "Nutrition Science and the Two World Wars," 149.

39. Sir William Beveridge, *British Food Control* (London: Humphry Milford, 1928), 194; Teich, "Science and Food during the Great War: Britain and Germany," 106, 110–111.

40. See especially Francis G. Benedict and Edward P. Cathcart, *Muscular Work: A Metabolic Study with Special Reference to the Efficiency of the Human Body as a Machine* (Washington, D.C.: Carnegie Institute, 1913). Cathcart had actually left Glasgow

to become professor of physiology at London Hospital in 1914, but he returned to Glasgow as professor in 1919. Major Robert Blackham of the Royal Army Medical Corps had conducted earlier, unsuccessful experiments on soldiers' calorific requirements, designed to reduce ration allowances, in 1908.

41. Sir W. G. Macpherson, W. H. Horrocks, and W. W. O. Beveridge, *Medical Services: Hygiene of the War* (London: HMSO, 1923), vol. 2, chap. 4; E. P. Cathcart and J. B. Orr, *Energy Expenditure of the Infantry Recruit in Training* (London: Miscellaneous Official Publications, 1919). In 1914, with Cathcart's help, Orr had become an officer in the Royal Army Medical Corps. Lord Boyd Orr, *As I Recall: The 1880s to the 1960s* (London: MacGibbon & Kee, 1966), 62–91.

42. See R. H. Plimmer, *Analyses and Energy Values of Foods* (London: HMSO, 1920).

43. Cited in Mark Harrison, "The Fight against Disease in the Mesopotamia Campaign," in H. Cecil and P. H. Liddle (eds.), *Facing Armageddon: The First World War Experienced* (London: Leo Cooper, 1996), 484. Macpherson, Horrocks, and Beveridge, *Medical Services,* vol. 2, chap. 3.

44. Later published as *Studies of Rickets in Vienna, 1919–22* (London: Medical Research Council, 1924). See H. M. Sinclair, "Chick, Dame Harriette (1875–1977)," in David F. Smith (ed.), *Oxford Dictionary of National Biography* (Oxford University Press, 2004), http://www.oxforddnb.com/view/article/30924.

45. The committee consisted of F. G. Hopkins, Harriette Chick, J. C. Drummond, Edward Mellanby, and Arthur Harden. Medical Research Committee, *Report on the Present State of Knowledge concerning Accessory Food Factors (Vitamines)* (London: HMSO, 1919).

46. All cited in Smith, "Nutrition Science and the Two World Wars," 150.

47. See Bryan Turner, "The Discourse of Diet," *Theory, Culture and Society* 1 (1982), 22–32; Turner, "The Government of the Body: Medical Regimens and the Rationalisation of Diet," *British Journal of Sociology* 33 (1982): 254–269; Ken Albala, *Eating Right in the Renaissance* (Berkeley: University of California Press, 2002); Steven Shapin, "Trusting George Cheyne: Scientific Expertise, Common Sense, and Moral Authority in Early Eighteenth-Century England Dietetic Medicine," *Bulletin of the History of Medicine* 77, no. 2 (2003): 263–297.

48. The Society of Public Analysts was founded in 1874, along with its professional journal, the *Analyst.* See Francis Vacher, *The Food Inspector's Handbook* (London: Record Press, 1893); O. W. Andrews, *Handbook of Public Health Laboratory Work and Food Inspection* (London: Bailliere, Tindall & Cox, 1901). My thanks go to Chris Otter for reminding me of the compromised and uneven nature of the move to the laboratory.

49. Sir Edward Sharpey-Schafer, *History of the Physiological Society during its First Fifty Years, 1876–1926* (London: Physiological Society, 1927). Gerald L. Geison,

Michael Foster and the Cambridge School of Physiology: The Scientific Enterprise in Late Victorian Society (Princeton, N.J.: Princeton University Press, 1978); Terrie M. Romano, *John Burdon Sanderson and the Culture of Victorian Science* (Baltimore, Md.: Johns Hopkins University Press, 2002).

50. The club became a society when it began publishing the *Biochemical Journal* in 1913, and by 1944 it boasted 1,017 members. R. H. A. Plimmer, *The History of the Biochemical Society, 1911–1949* (Cambridge, England: Biochemical Society, 1949).

51. Graeme Gooday, "The Premisses of Premises: Spatial Issues in the Historical Construction of Laboratory Credibility," in Crosbie Smith and Jon Agar (eds.), *Making Space for Science: Territorial Themes in the Shaping of Knowledge* (Houndmills, U.K.: Macmillan, 1998).

52. Rowett Institute, *First Report, 1922* (Aberdeen: Milne & Hutchison, 1922); Mark W. Weatherall, "The Foundation and Early Years of the Dunn Nutritional Laboratory," in Smith, *Nutrition in Britain,* 29–52.

53. Sally M. Horrocks, "The Business of Vitamins: Nutrition Science and the Food Industry in Inter-war Britain," in Kamminga and Cunningham, *Science and Culture of Nutrition,* 235–258; Horrocks, "Nutrition Science and the Food and Pharmaceutical Industries in Interwar Britain," in Smith, *Nutrition in Britain,* 53–74.

54. Orr, *As I Recall,* 96–99.

55. Rowett Institute, *First Report, 1922,* 21.

56. On laboratory equipment and equations as "immutable mobiles" that enabled transferable systems of measurement, see Bruno Latour, *Science in Action: How to Follow Scientists and Engineers through Society* (Cambridge, Mass: Harvard University Press, 1987); Latour, *Pandora's Hope: Essays on the Reality of Science Studies* (Cambridge, Mass: Harvard University Press, 1999), 102, 307. For a brilliant discussion of their mutable immobility, see Chris Otter, *The Government of the Eye: A Political History of Light and Vision in Britain, 1800–1900* (Chicago: Chicago University Press, 2007), chap. 3.

57. R. H. A. Plimmer, *Practical Organic and Bio-Chemistry* (London: Longmans, Green, 1926), 284.

58. W. R. Aykroyd, *Human Nutrition and Diet* (London: Thornton Butterworth, 1937), 97.

59. Ibid., 26.

60. Hence the interest in investigating the "tropical" metabolic rates of Australian aboriginals—see Warwick Anderson, *The Cultivation of Whiteness: Science, Health and Racial Destiny in Australia* (Melbourne: Melbourne University Press, 2002), 164.

61. The quest for the perfect mouthpiece or respiratory valve was characteristic of how small elements of laboratory instrumentation were subject to perpetual

failure. A variety of designs used materials such as mica, rubber, brass, and leather. Some scientists abandoned working with mouthpieces, instead preferring glass or rubber nose-pieces or even rubber or metal face masks. F. W. Lamb, *An Introduction to Human Experimental Physiology* (London: Longmans, Green, 1930), 195–197.

62. Michael Worboys, "The Discovery of Colonial Malnutrition between the Wars," in David Arnold (ed.), *Imperial Medicine and Indigenous Societies* (Manchester: Manchester University Press, 1988); David Arnold, "The 'Discovery' of Colonial Malnutrition and Diet in Colonial India," *Indian Economic and Social History Review* 31, no. 1 (1994): 1–26.

63. An example of a less meteoric rise: F. W. Fox, trained at University College, London, set up the new Biochemical Department of the South African Institute for Medical Research in 1925, shaping nutritional research in South Africa for a generation. See Diana Wylie, *Starving on a Full Stomach: Hunger and the Triumph of Cultural Racism in Modern South Africa* (Charlottesville: University of Virginia Press, 2001), 141.

64. D. McCay, *Investigations on Bengal Jail Dietaries: With Some Observations on the Influence of Dietary on the Physical Development and Well-Being of the People of Bengal* (Calcutta: Superintendent Government Print, 1910).

65. H. M. Sinclair, *The Work of Sir Robert McCarrison, with Additional Introductory Essays by W. R. Aykroyd and E. V. McCullom* (London: Faber and Faber, 1953); Sinclair, "McCarrison, Sir Robert (1878–1960)," in Andrew A. G. Morrice (ed.), *Oxford Dictionary of National Biography* (Oxford: Oxford University Press, 2004), http://www.oxforddnb.com/view/article/34678.

66. Robert McCarrison, "Problems of Nutrition in India" (1932), in Sinclair, *The Work of Sir Robert McCarrison,* 267–268; McCarrison, *Nutrition and National Health: Being the Cantor Lectures Delivered before the Royal Society of Arts 1936* (London: Faber and Faber, [1936] 1944), 21.

67. Robert McCarrison, "Memorandum on Malnutrition as a Cause of Physical Inefficiency and Ill-Health among the Masses in India" (1926), in Sinclair, *The Work of Sir Robert McCarrison,* 261.

68. The phrase *religious prejudice* is taken from McCarrison, *Problems of Nutrition in India,* 262, 277.

69. E. M. Collingham, *Imperial Bodies: The Physical Experience of the Raj, c. 1800–1947* (Cambridge: Polity, 2001), 156–157.

70. They "fared little or no better" than those fed on a Madrasi diet. McCarrison, *Nutrition and National Health,* 24–25; Robert McCarrison, "A Good Diet and a Bad One: An Experimental Contrast," *Indian Journal of Medical Research* 14, no. 3 (1927): 649–654.

71. W. A. Murray, *The Poor White Problem in South Africa: Report of the Carnegie Commission* (Stellenbosch, South Africa: Pro Ecclesia, 1932), viii, x, xvii, xx, xiv.

72. Ibid., pt. 4, *Health Factors in the Poor White Problem,* 7. Subsequent studies indicated no further deterioration in the nutritional health of South Africa's poor whites, especially by comparison with the deepening trough of malnutrition among non-Europeans. Wylie, *Starving on a Full Stomach,* 148.

73. Anderson, *The Cultivation of Whiteness,* chap. 5.

74. The cabinet committee believed that the "improvement of agriculture and animal husbandry . . . will almost certainly be accompanied by an improvement in the health and working capacity of the natives themselves." J. Boyd Orr and J. L. Gilks, *Studies in Nutrition: The Physique and Health of Two African Tribes* (London: HMSO, 1931), 12.

75. J. L. Gilks and J. Boyd Orr, "The Nutritional Condition of the East African Native," *Lancet* 29, no. 5402 (12 March 1927): 561–562. The Masai male was five inches taller, twenty-three pounds heavier, and, "as determined by the dynamometer," 50 percent stronger than his Kikuyu counterpart. Orr and Gilks, *Studies in Nutrition,* 9. Cynthia Brantley, "Kikuyu-Maasai Nutrition in 1928 Kenya," *International Journal of African Historical Studies* 30, no. 1 (1997): 49–86.

76. The Sub-Committee on Dietetics, chaired by Walter Elliot, M.P. (a personal friend of Orr's who had worked with him on animal nutrition in the early days at Rowett and was now a Conservative M.P. and a minister in the Department of Agriculture), included Hardy, Hopkins, Cathcart, and Orr. Worboys, "The Discovery of Colonial Malnutrition between the Wars," 212–213.

77. M. Havinden and D. Meredith, *Colonialism and Development: Britain and Its Tropical Colonies, 1850–1960* (New York: Routledge, 1993). Stephen Constantine, *The Making of British Colonial Development Policy, 1914–1940* (London: Frank Cass, 1984); Frederic Cooper, "Modernizing Bureaucrats, Backward Africans, and the Development Concept," in F. Cooper and R. Packard (eds.), *International Development and the Social Sciences: Essays on the History and Politics of Knowledge* (Berkeley: University of California Press, 1997).

78. Audrey I. Richards, *Hunger and Work in a Savage Tribe: A Functional Study of Nutrition among the Southern Bantu* (Cleveland, Ohio: World, [1932] 1964); Lord Hailey, *An African Survey: A Study of Problems Arising in Africa South of the Sahara* (Oxford: Oxford University Press, 1938). Established in 1926, the IIALC later became the International African Institute.

79. Economic Advisory Council, Committee on Nutrition in the Colonial Empire. *First Report,* pt. 1, *Nutrition in the Colonial Empire* (London: HMSO, 1939), 4.

80. See Cynthia Brantley, *Feeding Families: African Realities and British Ideas of Nutrition and Development in Early Colonial Africa* (Portsmouth, N.H.: Heinemann, 2002).

81. E. Burnett and W. R. Aykroyd, "Nutrition and Public Health," *Quarterly Bulletin of the Health Organisation of the League of Nations* 4 (June 1935): 1–140. Paul

Weindling, "The Role of International Organizations in Setting Nutritional Standards in the 1920s and 1930s," in Kamminga and Cunningham, *Science and Culture of Nutrition,* 319–332.

82. CNCE, *First Report,* 156, 151; Hailey, *An African Survey,* 961. During the 1930s, investments on medical and public health schemes came second only to transport and communication systems in the expenditure of colonial development funds. The importance of such investments grew during the decade, and by 1939 more was being spent on public health and welfare than on transport infrastructures. Havinden and Meredith, *Colonialism and Development,* chaps. 7 and 8.

83. CNCE, *First Report,* 14.

84. My emphasis. On the equal importance of education to this shift, see Corrie Decker, "Investing in Ideas: Girls' Education in Colonial Zanzibar" (Ph.D. diss.; University of California, Berkeley, 2007).

85. CNCE, *First Report,* 166, 151, 167. Hailey, *An African Survey,* 1123, 961.

86. Audrey Richards, *Land, Labour and Diet in Northern Rhodesia: An Economic Study of the Bemba Tribe* (London: Oxford University Press, 1951), 6.

87. Ibid., 5.

88. Brantley, *Feeding Families.*

89. CNCE, *First Report,* 106, 163.

90. Richards, *Land, Labour and Diet in Northern Rhodesia,* xii.

91. Richards, *Hunger and Work in a Savage Tribe,* 1. Malinowski's preface credited Richards with pioneering a new field of study, "the social and cultural functions of nutritive processes," ix.

92. See Tom Harrisson, *Savage Civilisation* (London: Gollancz, 1937), which was written very much under the sign of Malinowski, who later authorized Harrisson's "anthropology of ourselves" through Mass-Observation. Charles Madge and Tom Harrisson, *Mass-Observation: First Year's Work, 1937–38: With an Essay on a Nation-Wide Intelligence Survey by Bronislaw Malinowski* (London: Drummond, 1938).

93. Richards, *Hunger and Work in a Savage Tribe,* 8. See also Richards, *Land, Labour and Diet in Northern Rhodesia,* 7, 3, for her growing ambivalence about the role of nutritional science in colonial development.

94. Chandra Chakraberty, *Food and Health* (Calcutta: Ramchandra Chakraberty, 1922), 1; B. S. Gopala, *Universal Uncooked Food for Human Health, Economy, Contentment and Racial Efficiency* (Rajahmundry: Saraswathi Power Press, 1939).

95. These writings were subsequently collected and published as M. K. Gandhi, *Diet and Diet Reform* (Ahmedabad: Navajivan, 1949). The debate with McCarrison took place in 1929.

96. Ibid., 18, 19.

97. Ibid., 24 (emphasis in the original), 26. For similar attempts to indigenize

nutritional science, see Chakraberty, *Food and Health;* B. S. Gopala, *Universal Uncooked Food for Human Health.*

98. Gandhi, *Diet and Diet Reform,* 24

5. Hungry England and Planning for a World of Plenty

1. Vera Meynell, "Hungry England," *Week-End Review* 7, no. 152 (4 February 1933): 117.

2. *Daily Worker,* 30 January 1933, quoted in Allen Hutt, *The Condition of the Working Class in Britain* (London: Martin Lawrence, 1933), 153.

3. Fenner Brockway, *Hungry England* (London: Gollancz, 1932). Brockway, born in Calcutta to missionary parents, began his career as a journalist on the *Daily News* but made his name as a pacifist during the Great War. Elected an M.P. for the Independent Labour Party in 1929, he lost his seat in 1931, when the Labour Party refused to endorse him or his fellow ILP rebels. David Howell, "Brockway, (Archibald) Fenner, Baron Brockway (1888–1988)," *Oxford Dictionary of National Biography,* Oxford University Press, 2004, http://www.oxforddnb.com/view/article/39849.

4. "Hungry England: An Inquiry," *Week-End Review,* 1 March 1933, 264. The debate ran from 4 February through to the inauspicious publication of committee's report on April Fools' Day, "'Hungry England' Inquiry: Report of Committee," *Week-End Review,* 1 April 1933.

5. Political and Economic Planning (henceforth PEP), *Planning: The Measurement of Needs,* no. 29 (London: St. Clements, 19 June 1934), 2.

6. Ross McKibbin has argued that "the old way of personal observation [and] . . . sensational revelations . . . did not reach its apotheosis until *The Road to Wigan Pier*"; see his "Social Class and Social Observation in Edwardian England," *Transactions of the Royal Historical Society* 28 (1978): 175. Even the historian R. H. Tawney, who worked at the center of social science that was the London School of Economics, complained that what "doctors understand by malnutrition is what the plain man calls starvation." See M. E. Bulkley, *The Feeding of School Children* (London: Bell and Sons, 1914), xiii.

7. The term is from J. B. Priestley, *An English Journey: Being a Rambling but Truthful Account of What One Man Saw and Heard and Felt and Thought during a Journey through England during the Autumn of the Year 1933* (London: Heinemann, 1934), 397–413.

8. As quoted from Harry Pollitt's introduction to Allen Hutt, *The Condition of the Working Class in Britain* (London: Martin Lawrence, 1933), xii.

9. On the invention of "the North," see Beatrix Campbell, "Orwell Re-

Visited" in R. Samuel (ed.), *Patriotism: The Making and Unmaking of British National Identity* (London: Routledge, 1989), 3:227–232; Philip Dodd, "'Lowryscapes': Recent Writings about 'the North,'" *Critical Quarterly* 32 (Summer 1990): 17–28; and Dave Russell, *Looking North: Northern England and the National Imagination* (Manchester: Manchester University Press, 2004).

10. George Orwell, *The Road to Wigan Pier* (London: Penguin, [1937] 1979), 98, 94.

11. Orwell in Burma, Brockway in India: see Orwell, *The Road to Wigan Pier,* 54; Brockway, *Hungry England,* 188.

12. See Tom Harrisson, introduction to Bob Willcock, "Polls Apart" unpublished Mass-Observation survey, 1947, 2.

13. Humphrey Spender, *Worktown People: Photographs from Northern England, 1937–38* (Bristol: Falling Wall, 1985), 16; Julian Trevelyan, *Indigo Days* (London: MacGibbon & Kee, 1957), 85.

14. Brockway, *Hungry England,* 114.

15. Priestley, *An English Journey,* 409. See also Max Cohen, *I Was One of the Unemployed* (London: Gollancz, 1945), 7.

16. Brockway, *Hungry England,* 65, 109, 120. The future Conservative prime minister Harold Macmillan insisted "that the formal arrays of figures in the statistical tables which have been compiled relate to living men and women, not to abstractions," in Pilgrim Trust, *Men Without Work: A Report Made to the Pilgrim Trust* (Cambridge: Cambridge University Press, 1938), vii; Jurgen Kuczynski, *Hunger and Work: Statistical Studies* (London: Lawrence and Wishart, 1938), viii.

17. F. Greene (ed.), *Time to Spare: What Unemployment Means—by Eleven Unemployed* (London: Allen and Unwin, 1935), 10, 14.

18. Authenticity was, of course, scripted. Most of the "memoirs" were "written by the unemployed themselves" but when they had "much to say, but little or no power of saying it, . . . their narrative has been taken down verbally by intermediaries, thus producing a memoir of conversational flavour." H. L. Beales and R. S. Lambert (eds.), *Memoirs of the Unemployed* (Wakefield, U.K.: EP, [1934] 1973), 13. The "memoirs" were first published in the *Listener.*

19. Greene, *Time to Spare,* 83.

20. *The Long Summer,* episode 6, "The Facts" (Uden Associates, 1993).

21. *North Mail and Newcastle Chronicle,* 13 October 1936. The special correspondents identified are George Walker for the *South Shields Gazette,* Sidney Sterch for the *North Mail,* and, most famously, Ritchie Calder for the *Daily Herald.*

22. *Daily Herald,* 30 October 1936.

23. E. Wright Bakke, *The Unemployed Man: A Social Study* (London: Nisbet, 1933), 298, viii.

24. Ross McKibbin, "The 'Social Psychology' of Unemployment in Interwar Britain," in *Ideologies of Class: Social Relations in Britain, 1880–1950* (Oxford: Oxford University Press, 1990).

25. Quoted in David Smith, "Nutrition in Britain in the Twentieth Century" (Ph.D. Dissertation, University of Edinburgh, 1986), 115, 116.

26. Advisory Committee on Nutrition (ACN), Ministry of Health, *Memorandum to the Minister of Health on the Criticism and Improvement of Diets* (London: HMSO, 1932), 9. The ACN was chaired by Major Greenwood, who had been a medical officer at the Ministry of Health until 1927 and had previously worked closely with Cathcart.

27. "'Hungry England' Inquiry: Report of Committee," *Week-End Review,* 1 April 1933, 357, 358.

28. The BMA Committee included Mottram, G. C. M. McGonigle (on whom more later), and G. P. Crowden of the London School of Hygiene and Tropical Medicine.

29. Ministry of Health, *Nutrition: Report of Conference between Representatives of the Advisory Committee on Nutrition and Representatives of a Committee Appointed by the British Medical Association* (London: HMSO, 1934), 4, 7.

30. Ibid., 4, 5. The ACN never fully recovered from the controversy. Although it was reconstituted in 1935, it was effectively left inactive by the Ministry of Health. David F. Smith, "Nutrition Science and the Two World Wars," in David F. Smith (ed.), *Science, Scientists and Politics in the Twentieth Century* (London: Routledge, 1996), 153.

31. G. C. M. McGonigle and J. Kirby, *Poverty and Public Health* (London: Gollancz, 1936); J. B. Orr, *Food, Health and Income: Report on Adequacy of Diet in Relation to Income* (London: Macmillan, 1936); McCarrison, *Nutrition and National Health: Being the Cantor Lectures Delivered before the Royal Society of Arts 1936* (London: Faber and Faber, [1936] 1944).

32. PEP, "The Malnutrition Controversy," *Planning* 88 (15 December 1936): 2. The subcommittee of PEP Health Group on Nutrition included Crowden and Julian Huxley.

33. McGonigle and Kirby, *Poverty and Public Health,* 142; PEP, "The Malnutrition Controversy," 8.

34. James Vernon, "The Ethics of Hunger and the Assembly of Society: The Techno-Politics of the School Meal in Modern Britain," *American Historical Review* 110, no. 3 (June 2005): 693–725.

35. "Health of the School Child: Annual Report of the Chief Medical Officer of the Board of Education for 1908," Parliamentary Papers (1909), Cd. 5426, xxiii.

36. Bulkley, *The Feeding of School Children,* 170–171; Barbara Drake, *Starvation in the Midst of Plenty: A New Plan for the State Feeding of School Children,* Fabian tract no.

240 (London: Fabian Society, 1933), 9–10; Save the Children Fund, *Unemployment and the Child: Being the Report of an Enquiry Conducted by the Save the Children Fund into the Effects of Unemployment on the Children of the Unemployed and on Unemployed Young Workers in Great Britain* (London: Longmans, Green, 1933), 76–77.

37. Quotations from Bernard Harris, *The Health of the Schoolchild: A History of the School Medical Service in England and Wales* (Buckingham, U.K.: Open University Press, 1995), 130–131; John Hurt, "Feeding the Hungry Schoolchild in the First Half of the Twentieth Century," in D. J. Oddy and D. S. Miller (eds.), *Diet and Health in Modern Britain* (London: Croom Helm, 1985), 195.

38. Board of Education, Minutes of Meeting of Medical Staff Committee, 28 September 1934, NA, ED50/78 (M456/171). The inquiry was conducted by Dr. R. H. Simpson, Chief School Medical Officer of London County Council. According to a memo to Newman, Simpson's report "fully confirms what . . . we have recognised for some time that the summary of these returns published annually will not bear detailed examination." Board of Education, "Memo to Sir G. Newman from Cecil Maudsley 10.4.34 on Dr Simpson's Report on Standards of Nutrition," NA, ED50/51 (M456/150). See also Board of Education, Minutes of Meeting of Medical Staff Committee, 28 Sept 1934, NA, ED50/78 (M456/171).

39. Helen Jardine, Audrey Russell, F. Louis, S. Leff, and F. Le Gros Clark, "Statement of Aims," *Bulletin of the Committee against Malnutrition* 1 (March 1934): 2; "The Official Meaning of Malnutrition," *Bulletin of the Committee against Malnutrition* 9 (July 1935): 28–31; "Memorandum to the Advisory Committee on Nutrition from the Committee against Malnutrition," *Bulletin of the Committee against Malnutrition* 10 (September 1935): 49–51; McGonigle and Kirby, *Poverty and Public Health,* 144–145; R. H. Jones, "Physical Indices and Clinical Assessments of the Nutrition of Schoolchildren," *Journal of the Royal Statistical Society* 101, no. 1 (1938).

40. Quoted in Harris, *The Health of the Schoolchild,* 133.

41. The inaugural publication of the CAM argued that the "whole trend of modern investigation disproves the possibility of fixing minimum standards." Helen Jardine, Audrey Russell, F. Louis, S. Leff, and F. Le Gros Clark, "Statement of Aims," *Bulletin of the Committee against Malnutrition* 1 (March 1934): 2. The authors insisted that minimum standards were unscientific, for they ignored individual variations and were based on snapshot, short-term studies that were incapable of tracking long-term consequences for nutritional health. *Bulletin of the Committee against Malnutrition* 6 (January 1935): 6.

42. For McCarrison's argument, see his *Nutrition and National Health,* 65–66. See also McGonigle and Kirby, *Poverty and Public Health,* 147.

43. The first two League of Nations conferences on the standardization of vitamins were held in London in 1931 and 1934, with Edward Mellanby as chair, Jack Drummond as participant, and Harriette Chick and W. R. Aykroyd as the technical

secretaries. "Second Conference on Vitamin Standardisation," *Quarterly Bulletin of the Health Organisation of the League of Nations* 3, no. 3 (1934): 428–440. Similarly, Cathcart had chaired the first conference on calorific requirements at Rome in 1932. "Conference of Experts for the Standardisation of Certain Methods Used in Making Dietary Studies," *Quarterly Bulletin of the Health Organisation of the League of Nations* 1 (1932): 477. Mellanby chaired the subsequent meetings, in 1935 and 1936, when the focus shifted to a general consideration of food requirements. See "Report on the Physiological Bases of Nutrition," *Quarterly Bulletin of the Health Organisation of the League of Nations* 5 (1936): 391. See also Paul Weindling, "The Role of International Organizations in Setting Nutritional Standards in the 1920s and 1930s," in Harmke Kamminga and Andrew Cunningham (eds.), *The Science and Culture of Nutrition, 1840–1940* (Amsterdam: Rodopi, 1995), 319–332.

44. "The Most Suitable Methods of Detecting Malnutrition," *Quarterly Bulletin of the Health Organisation of the League of Nations* 2 (1933). See also E. J. Bigwood, *Guiding Principles for Studies on the Nutrition of Populations* (Geneva: League of Nations Technical Commission on Nutrition, 1939), 143–146; E. Burnett and W. R. Aykroyd, "Nutrition and Public Health," *Quarterly Bulletin of the Health Organisation of the League of Nations* 4, no. 2 (1935): 323–474.

45. Bigwood, *Guiding Principles,* 155.

46. Mellanby was chair of a committee of eight that included Aykroyd, Chick, and Orr. Bigwood, *Guiding Principles,* 147, 177, 175.

47. "Wages and the expenditure of money are always shrouded in thick darkness, but all details connected with food are trebly secure from observant eyes, however kindly." Margaret Loane, *From Their Point of View* (London: Edward Arnold, 1908), 74–75.

48. A. F. Wells, *The Local Social Survey in Great Britain* (London: Allen and Unwin, 1935), 32. By comparison with the handful of surveys before the war, Wells catalogues 156 conducted between 1918 and 1935.

49. David Vincent, *Poor Citizens: The State and the Poor in Twentieth-Century Britain* (Harlow, U.K.: Longman, 1991), 75–79; Vincent, *The Culture of Secrecy: Britain, 1832–1998* (Oxford: Oxford University Press, 1998), 142–154.

50. Herbert Tout, *The Standard of Living in Bristol: A Preliminary Report of the Work of the University of Bristol Social Survey* (Bristol: Arrowsmith, 1938), 24. On payments to keep a diary of food expenditure, see Maud F. Davies, *Life in an English Village: An Economic and Historical Survey of the Parish of Corsley in Wiltshire* (London: Fisher Unwin, 1909), 101.

51. Tout, *The Standard of Living in Bristol,* 14–15.

52. For examples, see Barbara Drake, *Starvation in the Midst of Plenty,* 5–7; D. Caradog Jones, *The Social Survey of Merseyside* (Liverpool: Liverpool University Press, 1934), 1:155–159; Pilgrim Trust, *Men without Work: A Report Made to the Pil-*

grim Trust (Cambridge: Cambridge University Press, 1938), 100–135; and Tout, *The Standard of Living in Bristol,* 16–17.

53. B. S. Rowntree, *The Human Needs of Labour* (London: Longmans, Green, 1937), 72; *Poverty and Progress: A Second Social Survey of York* (London: Longmans, Green, 1942), 173–176. In contrast, Bowley did not revise his coefficient scale for his repeat study, in order not to weaken the comparison. A. L. Bowley and Margaret L. Higg, *Has Poverty Diminished? A Sequel to 'Livelihood and Poverty'* (London: King & Son, 1925), 33–34.

54. Mottram, "The Fundamentals of Dietetics" in Greene, *Time to Spare,* 136.

55. Wal Hannington, *The Problem of the Distressed Areas* (London: Gollanz, 1937), 57. In January 1937 the National Unemployed Workers Movement (NUWM) even organized its own dietary survey, by means of a questionnaire headed "The Housewives Minimum," to catalogue the actual conditions in which families of the unemployed had to live. See Chapter 8 for a discussion of the NUWM and its hunger marches.

56. Ibid., 58. See also Somerville Hastings, *A National Physiological Minimum,* Fabian tract no. 241 (London: Fabian Society, 1934), 3.

57. Hannington, *The Problem of the Distressed Areas,* 61, 60.

58. In Beales and Lambert, *Memoirs of the Unemployed,* 270.

59. Orwell, *The Road to Wigan Pier,* 86. See also Kuczynski, *Hunger and Work,* 5.

60. Orr, *Food, Health and Income;* McGonigle and Kirby, *Poverty and Public Health*; League of Nations, *Interim Report of the Mixed Committee on the Problem of Nutrition,* vol. 1, *The Problem of Nutrition* (Geneva: League of Nations, 1936). See also League of Nations, *Report of the International Labour Office on Workers' Nutrition and Social Policy* (Geneva: League of Nations, 1936).

61. J. B. Orr, *The National Food Supply and Its Influence on Public Health* (London: King & Son, 1934). See also Ritchie Calder's introduction to Orr, *As I Recall* (London: MacGibbon & Kee, 1966), 15.

62. J. B. Orr, foreword to N. Gangulee, *Health and Nutrition in India* (London: Faber and Faber, 1939), 5.

63. PEP, "What Sort of Plenty?" *Planning* 44 (12 February 1935): 2; PEP, "The Malnutrition Controversy." On PEP and its critical place in the emergence of British social democracy, see *Fifty Years of Political and Economic Planning: Looking Forward, 1931–1981* (London: Heinemann, 1981); Daniel Ritschel, *The Politics of Planning: The Debate on Economic Planning in Britain in the 1930s* (Oxford: Clarendon, 1997).

64. Even those who sought practical advice on dieting and child-rearing had little time for "scientific subjects such as 'vitamins,' 'food values,' 'proper nutrition.'" Sir William Crawford and H. Broadley, *The People's Food* (London: Heinemann, 1938), 85–86.

65. The first professional advertising organizations were the Association of

British Advertising Agents (1917), the Incorporated Society of British Advertisers (1920), the Advertising Association of Great Britain (1926), and the Institute of Incorporated Practitioners in Advertising (1927). See T. R. Nevett, *Advertising in Britain: A History* (London: Heinemann, 1982). On Crawford, see the hagiographical G. H. Saxon Mills, *There is a Tide . . . The Life and Work of Sir William Crawford, K.B.E.; Embodying a Historical Study of Modern British Advertising* (London: Heinemann, 1954).

66. Stephen Constantine, *Buy and Build: The Advertising Posters of the Empire Marketing Board* (London: HMSO, 1986).

67. Crawford and Broadley, *The People's Food,* xi, 305, 304.

68. Peter Miller and Nikolas Rose, "Mobilizing the Consumer: Assembling the Subject of Mass Consumption," *Theory, Culture and Society* 14, no. 1 (1997): 1–36.

69. Crawford and Broadley, *The People's Food,* 314–315, 30.

70. Children's Nutritional Council, "Social Nutrition," *Wartime Nutrition Bulletin* 34 (February–March 1945): 1–2.

71. F. Le Gros Clark and R. M. Titmuss, *Our Food Problem and Its Relation to Our National Defences* (London: Penguin, 1939); J. B. Orr and D. Lubbock, *Feeding the People in Wartime* (London: Macmillan, 1940); Charles Smith, *Britain's Food Supplies in Peace and War* (London: Fabian Society, 1940); George Walworth, *Feeding the Nation in Peace and War* (London: Allen and Unwin, 1940). The following paragraph owes much to David Smith's work; see David Smith, "Nutrition Science in Britain in the Twentieth Century" (Ph.D. diss., University of Edinburgh, 1987); Smith, "Nutrition Science and the Two World Wars," in David F. Smith (ed.), *Nutrition in Britain: Science, Scientists and Politics in the Twentieth Century* (London: Routledge, 1997), 142–165; Smith, "The Rise and Fall of the Scientific Food Committee," in David F. Smith and Jim Phillips (eds.), *Science, Policy and Regulation in the Twentieth Century* (London: Routledge, 2000), 101–116.

72. Between 1941 and 1943 there were fifteen general surveys of food consumption, twenty-three surveys of food consumption among special groups, forty-three surveys about states of nutrition, thirty-one surveys into hemoglobin levels, and fifteen surveys on the effects of dietary supplements. Ministry of Food, "Bureau of Nutrition Surveys: Nutrition Society," NA, MAFF98/149.

73. He also introduced such nutritional techniques to the food industry as fortifying bread and margarine with vitamins, increasing the extraction rate of flour from wheat, and using dehydrated or powdered eggs, milk, and vegetables. Like Drummond, several members of his committee had prior experience in the commercial sector: Dr. Magnus Pyke at Vitamins and Agricultural Foods, L. Barton at Heinz, and Dr. G. Mills at Lever Brothers. For a succinct summary of the work of Drummond's division, see "Permanent Record of the Work of Scientific Adviser's Division," NA, MAFF223/30. The most complete accounts are Ministry of Food,

How Britain Was Fed in War Time (London: HMSO, 1946); R. J. Hammond, *Food: History of the Second World War,* 3 vols. (London: HMSO, 1951–1962).

74. Established in 1940, this committee considered a huge range of special groups, including vegetarians, diabetics, invalids, Jewish consumptives, and those with terminal illnesses. Ministry of Food, "Medical Research Council (Special Diets) Advisory Committee," MAFF98/15.

75. Ministry of Food, *How Britain Was Fed in War Time,* 47, 46.

76. Arnold Baines, "How the National Food Survey Began," in Ministry of Agriculture, Food and Fisheries (MAFF), *Fifty Years of the National Food Survey, 1940–1990* (London: HMSO, 1991), 17–23. Abrams became the doyen of market researchers in the postwar period and established the professional association the Market Research Society. Michael Warren, "Abrams, Mark Alexander (1906–1994)," *Oxford Dictionary of National Biography,* Oxford University Press, 2004, http://www.oxforddnb.com/view/article/54696.

77. Ministry of Food, *Annual Report of the National Food Survey Committee: Domestic Food Consumption and Expenditure, 1950; with a Supplement on Food Expenditure by Urban Working Class Households, 1940–1949* (London: HMSO, 1952), 5.

78. Abrams used forty women employees as research assistants, but the choice of location was limited by the inability to recruit trained investigators in certain localities, especially rural ones. Ministry of Food, *The Urban Working-Class Household Diet, 1940 to 1949: First Report of the National Food Survey Committee* (London: HMSO, 1951), 94.

79. Ibid., 98. Dorothy Hollingsworth was recruited for this job in 1941. By 1956 the punch cards for 1940 to 1943 had become so worn from frequent analysis that they were unreadable by the Hollerith machines. Dorothy Hollingsworth, "How Nutritional Knowledge was Applied," in MAFFF, *Fifty Years of the National Food Survey, 1940–1990,* 24–31.

80. Mark Abrams, *Social Surveys and Social Action* (London: Heinemann, 1951). For a suggestive account of the machinery and politics of governmental information, see Jon Agar, *The Government Machine: A Revolutionary History of the Computer* (Cambridge, Mass.: MIT Press, 2003).

81. Thanks go to Laura DuMond Beers for allowing me to cite "Cooper's Snoopers and the Ministry of Information in WW2 Britain," an unpublished paper presented to the Pacific Coast Conference on British Studies, University of California, Berkeley, March 2002. See also her "Whose Opinion? Changing Attitudes towards Opinion Polling in British Politics, 1937–1964," *Twentieth-Century British History* 17, 2 (2006): 177–205.

82. Ian McLaine, *The Ministry of Morale: Home Front Morale and the Ministry of Information in World War Two* (London: Allen and Unwin, 1979); Louis Moss, *The Government Social Survey: A History* (London: HMSO, 1991).

83. The Ministry of Food's Survey Branch claimed that the Plymouth incident was unrepresentative, with only forty or fifty letters of complaint from the many thousands of households surveyed in 1943. NA, MAFF102/58. A year earlier, its own investigation of attitudes toward its surveys had found 73 percent "interested and cooperative," 12 percent "doubtful but cooperative," 12 percent "uninterested but cooperative," 3 percent "doubtful or uninterested and not cooperative." Moss, *The Government Social Survey,* 6.

84. There were 2,131 refusals, with an additional 523 logbooks returned incomplete. Ministry of Food, *Annual Report of the National Food Survey Committee,* 90.

85. PEP, "Government Information Services," *Planning* 230 (2 February 1945): 15. The Wartime Social Survey boasted a permanent staff of over a hundred by 1943. Moss, *The Government Social Survey,* 7.

86. PEP, "Government Information Services," 22, 2.

87. Memo from Harrisson to E. F. Nash, Distribution Plans Division, 17 February 1944, NA, MAFF102/58.

88. In the autumn of 1943 a blank space was inserted in logbooks, in which subjects were invited to freely comment on any aspect of the food position. "The results were often difficult to classify, partly because they are frequently vague and sometimes ambiguous." Memo on Wartime Food Survey for Scientific Adviser's Division, June 1944, NA, MAFF98/145, 13.

89. The sample ranged in size from 1,082 to 1,513. Ministry of Food, "Reports on Enquiries into the Readership of 'Food Facts.' Prepared for Ministry of Food by the British Market Research Bureau Limited," NA, MAFF223/23.

90. The Ministry of Health survey, which sampled two thousand consumers in 1942–43, is cited in Children's Nutritional Council, "Social Nutrition," 3.

91. Ministry of Food, *How Britain Was Fed in War Time,* 50; Ministry of Food, *The Advertising, Labelling and Composition of Food* (London: HMSO, 1949), 64–65. These standards were extended by the Labelling of Food Order in 1946.

92. J. B. Orr, *Fighting For What? To 'Billy Boy' and All the Other Boys Killed in the War* (London: Macmillan, 1942), v.

93. Ministry of Food, *How Britain Was Fed in War Time,* 49.

94. "Draft White Paper on Post-War Food Policy," 15 February 1945, NA, MAFF128/17.

95. Between 1919 and 1926 McCarrison wrote all but two of the 27 papers published at Coonor. Between 1935 and 1945 80 percent of its 167 publications had been written by Indians. On the indigenization of Coonor and Indian science more broadly, see Sinclair, *The Work of Sir Robert McCarrison,* xi–xxix; David Arnold, *Science, Technology and Medicine in Colonial India* (Cambridge: Cambridge University Press, 2000).

96. On the scale of the work it funded, see W. R. Aykroyd, *Note on the Results*

of Diet Surveys in India (New Delhi: Indian Research Fund Association, 1939); Nagendranath Gangulee, *Bibliography of Nutrition in India* (Oxford: Oxford University Press, 1940); Nutrition Advisory Committee, *Results of Dietary Surveys in India 1935–1948,* Special Report no. 20 (New Delhi: Indian Council of Medical Research, 1951).

97. Gangulee, *Health and Nutrition in India*, iv, 306.

98. Nutrition Advisory Committee, Report of the 12th Meeting of the Nutrition Advisory Committee of the Indian Research Fund Association, held in New Delhi on 24 November 1944, 109, 110, BL, V/26/830/8.

99. Nutrition Advisory Committee, Report of the 11th Meeting of the Nutrition Advisory Committee of the Indian Research Fund Association, held in New Delhi on 27–28 March 1944, BL, ibid.

100. Quoted in Amy Moore, *Hunger and Deadlock in India* (London: Socialist Commentary, 1943), 1.

101. Famine Inquiry Commission, *Report on Bengal Famine* (Delhi, Government of India, 1945), 71; K. Santhanam, *The Cry of Distress: A First-Hand Description and an Objective Study of the Indian Famine of 1943* (New Delhi: Hindustan Times, 1944), 55.

102. Freda Bedi, *Bengal Lamenting* (Lahore: Lion, 1944), 6, 108.

103. Several of these, like Santhanam's and Bedi's, were subsequently published as books. See also Santosh Kumar Chaterjee, *The Starving Millions* (Calcutta: Asoka Library, 1944).

104. "Partial Starvation and Its Treatment," *Lancet* 245, no. 6345 (24 March 1945): 375. Starting in December 1943, India's Nutrition Advisory Committee funded clinical research into the treatment of the starving and destitute at the All-India Institute of Hygiene and Public Health, Calcutta. Nutrition Advisory Committee, Report of the 10th Meeting of the Nutrition Advisory Committee of the Indian Research Fund Association, held in New Delhi on 13–14 December 1943," BL, V/26/830/8, 3.

105. Famine Relief Committee, *Report for the Year 1943/44* (London: St. Clements, 1944), 6. On the medical critics, see *Lancet* 242, no. 6275 (4 December 1943): 704; *Lancet* 243, no. 6299 (29 April 1944): 576; *Lancet* 245, no. 6355 (9 June 1945): 723.

106. Maggie Black, *A Cause for Our Times: Oxfam, the First Fifty Years* (Oxford: Oxfam Publications, 1992). For the pacifist position, see Roy Walker, *Who Starves? A Discussion on Blockade* (London: Peace Pledge Union, 1940); Walker, *Famine over Europe: The Problem of Controlled Food Relief* (London: Andrew Dakers, 1941). Save the Children Fund had been established in 1920 to assist the estimated seventeen million starving and stunted children in Central Europe, whose deprivation had been caused in part by the blockade.

107. Famine Relief Committee, *Hunger in Europe: A Statement of the Case for Controlled Food Relief in German-Occupied Countries* (London: Famine Relief Committee, 1942), 1. Initially focused on Belgium and Greece, the organization later embraced Poland, France, and Holland. There is no scholarly treatment of this humanitarian campaign, which spawned Oxfam (Oxford Committee for Famine Relief).

108. Famine Relief Committee, *A Year's Work: An Account of Efforts to Obtain Permission for Controlled and Limited Food Relief in German-Occupied Countries* (London: Famine Relief Committee, 1943), 4–5, 7. For an account of the activities of one local committee, see Manchester and Salford Famine Relief Committee Minute Books, Manchester Central Reference Library Archives, M599/4/1/1–3.

109. Famine Relief Committee, *Report for the Year 1943/44*, 6.

110. G. H. Bourne, *Starvation in Europe* (London: Allen and Unwin, 1943), 5.

111. Ministry of Food, "Scientific Adviser's Division: Europe, General," NA, MAFF98/141.

112. The creation of the U.N. Relief and Rehabilitation Agency in November 1943 was also critical. Henri A. van der Zee, *The Hunger Winter: Occupied Holland, 1944–45* (London: Norman and Hobhouse, 1982); for Drummond's own account, see Jack Drummond, *Malnutrition and Starvation in Western Netherlands, September 1944–July 1945*, pt. 1 (The Hague: General State Printing Office, 1948).

113. Sir Jack Drummond, *Problems of Malnutrition and Starvation during the War* (Nottingham: Clough and Son, 1946), 17–18; Royal Society of Medicine, "Nutrition in Enemy Occupied Europe," *Lancet* 242, no. 6275 (4 December 1943): 703–704; Medical Women's Federation, "Problems of Health in Europe," *Lancet* 243, no. 6296 (29 April 1944): 576–577; "Partial Starvation and Its Treatment," 375–376. Drummond was also aware of similar experiments at University of Minnesota's Laboratory of Physiological Hygiene, where they were starving conscientious objectors, to explore the morphological, chemical, physiological, and psychological effects of starvation, as he later wrote in the foreword to Ancel Keys, Josef Brazek, Austin Henschel, Olaf Micklesen, and Henry L. Taylor, *The Biology of Starvation*, 2 vols. (Minneapolis: University of Minnesota Press, 1950).

114. Drummond, "Interim Report of F-Treatment for Cases of Starvation and Related Food Matters Concerning W. and N.W. Holland" NA, MAFF128/16.

115. *Lancet* 245, no. 6354 (9 June 1945): 723–724.

116. Ibid., 724; Drummond, *Problems of Malnutrition and Starvation during the War*, 18–19.

117. Drummond, foreword, Ancel Keys et al., *The Biology of Starvation*, 1:xiv.

118. Drummond, "Interim Report of F-Treatment for Cases of Starvation and Related Food Matters concerning W. and N. W. Holland," NA, MAFF128/16. W. R. Aykroyd, *The Conquest of Famine* (London: Chatto and Windus, 1974), chap. 11; World Health Organization, technical report, series no. 45, *Prevention and Treat-*

ment of Severe Malnutrition in Times of Disaster (World Health Organization: Geneva, 1951). Much of this report was written by Ancel Keys of the Minnesota starvation experiments.

119. For an interesting discussion of the discovery and conceptualization of "world hunger" during the 1930s and 1940s, see Frank Trentmann, "Coping with Shortage: The Problem of Food Security and Global Visions of Coordination, c. 1890s–1950," in Frank Trentmann and Flemming Just, eds., *Food and Conflict in the Age of the Two World Wars* (London: Palgrave, 2006), 27–35.

120. Orr, *As I Recall*, 163.

121. Tim Boon, "Agreement and Disagreement in the Making of 'A World of Plenty'" in Smith, *Nutrition in Britain*, 166–189.

122. J. B. Orr and David Lubbock, *The White Man's Dilemma: Food and the Future* (London: Allen and Unwin, 1953), 7.

123. Orr, *Fighting for What?*; J. B. Orr, *Food and the People* (London: Macmillan, 1943).

124. F. Le Gros Clark, *Feeding the Human Family* (London: Sigma, 1947).

125. Food and Agriculture Organization of the United Nations (FAO), *Proposals for a World Food Board* (Washington, D.C.: FAO, 1946). See also the preliminary discussions in FAO, *Report of the Special Meeting on Urgent Food Problems Washington, D.C., May 20–27, 1946* (Washington, D.C.: FAO, 1946).

126. Orr and Lubbock, *The White Man's Dilemma*, 102. Orr's colleague De Castro insisted that the world of plenty would "be matched by new social structures, which will guarantee that attainment of a new stage in the universal search for happiness and social well-being." Jose De Castro, *Geography of Hunger, with a Foreword by Lord Boyd Orr* (London: Gollancz, 1952), 258.

127. British nutritionists were, once again, at the forefront of these efforts: Dr. Isabella Leitch (still director of the Commonwealth Bureau of Animal Nutrition at Rowett), B. S. Platt (now director of the Human Nutrition Unit at the London School of Hygiene and Tropical Medicine), Margaret Read (now working in the Colonial Department of the University of London's Institute of Education), and Le Gros Clark (still secretary of the Children's Minimum Council) regularly contributed to or drafted the Nutrition Division's publications.

128. FAO, Nutritional Studies, *Dietary Surveys: Their Technique and Interpretation* (Washington, D.C.: FAO, 1949); FAO, Nutritional Studies, *Food Composition Tables for International Use* (Washington, D.C.: FAO, 1949).

129. The "universal" standard was based on a man or woman of twenty-five years old, in good health and well nourished, living in a temperate climate, with the man working in light industry and the woman engaged in either general household or light industrial work! Coefficients were abandoned for a detailed breakdown of requirements for infants, children, and adolescent boys and girls, as well as preg-

nant and lactating women. FAO, Nutritional Studies, *Calorie Requirements* (Washington, D.C.: FAO, 1950).

130. FAO, Nutritional Studies, *Teaching Better Nutrition: A Study of Approaches and Techniques* (Washington, D.C.: FAO, 1950), 4, 11–12. The phrase *nutrition-conscious* is Aykroyd's description of U.S. wartime programs in nutritional education; see Famine Inquiry Commission, *Final Report* (Madras: Government Press, 1945), 229.

131. Malcolm Muggeridge, *The Thirties: 1930–1940 in Great Britain* (London: Collins, [1940] 1967), 281, 282.

6. Collective Feeding and the Welfare of Society

1. Valerie Johnston, *Diets in Workhouses and Prisons* (New York: Garland, 1985). For work on prison and military diets in India, see David Arnold, "The 'Discovery' of Colonial Malnutrition and Diet in Colonial India," *Indian Economic and Social History Review* 31, no. 1 (1994), 1–26.

2. *Times,* 27 October 1843, 4.

3. Lyon Playfair, the distinguished chemist and student of Justus von Liebig, advised the Poor Law Board in 1850, and Dr. Edward Smith, a medic with a keen interest in diet, was appointed its medical inspector in 1865. See Edward Smith, *Dietaries for the Inmates of Workhouses* (London: Walton, 1866); Smith, *A Guide to the Construction and Management of Workhouses* (London: Knight, 1870). It is clear that despite Chadwick's best efforts, workhouse dietaries varied enormously from locality to locality and became more generous under Smith's direction.

4. Keith Laybourn, "The Issue of School Feeding in Bradford, 1904–1907," *Journal of Educational Administration and History* 14, no. 2 (July 1982): 30–38. Bradford's school meal service quickly became the model to be emulated both at home and abroad; see Louise Stevens Bryant, *School Feeding: Its History and Practice at Home and Abroad* (London: Lippincott, 1913).

5. Charles E. Hecht (ed.), *Rearing an Imperial Race* (London: St. Catherine's, 1913); *Inter-Departmental Committee on Physical Deterioration: Report and Appendix,* Parliamentary Papers (1904), Cd. 2175, xxxii; *A Bill to Provide Secular Education and Periodical Medical Examination and Food for Children Attending State-Supported Schools,* Parliamentary Papers (1906), 143: ii, 199.

6. John Stewart, "Ramsay MacDonald, the Labour Party and Child Welfare, 1900–1914," *Twentieth-Century British History* 4, no. 2 (1993): 105–125; Stewart, "'This Injurious Measure': Scotland and the 1906 Education (Provision of Meals) Act," *Scottish Historical Review* 78, no. 1 (1999): 76–94.

7. Sir Noel Curtis-Bennett, *The Food of the People: Being the History of Industrial Feeding* (London: Faber and Faber, 1949), chap. 7; Anson Rabinbach, *The Human Motor: Energy, Fatigue, and the Origins of Modernity* (Berkeley: University of California

Press, 1992); Jakob Tanner, *Factory Meal: Nourishing Science, Industrialism and People Nutrition in Switzerland, 1890–1950* (Zurich: Chronos, 1999).

8. See the collections in the Documentary Photography Archive at the Greater Manchester Record Office, D170/1/21.

9. I have examined the nutritional technopolitics of the school meal more fully in James Vernon, "The Ethics of Hunger and the Assembly of Society: The Techno-Politics of the School Meal in Modern Britain," *American Historical Review* 110, no. 3 (June 2005): 693–725.

10. See M. E. Bulkley, *The Feeding of School Children* London: Bell and Sons, 1914), 64–69. On the growth of the school medical service, see Bernard Harris, *The Health of the Schoolchild: A History of the School Medical Service in England and Wales* (Buckingham, U.K.: Open University Press, 1995), 56, 123–124.

11. Charles Segal, *Penn'orth of Chips: Backward Children in the Making* (London: Gollancz, 1939), 122–123; Barbara Drake, *Starvation in the Midst of Plenty: A New Plan for the State Feeding of School Children,* Fabian tract no. 240 (London: Fabian Society, 1933), 15–16.

12. Whereas one child in thirty was fed at school at the beginning of the war, by its end one in three was receiving meals, even if only 14 percent of those were free. Richard Titmuss, *Problems of Social Policy* (London: HMSO, 1950), 510.

13. John Burnett, "The Rise and Decline of School Meals in Britain, 1860–1990," in J. Burnett and D. Oddy (eds.), *The Origins and Development of Food Policies in Europe* (Leicester: Leicester University Press, 1994), 66; Harris, *The Health of the Schoolchild,* 196–197.

14. "Report of the Welfare and Health Section for the Year Ending 1917," NA, MUN5/94/346/39. The best account we have of these developments is Angela Woollacott, *On Her Their Lives Depend: Munitions Workers in the Great War* (Berkeley: University of California Press, 1994).

15. "No man," Lloyd George wrote of Rowntree and his appointment, "could have been found better qualified by sympathy and experience for the task." Lloyd George, foreword to Dorothea Proud, *Welfare Work: Employers' Experiments for Improving Working Conditions in Factories* (London: Bell and Sons, 1916), xii.

16. Their work formed the scientific backbone of the committee's twenty-one memoranda, and of its Final Report, issued at the end of 1917, which sold a remarkable 210,000 copies. H. M. Vernon, *The Health and Efficiency of Munition Workers* (London: Oxford University Press, 1940), 2–3.

17. Edgar L. Collis and Major Greenwood, *The Health of the Industrial Worker* (London: Churchill, 1921), 246, 258, 243.

18. See his foreword, ibid., xviii, xix.

19. Daniel Ussishkin, "Morale: Social Citizenship and Democracy in Modern Britain" (Ph.D. diss., University of California, Berkeley, 2007), chap. 3.

20. Quoted in Vernon, *Industrial Fatigue and Efficiency,* 247.

21. Quoted in Woollacott, *On Her Their Lives Depend,* 64–65.

22. Vernon, *The Health and Efficiency of Munition Workers;* Curtis-Bennett, *The Food of the People,* 253; Industrial Welfare Society, *Canteens in Industry: A Guide to Planning, Management and Service* (London: Industrial Welfare Society, 1940).

23. Ministry of Food, *How Britain Was Fed in War Time* (London: HMSO, 1946), 43. As a percentage of the total number of 170,000 factories, this was still not especially impressive. Labour Research Department, *Canteens in Industry* (London: Workers Pocket Series, 1941), 4.

24. Collis and Greenwood, *The Health of the Industrial Worker,* 267; Curtis-Bennett, *The Food of the People,* 300.

25. F. Le Gros Clark, *Social History of the School Meals Service* (London: National Council of Social Services, 1948), 2.

26. Eddie Williams, *School Milk and Meals* (Monmouth, U.K.: Rogerstone, 1944), 3; Bulkley, *The Feeding of School Children,* 199.

27. Quoted in Bryant, *School Feeding,* 74; Austin Priestman, *The Work of the School Medical Officer* (London: Oxford University Press, 1914), 4; Williams, *School Milk and Meals,* 3.

28. Proud, *Welfare Work,* 123.

29. Collis and Greenwood, *The Health of the Industrial Worker,* 261–263. See also Proud, *Welfare Work,* 119–126, 188–199; Canteen Committee of the Central Control Board (Liquor Traffic), *Feeding the Munitions Worker* (London: HMSO, 1916); Health of Munitions Workers Committee, "Canteen Construction and Equipment," memorandum no. 6, Cd. 8199, 1916.

30. Tom Harrisson diary, 25 November 1941, MO, TC67/3/D, "British Restaurants and Canteens."

31. Only postwar developments have been studied in Andrew Saint, *Towards a Social Architecture: The Role of School-Building in Post-War England* (New Haven, Conn.: Yale University Press, 1987).

32. The initial 1906 Report on the Education (Provision of Meals) Act noted: "To many of the poorest children a well ordered meal, with its accompaniments of clean table-cloths, clean crockery, and seemliness of behaviour, is almost unknown; and it is hoped, with some confidence, that the object lessons supplied by the meals provided . . . will have more than a transitory effect upon the behaviour of the children who have received them." Quoted in Hecht, *Rearing an Imperial Race,* 17.

33. Bulkley, *The Feeding of School Children,* 76–106.

34. George Rainey, "Paris and London," in Hecht, *Rearing an Imperial Race,* 421; Williams, *School Milk and Meals,* 5.

35. Segal, *Penn'orth of Chips,* 92.

36. "Particulars regarding the Provision of School Canteens (as Distinct From Feeding Centres), 1936," NA, ED50/219.

37. "Provision of Meals": Report of Edna Langley to Dr. Glover, 4 April 1939, NA, M501/262.

38. These designs probably originated in the Ministry of Works Experimental Building Research Station in Watford. One of these model canteen kitchens, complete with all the latest equipment from the newly produced *Catalogue of School Canteen Equipment* and sample wall finishes, was exhibited behind the Tate Gallery, where district school inspectors and LEA officials were invited to inspect it. See September 1943 memos from Agnes Miller and Miss Langley, as well as circular letter to LEAs, 13 October 1943, NA, ED50/219.

39. See C. Cameron, "School Canteens and Kitchens," 20 September 1943; and "Comments on the Draft Explanatory Memorandum to the Proposed Town and Country Planning Order," 8 January 1944, NA, HLG71/899.

40. "Ministry of Works Organisation: The Present Position," 1, NA, ED150/156; "The Standards for School Premises Regulations, 1951," Statutory Instruments, no. 1753"; Medical Research Council and Building Research Group: Joint Committee on Lighting and Vision: Proposed New Regulations for the Lighting of Schools," NA, ED150/25.

41. Only 25.5 percent of schools boasted their own dining room built for the purpose. *Report of an Inquiry into the Working of the School Meals Service, 1955–56* (London: HMSO, 1956).

42. On the competing merits of different materials and arrangements, see Willard Stanley Ford, *Some Administrative Problems of the High School Cafeteria* (New York: Columbia University, 1926); and Ministry of Works, *School Furniture and Equipment* (London: HMSO, 1946). Laminated and stackable tables and chairs became the focus, beginning in the 1950s; see London County Council, *School Furniture* (London: London County Council, 1958).

43. Bryant, *School Feeding,* 56; Priestman, *The Work of the School Medical Officer,* 3; Hecht, *Rearing an Imperial Race,* 400.

44. Work overseen by its senior engineer in conjunction with its senior catering adviser. "Ministry of Works Organisation: The Present Position," 1, NA, ED150/156. See, for example, Ministry of Education, *School Meals Service: Equipment Catalogue, 1947* (London: HMSO, 1947).

45. See the entire file of correspondence in "Wartime Meals: School Canteen Equipment: West Bromwich," 1943, NA, MAFF900/103. See also "Care and Maintenance of Insulated Containers," *School Meals Service: Canteen Leaflet,* no. 4 (1951).

46. J. W. Beeson (director of education, Norwich) to W. D. Pile, 19 June

1952; Norwich city architect, "Memorandum, School Meals Service—Kitchen and Dining Rooms: Insulation and Prevention of Condensation," 23 May 1952, NA, ED150/104. By the mid-1950s the kitchens' wooden working surfaces had also fallen afoul of the Ministry of Health's new Food Hygiene Regulations, which recommended use of formica or stainless steel tops. W. B. Ashplant to A & B General, "Food Hygiene Regulations, 1955," 12 October 1956, NA, ED150/156.

47. A. F. B. Nail (assistant technical director, British Standards Institute (BSI)) to Johnston Marshall (chief architect, Ministry of Education), 5 November 1953, NA, ED150/80; G. Weston (technical director, BSI) to W. D. Pile, "School Furniture Press Conference," 7 October 1955, ibid.; BSI, "Sub-Committee—Dining Tables and Chairs of Technical Committee—School Furniture, Revised Draft Standard for School Dining Tables and Chairs," April 1955, ibid.

48. Proud, *Welfare Work,* 196, 193.

49. Drake, *Starvation in the Midst of Plenty,* 16; London County Council, *Meals for School Children* (London: London County Council, 1947), 5. See also London County Council, *Education in London, 1945–1954: A Report by the Education Officer* (London: London County Council, 1954), 87.

50. F. Le Gros Clark, *The School Child's Taste in Vegetables: An Inquiry Undertaken by F. LeGros Clark, BA, and Presented to the Education Committee* (Hertford: Hertfordshire County Council, 1943), 13, 14.

51. Priestman, *The Work of the School Medical Officer,* 13, 4.

52. Quoted in Segal, *Penn'orth of Chips,* 93.

53. See, for example, the Board of Education's 1914 circular no. 856, 7–10. Brinson to Maudsley, 23 March 1937, "Dietaries; The Oslo Breakfast; The London Health Dinner," 1937–1943, NA, ED50/219.

54. These included supervisors, cook-supervisors, cook-caterers, cooks in charge, cooks, assistant cooks, kitchen assistants, storekeepers. Board of Education, "Staff for the School Meals Service," circular no. 1631 (24 June 1943); "Special Services General Files: Staffing of School Canteens and Kitchens, 1947–52," NA, ED50/502.

55. Note the way that both the already cited *School Canteen Handbook* (1940) and *Balanced Menus for School Canteen Dinners,* 2nd ed. ([1947] 1958) were written in collaboration with domestic science experts (in addition to being Surrey County Council's school meals officer, Morkam was the former head of Wimbledon Technical College's Domestic Science Department). London County Council's *Meals for School Children* (1947) was written by W. J. O. Newton, its chief officer of meals services. There were many other such publications.

56. Deborah Thom, *Nice Girls and Rude Girls: Women Workers in World War I* (London: Tauris, 1998), 169. Woollacott has detailed the range of voluntary effort, which included the "YMCA (England), the YWCA (in both England and Scotland),

the YW&WCA (Scotland), the National People's Palace Association, the Salvation Army, the Church of England Temperance Society, the Church Army, the British Women's Temperance Association (Scotland), the Glasgow Union of Women Workers, the Women's Volunteer Reserve, and the Women's Legion." Woollacott, *On Her Their Lives Depend,* 64.

57. Thom, *Nice Girls and Rude Girls,* 131. Woollacott, "Maternalism, Professionalism and Industrial Welfare Supervisors in World War I Britain," *Women's History Review* 3 (March 1994): 29–56.

58. Proud, *Welfare Work,* 124.

59. Collis and Greenwood, *The Health of the Industrial Worker,* 264–265.

60. *Canteens in Industry,* cited in Curtis-Bennett, *The Food of the People,* 277, 251–253.

61. "Report of the Superintendent Inspector of Canteens," Ministry of Labour Factory Inspectors Department, 1944, cited in Curtis-Bennett, *The Food of the People,* 277. Le Gros Clark lamented the lack of inspection regimes, for they ensured the responsible provision of services. F. Le Gros Clark, "The Principles of Canteen Inspection," *Food Manufacture* 18 (1943): 36–38, WA, GC/145/D.23.

62. One catering firm armed a team of nutritionists with a mobile laboratory to analyze the meals served in its canteens. Curtis-Bennett, *The Food of the People,* 12, 271.

63. Publications aimed at this newly professionalized sector included M. B. Neary, *Canteen Management and Cookery* (London: John Miles, 1940); Catherine H. MacGibbon, *Canteen Management* (Christchurch: Whitcombe and Tombs, 1941); John Douglas Mitchell, *Successful Canteen Management* (London: Practical Press, 1946); Empire Tea Bureau, *The Small Canteen: How to Plan and Operate a Modern Meal Service* (London: Oxford University Press, 1947); Dick T. Kennedy, *Industrial Catering and Canteen Management* (London: MacClaren & Sons, 1949); Jack Hampton, *Canteen Cookery* (London: Practical Press, 1953). See also the journal *Nutrition and Canteen Catering,* published in London starting in 1946.

64. Labour Research Department, *Canteens in Industry,* 6–7.

65. As reported in the *New Propellor* (January 1943), quoted in Labour Research Department, *Works Canteens and the Catering Trade: Food Problems, Workers' Control of Canteens, Catering Workers and Employers' Profits* (London: Labour Research Department, 1943), 15.

66. Labour Research Department, *Works Canteens and the Catering Trade,* 11–12. Of those 14 million workers, only 2.5 million received a hot meal.

67. For these competing explanations, see Labour Research Department, *Works Canteens and the Catering Trade;* and Eleanor Umney, "A Few Notes from Experience," 1 February 1942 (welfare officer in Letchworth), MO, TC67/3/D, "British Restaurants and Canteens."

68. On the growing popularity of porridge at home, given its use in school breakfasts, see Bulkley, *The Feeding of School Children,* 200.

69. Ernie Benson, *To Struggle Is to Live: A Working-Class Autobiography,* 2 vols. (Newcastle, U.K.: People's, 1979), 1:39.

70. Le Gros Clark, *The School Child's Taste in Vegetables,* 11.

71. Kathleen Dayus, *Her People* (London: Virago, 1982), 15; Nancy Sharman, *Nothing to Steal: The Story of a Southampton Childhood* (London: Kaye and Ward, 1977), 39; Benson, *To Struggle Is to Live,* 44–45; J. G. Atherton, *Home to Stay: Stretford in the Second World War* (Manchester: Richardson, 1991), 6, 15.

72. The survey was conducted by www.friendsreunited.com and *BBC Good Food* magazine, where the results were published in September 2003, p. 105.

73. E. R. Hartley, *How to Feed the Children: Bradford's Example* (Bradford, 1908), quoted in Laura Mason, "Learning How to Eat in Public: School Dinners," in *Oxford Symposium on Food and Cookery: Public Eating* (London: Prospect, 1991), 209.

74. Quoted in Mason, "Learning How to Eat in Public," 208.

75. For characteristic examples from the testimonies of the poor, see Grace Foakes, *Between High Walls: A London Childhood* (London: Shepheard-Walwyn, 1972), 39; Benson, *To Struggle Is to Live,* 39; Fenner Brockway, *Hungry England* (London: Gollancz, 1932), 32.

76. See Barbara Vaughan, *Growing Up in Salford 1919–1928* (Manchester: Richardson, 1983), 9; Mary H. Dagnah, *Castel Hall Revisited: Stalybridge in the 1930s* (Manchester: Richardson, 1995), 5.

77. The most extensive discussion of these can be found in Marion Roberts, "Private Kitchens, Public Cooking," in Matrix, *Making Space: Women and the Man-Made Environment* (London: Pluto, 1986), 106–119.

78. War Emergency Workers National Committee, "National Kitchens," NMLH, WNC14/2.

79. L. Margaret Barnett, *British Food Policy during the First World War* (London: Allen and Unwin, 1985), 151.

80. C. S. Peel, *A Year in Public Life* (London: Constable, 1919), 189.

81. Pember Reeves was a member of the National Union of Women's Suffrage Society and the Women's Trade Union League and established the Fabian Women's Group in 1907, the year before her husband became director of the London School of Economics. Peel was the author of various books, such as *Ten Shillings a Head for House Books: An Indispensable Manual for Housekeepers* (London: Constable, 1900) which went through nine editions by 1912; *The New Home: Treating of the Arrangement, Decoration and Furnishing of a House of Medium Size to Be Maintained by a Moderate Income* (1903); *How to Keep House* (1910); *Marriage on Small Means* (1914); and *Learning to Cook: The Book of "How" and "Why" in the Kitchen* (1915). She had also pro-

duced a series of cookbooks, such as *Entrees Made Easy* (1905), *Puddings and Sweets* (1905), and *Fish and How to Cook It* (1907). On Manley, see "Memorandum on Work in Connection with Food Economy and Control, carried out by Miss Kate Manley, O.B.E.," "Women, War, and Society" microfilm collection, IWM, pt. 4, Food, 3/9.

82. Peel, *A Year in Public Life,* 191; C. S. Peel, *How We Lived Then, 1914–1918: A Sketch of Social and Domestic Life in England during the War* (London: John Lane, the Bodley Head, 1929), 83–85.

83. F. W. Spencer, "Report on National Kitchens," NMLH, CC/NK/131/2. For the increasing regulation and interrogation of Spencer's National Kitchen Division by the newly formed Consumer Council, see NMLH, CC/NK/105/113. For the barrage of negative reports, see NMLH, CC/NK/161–227.

84. Dilwyn Porter, "Jones, (William) Kennedy (1865–1921)," *Oxford Dictionary of National Biography* (Oxford: Oxford University Press, 2004), http://www.oxforddnb.com/view/article/46376.

85. Peel, *A Year in Public Life,* 189. Spencer glumly admitted that the working classes regarded them "as charitable institutions comparable with Soup Kitchens of years ago." Spencer, "Report on National Kitchens," 7.

86. This was such a problem that Spencer even designed an insulated "water-jacketed carrier." Spencer, "Report on National Kitchens," 5.

87. Ministry of Food official, as quoted in Barnett, *British Food Policy during the First World War,* 151.

88. National Kitchen Advisory Committee, 15 October 1919, NMLH, CC/NK/328. The advisory committee formed by Jones consisted of himself, Pember Reeves, Peel, Mrs. Jessy Mair (all from the ministry), and Phillips. See also Alex J. Philip, *Rations, Rationing and Food Control* (London: Book World, 1918), 110; and H. W. Clemesha, *Food Control in the North-West Division* (Manchester: Manchester University Press, 1922), 31.

89. Peel, *How We Lived Then,* 85.

90. See Jane Lewis and Barbara Brookes, "The Peckham Health Centre, PEP and the Concept of General Practice during the 1930s and 1940s," *Medical History* 27 (1983): 151–161; Lesley A. Hall, "Archives of the Pioneer Health Centre, Peckham, in the Wellcome Library," *Social History of Medicine* 14, no. 3 (2001): 525–538; Philippa Grand, "'Between Work and Sleep': The Problem of Leisure and Civil Society in Interwar Britain" (Ph.D. diss., University of Manchester, 2002), chap. 4; and David Matless, *Landscape and Englishness* (London: Reaktion, 2004).

91. George Scott Williamson, "A Scientific Enquiry into Social Disintegration," n.d., 1–7, WA, SA/PHC/B.1/1/6.

92. "The Basis of Planning: A Lecture Given at the School of Planning and Research for National Development by Dr Scott Williamson," *Architectural Association Journal* (November 1936): 182–186, WA, SA/PHC/D.2/4/2.

93. George Scott Williamson, "Health: Need for Experimental Approach," scrap note, 1939, p. 3, WA, SA/PHC/B.3/12.

94. The early motto of the experiment was "Peaceful Homes, Adequate Parenthood, Healthy Babies, Useful Citizenship." The "Women's Work and Hobbies" room was dedicated to Peel, whose "knowledge and appreciation of the Old Centre led her to work unceasingly for the realisation of the present building." See the handwritten notes in the box WA, SA/PHC/3/1.

95. She remarked on those "well-fed being lively and amiable while those ill-fed were quarrelsome and of uncertain temper." Innes Hope Pearse, "Statement on the Relation of Oakley House to the Pioneer Health Centre," p. 1, WA, SA/PHC/B4/1.

96. Innes Hope Pearse and George Scott Williamson, *The Case for Action: A Survey of Everyday Life under Modern Industrial Conditions with Special Reference to the Question of Health,* 3rd ed. (London: Faber and Faber, 1938), 52. On the politics of their organicism, see Matless, *Landscape and Englishness.*

97. Pearse, "Statement on the Relation of Oakley House," 3.

98. Pearse and Williamson, *The Case for Action,* 136.

99. George Scott Williamson, "Self-Service," May 1938, WA, SA/PHC/B.3/12; Innes Hope Pearse and Lucy H. Crocker, *The Peckham Experiment: A Study in the Living Structure of Society* (New Haven, Conn.: Yale University Press, 1945), 57, 74–75.

100. Minute Book, 1 February 1934, WA, SA/PHC/A.1/3.

101. Pearse and Crocker, *The Peckham Experiment,* 74–75.

102. "The Peckham Experiment: What Next?" 1947, WA, SA/PHC/B.5/23/5; G. Scott Williamson and Innes H. Pearse, *The Passing of Peckham* (London: Associates of Peckham, 1951), 1–2.

103. *Report of an Inquiry into the Working of the School Meals Service,* 8.

104. Sir Thomas G. Jones, *The Unbroken Front: Ministry of Food, 1916–1944: Personalities and Problems* (London: Everybody's Books, 1944). Mass-Observation claimed, however, that the first canteen opened in Liverpool during the summer of 1940, before the Blitz. Charles Madge, "British Restaurants," 22 January 1942, iii, MO, TC67/3/d, "British Restaurants and Canteens."

105. There were huge variations in provision between localities and an enormous gulf between London and the rest of England, Scotland, Wales, and Northern Ireland. Labour Research Department, *Works Canteens and the Catering Trade,* 18–21. See also the rather different but more detailed December 1941 figures provided to Mass-Observation by the Ministry of Food in Madge, "British Restaurants," i.

106. F. Le Gros Clark, *The Communal Restaurant: A Study of the Place of Civic Restaurants in the Life of the Community* (London: London Council of Social Services, 1943), 25, 5 (emphasis in the original).

107. Ibid., 24; Madge, "British Restaurants," iii.

108. Tom Harrisson, "Housewives' Feelings about Food," 24 April 1942, p. 6, MO, TC67/3/d, "British Restaurants and Canteens."

109. "British Restaurant Diary W.00.3. Worcester Jan 1942," in MO, TC67/3/ d, "British Restaurants and Canteens."

110. Le Gros Clark, *The Communal Restaurant*, 24.

111. Ibid., 21.

112. MO, TC67/3/d, "British Restaurants and Canteens."

113. Le Gros Clark, *The Communal Restaurant*, 6, 7–8, 12–13, 19.

114. Ina Zweiniger-Bargielowska, *Austerity in Britain: Rationing, Controls, and Consumption 1939–1959* (Oxford: Oxford University Press, 2000), 74. Mass-Observation's survey found that of the 33 percent who had been to a British Restaurant 96 percent had "liked it," despite odd complaints about the speed of service and cramped accommodation. Harrisson, "Housewives' Feelings about Food," 6, 5.

115. Only 1.3 percent of housewives had ever eaten in a British Restaurant, and while 4 percent disapproved of them, only 40 percent approved (56 percent had no opinion). All figures from Ina Zweiniger-Bargielowska, *Austerity in Britain*, 33, 74, 114. See also Steven Fielding, Peter Thompson and Nick Tiratsoo *"England Arise!": The Labour Party and Popular Politics in 1940s Britain* (Manchester: Manchester University Press, 1995), 108–110.

116. Ministry of Food, "British Restaurants: Yiewsley and West Drayton Urban District," NA, MAFF900/112.

117. Le Gros Clark, *The Communal Restaurant*, 21; Ministry of Food, "Nutritional Survey of British Restaurants: General," NA, MAFF98/61.

118. James Devon, *Lets Eat!* (London: War Facts, 1944), 16, 12–13.

119. "Altogether the canteen is an important factor in the social education of members." *Community Centres* (London: HMSO, 1944), quoted in F. Le Gros Clark, *Community Restaurants in Design* (London: London Council of Social Services, 1945), 12, 4.

120. Managers had to remember "to satisfy the tastes and prejudices of the community they will have to serve." Le Gros Clark, *Community Restaurants in Design*, 4.

121. Barnett, *British Food Policy during the First World War.*

122. See Angus Calder, *The People's War* (London: Jonathan Cape, 1969); and, most recently, Sonya Rose, *Which People's War? National Identity and Citizenship in Britain, 1939–1945* (Oxford: Oxford University Press, 2003).

123. Ministry of Food, *How Britain Was Fed in War Time* (London: HMSO, 1946);

R. J. Hammond, *Food: History of the Second World War,* 3 vols. (London: HMSO, 1951–1962). See also Jones, *The Unbroken Front.*

124. The most comprehensive account of the administrative machinery and politics of food rationing is Zweiniger-Bargielowska, *Austerity in Britain.*

125. Only between 54 and 64 percent of families claimed their entitlements, but levels of consumption were significantly lower, with only 27 percent of children actually consuming their daily requirements. See J. E. Fothergill, "The Uptake of Welfare Foods: Report of an Inquiry Carried Out by the Social Survey in April 1951 for the Ministry of Food," September 1951, NA, M501 (24)/7, ii.

126. Carolyn Steedman, *Landscape for a Good Woman: A Story of Two Lives* (1986), 122, 2. I am indebted here to Bruce Robbins's perceptive reading of this text in "The Health Visitor: Identity, Injustice, and the Welfare State," a paper presented to "States of Welfare," a Mellon Foundation Conference at the Unit of Criticism and Interpretive Theory at University of Illinois, Urbana-Champaign, 10–11 March 2006.

7. You Are What You Eat

1. Board of Education, *Health of the Schoolchild, 1926* (London: HMSO,1927), cited in David Smith and Malcolm Nicolson, "Nutrition, Education, Ignorance and Income: A Twentieth-Century Debate," in Harmke Kamminga and Andrew Cunningham (eds.), *The Science and Culture of Nutrition, 1840–1940* (Amsterdam: Rodopi, 1995), 297.

2. F. Le Gros Clark (ed.), *National Fitness: A Brief Essay on Contemporary Britain* (London: Macmillan, 1938), 114.

3. A point first compellingly made in Denise Riley, *"Am I That Name?" History and the Category of "Women" in History* (Basingstoke, U.K.: Macmillan, 1988).

4. B. S. Rowntree, *Poverty: A Study of Town Life* (London: Macmillan, 1901), 141–142, 74, 105.

5. B. S. Rowntree, *The Human Needs of Labour* (London: Longmans, Green, 1937), 127.

6. B. S. Rowntree, *Poverty and Progress: A Second Social Survey of York,* 2nd ed. (London: Longmans, Green, 1942), 26.

7. Among many examples, see *Report of the Inter-Departmental Committee on Physical Deterioration,* vol. 1, *Report and Appendix* (London: HMSO, 1904), 41; Pilgrim Trust, *Men without Work: A Report Made to the Pilgrim Trust* (Cambridge: Cambridge University Press, 1938), 115, 128. As Paul Johnson and Ross McKibbin have argued, middle-class social investigators utterly failed to comprehend the ways in which conspicuous and seemingly unnecessary forms of expenditure were intricately tied to the maintenance of working-class self-respect and cultural capital.

Paul Johnson, *Saving and Spending: The Working-Class Economy in Britain, 1870–1939* (Oxford: Clarendon, 1985), 6; Ross McKibbin, "Social Class and Social Observation in Edwardian England," *Transactions of the Royal Historical Society* 28 (1978): 175–199.

8. D. N. Paton, J. G. Dunlop, and E. M. Inglis, *A Study of the Diet of the Labouring Classes in Edinburgh* (Edinburgh: Otto Schulze, 1900), cited in Smith and Nicolson, "Nutrition, Education, Ignorance and Income," 289; *Report of the Inter-Departmental Committee on Physical Deterioration,* 1:40.

9. For examples, see Pilgrim Trust, *Men without Work,* 114; PEP, "The Malnutrition Controversy," *Planning* 88 (15 December 1936): 12–13. For the rare advocate of the housewife, see Maud Pember Reeves, *Round about a Pound a Week* (London: Virago, [1913] 1979), 75, 144.

10. Mary Poovey, *Making a Social Body: British Cultural Formation, 1830–1864* (Chicago: Chicago University Press, 1995); Eileen Yeo, *The Contest for Social Science: Relations and Representations of Gender and Class* (London: Rivers Oram, 1996); Ellen Ross, *Love and Toil: Motherhood in Outcast London, 1870–1918* (Oxford: Oxford University Press, 1993); Jane Lewis, "The Working-Class Wife and Mother and State Intervention, 1870–1918," in Jane Lewis (ed.), *Labour and Love: Women's Experience of Home and Family, 1850–1914* (Oxford: Oxford University Press, 1986).

11. Nikolas Rose, *Powers of Freedom: Reframing Political Thought* (Cambridge: Polity, 1999), 128–130, 213–215.

12. Rowntree, *Poverty,* 223–225.

13. See Pember Reeves, *Round about a Pound a Week,* 10–15, for a detailed picture of grappling with accounts. See also Bowley's telling remark that "few people have the patience, perseverance, willingness and skill to keep such accounts." A. L. Bowley, *The Nature and Purpose of the Measurement of Social Phenomena* (London: King & Son, 1915), 139–140.

14. Max Cohen, *I Was One of the Unemployed* (London: Gollancz, 1945), 102.

15. Sir William Crawford and H. Broadley, *The People's Food* (London: Heinemann, 1938), 314. Their survey, however, included all social classes, not, as with its predecessors, just the working class.

16. Kathryn Hughes, *The Short Life and Long Times of Mrs Beeton* (London: Harper, 2006).

17. June Purvis, "Domestic Subjects since 1870," in Ivor Goodson (ed.), *Social Histories of the Secondary Curriculum* (London: Falmer, 1985); Ann Marie Turnball, "Learning Her Womanly Work: The Elementary School Curriculum, 1870–1914," in Felicity Hunt (ed.), *Lessons for Life: The Schooling of Girls and Women, 1850–1950* (Oxford: Blackwell, 1987).

18. The "National" provided cooking courses and advice to the prison commissioners, the local government board, and the army. By 1913 it claimed to have sup-

plied 75 percent of London County Council's elementary cooking teachers. Dorothy Stone, *The National: The Story of a Pioneer College, The National Training College of Domestic Subjects* (London: Robert Hale, 1976), 91–92, 62–63, 95–97, 106.

19. Helen Sillitoe, *A History of the Teaching of Domestic Subjects* (London: Methuen, 1933), 27, 44.

20. Ibid., 41, 44; Anne Clendinning, *Demons of Domesticity: Women and the English Gas Industry, 1889–1939* (Aldershot: Ashgate, 2004), 32.

21. Anna Davin, *Growing Up Poor: Home, School and Street in London, 1870–1914* (London: Rivers Oram, 1996), 149.

22. Cooking classes, it stipulated, should focus on economy, practicality, and nutritional knowledge; see *Report of the Inter-Departmental Committee on Physical Deterioration,* 1:43.

23. Sillitoe, *A History of the Teaching of Domestic Subjects,* 129–131. Board of Education, *Special Report on the Teaching of Cookery to Public Elementary School Children* (London: HMSO, 1907).

24. Board of Education, *General Report on the Teaching of Domestic Subjects to Public Elementary School Children in England and Wales, by the Chief Woman Inspector of the Board of Education* (London: HMSO, 1912), 38.

25. "Women, War, and Society" microfilm collection, IWM, pt. 2, Education Files, 2/9/6, Household and Social Science Department, King's College for Women; Nancy L. Blakestead, "King's College of Household and Social Science and the Origins of Dietetics Education," in David F. Smith (ed.), *Nutrition in Britain: Science, Scientists and Politics in the Twentieth Century* (New York: Routledge, 1997), 75–98.

26. It has been estimated that by the 1890s over half a million women worked in what we might call the inspection business, on either a professional or a voluntary basis. Martha Vicinus, *Independent Women: Work and Community for Single Women, 1850–1920* (London: Virago, 1985), 211–212.

27. Deborah Dwork, *War Is Good for Babies and Other Young Children: A History of the Infant and Child Welfare Movement in England, 1898–1918* (London: Tavistock, 1986), 147, 154, 167.

28. Clendinning, *Demons of Domesticity.*

29. I am heavily indebted here to Michael Buckley's forthcoming doctoral dissertation, "Recipe for Reform: Food, Economy and Citizenship in First World War Britain." Parallel efforts were made by, among others, the National Training College of Domestic Subjects, the National Union of Women's Suffrage Societies (whose Patriotic Housekeeping Exhibition in November 1915 focused specifically on menus and foodstuffs that maximized nutritional value and minimized cost and waste), and the British Commercial Gas Association. "Women, War, and Society"

microfilm collection, IWM, pt. 4, Food, 1/25; Stone, *The National,* 128–129, 136; Clendinning, *Demons of Domesticity,* 186–189.

30. Lady Chance, "An Account of the Work of the National Food Economy League," and National Food Fund, "The National Food Fund and Its Work," both in the "Women, War, and Society" microfilm collection, IWM; "Classes in Household Economy," *Times,* 12 March 1915. Scotland had its own Patriotic Food League.

31. On the Board of Education's early activities, see "Memorandum on Work in Connection with Food Economy and Control, carried out by Miss Kate Manley, O.B.E.," "Women, War, and Society" microfilm collection, IWM, pt. 4, Food, 3/9.

32. For a recent account that charts the emergence of consumer rights in formal political terms, see Matthew Hilton, *Consumerism in Twentieth-Century Britain: The Search for a Historical Movement* (Cambridge: Cambridge University Press, 2003).

33. Lady Chance, "An Account of the Work of the National Food Economy League."

34. These publications were priced accordingly. See, for instance, *Patriotic Food Economy for the Well-to-Do* (6d); *Handbook for Housewives* (2d); *Housekeeping on 25/- a Week* (1d). See also "Syllabus for Working Women" and "Syllabus for Mistresses and Cooks," "Women, War, and Society" microfilm collection, IWM.

35. *Handbook for Housewives,* 3, 4.

36. *Patriotic Food Economy for the Well-to-Do,* 4, 2, 11.

37. Despite the criticisms of the Food (War) Committee, see Mikulas Teich, "Science and Food during the Great War: Britain and Germany," in Kamminga and Cunningham, *The Science and Culture of Nutrition,* 227.

38. C. S. Peel, *A Year in Public Life* (London: Constable, 1919), 106–107.

39. Here, for a work echoing the advice of the Food (War) Committee, see T. B. Wood and F. G. Hopkins, *Food Economy in War Time* (Cambridge: Cambridge University Press, 1917), 35.

40. Peel, *A Year in Public Life,* 126, 26–27, 28.

41. "Report on Cookery Section of the Ministry of Food," n.d., National Museum of Labour History (NMLH), CC/NK/4.ii; "Memorandum on Work in Connection with Food Economy and Control" 3. On the media-savvy Kennedy Jones, see Sir Thomas G. Jones, *The Unbroken Front: Ministry of Food, 1916–1944: Personalities and Problems* (London: Everbody's Books, 1944).

42. Margaret L. Barnett, *British Food Policy during the First World War* (London: Allen and Unwin, 1985), 76–77, 117.

43. Jones, *The Unbroken Front,* 4; Derek J. Oddy, *From Plain Fare to Fusion Food: British Diet from the 1890s to the 1990s* (Woodbridge: Boydell, 2003), 77–78.

44. Ibid., 23; Peel, *A Year in Public Life,* 167.

45. Oddy, *From Plain Fare to Fusion Food,* 82. The conversation in Figure 7.1 runs like this: "My dear, I've been lecturing on food economy, and I'm dying for tea!" / "You poor dear!" / "As I've been telling them, it's the amount of unnecessary food that people eat— / Thank you, I will—as I was saying— / The servants eat so much!" / "Just what I find!" / "If people would only deny themselves to ever so small an extent!" / "Don't be afraid of it, it's home made[.]" / "My dear, I see no sign of self-denial anywhere[.]" / "I'm afraid you're right—I'll just ring for some more bread and butter."

46. Peel, *A Year in Public Life,* 126, 91.

47. "When at a cookery demonstration a bean was suggested as a substitute for the meat which it was so difficult to obtain, a good lady laughed ironically, "Give me 'usbin' that muck? Yes, I don't think!' Whilst another added, 'Give 'im beans, an' get a black eye for me pains!'" Peel, *How We Lived Then,* 91.

48. NMLH, Consumers' Council 1918–1920, CC/NK/2. By 1920 it was claimed that some three thousand had been reeducated as cooking instructors.

49. Stone, *The National,* 128–129, 136; "Memorandum on Work in Connection with Food Economy and Control," "Women, War, and Society" microfilm collection, IWM, pt. 4, Food, 3/9, "Household and Social Science Department, King's College for Women, Appointments Gained by Past Students," ibid., Education files, 2/9/4; Sillitoe, *A History of the Teaching of Domestic Subjects,* chap. 15.

50. Philippa C. Easdaile, "Memorandum on the Teaching of Domestic Science in England and Its Application to Work in the Colonies," forwarded by W. Ormsby-Gore of the Colonial Office to British resident, Zanzibar, 21 April 1937, Zanzibar National Archives, AB 1/395 Secretariat, Domestic Science, 1937. My thanks to Corrie Decker for this memo.

51. Despite a rich historiography on domestic science in the United States, there has been a dearth of similar work on Britain. See, however, Clendinning, *Demons of Domesticity;* Judy Giles, *The Parlour and the Suburb: Domestic Identities, Class, Femininity and Modernity* (Berg: New York, 2004); Dena Attar, *Wasting Girl's Time: The History and Politics of Home Economics* (London: Virago, 1990).

52. V. H. Mottram, *Food and the Family* (London: Nisbet, 1925); V. H. Mottram and W. M. Clifford, *Properties of Food: A Practical Text-Book for Teachers of Domestic Science* (London: University of London Press, 1929).

53. Established in 1917, the People's League of Health appears to have quickly taken up the nutritional question. See Eric Pritchard, *Principles of Diet: The People's League of Health Pamphlets* (London: Bailliere, Tindall & Cox, 1921).

54. Mottram, *Food and the Family,* 17–18, x. For a similar story of popularization, see Harmke Kamminga, "'Axes to Grind': Popularising the Science of Vitamins, 1920s and 1930s," in D. F. Smith and J. Phillips (eds.), *Food, Science, Policy and*

Regulation in the Twentieth Century: International and Comparative Perspectives (London: Routledge, 2000), 83–100; Rima D. Apple, *Vitamania: Vitamins in American Culture* (New Brunswick, N.J.: Rutgers University Press, 1996).

55. Here is Mottram's explanation of how to calculate a family's calorific needs: "Assuming father to be a clergyman, his index will be 1.0; his wife's 0.83; the children, whom we will assume to be nine, twelve and fourteen years of age, the last being a boy, will need indices of 0.6, 0.7 and 1.0. Assuming there to be two maids each with an index of 0.83. The total index will be $1.0 + 0.83 + 0.6 + 0.7 + 1.0 + 0.83 + 0.83$ or 5.79, i.e., the family counts as 5.79 adult males. The total calorie need per day will be 3,000 x 5.79 or 17,370, or per week, 121,590. The amount supplied in food taken during the week should cover this weekly need; if it does not, trouble will be brewing somewhere." Got it? Mottram, *Food and the Family,* 140.

56. Violet G. Plimmer, *Food Values at a Glance and How to Plan a Healthy Diet* (London: Longmans, Green, 1935), 5.

57. Ibid., 13; R. H. A. Plimmer and Violet A. Plimmer, *Food, Health and Vitamins* (London: Longmans, Green, 1928), vii.

58. Rima D. Apple, *Perfect Motherhood: Science and Childrearing in America* (Piscataway, N.J.: Rutgers University Press, 2006).

59. Sally Horrocks, "The Business of Vitamins: Nutrition Science and the Food Industry in Interwar Britain," in Kamminga and Cunningham, *The Science and Culture of Nutrition,* 247–248.

60. Plimmer and Plimmer, *Food, Health and Vitamins,* 89, 6. On the rise between the wars of the male cult of reducing, see Ina Zweiniger-Bargielowska, "'The Culture of the Abdomen': Obesity and Reducing in Britain, c. 1900–1939," *Journal of British Studies* 44, no. 2 (April 2005): 239–273.

61. George Newman, *On the State of Public Health, 1932* (London: HMSO, 1933), 140n47. On the organic movement see David Matless, *Landscape and Englishness* (London: Reaktion, 1998), chaps. 3 and 4.

62. Mottram and Clifford, *Properties of Food,* 205. On interwar critiques of mass consumer culture, see D. L. LeMahieu, *A Culture for Democracy: Mass Communication and the Cultivated Mind in Britain between the Wars* (Oxford: Clarendon, 1988). For a particular view of the "mob instinct" of the consumer in interwar Britain, see Percy Redfern (ed.), *Self and Society: First Twelve Essays; Social and Economic Problems from the Hitherto Neglected Point of View of the Consumer* (London: Ernest Benn, 1930), 4.

63. Mottram and Clifford, *Properties of Food,* 206.

64. PEP, *Planning: What Consumers Need* 36 (23 October 1934), 12. Much of PEP's discussion of the need for consumer rights and protection were illustrated

through reference to foods. Committee against Malnutrition, "Memorandum to the Advisory Committee on Nutrition from the Committee Against Malnutrition," Bulletin of the Committee against Malnutrition, 10 (September 1935), 51.

65. Crawford and Broadley, *The People's Food,* 303, 304, 86.

66. Fabian Society, "National Nutritional Conference," BLPES, K25/1.

67. Siegfried Giedion, *Mechanization Takes Command: A Contribution to Anonymous History* (New York: Norton, 1948). See also Leif Jerram, "Buildings, Spaces, Politics: The City of Munich and the Management of Modernity, 1900–1930" (Ph.D. diss., University of Manchester, 2000); "Kitchen Technologies," special issue, *Technology and Culture* 43, no. 4 (2002).

68. The following paragraphs in the text draw heavily on Deborah S. Ryan, *The Ideal Home through the 20th Century: Daily Mail—Ideal Home Exhibition* (London: Hazar, 1997).

69. *Daily Mail Ideal Labour-Saving Home* (London: Associated Newspapers, 1920).

70. Ryan, *The Ideal Home,* 34.

71. She had earlier published her own models in Dorothy Peel, *The Labour-Saving House* (London: John Lane, the Bodley Head, 1917). See Chapter 6 for Peel's *Daily Mail* cookbooks.

72. Tom Jeffrey and Keith McClelland, "A World Fit to Live In: The *Daily Mail* and the Middle Classes, 1918–1939," in J. Curran, A. Smith, and P. Wingate (eds.), *Impacts and Influences: Essays on Media Power* (London: Methuen, 1987), 27–52. In 1921 the Ideal Home Exhibition was temporarily renamed the Daily Mail Efficiency Exhibition.

73. Ryan, *The Ideal Home,* 16. Mark Sandberg has suggestively written: "Domestic display has a long history, to be sure, but at some point in the early twentieth century, the idea of trying out space imaginatively before 'buying' it, began to be widely assimilated . . . The model home, I would propose, is the site for this transformation, and facilitated the spread of a modern logic of housing that saw fit between body and space as something performed, not given." Mark B. Sandberg, "Temporary Housing; Model-Home Spectators and Housing Exhibitions in the Early Scandinavian Design Movement," unpublished paper, February 2004.

74. Ryan, *The Ideal Home,* 55, 17. The colonial and postcolonial careers of ideal-home exhibitions are just beginning to receive attention; see the forthcoming doctoral dissertation of Bianca Murillo at University of California, Santa Barbara, on the *Daily Graphic*'s Ideal Home Exhibition in Accra, Ghana, which attracted fifty thousand visitors in 1967.

75. See Barbara Vaughan, *Growing Up in Salford, 1919–1928* (Manchester: Neil Richardson, 1983), 24; "Papers from the Mass-Observation Archive at the University of Sussex," microfilm 78388, pt. 1, reel 33, W42/J.

76. David Jeremiah, *Architecture and Design for the Family in Britain, 1900–1970* (Manchester: Manchester University Press, 2000), 106.

77. By 1932 there were twenty-five weekly and fourteen monthly magazines for women. *Woman's Weekly* had over a million readers. Ross McKibbin, *Classes and Cultures: England, 1918–1951* (Oxford: Oxford University Press, 2000), 508. I draw here on *Ragtime to Wartime: The Best of Good Housekeeping, 1922–1939* (London: Ebury, 1986).

78. Clendinning, *Demons of Domesticity,* 268–270.

79. Georgie Boynton Child, The *Efficient Kitchen: Definite Directions for the Planning, Arranging and Equipping of the Modern Labor-Saving Kitchen—A Practical Book for the Homemaker* (New York, Robert McBride, 1925); Charles R. Darling, *Modern Domestic Scientific Appliances: Being a Treatise for the Guidance of Users and Manufacturers of Domestic Appliances, Architects and Teachers of Domestic Science, with Special Regard to Efficiency, Economy and Correct Method of Use* (London: Spon, 1932).

80. A mission not limited to the middle-class home. An EAW survey in 1935 estimated that domestic electrification could reduce the hours of housework for working-class women by 73 percent, from 26.5 hours a week to just over 7 hours. Caroline Davidson, *A Woman's Work Is Never Done: A History of Housework in the British Isles, 1650–1950* (London: Chatto and Windus, 1986), 42–43.

81. On the EAW and Haslett see Suzette Worden, "Powerful Women: Electricity in the Home, 1919–1940," in Judy Attfield and Pat Kirkham (eds.), *A View from the Interior: Feminism, Women and Design* (London: Women's Press, 1989), 128–143; Rosalind Messenger, *The Doors of Opportunity: A Biography of Dame Caroline Haslett* (London: Femina, 1967); Davidson, *A Woman's Work Is Never Done,* 40–42. By 1940 the EAW had eighty-five branches and nine thousand members.

82. Quoted in Jeremiah, *Architecture and Design for the Family,* 69.

83. Worden, "Powerful Women," 144; Messenger, *The Doors of Opportunity,* 79–82. Under Haslett's direction the EAW forged close links with the Association of Teachers of Domestic Science, holding an annual conference for them from 1930 and offering diplomas from 1933.

84. Established in 1934 the Women's Gas Council followed the EAW's lead and sought to bridge the divide "between the scientist and the housewife and link the manufacturer with the consumer." By 1939 it had recruited thirteen thousand housewives to its regular weekly meetings in branch showrooms to discuss general issues of home management and the specific contribution of gas technologies to them. Clendinning, *Demons of Domesticity,* 285.

85. A variety of women's organizations were represented, such as the National Council of Women, the Women's Co-Operative Guild, and the Women's Labour League, which had earlier published the pamphlet *The Working Women's House.* Ministry of Reconstruction Advisory Council, *Women's Housing Subcommittee, First Interim*

Report, Cd. 9166 (London: HMSO, 1918); Ministry of Reconstruction Advisory Council, *Final Report,* Cd. 9232 (London: HMSO, 1919). See Barbara McFarlane, "Homes Fit for Heroines: Housing in the Twenties," in Matrix, *Making Space: Women and the Man-Made Environment* (London: Pluto, 1986), 26–36.

86. Alison Ravetz, *The Place of Home: English Domestic Environments, 1914–2000* (London: Chapman and Hall, 1995), chap. 8.

87. Alison Ravetz, "A View for the Interior," in Attfield and Pat Kirkham, *A View from the Interior,* 198.

88. Ibid. The *Daily Mail's Book of Britain's Post-War Homes,* by Mrs. Pleydell Bouverie, was also published in 1944 after an extensive three-year survey to find the "house that women want." Ryan, *The Ideal Home,* 89.

89. Cited in Marion Roberts, "Private Kitchens, Public Cooking," in Matrix, *Making Space,* 107.

90. PEP, *Report on the Market for Household Appliances* (1945), cited in Helene Reynard, *Domestic Science as a Career* (London: Southern Editorial Syndicate, 1947), chap. 13.

91. Cited in Marion Roberts, "Private Kitchens, Public Cooking," in Matrix, *Making Space,* 107.

92. F. Le Gros Clark, "Memorandum on the 'Food Advice' Work of the Ministry of Food," April 1946, 1, WA, GC/145/04. Historians have entirely neglected the work of the Food Advice Division.

93. Ministry of Food, "Food Advice Information Service," NA, MAFF102/ 36 1.

94. See, for a full list of these materials, ibid., November 1951. The nostalgic or curious can sample many of Food Advice Division recipes in cookbooks written by one of its members; see Marguerite Patten, *We'll Eat Again: A Collection of Recipes from the War Years* (London: Hamlyn, 2002); *Post-war Kitchen: Nostalgic Food and Facts from 1945–1954* (London: Hamlyn, 2000); *Victory Cookbook: Nostalgic Food and Facts from 1940–1954* (London: Bounty, 2002).

95. Sian Nicholas, *The Echo of War: Home Front Propaganda and the Wartime BBC, 1939–45* (Manchester: Manchester University Press, 1996), 82.

96. For characteristic examples, see Barbara A. Callow, *Good Health on War-Time Food* (London: Oxford University Press, 1941); Ministry of Food, *Wise Eating in Wartime* (London: HMSO, 1943); Edinburgh Children's Nutritional Council, *It Should Be the Aim of All Housewives to Secure for the Family a Well-Balanced Diet* (Edinburgh: Children's Nutritional Council, 1944); Ministry of Food, *The ABC of Cookery* (London: HMSO, 1945).

97. Le Gros Clark, "Memorandum on the 'Food Advice' Work of the Ministry of Food," 1. Mass-Observation's early report on reactions to the ministry's publicity campaigns found that most unfavorable comment was "based upon resentment as to

the fact that the Ministry should condescendingly inform 'them.'" MO, TC67/2/A, Ministry of Food—Publicity Campaign Questionnaire, May 1940.

98. L. S. Horton, "Memorandum on Food Advice Centres," 19 January 1941, NA, MAFF102/1; N. Bamworth, Food Economy Division, to H. P. Blunt, Public Relations Division, Ministry of Food, 4 April 1941, in "Food Education Campaigns: Establishment of Food Advice Centres," NA, MAFF102/1.

99. The figure rose to 23,567 by the end of 1947. See James Hinton, *Women, Social Leadership and the Second World War: Continuities of Class* (Oxford: Oxford University Press, 2003), 168.

100. "Guidance Notes for Grand Openings of Food Advice Centres, March 1941," in Ministry of Food, Food Education Campaigns. Freddie "Ricepud" Grisewood, host of the BBC *Kitchen Front* show, traveled the country, opening Food Advice Centres, often to large audiences that spilled out onto the pavement and road outside. See Norman Longmate (ed.), *The Home Front: An Anthology of Personal Experience, 1938–1945* (London: Chatto and Windus, 1981), 154.

101. L. S. Horton, "Memorandum on Food Advice Centres," 19 January 1941, 1–3, NA, MAFF102/1.

102. Ministry of Food, Food Advice Division—National Training Colleges of Domestic Subjects, General Correspondence, NA, MAFF900/151; Stone, *National,* chaps. 39–40.

103. F. Chapman to Miss McKean, Weekly Report: Doncaster, 1 May 1943; Resume of Work Done in Eastern Division—both in NA, ibid.; Cardiff: Cookery Demonstrations, Lectures on Nutrition, Film Shows; Permanent Records of Divisional Food Advice Activities, 1940–1949: Midland Division; Food Advice Service in South Wales; Ministry of Food, Food Advice Centre, 79 St Johns Road, London, SW11—all in NA, MAFF102/30.

104. Ministry of Food, "Food Advice Centre—Doncaster," NA, MAFF900/152; Ministry of Food, "'News of the World' Exhibition," NA, MAFF128/16.

105. F. Le Gros Clark, "Memorandum on the 'Food Advice' Work of the Ministry of Food," 5.

106. In April 1946 fewer than half of the 22,300 food leaders were registered as trained. Just as there were considerable regional variations in the food leader scheme (Scotland and London between them accounted for less than 10 percent of the total), so the preponderance of certain organizations varied from locality to locality. In Newcastle 30 percent of Food Leaders belonged to the WVS, with a further 40 percent being professional women. Ibid., 2, 4.

107. Hinton has suggested that reliance on middle-class voluntary groups like the WVS made that contact even less likely. Hinton, "Women, Social Leadership and the Second World War," 168–175.

108. MO, TC/67/2A, Ministry of Food—Publicity Campaign Questionnaire,"

May 1940; ibid., "The Kitchen Front Exhibition: Investigation into the Public's Knowledge of Energy, Body-Building and Protective Foods."

109. It is true that 10 percent of working-class homes still lacked a wireless to hear it. Ibid., "April 1940: Gert and Daisy's BBC Talks."

110. Home Intelligence Special Report, no. 44, "Housewives' Attitudes towards Official Campaigns and Instructions," 14 May 1943, NA, INF1/293. Also cited in Ina Zweiniger-Bargielowská, *Austerity in Britain: Rationing, Controls, and Consumption 1939–1959* (Oxford: Oxford University Press, 2000), 111–112.

111. Ministry of Food, "Reports on Enquiries into the Readership of 'Food Facts,' prepared for Ministry of Food by the British Market Research Bureau Limited, a branch of J. Walter Thompson Co. Ltd," NA, MAFF223/23.

112. For instance, the supervisor of Doncaster's Food Advice Centre complained that Gert and Daisy's recent demonstration there had undone much good work by their too-liberal use of ingredients like eggs and sugar. Ministry of Food, "Food Advice Centre—Doncaster," NA, MAFF900/152. Woolton personally received thirteen thousand letters in 1941. *Times,* 12 January 1942.

113. "The Kitchen Front Exhibition"; Wartime Social Survey, Food during the War, February 1942–October 1943, NA, RG23/9A.

114. Le Gros Clark, "Memorandum on the 'Food Advice' Work of the Ministry of Food," 10.

115. Ministry of Food, "State of Nutrition in UK," NA, MAFF98/68.

116. For examples, see J. G. Atherton, *Home to Stay: Stretford in the Second World War* (Manchester: Neil Richardson, 1991); Barbara Atkinson, *The Home Front: Life in Ashton during World War II* (Ashton, U.K.: Tameside Leisure Services, 1995).

117. The General Ration Book (R.B.1) was issued to adults, whereas children under six had the Infants Ration Book (R.B.2) and children between five and eighteen the Children's Ration Book (R.B.4). Straight rationing, which required the housewife to register with a particular retailer for supplies, applied to bacon, ham, butter, sugar, meat, tea, margarine, cooking fats, preserves, and cheese by 1941. Points rationing, in which consumers received sixteen points every four weeks to spend as and where they saw fit on a variety of foods (extended by 1942 to canned foods, dried foods, rice, tapioca, condensed milk, breakfast cereals, biscuits, and oats). Fruit, vegetables, fish, and bread were all unrationed.

118. The Ministry of Food was always careful to validate the patriotic efforts of the housewife in mastering the disciplines of rationing: "There were ration books to be remembered, points values and validity to be watched, occasional supplies of oranges and other rarities to be tracked down. Much time was spent in queues, even for the ordinary rations." Ministry of Food, *How Britain Was Fed in War Time,* 49–50.

119. For an extensive discussion of attitudes toward food rationing and the poli-

tics of the black market, see Zweiniger-Bargielowska, *Austerity in Britain,* 69–86, 160–177.

120. James Hinton, "Militant Housewives: The British Housewives' League and the Attlee Government," *History Workshop Journal* 38 (1994): 129–156; Joe Moran, "Queuing Up in Post-War Britain," *Twentieth-Century British History* 16, no. 3 (2005): 283–305.

121. See Ministry of Food, *Manual of Nutrition* (London: HMSO, 1945), of which new updated editions were published in 1947 and 1953; F. Le Gros Clark and Margaret E. Gage, *Planning Meals: Introductory Book for the Use of Beginners* (London: Association of Teachers of Domestic Subjects, 1951).

122. Quoted in Sonya Rose, *Which People's War? National Identity and Citizenship in Britain, 1939–1945* (Oxford: Oxford University Press, 2003), 34.

123. *Family Cooking: A Guide to Kitchen Management and Cooking for the Family* (Dublin: Parkside, 1947), 5.

124. Helene Reynard, *Domestic Science as a Career* (London: Southern Editorial Syndicate, 1947), 11, 12, 100.

125. James Devon, *Let's Eat!* (London: War Facts, 1944), 3, 7.

126. Atherton, *Home to Stay,* 11. On the long-delayed and largely toothless 1938 act, which remained chiefly concerned with questions of adulteration, not advertising, see Michael French and Jim Phillips, *Cheated Not Poisoned? Food Regulation in the United Kingdom, 1875–1938* (Manchester: Manchester University Press, 2000).

127. Ministry of Food, *The Advertising, Labelling and Composition of Food* (London: HMSO, 1949), 9.

128. Ministry of Food, *How Britain Was Fed in War Time,* 50; Ministry of Food, *The Advertising, Labelling and Composition of Food,* 64–65. The Labelling of Food Order extended these standards in 1946.

129. Carolyn Steedman, *Landscape for a Good Woman: A Story of Two Lives* (New Brunswick, N.J.: Rutgers University Press, 1986); Zweiniger-Bargielowska, "Rationing Austerity and the Conservative Party Recovery after 1945," *Historical Journal* 37, no. 1 (1994): 176–917; Zweiniger-Bargielowska, *Austerity in Britain.*

8. Remembering Hunger

1. Aneurin Bevan, *In Place of Fear* (London: Heinemann, 1952). Bevan was one of the few Labour M.P.'s to support unemployed hunger marchers between the wars.

2. *Hansard,* 5th series, Commons, (1947–48), 444:1632, 1635.

3. Jon Lawrence, "Labour—the Myths It Has Lived By," in D. Tanner, P. Thane, and N. Tiratsoo (eds.), *Labour's First Century* (Cambridge: Cambridge Uni-

versity Press, 2000), 349. For examples, see Francis Williams, *The Rise of the Labour Party* (London: Labour Party, 1946); Williams, *Fifty Years' March: The Rise of the Labour Party* (London: Odhams, 1949); *Marching On, 1900–1950: Golden Jubilee of the Labour Party* (London: Labour Party, 1950).

4. Geoff Eley, "*Distant Voices, Still Lives:* The Family Is a Dangerous Place; Memory, Gender, and the Image of the Working Class," in Robert Rosenstone (ed.), *Revisioning History: Film and the Construction of New Past* (Princeton, N.J.: Princeton University Press, 1995), 30.

5. From its creation in 1921 through to 1929 this organization had the slightly more cumbersome name of the National Unemployed Workers' Committee Movement.

6. Ellen Wilkinson, *The Town That Was Murdered: The Life-Story of Jarrow* (London: Gollancz, 1939), 7.

7. A classic example is Noreen Branson and Margot Heinemann, *Britain in the Nineteen Thirties* (London: Weidenfeld and Nicolson, 1971).

8. For testimonies of those involved, see Wal Hannington, *The Insurgents in London* (London: Southwark, 1923); Hannington, *Unemployed Struggles, 1919–1936: My Life and Struggles amongst the Unemployed* (Wakefield, U.K.: EP, [1936] 1973); Bob Edwards, *Hunger Marches and Hyde Park* (London: Jones, 1983); Robert Davies, "Hunger March: The Story of a Short and Long Unemployed March to Preston and to London," Manuscript, Working Class Movement Library, n.d.); Ian MacDougall (ed.), *Voices from the Hunger Marches: Personal Recollections by Scottish Hunger Marchers of the 1920s and 1930s,* 2 vols. (Edinburgh: Polygon, 1990–1991).

9. For accounts of the 1933 marches, see Harry McShane, *Three Days That Shook Edinburgh: Story of the Historic Scottish Hunger March* (Edinburgh: AK, [1933] 1994); Phil Harker, *Lancashire's Fight for Bread! Story of the Great Lancashire Hunger March* (Manchester: Lancashire Marchers' Committee, 1933).

10. Peter Kingsford, *The Hunger Marchers in Britain, 1920–1939* (London: Lawrence and Wishart, 1982); Richard Croucher, *We Refuse to Starve in Silence: A History of the National Unemployed Workers Movement* (London: Lawrence and Wishart, 1987); W. Gray, M. Jenkins, E. Frow, and R. Frow, *Unemployed Demonstrations, Salford and Manchester, 1931* (Salford: Working Class Movement Library, 1981); H. Davies, *Ten Lean Years: Unemployed Struggles and the NUWM in Nottingham* (Middlesborough, U.K.: n.p., 1984).

11. John Burnett, *Idle Hands: The Experience of Unemployment, 1790–1990* (London: Routledge, 1994), 262. This paragraph owes much to Burnett's guidance through the thickets of legislation. See also Croucher, *We Refuse to Starve in Silence;* David Vincent, *Poor Citizens: The State and the Poor in Twentieth-Century Britain* (London: Longman, 1991).

12. Digby argues that the real battle against a punitive conception of unem-

ployment relief came not from the NUWM but from the highly politicized local boards of guardians and public assistance committees; see Anne Digby, "Changing Welfare Cultures in Region and State," *Twentieth Century British History* 17, no. 3 (2006): 297–322.

13. Croucher, *We Refuse to Starve in Silence,* chap. 1. On continental Europe and British exceptionalism, see Adrian Gregory, "Peculiarities of the English? War, Violence and Politics, 1900–1939," *Journal of Modern European History* 1, no. 1 (2003): 44–59.

14. Hannington, *Unemployed Struggles,* 85, 81.

15. Kingsford, *The Hunger Marchers in Britain,* 50.

16. "The Press with almost the sole exception of the *Daily Herald* and the Liberal newspapers represented the unemployed as people too idle to seek work, and 'the dole' as a comfortable wage." Robert Graves and Alan Hodge, *The Long Weekend: A Social History of Great Britain, 1918–1939* (New York: Norton, 1963), 246.

17. For good examples of the tropes of heroic struggle, selfless sacrifice, and manly endurance, see Harry McShane, *Three Days That Shook Edinburgh,* 7, 14–15; Hannington, *Unemployed Struggles,* 81, 184.

18. *Socialist* 12 (November 1936): 1.

19. "Previously it had been a shameful thing to apply for relief to the Guardians . . . But we insisted that in the new circumstances it would be a point of honour to demand from a country which was denying us the right to a living wage, and in an increasing number of cases the right even to a job." Arthur Horner, *Incorrigible Rebel* (London: MacGibbon & Kee, 1960), cited in Matt Perry, *Bread and Work: Social Policy and the Experience of Unemployment* (London: Pluto, 2000), 122.

20. Croucher's *We Refuse to Starve in Silence* is particularly effective at detailing the NUWM's work on the politics of relief administration. See also Perry, *Bread and Work,* 104.

21. MacDougall, *Voices from the Hunger Marches,* 1:4.

22. A women's contingent consisting of eight women from Barnsley and fourteen from Bradford marched under Brown's leadership from Bradford to Sheffield, where, presumably thought to be lacking the stamina of men, they were bundled onto a coach to Luton, before resuming the march to London and meeting with the Labour M.P.'s Jennie Lee and Marion Phillips. Croucher, *We Refuse to Starve in Silence,* 112.

23. Perry, *Bread and Work,* 78.

24. See Maud Brown, *Stop This Starvation of Mother and Child* (London: NUWM, 1935).

25. *Shields Daily Gazette,* 25 July 1936, 5. "The Jarrow March," Ellen Wilkinson Press Cuttings, NMLH, W1/7.

26. *Daily Herald,* 28 February 1934, 2.

27. "Communist Plot in London: The Truth about Tomorrow's March of Unemployed; Organised Plot to Provoke a Riot at Dictation of Moscow." Special Branch reports on the police and political records of twenty-one NUWM leaders were published the following day in the rest of the press. Kingsford, *The Hunger Marchers in Britain,* 52–53; Hannington, *Unemployed Struggles,* 84.

28. A more favorable response was evident among the local and regional press, especially those covering what was often referred to as the pilgrimage of local men. Press Cuttings, NMLH, CP/IND/HANN/02/04–05.

29. Royden Harrison, "New Light on the Police and Hunger Marchers," *Bulletin of the Society for the Study of Labour History* 37 (Autumn 1978): 17–49.

30. Many historians have focused on the states' repressive response to the NUWM. See, for examples, ibid.; R. Hayburn, "The Police and the Hunger Marchers, *International Review of Social History* 17, no. 3 (1972): 625–644; John Stevenson, "The Politics of Violence," in G. Peele and C. Cook (eds.), *The Politics of Reappraisal, 1918–1939* (London: Macmillan, 1975); John Halstead, Royden Harrison, and John Stevenson, "The Reminiscences of Sid Elias," *Bulletin of the Society for the Study of Labour History* 38 (Spring 1979): 35–48; Gray, Jenkins, Frow, and Frow, *Unemployed Demonstrations, Salford and Manchester.*

31. Hannington claimed that not since the Chartists had the state so persecuted a political leader through the use of spies and agents provocateurs. Hannington, *Unemployed Struggles,* 141.

32. Croucher, *We Refuse to Starve in Silence,* 125–143. On the National Council for Civil Liberties, see Gerald Anderson, *Fascists, Communists and the National Government: Civil Liberties in Great Britain, 1931–1937* (Columbia: University of Missouri Press, 1983); Mark Lilly, *The National Council for Civil Liberties: The First Fifty Years* (London: Macmillan, 1984); K. D. Ewing and C. A. Gearty, *The Struggle for Civil Liberties: Political Freedom and the Rule of Law in Britain, 1914–1945* (New York: Oxford University Press, 2000). Issues of civil rights—to public assembly, to petition and freedom of speech—had been uppermost for the unemployed in the protests during the 1880s. Trafalgar Square had been closed to public meetings following the Bloody Sunday clash there in November 1887—hence the symbolism of meetings by hunger marchers there, under the eye of Tom Mann, forty years later. See Jose Harris, *Unemployment and Politics: A Study in English Social Policy, 1886–1914* (Clarendon: Oxford, 1972), chap. 2.

33. On this political construction of unemployment, see Croucher, *We Refuse to Starve in Silence,* 14–16; Perry, *Bread and Work,* 64–65. On the discovery of the North and the hunger of its working classes, see Chapter 2.

34. Kingsford, *The Hunger Marchers in Britain,* 41.

35. Ibid., 197, 191.

36. Valentine Cunningham, *British Writers of the Thirties* (Oxford: Oxford University Press, 1988), 247.

37. *North Mail and Newcastle Daily Chronicle,* 3 November 1936, in National Hunger March Cuttings, NMLH, CP/IND/HANN/O5; Kingsford, *The Hunger Marchers in Britain,* 212–213.

38. Hugh Montgomery-Massingberd and David Watkin, *The London Ritz: A Social and Architectural History* (London: Aurum, 1980), 92–93. My thanks to Judy Walkowitz for this quotation. See also Graves and Hodge, *The Long Week-End,* 391.

39. My thanks to Fiona Flett, "The Nation and the North: Perceptions of 'The North' through the Jarrow March, 1936" (B.A. thesis, University of Manchester, 1995).

40. She dismissed as "absurd" the hopes of one alderman, who wanted to accept "every unemployed man who can to march to London." Ellen Wilkinson, "The Jarrow March," Ellen Wilkinson Press Cuttings, NMLH, W1/7; *Shields Daily Gazette,* 25 July 1936, 5; *Shields Daily Gazette,* 29 September 1936. All press citations that follow are from this collection unless otherwise stated.

41. *Northern Echo,* 8 September 1936.

42. *South Shields Gazette,* 9 October 1936; *Liverpool Daily Post,* 15 October 1936.

43. *Yorkshire Post,* 6 October 1936; *Daily Independent,* 16 October 1936.

44. *Northampton Daily Chronicle,* 6 October 1936.

45. There were in fact two petitions: one from Jarrow, with 12,000 signatures, the other from Tyneside, with 68,500 signatures. Jarrow's was presented by its Labour M.P., Wilkinson; Tyneside's by its Conservative M.P., Sir Nicholas Doyle. Numerous religious services were held along the route of the march, and the marchers always rested on Sunday. *South Shields Gazette,* 5, 9, and 12 October 1936.

46. National Hunger March Cuttings, NMLH, CP/IND/HANN/O5; *Daily Sketch,* 15 October 1936.

47. *Eastern Press,* 17 October 1936; *Sheffield Independent,* 14 October 1936; *Sunday Express,* 15 October 1936.

48. *Spectator,* 30 October 1936.

49. Wilkinson, *The Town That Was Murdered,* 204.

50. *Eastern Press,* 17 October 1936.

51. For examples, see *South Shields Gazette,* 9 October 1936; *East Ham Echo,* 13 November 1936; *Star,* 14 October 1936; and *Daily Mirror,* 29 October 1936.

52. *Morning Post,* 31 October 1936.

53. Wilkinson, *The Town That Was Murdered,* 208; *Sunday Referee,* 4 October 1936.

54. For characteristic statements, see John Lochmore in MacDougall, *Voices*

from the Hunger Marches, 2:327; Kingsford, *The Hunger Marchers in Britain, 1920–1940,* 221.

55. Stephen Fielding, "What Did 'the People' Want? the Meaning of the 1945 General Election," *Historical Journal* 35, no. 3 (1992): 623–640; Tony Mason and Peter Thompson, "'Reflections on a Revolution'? The Political Mood in Wartime Britain," in N. Tiratsoo (ed.), *The Attlee Years* (London: Pinter, 1991): 54–70; S. Fielding, P. Thompson, and N. Tiratsoo, *England Arise! The Labour Party and Popular Politics in 1940s Britain* (Manchester: Manchester University Press, 1991).

56. Gareth Stedman Jones, "Why Is the Labour Party in a Mess?" in *Languages of Class: Studies in English Working Class History, 1832–1982* (Cambridge: Cambridge University Press, 1983), 246.

57. With apologies to Stedman Jones, "Why Is the Labour Party in a Mess?" 242.

58. T. S. Ashton, "The Treatment of Capitalism by Historians," in F. A. Hayek (ed.), *Capitalism and the Historians* (Chicago: Chicago University Press, 1952), 55.

59. W. H. Chaloner, *The Hungry Forties: A Reexamination* (London: Routledge and Kegan Paul, 1957); A. C. Howe, "Towards the 'Hungry Forties': Free Trade in Britain, c. 1880–1906," in E. Biagini (ed.), *Citizenship and Community: Liberals, Radicals and Collective Identities in the British Isles, 1865–1931* (Cambridge: Cambridge University Press, 1996), 193–218; Biagini (ed.), *Free Trade and Liberal England, 1846–1946* (Oxford: Oxford University Press, 1998); Frank Trentmann, "The Erosion of Free Trade: Political Culture and Political Economy in Great Britain, c. 1897–1932" (Ph.D. diss., Harvard University, 1998).

60. Jane Cobden Unwin, *The Hungry Forties: Life under the Bread Tax; Descriptive Letters and Other Contemporary Witnesses* (London: Unwin, 1904).

61. William Chadwick, "the last of the Manchester Chartists," was employed by the Free Trade Union to "tell an audience what Protection was like because he had himself experienced its evils . . . When he described the 'Hungry Forties,' he spoke of days when he and Hunger were 'weel-acquaint.'" T. Palmer Newbould, *Pages from a Life of Strife* (London: Frank Palmer, 1911), ix; Allen Clarke, *The Men Who Fought Us in the Hungry Forties* (Manchester: Cooperative Newspaper Society, 1914); Lilian Dalton, *Sons of Want: A Story of the Hungry "Forties"* (London: Sheldon, 1930). G. D. H. Cole and R. W. Postgate, *The Common People, 1746–1946* (London: Methuen, 1938), devoted a whole chapter to the "Hungry Forties." Richard Hoggart had "not forgotten the memory of the 'Hungry Forties,'" which his grandmother had taught him between the wars. Richard Hoggart, *The Uses of Literacy* (New Brunswick, N.J.: Rutgers University Press, [1957] 1998), 60. Clapham was the first to try to dispel the "legend" in his *Economic History of Modern Britain: The Early Railway Age, 1820–1850* (Cambridge: Cambridge University Press, 1926), vii.

Others soon followed suit; see Montague Fordham, *Britain's Trade and Agriculture* (London: Allen Unwin, 1932), 28–29.

62. On the hegemonic influence of Toynbee's *Lectures on the Industrial Revolution in England* (London: Rivingtons, 1884), see Gareth Stedman Jones, *An End to Poverty? A Historical Debate* (London: Profile, 2004), 227–231.

63. W. H. Auden, "1st September 1939," in *Another Time* (London: Faber and Faber [1940], 2007); Malcolm Muggeridge, *The Thirties: 1930–1940 in Great Britain* (London: Collins, [1940] 1967); Graves and Hodge, *The Long Weekend.*

64. J. B. Priestley, *Out of the People* (London: Collins, 1941); George Orwell, *The Lion and the Unicorn* (London: Secker and Warburg, 1941). The best of recent accounts of the radicalization thesis and its critics is Fielding, Thompson, and Tiratsoo, *England Arise!.* See also John Baxendale and Christopher Pawling, *Narrating the Thirties: A Decade in the Making, 1930 to the Present* (Basingstoke, U.K.: Macmillan, 1996), 46–78, 116–139.

65. Cited in Christopher Waters, "Autobiography, Nostalgia and the Changing Practices of Working Class Selfhood," in G. K. Behlmer and F. M. Levanthall (eds.), *Singular Continuities: Tradition, Nostalgia, and Identity in Modern British Culture* (Stanford, Calif.: Stanford University Press, 2000), 178–195.

66. Peter Hennessy, *Never Again: Britain, 1945–51* (New York: Pantheon, 1992).

67. Speech of 3 July 1948, Wikipedia.

68. *Let Us Win Through Together: A Declaration of Labour Policy for the Consideration of the Nation, 1950,* http://www.psr.keele.ac.uk/area/uk/man/lab50.html.

69. *Labour Party Election Manifesto, 1951,* http://www.psr.keele.ac.uk/area/uk/man/lab51.htm.

70. H. G. Nicholas, *The British General Election of 1950* (London: Macmillan, 1951), 213, 241; cited in Baxendale and Pawling, *Narrating the Thirties,* 154.

71. Ina Zweiniger-Bargielowska, *Austerity in Britain: Rationing, Controls, and Consumption, 1939–1955* (Oxford: Oxford University Press, 2000).

72. *Sunday Express,* 20 February 1956.

73. It was an analysis that both Richard Crossman and Harold Wilson on the right shared, as did Hall and Thompson on the "new Left." Crossman and Wilson used the thirties to dismiss the relevance of class politics in the affluent age, while Hall and Thompson used them to highlight "the shallowness, apathy and materialism of the Fifties." Baxendale and Pawling, *Narrating the Thirties,* 161.

74. For an early example expressly legitimating the emergent welfare state, see Max Cohen, *I Was One of the Unemployed,* foreword by William Beveridge (London: Gollancz, 1945).

75. Carolyn Steedman, "State-Sponsored Autobiography," in B. Conekin, F.

Mort, and C. Waters (eds.), *Moments of Modernity? The Reconstruction of Postwar Britain* (London: Rivers Oram, 1998), 41–54. See also James Vernon, "Telling the Subaltern to Speak: Social Investigation and the Formation of Social History Twentieth Century Britain," *Proceedings of the International Congress History under Debate, Santiago de Compostela, July 1999* (Santiago de Compostela: University of Santiago de Compostela, 2000).

76. The list always includes John Osborne's *Look Back in Anger* (1956), Colin Wilson's *The Outsider* (1956), John Braine's *Room at the Top* (1957), Alan Sillitoe's *Saturday Night, Sunday Morning* (1958), and Dennis Potter's *Glittering Coffin* (1960)—most of which were also made as films. In the words of David Edgar, they spoke to "the generation too young to have the 1944 Education Act, who had escaped from the lower middle and working classes but had not been accepted by the class they had joined. Jimmy Porter [the central character of Osborne's *Look Back in Anger*] is the most vivid representative of the children for whom the welfare state had provided an invalid passport; it got them out of a background they despised, but appeared not to allow them entry into a new world in which they felt comfortable." David Edgar, "Stalking Out," *London Review of Books,* 20 July 2006, 10.

77. Stuart Hall, "A Sense of Classlessness," *Universities Left Review* 5 (1958): 26–32; Raphael Samuel, "Class and Classlessness," *Universities Left Review* 6 (1959). The best account of these discussions is Dennis Dworkin, *Cultural Marxism in Postwar Britain: History, the New Left, and the Origins of Cultural Studies* (Durham, N.C.: Duke University Press, 1997).

78. Robert Hewison, *In Anger: Culture in the Cold War 1945–60* (London: Weidenfeld and Nicolson, 1981), 141.

79. Up until the late 1960s the WEA had twice as many students enrolled as the university sector. See Michael Sanderson, "Education and Social Mobility," in P. Johnson (ed.), *Twentieth Century Britain* (London: Longman, 1994), 380–382; Jonathan Rose, *The Intellectual Life of the British Working Classes* (New Haven, Conn.: Yale University Press, 2001), 256–297.

80. Edward Thompson, *The Making of the English Working Class* (New York: Vintage, [1966] 1981), 12.

81. Hoggart, *The Uses of Literacy.*

82. Steedman, "State-Sponsored Autobiography," 49. At the History Workshop conference at Ruskin College, Oxford, in 1969 Stephen Yeo asserted, "The assumption underpinning all of this work IS that for working people to speak for themselves, about their own history, IS somehow a political act in itself." Lin Chun, *The British New Left* (Edinburgh: Edinburgh University Press, 1993), 166.

83. Carolyn Steedman, *Landscape for a Good Woman* (Newark, N.J.: Rutgers University Press, 1987).

84. Chun, *The British New Left,* 166. For other accounts of the formation

of working-class historians, see Patrick Joyce, "More Secondary Modern than Postmodern," *Rethinking History* 5, no. 3 (2001): 367–382; Peter Bailey, *Popular Culture and Performance in the Victorian City* (Cambridge: Cambridge University Press, 2003), chap. 1; Geoff Eley, *A Crooked Line: From Cultural History to the History of Society* (Ann Arbor: University of Michigan Press, 2005); chap. 1.

85. Jed Esty, *A Shrinking Island: Modernism and National Culture in England* (Princeton, N.J.: Princeton University Press, 2004).

86. Christopher Waters, "Autobiography, Nostalgia and the Changing Practices of Working Class Selfhood," in G. K. Behlmer and F. M. Leventhall (eds.), *Singular Continuities: Tradition, Nostalgia, and Identity in Modern British Culture* (Stanford, Calif.: Stanford University Press, 2000), 180; D. Morley and K. Worpole (eds.), *The Republic of Letters: Working Class Writing and Local Publishing* (London: Comedia, 1982).

87. It ends with "two great beginnings, one in the Trade Union movement and the other in the WEA . . . She has drawn strength from both movements and has repaid both with a lifetime of service and devotion." Alice Foley, *A Bolton Childhood* (Manchester: M/C University Extra-Mural Department and N.W. District of the Workers Education Association, 1973), 92.

88. Ernie Benson, *To Struggle Is to Live: A Working Class Autobiography*, vol. 1 (Newcastle: People's, 1979). Benson was taught by the veteran labor historian John Halstead at the WEA. He also thanked the Frows. Eddie Frow's leadership of the NUWM in Salford was immortalized by Walter Greenwood in *Love on the Dole*. Together they formed the Working Class Movement Library in Salford, where I read Benson's book.

89. Benson, *To Struggle Is to Live*, vol. 2, *Starve or Rebel, 1927–1971* (Newcastle: People's, 1980), 5. See also Kathleen Dayus, *Her People* (London: Virago, 1982).

90. The oral history material I draw from in the following pages is from the collections of the North-West Sound Archive, established in Manchester in 1979.

91. Waters, "Autobiography, Nostalgia and the Changing Practices of Working Class Selfhood," 185–186. On nineteenth-century working class and autodidact autobiography see David Vincent, *Bread, Knowledge and Freedom: A Study of Nineteenth-Century Working Class Autobiography* (London: Europa, 1981); J. Burnett, D. Vincent, and D. Mayall, *The Autobiography of the Working Class* (New York: New York University Press, 1984–1989).

92. Jimmy Jones, testimony (1974), NWSA, no. 834.

93. Testimony (1981), NWSA, no. 85.

94. "But I'll tell you this much, I wouldn't like to go through it again; I couldn't face that life again because it was that hard." Mary Burnett, testimony (n.d.), NWSA, no. 1999.0337.

95. Mrs. Mawson, testimony (n.d.), NWSA, no. 1998.0164. Although her fa-

ther was a shopkeeper, he too "was out of work and then we were so hungry, my mother gave us three slices of bread each at a meal and no more and nothing else; there wasn't any money . . . My mum went down to six stone."

96. Testimony (1982), NWSA, no. 88c.

97. Steedman, *Landscape for a Good Woman,* 39, 46.

98. "I've not been hungry for years. Not like we used to be as kids, when finding that bit extra to eat was all you could think of." Gilda O'Neil, *My East End: Memories of Life in Cockney London* (London: Viking, 1999), 291.

99. Grace Foakes, *My Part of the River* (London: Shepheard-Walwyn, 1974), 107. "To live and to know that you had neighbours who cared about you and on whom you could rely as friends and helpers indeed made up for the lack of money and material things."

100. Mary H. Dagnah, *Castle Hall Revisited: Stalybridge in the 1930s* (Manchester: Neil Richardson, 1995), 3. Also Testimony (1981), NWSA, no. 85.

101. Arthur Barton, *Two Lamps in Our Street: A Time Remembered* (Hutchison, U.K.: Hutchison New Authors, 1967), 19–20.

102. "There were no luxuries-kind-of-thing, you know. I mean, we enjoyed a luxury like they don't now—you know what I mean?" Miss Healy, testimony (1982), NWSA, no. 129. On the importance of "something tasty" and a "good table," see Hoggart, *The Uses of Literacy,* 21.

103. William Woodruff, *The Road to Nab End: An Extraordinary Northern Childhood* (London: Abacus, [1993] 2002), 41–42.

104. On the hunger strike and the dissolution or staging of the self, see Maud Ellmann, *The Hunger Artists: Starving, Writing, and Imprisonment* (Cambridge, Mass.: Harvard University Press, 1993). For examples, see Sylvia Pankhurst, *The Suffragette Movement: An Intimate Account of Persons and Ideals* (London: Virago, [1931] 1977), 444, 474; Frank Gallagher, *Days of Fear* (John Murray: London, 1928), 21–40; Paedar O'Donnell, *The Gates Flew Open* (London: Jonathan Cape, 1932), 191–211.

105. Cohen, *I Was One of the Unemployed,* 29–30. Knut Hamsun's *Hunger,* first translated into English in 1899, is a classic modernist account of a writer's battle against the physical and psychic hinterlands of hunger.

106. Here I echo Waters's suggestion that "there *is* a notion of self in these works, maybe not a self marked by psychological depth . . . but a self discovered in a rich and elaborately textured community." Christopher Waters, "Autobiography, Nostalgia and Working Class Selfhood in Post-War Britain," paper presented to the Department of History, George Washington University, October 1999.

107. Hoggart, *The Uses of Literacy,* 73.

108. Nancy Sharman's uncle took her to political meetings and, she wrote,

"[told me] how different things were going to be when I grew up, working class people were going to change the social face of England, there would be enough for all to eat, there would be no unemployment." Nancy Sharman, *Nothing to Steal: The Story of a Southampton Childhood* (London: Kaye and Ward, 1977), 53; Woodruff, *The Road to Nab End,* 365–372.

109. Ifan Edwards, *No Gold on My Shovel* (London: Porcupine, 1947), 187.

110. Cohen, *I Was One of the Unemployed,* 20.

111. Woodruff, *The Road to Nab End,* 382–386.

112. The point is made in Liz Stanley, "Women Have Servants and Men Never Eat: Issues in Reading Gender, Using the Case-Study of Mass-Observation's 1937 Day-Diaries," *Women's History Review* 4, no. 1 (1995): 85–102.

113. "Mothers often figure in the autobiographical literature as heroic and self-sacrificing, deserving more than could ever be done for them in return. Fathers seldom loom as large or evoke such loyalty, especially if their response to stress in earlier days involved much drink or violence. Anna Davin, *Growing Up Poor: Home, School and Street in London, 1870–1914* (London: Rivers Oram, 1996), 26.

114. Hoggart, *The Uses of Literacy,* 29–31.

115. See, on fatherless families, ibid.; and Sharman, *Nothing to Steal.* On distant, absent, or drunken fathers, see Grace Foakes, *Between High Walls: A London Childhood* (London: Shepheard-Walwyn, 1972); Albert S. Jasper, *A Hoxton Childhood* (London: Barrie and Rockcliff, 1969); Jean Rennie, *Every Other Sunday* (Bath: Chivers, 1979); Pat O'Mara, *The Autobiography of a Liverpool Irish Slummy* (Liverpool: Bluecoat, 1994); Foley, *A Bolton Childhood;* and Woodruff, *The Road to Nab End.*

116. "We had a bit of bread and jam, or brown sauce on bread or a bit of relish. I used to watch my dad eat his herrings and he used to look at me and break me a bit off. They were hungry times, very hard times." O'Neil, *My East End,* 196.

117. "Unlike mother, father seemed oblivious of the famine that now stared us in the face . . . He never seemed to realize that his family was getting hungrier and hungrier . . . If there was no work you went hungry. You didn't beg and you didn't steal . . . You didn't complain, whine or whimper; it was a matter of pride. As for the rich, by his lights, it was their job to leave the poor alone. Charity from 'them' would have hurt. Fortunately for us, it was an attitude that mother didn't share. Come what may she was not going to see her children starve." Woodruff, *The Road to Nab End,* 47.

118. Dayus, *Her People;* Ray Forsberg, *Means Test Kid* (Beverley, U.K.: Hulton, 1985).

119. Foakes, *My Part of the River,* 8.

120. Rennie, *Every Other Sunday,* 8.

121. Davin, *Growing Up Poor,* 185–186. Children do not generally seem to have

rationalized theft in the way that an unemployed East Anglian carpenter did: "I don't intend to see my wife or boys starve, and I don't intend to starve myself . . . If I'm not allowed to earn bread I shall take it. As long as I am a free man I shall get it, and I shall get it from those who have got more than their fair share and don't know better what to do with it than to spend it on dress and banquets for their own bellies. There may be no sense or justice in theft, but there's less still in charity." H. L. Beales and R. S. Lambert (eds.), *Memoirs of the Unemployed* (Wakefield, U.K.: EP, [1934] 1973), 193.

122. Dayus, *Her People,* 16–18. See also Benson, *To Struggle Is to Live,* 1:54–55; Sharman, *Nothing to Steal,* 57–58.

123. Foley, *A Bolton Childhood,* 47; Jones, testimony (1974), NWSA, no. 834.

124. Joe Loftus, "Lee Side," cited in Burnett, *Idle Hands,* 261.

125. C. L. Mowat, *Britain between the Wars, 1918–1940* (London, [1955] 1967), 432.

126. Thompson, *The Making of the English Working Class,* 207–212; Raphael Samuel, "British Marxist Historians, 1880–1980: Part 1," *New Left Review* 120 (1980): 21–96; Bill Schwarz, "'The People' in History: The Communist Party Historians Group, 1946–1956" in Richard Johnson, Gregor McLennan, Bill Schwarz, and David Sutton (eds.), *Making Histories: Studies in History Writing and Politics* (London: Hutchison, 1982).

127. For some examples among many, see John Burnett, *Plenty and Want: A Social History of Diet in England from 1815 to the Present Day* (London: Nelson, 1966); D. H. Aldcroft, *The Interwar Economy, 1919–1939* (New York: Columbia University Press, 1970); John Stevenson, *Social Conditions between the Wars* (Harmondsworth, U.K.: Penguin, 1977); Jay Winter, "Unemployment, Nutrition and Infant Mortality in Britain, 1920–1950," in *The Working Class in Modern British History* (Cambridge: Cambridge University Press, 1983), 232–255; Miriam Glucksman, *Women Assemble: Women Workers and the New Industries in Interwar Britain* (London: Routledge, 1990).

128. Charles Webster, "Healthy or Hungry Thirties?" *History Workshop Journal* 13 (1982): 111. Andrew Thorpe was right that scholars like Webster sought to "present the Thirties in an unfavourable light in order to delegitimise Thatcherism." Andrew Thorpe, *Britain in the 1930s* (London: Longman, 1992), 4.

129. Stephen Constantine, *Unemployment in Britain between the Wars* (London: Longman, 1980), 84. Many of the works cited here are a product of the recent renewal of interest in the thirties.

130. Tony Mason, "'Hunger is a Very Good Thing': Britain in the 1930s," in N. Tiratsoo (ed.), *From Blitz to Blair: A New History of Britain since 1939* (London: Weidenfeld and Nicolson, 1997): 1–24; Baxendale and Pawling, *Narrating the Thirties.*

Conclusion

1. This point is well analyzed in R. English and M. Kenny (eds.), *Rethinking British Decline* (New York: St. Martin's Press, 2000).

2. P. Wilmot and M. Young, *Family and Kinship in East London* (London: Routledge, 1957); B. Abel-Smith and P. Townsend, *The Poor and the Poorest: A New Analysis of the Ministry of Labour's Family Expenditure Surveys of 1953–54 and 1960* (London: Bell, 1965). It was this moment that organizations such as Help the Aged (1961), the Child Poverty Action Group (1965) and Shelter (1966) were established. David Vincent: *Poor Citizens: The State and the Poor in Twentieth-Century Britain* (London: Longman, 1991).

3. Fred Cooper, *Africa since 1940: The Past of the Present* (New York: Cambridge University Press, 2002); Jenny Edkins, *Whose Hunger? Concepts of Famine, Practices of Aid* (Minneapolis: University of Minnesota Press, 2000).

Index